Eyes on City Hall

Eyes on City Hall

A Young Man's Education in New York Political Warfare

Evan J. Mandery

with fifteen original illustrations
by Rob Shepperson and
four political cartoons
by R. J. Matson

A Member of the Perseus Books Group

Paperback first published in 2001 in the United States of America by Westview Press, 5500 Central Avenue, Boulder, Colorado 80301-2877, and in the United Kingdom by Westview Press, 12 Hid's Copse Road, Cumnor Hill, Oxford OX2 9JJ
Hardback published in 1999 under the title *The Campaign.*

Find us on the World Wide Web at www.westviewpress.com

A CIP catalog record for this book is available from the Library of Congress.
ISBN 0-8133-9815-0 (pbk.)

Designed by Heather Hutchison

The paper used in this publication meets the requirements of the American National Standard for Permanence of Paper for Printed Library Materials Z39.48-1984.

10 9 8 7 6 5 4 3 2 1

Contents

Foreword

BY FRAN REITER

At the beginning of 1997, Evan Mandery was a young, practicing attorney with very limited political experience and a yen to jump into a real campaign. I, on the other hand, was a seasoned *pol*, the former State Chair of New York's Liberal Party, and a former, some-time campaign operative who had found nirvana in government service as one of NYC Mayor Rudy Giuliani's Deputy Mayors. Unlike Evan, I had no desire to jump into any campaign. So I didn't jump. I was, however, nudged. Shortly after Evan voluntarily joined Manhattan Borough President and Democratic mayoral candidate Ruth Messinger's campaign as Research Director, Mayor Giuliani *asked* me to leave his government and serve as his re-election campaign manager. To the uninformed, this might sound like a great honor. Suffice it to say that when asked by a sitting Mayor, who also happens to be your boss, to do something, you tend to say yes. By mid-March 1997, I was an ex-Deputy Mayor sitting virtually alone in an office that would eventually house a typically chaotic campaign headquarters.

Despite the fact that Evan was a willing participant in Campaign '97 and I somewhat less so, and while the positions we held in our respective campaigns were very different, and finally, while we worked for candidates diametrically opposed to one another, Evan is, in many respects, a kindred spirit and, ultimately, a survivor who lived to tell his tale. And it is a tale of all campaign workers, irrespective of party or ideology.

Many books have been written about political campaigns, usually by professional political operatives or strategists, candidates, members of the media, or academics. These works are either overly theoretical (the academic approach) or self-indulgent, self-aggrandizing tomes, burdened with the enormous cynicism that eventually afflicts all political professionals. To my knowledge, *Eyes on City Hall* is the first of this genre to be written by a virtual political neophyte and, therefore, provides an important and interesting perspective. It is an honest, inside look at a major political contest, without any of the aforementioned baggage. This is both refreshing and enlightening—and something for which we should be grateful.

On a personal note, while reading the book two years after the campaign ended, I was able finally to think and talk about my own experience without my own emotional and cynical baggage (well, at least not as much) and to enjoy and learn from an account of the overall experience from the opponent's perspective.

But *Eyes on City Hall* is not a book simply to be enjoyed by those of us who were personally involved. On both a micro and macro level, it is a serious and important work that leads to greater understanding of the dynamics, strategies, and personalities of modern-day, big-money campaigns.

Campaigns are lived at the extremes, and the adrenaline pumps 24/7. The highs are very high and the lows very low—particularly since every event is played out in the media spotlight. (There is no right to privacy in a political campaign.) While successes along the way can be euphoric, small mistakes, errors in judgment, miscalculations, or a misspoken word often have enormous, negative ramifications, both for the effort and the individual perpetrator. As you will read, Evan and I both had such moments during the campaign.

Most staffers, not to mention volunteers, are true believers. They have to be, or they'd never put up with the crazy hours, no sleep, low (if any) pay, and miserable food—not to mention the candidate who, no matter how otherwise charming, inspirational, or statesmanlike, will periodically transform from Dr. Jekyll to Mr. (or Ms.) Hyde.

The diary format of *Eyes on City Hall* is a wonderful day-by-day illustration of a challenger versus incumbent campaign. It was widely believed by the professionals and the public that, barring an unforeseen catastrophe or scandal, Rudy Giuliani was a shoe-in for re-election. Therefore, of particular interest is the level of belief by the Messinger campaign's staff, not to mention the candidate herself, that the election was winnable, even at its lowest moments. Having served on winning and losing campaigns, I can attest to the fact that this is not unusual. Staffers always think their candidate can win. Such delusional behavior is necessary in order to maintain the energy level that campaigns demand. As you'll read, examples of self-deception abound, making it clear that this is not an environment for the mentally stable.

On a more macro level, there is the ever-present and much-debated issue of political fundraising: the need to raise millions of dollars in a relatively short period of time from an increasingly apathetic public and a business sector whose motives are always viewed with suspicion; the lengths a campaign will go to in raising the maximum, legal, allowable amount; and the role money (or the lack of money) plays in the political decision-making process.

Perhaps most interesting is the reliance of the Messinger campaign on a *gun for hire*, one of those very senior, well-paid campaign professionals who go from state to state, campaign to campaign, selling their services with little or no regard for who the candidate is, other than their political party affiliation, and not always that. Most, if not all, modern campaigns (Giuliani's included) hire professional media gurus, pollsters, and to a lesser extent, opposition researchers (Mandery, while paid as Research Director, was not in this category). Messinger, as is increasingly the case in today's campaigns, brought in a *gun for hire* as her campaign manager/chief political strategist. In my own experience through three Giuliani campaigns (losing in 1989 and winning in 1993 and 1997), only in the first months of the 1989 campaign was there reliance on paid, professional outsiders for campaign management, and in my opinion, the campaign never recovered from the experience. Thereafter, Giuliani relied on trusted close friends and associates for day-to-day management and most of the strategizing. I leave it to the reader to decide, irrespective of the fact that she lost, if Messinger's approach worked to her benefit.

Mandery treats me very fairly in his book, despite the fact that I refused to cooperate when he called me soon after the campaign was over, seeking an interview. I confess that, upon purchasing the book, I immediately looked up all references to me in the index and read those first. (I may be out of politics, but my ego and paranoia remain intact.) I finished the book by the next day, swallowed my embarrassment, called Evan, and confessed how much I had enjoyed it. After all that, to be asked to write this foreword for the paperback edition is indeed an honor and a vivid illustration of the bond we share.

For those not yet so cynical that they have given up all interest in politics and political contests, not to mention political *groupies*, *Eyes on City Hall* is an entertaining and informative work that goes beyond its obvious account of a major mayoral campaign, raising serious questions about the state of politics in America today. One last note: While, after twenty years of political activity and direct and indirect involvement in numerous campaigns, I have vowed never again to work on a campaign, they provided me with the greatest *highs* I have ever known and led to a short but wonderful career in public service. I'll never regret the experience. I don't believe Evan Mandery will either.

Preface

I VOLUNTEERED ON MY first political campaign in 1994. Mario Cuomo, running for governor of New York for a fourth time, was facing a tough race against George Pataki, a Republican state senator who, unlike Cuomo, favored the death penalty. I called the Cuomo campaign and expressed my desire to help, explaining that I had a better than average education in the hope that I would be given an interesting assignment. My offer was enthusiastically received. I was asked to report to an office in Garden City, Long Island, near where I was working as a lawyer at the time.

There I was locked in a small room to seal envelopes and make telephone calls. No one could have been less suited for the task than I. Even with a script provided by the campaign, my phone manner was extraordinarily bad. I began each call with a string of profuse apologies for bothering people at home. People often hung up before I could state the reason for my call. I wasn't very good at sealing envelopes either.

My colleagues were passionate and vibrant and all over seventy years old. They fed me constantly. Pizza. Cookies. Chips. I hardly had time to be hung up on before someone offered me more food. After work we would go out to a diner where my new friends would feed me more. They liked that I was Jewish. Mostly, I think, they liked that I was less than seventy. It felt much more like visiting my grandparents in Florida than working on a political campaign. I know now that I was part of a systematic process to stimulate voter turnout—a pull operation to be precise—but the work had only slightly more appeal to me than the game of mah-jongg to which my colleagues retired after dinner. I left the Cuomo campaign disenchanted. I had imagined politics to be so much more.

My second political experience was vastly different. As the research director on Ruth Messinger's 1997 New York City mayoral campaign against Rudy Giuliani, I was part of a universe of consultants and advisers who sat in think tanks and plotted strategic courses through the labyrinth of politics. They ate lots of food too, but in every other respect this world was everything the other was not. It was vibrant, fast-paced, and filled with complex characters each more colorful than the last. For nine months, I and twenty men and women worked hundred-hour weeks without respite in close quarters under almost constant pressure. Together we all saw the best and worst of political life, but I viewed it through a slightly different lens. Though I had followed politics for most of my life, I was the only senior member of the staff without significant campaign experience.

The universe I lived in for those nine months—and the one you are about to enter—is unusual. It is a universe where truth is fungible and moral conviction a mere asset, like good looks or personal wealth, a universe where corporeal restraints do not exist and people regularly become things they are not. It is a world scrutinized in exquisite detail by people as interested in the motivations behind actions as the actions themselves. Paranoia reigns. It is frenzied, oppressive, and exhilarating. And once you've lived in it, you can never view the world in the same way.

Though it was not an easy time to be a Democrat in New York, working for Ruth Messinger's campaign was the most fulfilling job I ever had. I did not go to work for Ruth to write a book. I went to work for her because I admired her as a smart, principled person who would be an effective and compassionate mayor. I still think all of these good things about her and more. Along the way, though, I realized that all of us were working in politics at a remarkable time in the evolution of campaigns—a time when campaigns were fundamentally changing the way the business of politics is practiced in America. How this is so seemed a story worth telling. To my mind, this is not a book about Ruth Messinger's campaign, but rather a book about political campaigns that is incidentally about the 1997 New York mayoral race.

I maintained this journal and offer it now with only the modest ambition of presenting a look at how modern campaigns go about the difficult and important business of defining themselves and shaping attitudes. Doubtless a hundred different people would have a hundred different views of the events I describe here. I make no special claim on history. This is what I experienced.

Evan J. Mandery

Eyes on City Hall

PART ONE

Jams, Jellies, and Other Tools of the Trade

January 28, 1997

Mine is an unusual political birth. The attending physician is neither an elected official nor a political insider of any sort; it is Nathan Lane, the Tony award–winning star of the hit Broadway musical *A Funny Thing Happened on the Way to the Forum!* "Good evening," he says, "and welcome to the Friends of Ruth Messinger. My name is Nathan Lane. My jams and jellies are on sale outside."

Approximately six hundred people attend this benefit, one of the first of the political season, and I could not be more excited to be among them. I was hired as research director for this campaign only two days ago and am still wide-eyed at the spectacle of politics. There is Jerrold Nadler, the corpulent congressman from the Upper West Side, munching on cheese balls. There is Mark Green, the New York City Public Advocate, who ran a losing campaign for Senate against Al D'Amato back in 1986. And in the corner, in his immaculately pressed black suit and thin white handkerchief, is David Dinkins, the bitter former mayor.

Truth be told, most people would not regard this event as much of a spectacle. No one seems especially happy to be here. The food is bland. Lane's best shot hardly causes a stir ("How many Freudian psychologists does it take to screw in a light bulb? Two. One to hold the other light bulb and the other to screw his mother. I mean his penis. The latter. The latter"). Other than Ruth, not a single politician addresses the crowd. Harry Belafonte says a few words, but has a sore throat and is unable to honor a decades-old promise to Ruth to sing for her campaign. The cast of *Smoky Joe's Cafe*, a somewhat less successful Broadway musical than *Forum*, puts on three snappy numbers, but it is hard to imagine that the twenty-something cast members, who grin absently throughout their performance, have much of a connection to Ruth Messinger, the last best guardian of Upper West Side liberalism.

But, to me, it makes no difference. I relish the ordinary. You can have Bill Clinton. Jerrold Nadler and the cast of *Smoky Joe's* are just fine with me.

The big subject in the air throughout the night is when Ruth will "come out," which is not what you might think. It refers to her formal declaration of candidacy. Ruth begins her remarks by saying, "Sounds like you're ready for a new mayor," which sounds like a declaration of candidacy to me. This

thought only proves my naïveté. Ruth's remarks, I am told, are a demonstration of serious intention to run, not a formal declaration of candidacy. According to the strategists at my table, there are many factors to consider in timing a formal declaration. It must, depending on circumstances, either coincide with other endorsements or not conflict with other endorsements. It should come at either a time of great strength or great weakness for the candidate or, in exceptional cases, a moment of neither great strength nor great weakness.

I am obviously not up to this sort of strategic decisionmaking yet. It is better left to the assembled armchair strategists, who are an impressive lot to say the least. I am seated directly across from a lifelong friend of Ruth's who had been a chief assistant U.S. Attorney in the Southern District of New York and a Bosnian war crimes prosecutor at the World Court. The senior partner in one of the city's most prestigious law firms is here too. Only a wonderful person could have such impressive friends.

I am, understandably I think, nervous at the prospect of meeting Ruth. I have just signed on to work nine months of hundred-hour weeks for a person I have never met. And someone told me that Ruth Messinger is the only politician he had ever met who did not like people. I have no idea what to expect.

It all works out fine. Ruth grasps my hand warmly as the campaign consultant, Jim Andrews, introduces me as her new research director. She is pleased to meet me, she says, and tells Jim that she has heard wonderful things about me from David Dinkins. What good fortune! My reputation has preceded me.

The problem is, I've never met the former mayor.

No bother. I'm raring to go.

January 29

I solicited an introduction to Jim Andrews from a college friend who had been Jim's research director on Harvey Gantt's second unsuccessful Senate campaign against Jesse Helms in North Carolina. I was bored with my job and, though I had no idea what being the research director for a campaign entailed, I figured it had to be more interesting than what I was doing at the time. Besides, I had always wanted to know what really goes on in a political campaign.

My friend warned me that the job would not be an easy one. He regarded Jim as a brilliant political strategist and thought that I would learn a lot from the experience, but quite candidly said that Jim could be a difficult person to work for. I went ahead anyway and arranged to meet Jim for dinner shortly after the first of the year. We met on a cloudy Thursday outside my office near City Hall. Jim, who was coming from a meeting with Ruth and her staff, was dressed in a collarless white button-front shirt and jeans. I concluded—correctly it turns out—that I was not scoring any points for wearing a suit.

It was quickly clear that Jim was an extraordinary person in many different respects. His intelligence was obvious. In a matter of minutes he displayed a command of New York City history that was especially remarkable for a man who had grown up in Rochester and lived in Chicago for most of his adult life. He spoke comfortably about New York and its political scene. His passion was obvious too. He made it clear that he didn't care for Republicans and that Rudy Giuliani was as bad as any of them. Jim was a populist, and Rudy Giuliani was their people's mayor, not his.

It was also clear, though, that Jim had some unusual idiosyncrasies. In the first five minutes of our time together, he went through three Old Gold cigarettes, a brand I had never heard of before. He would light the cigarette, take three puffs, and then extinguish it in apparent revulsion. A minute later, he would light another and go through the same routine. He rubbed at his eyes constantly. Every few minutes or so, he would raise his right thumb and forefinger to his nose, pinch the bridge, and shut his eyes tightly. He said something about having bad allergies.

His anger, about which I had been forewarned, seemed out of proportion to whatever it was directed at at the moment. He didn't just dislike Rudy Giuliani; he hated Rudy Giuliani—which seemed to me an overly strong reaction to someone he had never met. Seemingly trivial stuff set him off. When I referred to him as the "campaign manager," he raged that he was the "consultant," not the "campaign manager," and that the borough president's office was going to ruin his career if it continued to propagate this mistaken notion. The distinction was lost on me. To me, he seemed a tortured genius. He was clearly smart, and he was just as clearly a little off.

My interview over Heinekens and 7-Up (my 7-Up, Jim's Heinekens) consisted of a brief monologue during which Jim told me that working for him would be the hardest thing I would ever do, but that if I survived his "boot camp," I would be prepared to do anything in life. The speech was tailored toward a somewhat younger crowd, but it intimidated me all the same. I distressingly suspected that what he said might really be true. Perhaps working on this campaign really would be equal to the worst life has to offer.

The speech concluded, Jim reasonably asked me if I had any questions for him. I asked something about the nature of my responsibilities. Jim answered that I would be involved in every aspect of the campaign from polling to writing speeches and then asked if I had any other questions. I asked something about his perception of Ruth's chances. "The only two people in New York City who understand how vulnerable Rudy Giuliani is," he said, "are Ruth Messinger and Rudy Giuliani." Then he asked again if I had other questions. He solicited questions at least a dozen more times. When I tried to say that I had nothing more to ask, he was aghast.

"Are you sure you really want this job? You *must* have more questions."

I indulged him. I asked questions about things I neither knew anything about nor had any interest in learning. I asked what sort of interaction the research team would have with the press department. Do you think the mayor is vulnerable on education? I asked obsequious questions, the sort of questions asked by front-row sitters whom I used to ridicule in law school. Once at a meeting for summer associates at a (now defunct) firm where I worked, a colleague asked the managing partner, with impossible sincerity, "Where do you see the firm going in the next century?" After a half hour of questioning, "Where do you see the campaign going in the next century?" was all that was left in my arsenal. It made no sense of course, but I could think of nothing else to say. Better to ask that, let him regard me as insane, and lose the job than to continue the torture. Mercifully, he cut off. "I'll let you know in a few days."

Two days later, he called. "You can do it," he said. And with that ambiguous instruction, I became the director of research for the heady Messinger campaign.

January 30

My professional career has been a slow, steady descent down the scale of offices. After law school, I started as a law clerk for a federal judge in Honolulu in a lavish office with a magnificent view of the Pacific Ocean. From there, I went to the dignified, if stern, setting of a large New York City law firm. Out of the corner of my window, I could see Central Park. A year later, I was in the employ of the city working to fight mob corruption in the private garbage-collection industry. My neat but dingy office had a head-on view of the rooftop of a dirty, but distinguished, timeworn office building.

Now I am spending the day looking at a potential office for the campaign. There are mousetraps scattered across the rugs, which are stained with various unidentifiable substances. I test the toilet. It struggles to flush. There is a shower in the bathroom, where a fungus I cannot identify is thriving. I eye an office with a nice view of the Brooklyn Bridge, but am told that I will not have my own space. I will share a room with six or seven other yet-to-be-hired researchers. It looks out to a bleak wall.

Jim is quite enthusiastic about the office, which has just one redeeming feature: From certain angles, if you strain your neck, you can see the city's capitol. We'll be able to keep our eye on City Hall.

February 1

Unlike Jim and most of the people at the fund-raiser, I don't view this campaign as a crusade. Though I'm generally aware politically, my impression of Rudy Giuliani is formed almost entirely by three images.

The first is the most bizarre sight I've ever seen in politics. At Rudy's inaugural speech in 1994, his eight-year-old son, Andrew, stood by his side and mouthed the words to his father's speech. Amazingly, no one moved to seat the boy. For half an hour, the two Giulianis stood side by side matching each other's lip movements and gesticulations.

The second image is of a tough, arrogant, egotistical man who fought the mob as a prosecutor and reduced crime in the city as mayor. The third is of a tough, arrogant, egotistical man who drove a popular schools chancellor and an even more popular police commissioner out of town and cut hundreds of millions of dollars from the school budget. He seems to me to be an effective leader with bad priorities. I wouldn't vote for him, but I also wouldn't put him up there with the Newt Gingriches of the world.

My candidate is the Manhattan borough president, a job that had some cachet at one time in New York City's history, but is now mostly titular and a stepping-stone for higher office. David Dinkins and Robert Wagner were both borough president of Manhattan before they were mayor. Before becoming borough president in 1989, Ruth served as a member of the City Council for twelve years. She was widely regarded as among the best of the

City Council, an expert on the city budget, and an effective critic of the Koch administration.

I don't know all that much about Ruth yet, but what I do know I like very much. She's smart—she graduated magna cum laude from Radcliffe—and principled. She's pro-choice and against the death penalty; she led the fight to pass the city's gay-rights bill and helped write the city's campaign-finance law, which is widely regarded as one of the best in the country. She's known as a policy wonk, which makes me think she is the best sort of liberal, one who can ground her convictions in practicalities. She seems like a candidate worth fighting for, and I'm anxious to get to know her better.

Winning the election will be difficult. Giuliani is not well liked, but most people share my perception of him as an effective leader. Crime in New York City is down by 50 percent over the past three years. Whether Giuliani is responsible for the decline is a subject for an interesting theoretical discussion, but whatever the truth is, the people of New York give him tremendous credit for the drop. The economy is thought to be doing well too. Despite the fact that Democrats outnumber Republicans in New York City by more than five to one, Rudy leads all challengers in early polling by 15 points or more.

Getting the opportunity to face Rudy will be a tough task in itself. Three candidates have already thrown their hats into the ring to challenge Ruth for the Democratic nomination. Fernando Ferrer, the Bronx borough president, is well respected, has a strong base of support in the Bronx and the Latino community, and has already raised over $2 million. The Reverend Al Sharpton appears to be in the race for the long haul. Many people regard him as a race-baiter and distrust him for his role in the 1987 Tawana Brawley affair, but Sharpton has demonstrated in two consecutive Senate elections that he can mobilize the black vote. Sal Albanese is a little-known City Councilman from Bay Ridge, but he is smart and is waging a serious campaign as a populist.

Ruth is the apparent favorite, but it will be a bloody fight just to get to the general election. And if we make it through, my guess is that will only be the beginning of the carnage.

February 2

Though I'll be the first to admit this campaign is a long shot, I don't think it's quite as long a shot as most people believe. Though the campaign has not yet begun, the press has been relentlessly pessimistic about the quality of the Democratic field and the chances of any Democrat beating Giuliani in

November. When former police commissioner William Bratton passed on the race in December, an editorial in the *Daily News* said his decision left "a weak Democratic field even weaker." Surely, the *News* said, "a party that boasts 2.5 million registered voters can do better." In December, Bob Herbert of the *New York Times* quoted a Giuliani aide as saying there is no truth to the rumor that they crafted the Democratic field. Herbert said, conclusorily, that all of the strongest potential candidates had taken a pass on the race. Former mayor Ed Koch says the mayoral race "shapes up as hold your nose time." "It's a miserable choice," Koch says of the four Democrats.

The negativity doesn't seem justified. The past two mayoral elections in New York City have been decided by narrow margins. Giuliani lost to David Dinkins in 1989 by 47,080 votes. Dinkins received 917,544 votes, or 48.3 percent of the vote. Giuliani received 870,464 votes, or 45.8 percent, including 55,077 votes on the Liberal line. Dinkins's margin of victory was the smallest for a mayoral candidate in more than eighty years. In 1993, Giuliani defeated Dinkins by 53,581 votes. Giuliani received 930,236 votes, or 50.8 percent of the votes cast, including 62,469 votes on the Liberal party line. The votes on the Liberal line were greater than the difference in the election.

Giuliani is clearly a stronger candidate in 1997 than he was in 1993, but he's far from invulnerable. As recently as July of last year, Giuliani looked downright weak. His approval rating was a paltry 43 percent. He squeaked through a projected head-to-head matchup with Messinger 47–41 percent. In April 1996, his lead was only 5 points. Giuliani's numbers have come around a bit since then, but hardly enough, it seems, to justify the conclusion in the press that the race will be over before it begins. Jim thinks the opposite is true. Ruth has not yet spent a single dollar on television advertising, but she remains competitive in head-to-head matchups with the mayor. And, most important, when it comes time to vote, the overwhelming Democratic registration advantage will mean quite a bit.

Ira Kaufman, my best friend from high school, is brainwashed by the media and predicts that Ruth will be trounced. To me, it's unthinkable that she could lose by more than 2 points. We bet twenty dollars on a 4-point spread, and I feel guilty about taking advantage of my insider status.

This is easy money.

February 3

Today is my first official day of work. I arrive at 8:30, early by most people's standards, ungodly by those I am used to as an attorney. Jim is already at the office, dressed again in a collarless white shirt and jeans. "Are we working bankers' hours?" he snarls. One of the research department's functions will be to clip the papers each day for news about the campaign. We agree that will start tomorrow.

February 4

I'm in today at 7:30. I am able to get a seat on the 6 train, which is a story in itself. I'm used to riding with a *Daily News* crowd. These people are all reading the *Wall Street Journal*. They are also considerably better dressed than the straphangers I am used to traveling with. As I settle down with my copy of the *News*, I feel a little self-conscious about my casual attire and choice of reading material.

By 8:00, I'm set to fax the morning clips to Jim at his apartment, but he calls just as I'm set to send the papers through. "Where the fuck are my clips?" he growls. After only two days on the job, I now get a knot in the pit of my stomach each time Jim calls.

February 5

My first task is to recruit a staff and, after the past two days, I am determined to get this done sooner rather than later. During our interview, Jim asked me whether I thought I could recruit a staff. "Yes," I replied confidently.

I had no idea what I was getting into.

Here's the honest pitch to a twenty-two year old:

> Drop whatever you are doing and move to New York. You will work sixteen hours a day, seven days a week, for a tyrannical campaign manager and a candidate no one thinks has any chance of winning. We'll pay you $2,000 a month, which is barely enough to live on in Boise, let alone New York City, but we won't help out with moving expenses or transportation (in fact, if you are here, you've already paid your way to the interview). And by the way, you only have a day to decide. We need you to start immediately.

Incredibly, there is a small universe of people who are willing to consider such an offer. Since there's not much room for wage competition between campaigns, the trick is to lock up the few qualified people as quickly as possible.

I am especially terrible with the pitch. Perhaps someone with experience could credibly say, "Look, slave for me for a year, and if you do a good job, I'll make sure that you move on to a good job." I cannot. I have no connections in the political world. I'm not even sure I'll make it through the year myself. The only variation I can add to the pitch is, "On top of working a hundred hours a week for no pay, you'll work for someone who has never worked on a campaign before."

"We'll learn together," I told one qualified person last week with a reassuring smile, hoping that my candor would entice him. He took a job working on the New Jersey governor's race the next day.

February 6

No one tells me exactly what I am supposed to be doing, so for three days I pester my friend from the Gantt campaign with questions about what exactly will be expected of my staff and me. Three things, it appears: research on Ruth, research on each of our primary opponents and Rudy Giuliani, and monitoring the media. "Media monitoring" is a polite term for reading newspapers and watching television. What I have been doing for the past week—getting in at 7:00 in the morning to clip newspapers—is media monitoring.

The idea is to assess, as objectively as possible, the strengths and weaknesses of our candidate and our opponents. Armed with that information, we will be able to poll the strength of potential arguments we could make about both Ruth and our opponents, formulate responses to arguments that might be made about Ruth, and anticipate and develop counterresponses to arguments we may make about our rivals. A little bit like chess, there are offensive and defensive components to what we will do.

A training manual put out by the Democratic National Committee suggests that, of the two, the defensive component is more important. "When it comes to defense," the manual says, "there are a thousand places where disaster lurks. You had best know about as many of them as possible, so that you can respond when a television reporter calls you up at 4:00 and says, 'Your opponent is about to start running an ad saying . . . Is it true?'" It sounds rather ominous. The stakes are high and the work is imposing. Each of the research projects is individually daunting. As a group they seem monumental.

The first step in researching each candidate is to review every article in which the subject is quoted. Merely collecting the articles will be a difficult task, let alone reading through them all. I search an electronic database of news articles called NEXIS to get a sense of the scope of the project. Ruth's name has been mentioned in over twelve thousand articles since 1973 and that does not include magazine articles or journals or the *New York Post*, all of which are not registered with the service. Simply downloading the articles will take days. Going through the *New York Post*, which can only be searched on microfiche, will take weeks.

And that is only the first step. We will need to compile complete voting histories for each candidate. That could be done on computer if Messinger and Ferrer were members of Congress. But assembling voting records for former City Council members means reading through the voluminous City Council records for each year they served. We will also need to search for lawsuits in which any of the candidates are or have been involved, check their property holdings, corporate memberships, and any partnerships to which they belong, review their draft records, confirm their educational degrees, and follow up on any tip we get that sounds credible.

I decide to start with Ruth, but it seems to me like moving a mountain a pebble at a time. I cannot imagine finishing any sort of remotely thorough job in less than a year with twenty people, let alone the staff of four or five that I ultimately will have (that is, if I am ever able to recruit anyone at all). Even if I knew what I was doing, which I don't, this seems like an impossible task.

February 10

I'm starting to have second thoughts about whether this job was such a good idea. The hours don't bother me and, though I'm anxious about the work, I'm sure it will eventually sort itself out. People have survived campaigns before. But this is too much. Today they are telling me I have to wear a beeper.

Jim has a reputation for hiring attractive women as his assistants. Gayle, who has worked with Jim before, is no exception. She is helping Jim set up the campaign, which includes finding a new, attractive assistant to replace her when she returns to Washington. Gayle is a wonderful complement to Jim. She's tough, mean, and demanding.

"Evan, you have to wear this," she says.

I explain that I'm not a beeper guy. "Besides," I say, "I really don't see the point. I don't plan on being out of the office much and I have a telephone at home, so people will always be able to get in touch with me."

"You like to run, don't you?" she asks.

"Yes."

"Well, what if Jim wants to get in touch with you while you're running?"

I plead to be spared my fate. I can always run back, I say. I often run in parks and along rivers where there are no public phones; the beeper will accomplish nothing. But my appeals are to no avail.

The beeper is thrust upon me.

February 11

For the past week, the campaign has stood still while David Dinkins enjoyed a public flirtation with the idea of running for mayor for a third time.

Dinkins has done little in the three and a half years since he lost his reelection bid to Rudy Giuliani to position himself for another mayoral try. He teaches a public-policy class at Columbia University, hosts a weekly call-in radio show, and plays a lot of tennis. The radio program's title, *Dialogue with Dinkins,* reflects the gentlemanly deportment of its host, but it also betrays its painfully boring content. Callers who express views sympathetic to Dinkins are politely embraced. Callers who express positive views about the current mayor are politely dispatched. Paid advertisements are read politely. Everything is very polite. Ed Koch hosts a daily program that is a bit more "New York." Koch, who is modestly introduced as the city's "Mayor for Life," greets listeners by introducing himself as the city's "voice of reason" and delights in cutting callers off and calling them morons and idiots. My guess is that Koch's ratings are higher than Dinkins's and that Dinkins's radio program has not done much to bolster his image. On top of everything else, Dinkins underwent bypass surgery last year.

Still, the flirtation is a demonstration of considerable political strength, all the more impressive for its casualness. A *Daily News* poll shows Dinkins trailing Rudy by a mere 10 percent, 46 to 36 percent, in a hypothetical head-to-head matchup. None of the current candidates come within 15 points. A significant plurality of voters view Dinkins as the candidate with the best chance of beating Giuliani. The prospect of a Dinkins candidacy was more than enough to make the Messinger staff hunch around a radio two days ago and listen to Dinkins announce his decision. A positive decision would have ended the Messinger campaign before it began.

As it is, Dinkins is not running, and many people close to him say that he was never really serious about the idea of running again. Some suggest that he floated the idea to increase the ultimate impact of his endorsement, which was expected to go to Ruth. Others, more cynical, say that he wanted a brief return to the limelight. Whatever his motivations, for one week, David Dinkins flexed his political muscle, and no one laughed.

But David Dinkins the candidate is not fungible with David Dinkins the political asset. For all of his political strength, Dinkins, who is black, is a polarizing figure. According to the polls, although 36 percent of blacks have a strongly positive view of Dinkins, 31 percent of whites have a strongly negative view of him. In total, blacks like him by ten to one. Whites view him negatively by two to one. Blacks revere him. Whites see him as inept and spineless.

With dramatic flair, David Dinkins called Ruth yesterday at 5:30 in the morning to tell her he was endorsing her. He then called the other candidates immediately thereafter to let them know, at least from his standpoint, the bad news. The truth is, Dinkins's endorsement is a mixed blessing. It offers early credibility, which is important for fund-raising purposes and stature in the press. But it also creates a link—which Rudy Giuliani is certain to draw—between the endorsed candidate and the perceived failure of the Dinkins administration.

In the abstract, if you were building the ideal candidate to challenge Rudy Giuliani, David Dinkins's endorsement would probably be viewed as a liability, not an asset. A campaign might reasonably make the strategic decision not to seek out the endorsement. We never bothered with a strategic calculation of that sort. Ruth has invested tremendously in David Dinkins. In 1989, when Ed Koch was viewed (and proved to be) vulnerable in a Democratic primary, Ruth stepped aside in favor of Dinkins despite the fact that many viewed her as a formidable candidate. Dinkins and Messinger are friends, and no thought is ever given to doing anything other than accepting the former mayor's endorsement enthusiastically. At a press conference yesterday afternoon, Ruth stood beside Dinkins and told the city that New York "was made a safer, healthier, smarter and, yes[!], far better place" because of David Dinkins's years in City Hall.

The end result of the events of the past week is a picture on the front page of today's *New York Times* of the man the overwhelmingly white readership of the *Times* regards as the worst mayor in the history of the city hugging Ruth.

Dinkins could have waited until after 6:00 to call.

February 13

I am observing as Ruth is being prepped for next week's primary candidates' debate sponsored by the *New York Post*. It is the first major debate of the season and, if the number of people attending to the task is a measure of the importance ascribed to it, this is *quite* important. Jim is here. So is our media consultant, Mandy Grunwald, a star in the 1992 Clinton campaign, who is featured briefly in the movie *War Room*. Marla Romash, a former press secretary to Al Gore, is in the room too. I don't know her precise role. She seems to be acting as an image consultant of sorts. Ruth's press secretary, Lee Jones, is here, pacing back and forth with a look of unspeakable pain on his face. Lee was press secretary to both Ed Koch and David Dinkins before working for Ruth. Two current and one former member of Ruth's borough president office staff are here posing as the other candidates. Ruth's chief of staff, a delightfully nice person named Jan who, I'm told, once ran for mayor in Dayton, is making sure things run smoothly. Three or four other people I don't know are in the room too. I have no idea what their respective roles are, but they all seem to feel free to chime in with their thoughts whenever they like.

Everyone is throwing around jargon. The words appear before me in italics.

"Ruth, you need to remember to turn the answer back to the *message*."

"Think *offensively*, not *defensively*. It's important to use your answer for several purposes. Respond to the question asked, respond to an attack, and then *launch an attack at Rudy*."

Everyone except me nods his or her head in agreement at these ideas. We are going into battle and I do not understand the lingo.

As the jargon flies around the room, I thumb through a memo to Ruth from her consultants. It's twenty pages thick and has lots of italics and bold print. It's obviously important.

The first debate presents an opportunity and a challenge. It is important to understand and set clear goals.

Heavens. She pays for this? There's some real nonsense here. *Tone is important. Work to create the moment that focuses coverage. Relax*. The woman went to Harvard, for goodness sake.

There is some good stuff, though, including a few subtle things that might not be obvious even to an experienced candidate.

Ruth needs to *remember her audience*. In other words, Ruth needs to avoid the temptation to speak to the particular people in the room and, instead, speak to the people of New York (that is, to the television cameras). That's a good point.

Ruth needs to *get people thinking of her as mayor.* One consequence of that is a bit gauche. Ruth is coached to preface every answer to a policy question by saying, "As mayor, I will . . ." It makes me wince at first, but you get used to it after a while. The key point is to get Ruth speaking prospectively rather than retrospectively. People want to know what candidates will do, not what they've done.

Ruth also needs to remember *not to repeat charges*. Instead of saying, "You're wrong when you say I'm just another big-spending liberal," she should say, "Use whatever labels you want, I'm going to go right on fighting for the working people of this city." I suppose that goes in with thinking *offensively, not defensively.*

There's a lot for me to learn. Still, some of this stuff just seems so silly. *Key challenge to Giuliani: We need welfare reform that works, not welfare reform that makes things worse.*

Who could argue?

February 15

Jim, my boss, is among a handful of people in the country who make their living traveling from city to city running political campaigns. Lots of professionals make money off of politics, but only a few get involved in the day-to-day functions of a campaign. Media consultants and pollsters don't like to get their hands too dirty. Their function is self-contained. They work for too many people to make a large emotional investment in any one candidate. But Jim and his peers are in it to their chins—modern-day mercenary generals. There's plenty of blood in the battles they fight; the only difference is that usually no one dies. Years in the trenches seem to have taken their toll on Jim. He's twenty pounds too heavy and prematurely gray and smokes those Old Gold cigarettes by the carton. He drinks coffee by the quart, which he flavors with lots of sugar. Watching Jim's ritualistic sweetening of coffee is amusing. He puts in three measured teaspoons, then pours an additional copious helping of sugar directly from a box he keeps on his desk.

Jim was a graduate student in political science at the University of Chicago in the early 1980s, on track to becoming an academic, when he got involved in Chicago politics and "caught the bug," as they say in the politics (and, not coincidentally, theater) biz. He was deputy campaign manager on then-congressman Harold Washington's surprisingly successful mayoral campaign (Washington was the first black mayor in the history of Chicago) and then kicked around Chicago politics for several years. His own résumé puts it a bit more dramatically:

> Jim Andrews began his career in politics organizing Chicago's notorious river wards, then considered among the toughest political territories in America.

> Controlled for generations by powerful ward bosses with strong connections to organized crime, this area was a linchpin in Chicago's regular Democratic machine, routinely providing machine candidates with ten-to-one victory margins in primary elections. Two years after he began, Andrews elected the first independent Democrat ever to emerge from this area. Six years after he started, not one of the old bosses remained.

A job well done.

In the early 1990s, Jim caught his break when he hooked up with James Carville, Bill Clinton's 1992 campaign manager and the most famous of the itinerant political mercenary generals. Jim managed Clinton's New Jersey campaign (Clinton carried the state) and then stuck around the Garden State to manage the reelection campaign of Governor Jim Florio, also a client of Carville and his partner, Paul Begala. Florio lost by a slim margin amid allegations that Ed Rollins, another merc, had paid cash to suppress black voter turnout. Though Christie Todd Whitman pulled the election out, Rollins said the Florio campaign was the best campaign run against him in thirty years.

From New Jersey, Jim went south and managed the successful reelection campaign of another Carville client, Zell Miller, the governor of Georgia. Miller's opponent, Guy Millner, a multimillionaire and political newcomer, outspent Miller badly, but Miller weathered the storm. The following year, Jim went to Kentucky to manage the gubernatorial campaign of yet another Carville client, Bob Babbage. Babbage lost, but by then Jim had established himself as a player on the national scene.

In 1996, he consulted on two of the highest-profile campaigns in the nation, black architect Harvey Gantt's second try to unseat Jesse Helms in North Carolina and Minnesota senator Paul Wellstone's reelection bid. Wellstone won, but Gantt, who appeared close in many late polls, lost by 7 points. Two months later, Jim was in New York.

If old articles are any indication, Jim's aggressive management style is nothing new. Articles from Babbage's campaign refer to Jim as "imposing order on the seemingly chaotic campaign" and "cracking the whip" at Babbage headquarters. He'll clearly do most anything to win. He and Mandy Grunwald ran one ad during the Babbage campaign that deplored the fact (underlined in red on the television screen) that not one death sentence had been carried out in Kentucky since 1962. *The Louisville Courier-Journal* called it the "most misleading TV ad of the year." The ad implied that Kentucky had had a death-penalty law since 1962 and failed to enforce it. In fact, all state capital-punishment laws were ruled unconstitutional for a period during the early 1970s. During the Florio campaign, Jim sent three campaign staffers to Christie Todd Whitman's house to take pictures for television ads attacking Whitman's wealth.

Jim seems to relish maintaining a secretive, puppet-master status. He hates being referred to as the "campaign manager" and not as the "campaign consultant." That anger comes in part from a well-placed desire not to be the public face of any campaign with which he is associated and in part from a sincere belief that political consultants are not afforded the respect they are due as a profession. Whatever the reason, Jim succeeds in keeping out of the papers for the most part. But, not surprisingly, the occasional intemperate remark filters through. A 1994 ad by Guy Millner tried to link profits made by Zell Miller on investments in North Georgia to Whitewater. According to the *Atlanta Journal and Constitution,* Jim screamed into the phone, "This is just . . . false!" One can imagine the word replaced by ellipses. Jim called Millner "morally unfit" to be governor and likened him to a sloganeering parrot: "Millner reminds me of a well-trained tropical bird. All you hear is 'Squawk! I'm a businessman, not politician. Squawk!'"

Ironically, in 1993, when asked about candidate Whitman's economic plan, Jim—who says that Ruth is the victim of sexism in the press that manifests itself in the subtle questioning of her competence—used a phrase that his staff repeated throughout the Jersey campaign. "She hasn't a clue," he said.

He's clearly a complex man. He's clearly also someone you want to have on your side in a battle.

When Ruth's staff announced Jim's hiring, they said that they could have gotten themselves a gun for the campaign, but instead they got themselves an Uzi.

And that seems about right.

February 16

Ruth Messinger was born in 1940 on the Upper West Side of Manhattan. Her father was an accountant, and her mother worked for the Jewish Theological Seminary. She attended the Brearley School, an exclusive academy on the Upper East Side, where she was voted "Class Brain" and wore Adlai Stevenson buttons on her uniform. From there she went to Radcliffe, where she majored in government.

Ruth was independent from an early age. She had a fifty-dollar clothing allowance from the time she was twelve. By her senior year at Radcliffe she was married to a young medical student, Eli Messinger, whom she met at a settlement-house camp in upstate New York. She graduated magna cum laude and was voted Phi Beta Kappa. After Harvard, she followed Dr. Messinger to Oklahoma, where he served in the federal Public Health Service. There, she passed time by earning a masters degree in social work at the University of Oklahoma and by working as a director of child welfare for a local county. While in Oklahoma, she got her first taste of electoral politics working on the Senate campaign of Fred Harris, a progressive liberal Democrat.

Back in New York City, Ruth raised her three children and held various jobs around town. For a few years, she worked at an alternative school on the Upper West Side. In 1975, she got her political feet wet by running for a seat on the local community school board. A year later, she ran in a seven-way Democratic primary for the state Assembly, only to lose to now-congressman Jerrold Nadler by 73 votes. It was the last election she would lose in twenty years.

In 1977, she won the first of three terms on the City Council. During her twelve years as a councilwoman, she earned a reputation as a tireless worker and a fierce critic of the Koch administration. In 1983, the *Daily News* rated her the most effective member of the City Council. In 1989, after considering a run for mayor or comptroller, she ran to succeed David Dinkins as borough president and won with 83 percent of the vote. In 1993, she nearly repeated that performance, winning with 76 percent of the vote. From there, she turned her sights on the mayoralty.

Ruth is appealingly quirky. She used a chain letter to drum up support when she ran for school board in 1975 and took her first oath of office for the City Council at the subway station on 72nd and Broadway. For years while living in an Upper West Side brownstone with her family, she slept on a mattress on the floor.

By instinct, she is disinterested in appearances. One newspaper article described her as "a tall, thin, slightly clumsy figure with a legendary lack of interest in fashion." She pays more attention to her looks these days, but the gist of the comment is right. Though her hairstyle seems more mayoral now, her natural inclinations shine through. Despite her staff's protestations, Ruth still carries two handbags with her at almost all times and rarely has a conversation without reading something at the same time. She seems compelled to do several things at a time, including whatever crossword puzzle is at hand.

On a personal level, she is warm and caring, the sort of person who remembers birthdays and shows up at funerals for parents of staff members.

She loves to bake and offers cookies to friends on any good excuse. Around the borough president's office, they refer to her as St. Ruth.

It is, in short, difficult to imagine an odder couple than Jim and Ruth. She is genteel. He is brusque. She is a family person. He is not married and rarely mentions his relatives. She thinks of individual voters. He thinks of voters only in the aggregate. The Manhattan borough president's office is a model of sensitivity. Decisionmaking is an open process, the staff is culturally diverse, and all views are respected. Jim disdains political correctness; our campaign is, and will remain, a dictatorship. There is little sharing of information, no tolerance for dissenting opinions, and no tolerance for mistakes. Ruth leads by example and influences people through persuasion. Jim leads by fiat and drives people by intimidation. Ruth is a politician. Jim is a general.

But they share one important thing—an unquenchable desire to succeed.

February 18

Rudy Giuliani portrays himself as a reformer, but Jim believes one of the arguments we will have to make is that Rudy is nothing more than an ordinary politician. There's strong evidence in the papers this week suggesting the truth of that claim. Two of Giuliani's closest advisers are Herman Badillo, formerly a congressman and the Bronx borough president, and Ray Harding, the head of the Liberal party, which provided Giuliani's margin of victory in the 1993 campaign. Harding and Badillo are partners in a law firm that lobbies the city. Since Giuliani took office, the firm's roster of city-lobbying clients rose from three to sixty-eight.

It's no wonder. A manufacturer that sold defective garbage bags to the city evaded penalties after Ray Harding took up his cause with the city. A construction company that did shoddy work on two city-owned tenements got off the hook after it hired the law firm of Fischbein Badillo Wagner Harding.

Lobbying payments must be disclosed under city law, but Fischbein Badillo seems to be playing loose with the regulations. Local 1199, a hospital-workers' union that endorsed David Dinkins in 1993, paid $25,000 to Fischbein Badillo to help persuade the city not to award contracts to nonunion home health-care agencies. The law firm reported only $250 on its lobbying reports. Fischbein Badillo says the remainder of the money was for legal advice and not lobbying services, which may be true, but it all smells rather fishy. It's something my team will be looking into quite closely.

February 19

Freddie Ferrer makes it clear from the outset that today's debate is going to be a Giuliani-bashing session. "Rudy Giuliani the prosecutor," he says, "would not tolerate Rudy Giuliani the mayor." It's a good line. Ferrer likes it so much that he repeats it. "Let me say that again. Rudy Giuliani the prosecutor would not tolerate Rudy Giuliani the mayor."

Ferrer says he is "running against Rudolph Giuliani not only because he has failed as a governmental leader, but because he has failed as a moral leader as well." He likes that one so much, he says it again too. "As mayor, Rudolph Giuliani has failed New York as a moral leader."

The candidates all take Ferrer's lead in attacking Giuliani (though not in repeating themselves). Sal Albanese, invoking the image of Darth Vader, says, "The present mayor has long ago gone over to the dark side." Ruth describes a city with overcrowded schools, homelessness, and high unemployment. "This is Rudy Giuliani's New York," she says, "and it is a disgrace." Days earlier, in accepting David Dinkins's endorsement, Ruth (overzealously in the eyes of the *Post*, which called the attack a "cheap shot") faulted Giuliani for not talking about the fact that he belongs to the same party as Newt Gingrich, Jesse Helms, and David Duke. Sharpton clarifies today: "Giuliani's problem is not that he's Republican, his problem is that he's repugnant and he does not care about the people of the city of New York."

In total, the candidates attack Giuliani thirty-four times. Ferrer leads with sixteen mentions of the mayor. Ruth is close behind with twelve. No one attacks a fellow Democrat. Détente reigns.

I find the debate especially interesting, because, as I still know sufficiently little about the candidates, I am, for the most part, able to view it as would an ordinary voter.

Ruth is impressive, if a bit boring. She is quite specific in her criticism of the Giuliani administration, but vague when it comes to the details of what she would do differently. She calls the city's overcrowding crisis "a disgrace"—more than ninety thousand kids do not have regular classroom seats—but says nothing about how she would address the problem and how she would raise the money to do it.

She speaks of "new strategies" and "innovative programs," but the phrases have no content. "Giuliani has ignored the needs of New Yorkers and followed his whims," she says. "I'll listen to New Yorkers and stand up for them." Most of it sounds like platitudes. She pledges not to raise taxes, a promise I recognize as politically expedient but consider incredible, given what little I know of her history, and irresponsible.

She is far stronger on civil-rights issues. Ruth unhesitatingly says that she would perform gay marriages at City Hall. Her daughter, she explains, is married to a woman and is a wonderful mother.

She is at her absolute best on the death penalty. Freddie Ferrer gives a confusing response to a question about the death penalty, explaining that he had been against it, but changed his position after a Bronx police officer, Kevin Gillespie, was shot to death. "The facts had changed in that case," he explains. "This crime was particularly heinous and cold-blooded. Politicians, as you know, are not made out of wood. You react and respond to things as they come."

It's shoddy logic. One could plausibly contend that one's view on an issue like the death penalty had evolved, but Ferrer was making a different argument. Ferrer did not say that his view of the death penalty had changed; he said that the facts of the particular case had changed in a way to compel the use of the death penalty. If his view had not changed, then he must have always favored the death penalty in particularly egregious cases.

Ruth nails him on the waffle. "That is a moral position and I don't change my moral positions." Jim suggested the answer to her earlier in the week during a prep session. She has the good sense to use Jim's short statement and not to address the soundness of Ferrer's reasoning in depth. It makes her seem strong.

Sal Albanese spends most of his precious time talking about his personal history:

> I arrived in New York City when I was eight, having immigrated from Calabria, Italy, with my family. We settled in Park Slope, Brooklyn. Soon after, my father became disabled and my mother, employed as a garment worker, had to support us. Because of my mother's union, she received a living wage that sustained our family. The public schools provided me with a good education. Free tuition at the City University of New York allowed me to attend college and become a teacher in the New York City Public School System—where I served for eleven years.

It's a good story, and Albanese seems like a nice guy, but it's hard to figure out what he stands for. For that matter, it's hard to figure out what any of the candidates stand for. After an hour and a half, it's difficult to discern many differences among them. "Who has the most experience to be the mayor of New York?" Ferrer asks in his closing. It's a rhetorical question. He is referring to himself, of course, but one can hardly tell from the way the debate has gone. Ruth takes no chances on her turn. "Who has the experience, the vision, and the determination to lead New York?" she asks. "I am that person," she answers.

The clear winner in my mind is Al Sharpton (Rudy Giuliani agrees; though he did not watch the debate, he says Sharpton is "far and away the winner"). Reverend Al has the best line of the debate. Commenting on Giuliani's record on hiring minorities (the number of blacks in the mayor's office has been nearly cut in half since Rudy took office), he says, "This administration is like the Rocky Mountains. The higher up you go, the whiter it gets." And I find myself agreeing with him on most policy matters. He opposes tuition vouchers, promises to fight police abuse, criticizes special tax breaks for corporations, and admits that he would reluctantly raise taxes if necessary. I would vote for this person if only he were not saddled with Al Sharpton's history. He's funny and charismatic and, best of all, he puts the interests of the party first. Sharpton says he will drop out of the mayoral race if he doesn't win the primary outright rather than engage in a bruising runoff that would damage the party.

"I think that would be the right thing to do," Sharpton says after the debate. "Then we could unite the party and not go through a grueling runoff."

February 20

An unsettling tone in the coverage of the debate makes me wonder whether a tough incumbent is the only obstacle we are up against. The press clearly views the campaign as a long shot. That's neither surprising nor unreasonable. But the press seems to regard the Democrats' mere act of running as audacious.

The four candidates were "competing for the privilege of being shellacked in the fall" by Rudy Giuliani, writes Maureen Dowd of the *New York Times*. Fair enough. But, Dowd continues, "It is unfathomable to think of any of the Democratic candidates for mayor actually being mayor." "To paraphrase Pat Moynihan," she says, "the state of the Democratic Party in New York might best be described as defining competency down."

There's not a nice word to be found in the papers. Collectively, the candidates are portrayed as out of touch and extreme. "Applause was reserved for gay marriage, the rainbow curriculum and police brutality." "Close your eyes," writes *News* columnist Sidney Zion, "and you were back to 1972." Murray Kempton says he won't vote for Ruth because "she personifies the evil of lesser evilism."

The *Times* beat reporter, Adam Nagourney, says "the leading contenders made no obvious progress in distinguishing themselves," which is probably true, but he reports it as a matter of fact and not opinion. Even the Democrats are tepid. Ed Koch says, "I'm not suggesting I would have been much better than they were. I know I would have been much better." "It's spring training," David Dinkins says. Sal Albanese gets what comes closest to a compliment. Jack Newfield, a *Post* columnist, writes, "Most politicians are half people—hollow stumps of ambition and calculation. But Councilman Sal Albanese is almost a whole human being."

This is going to be fun.

February 23

The Reverend Al Sharpton is a bizarre dichotomy.

During the debate, Sharpton, whose sister is a lesbian, proudly declared that not only would he perform gay marriages in City Hall if elected, he was the only candidate who could perform them regardless of whether he won. In 1987, he called Ed Koch a faggot.

On hand the day Sharpton announced his candidacy for mayor was the Reverend Wyatt Tee Walker, former chief of staff to Martin Luther King, Jr., and pastor of Harlem's renowned Canaan Baptist Church. So too was Leonard Jeffries, a City College professor whose speeches are often tainted with antiwhite and anti-Semitic remarks. Throughout his life, Sharpton has at times demonstrated extraordinary strength and at others devolved into demagoguery.

In either case, it is an extraordinary life. Born in East New York, Brooklyn, Sharpton delivered his first sermon at the age of four to a congregation of more than nine hundred. He was ordained and licensed as a minister in the Pentecostal church at the age of ten. At about the same time he was ordained, Sharpton learned that his father was having an adulterous relationship with his mother's daughter from a previous marriage. Sharpton's father left the family and eventually had a child with Sharpton's half sister.

Sharpton's mother struggled to keep the family in the house in Queens to which they had moved, but, after living without heat and electricity for several months, she admitted that she could not make ends meet and moved the family back to the projects in Brooklyn. The family eventually settled in another apartment in Crown Heights.

Throughout it all, Sharpton somehow thrived. By his late teens, he counted Adam Clayton Powell, the famous Harlem congressman, and Jesse Jackson among his mentors. He corresponded regularly with Marcus Garvey's widow, whom he met on a preaching trip to Jamaica. By the early 1980s, Reverend Sharpton was a force in the black community.

He burst into the city's consciousness in 1987 when he, together with attorney Alton Maddox, defended a young woman named Tawana Brawley, who said that she had been abducted by a group of white men, smeared with feces, and dropped on the side of a road. Many felt that the claim was a hoax, and a yearlong investigation failed to disclose any suspects, but Sharpton was a daily presence on the evening news. From that point on, he was a presumed participant in any matter involving race relations in the city. He was at the forefront when subway vigilante Bernhard Goetz shot two black men, and again in 1993 when a Hasidic Jew lost control of his car and accidentally killed a black child, precipitating a riot and the retributive murder of a yeshiva student.

Sharpton was at his absolute finest in 1991 when a white detractor stabbed him. Sharpton publicly forgave the man and asked a judge to be lenient in sentencing the criminal. He was at his absolute worst in 1995 while picketing a Harlem clothing store whose white owner terminated the lease of a record store owned by an African American. Sharpton called the landlord a "white interloper." The crowd was a bit less temperate, shouting racial epithets like "Jew bastards" and "bloodsucking Jews." Eventually, a man named Abubunde Mulocko burst into the store armed with a .38, shot three whites and a Pakistani, and set fire to the building, killing seven more men, including a black security guard whom the protesters had taunted as a "cracker lover."

Sharpton had no connection to the arsonist, but the "white interloper" remark had not done anything to ease tension. Sharpton eventually apologized for the comment, but denied that he had intended to attack the owner of Freddy's Fashion Mart. Instead, he said, he had meant to attack all landlords not from Harlem.

Even Sharpton's political career has been a contradiction. In 1986, he endorsed Al D'Amato. Immediately after the endorsement press conference, Sharpton took D'Amato to see a building that housed a drug program sponsored by Sharpton's National Youth Movement. D'Amato agreed to secure a $500,000 grant from the Department of Housing to rehabilitate the building, which was run by the vice-chair of the National Youth Movement. Sharpton was later charged with defrauding the movement of more than $250,000. Six years later, Sharpton was among four Democrats vying for D'Amato's seat.

Whatever your view, two things are clear about the Reverend Alfred Sharpton. One is that he's a political force to be reckoned with. In his first run for political office, Sharpton ran third in a four-way Democratic primary, finishing ahead of then–city comptroller Elizabeth Holtzman. Sharpton won 15 percent of the total vote and 70 percent of the black vote. In 1996, he won 26 percent of the total vote in a primary against incumbent senator Daniel Patrick Moynihan. And his charm is undeniable. After a speech, a police officer's son asked Sharpton whether he would raise police salaries if elected. "Yeah, but I'd make them live in the city," Sharpton said.

"Sounds fair," said the boy, who was white.

Recalling the conversation to a *Washington Post* reporter later in the day, Sharpton shook his head. "He acted like he'd vote for me," Sharpton said. "You live long enough, you'll see everything."

• • •

Hours after a gunman shoots seven tourists on the observation deck of the Empire State Building, the mayor summons the heads of two major Jewish organizations to City Hall for a briefing on a threat to the safety and security of the Jewish community. The police commissioner tells them that security has been beefed up for high-profile Jewish institutions and individuals—even though the gunman has already shot himself in the head and there is no evidence that his action was tied to any group.

On the same day, Sal from Queens (not Albanese; he's from Brooklyn, you'll recall) telephones a radio station and says that he has an Uzi and wants to kill Al Sharpton. The police are contacted, but Sharpton doesn't exactly get equal treatment. No one gets around to telling the Reverend about the death threat for five days.

"I wish somebody from the Police Department had told me," Sharpton says.

"The Police Department is not going to be drawn into Al Sharpton's political agenda," a spokesperson for the police department replies.

February 25

The battle lines are now completely drawn. Rudy Giuliani put the last piece of his team in place yesterday, hiring a media consulting company called the Goodman Group, headed by Adam Goodman. Last week, Sal Albanese filled in his lineup by hiring Joe Slade White, a media consultant known for operating low-budget campaigns. We check Goodman and White out.

White seems clean and quirky. He got his start working for the 1972 McGovern campaign and did ads for billionaire Paul Allen's attempt to build a new stadium for the Seattle Seahawks. He lived on the Upper West Side for seventeen years, but has not previously worked on a New York City campaign. If he has been involved in any scandals, they haven't surfaced in the press.

Goodman seems a bit shadier (admittedly an imprecise term—I think working for a Republican is shady). In 1985 and 1986, Adam Goodman and his father produced more than a million dollars worth of ads for organizations headed by a man named Carl Channel, urging support for the Nicaraguan Contras and opposing some congressional candidates for refusing to support aid to the Contras. In 1987, Channel pled guilty to conspiring to defraud the government and fingered Oliver North as his coconspirator. One newspaper reported that some of the profits from arms sales to Iran had been diverted to groups that funded the ads.

Those charges were never proved, and the Goodmans consistently said that they did not know where Channel's money came from. And they said the accusations that they had worked for Oliver North were a "really bad rap." But at the same time, Adam Goodman admitted that he met with Oliver North on two occasions, including an event in 1985 at which Pat Buchanan and North gave a slide and map presentation to fifty of Channel's donors. Goodman also said that North gave them footage for one of the advertising films the agency produced.

Armed with this information, Lee Jones is out trying to persuade some reporter to write a story about Goodman's background. This is called "placing a story." An interesting concept, it is premised on the assumption that the press is smart, but lazy. If the story is interesting, reporters are sometimes happy to have a campaign do their work for them. Even though the information is from an obviously biased source, it has some reliability since the campaign has a long-term interest in being perceived as credible.

February 26

Making a guest appearance in the New York mayoral race today is Dick Morris, one of the stars of the national political scene. Morris, who got his start in politics working for liberals on the Upper West Side of Manhattan back when liberals were liberals, has represented a diverse set of clients ranging from Bill Clinton to Trent Lott. He is widely recognized as a major force behind Bill Clinton's shift to the center after the 1994 mid-term elections. Some regard him as President Clinton's savior (he certainly does), others as one of the policy architects of a welfare-reform plan that sent millions of children into poverty and rendered Bill Clinton indistinguishable from many Republicans.

Morris was disgraced during the 1996 presidential election by evidence that he had allowed a prostitute to listen in on conversations between him and the president. He was even more disgraced by evidence that he had a nasty foot fetish. Morris doesn't have much to do these days and is weighing in today on Giuliani's choice of Adam Goodman. Goodman "produces cuddly media," Morris says, and "can remedy the biggest weakness that Giuliani has, which is that people think he is a good mayor, but don't particularly like him as a person."

Morris reveals that he interviewed for the Giuliani job last year. That's especially interesting since Morris also met with Freddie Ferrer. Many had speculated that Morris was the force behind Ferrer's shift on the death penalty. Morris landed neither client, but he came close to achieving what seems to be his ultimate dream.

Perhaps someday Morris will be able to run against himself.

February 28

In my capacity as research director of the campaign, I've inherited a folder of memos from people with helpful suggestions for Ruth. The best of the lot is a five-page note from one of Ruth's friends outlining "strategic approaches." The memo "is a campaign strategy in the broadest sense" offered as an "outside perspective, with the intention that it be a constructive view."

"After careful observation and much thought," the author begins, "I've put together these notes on an overall strategy and perceptual framework for the fall election. Essentially there are four components: Define what the election is about. Define the perceptual framework. Identify the communication strategy and key issues. Tactical implementation of the strategy."

What precisely, you may ask, is the perceptual framework?

"Based on observations, conversations with voters, and polls, the perceptual battlefield has two dimensions: (1) personal warmth and working with others—Compassion/Abrasiveness—and (2) ability to get things done, to achieve goals—Effectiveness. The 'winning' perception is to be both compassionate and also effective."

The memo then places the candidates on a graph with the horizontal axis labeled "Bureaucratic/Ineffective" at the left and "Effective/Autocratic" at the right and the vertical axis labeled "Abrasive/Cold" at bottom and "Compassionate/Warm" at top. The four leading candidates are represented by points on the graph. Rudy Giuliani's dot is in the lower right-hand corner of the graph (quadrant IV for geometry majors), representing an effective but cold public figure. Ruth's dot is in the upper left-hand corner, depicting her as warm but ineffective. Freddie Ferrer is in the same

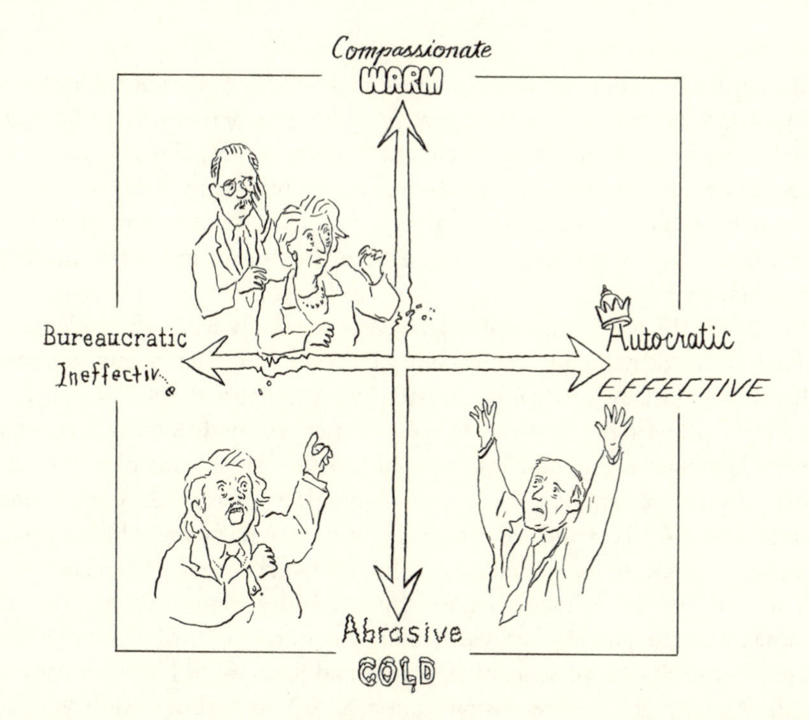

quadrant, though slightly higher and to the left of Ruth. That may simply be a space accommodation, but if it's intentional, it shows the author's sense that Ferrer is perceived as warmer and more ineffective than Ruth. Sharpton's dot is way down in the lower left-hand Neverland of ineffective, abrasive types. It's difficult to tell from the graph, but the author appears to regard Sharpton as slightly more abrasive than ineffective, but in any case his is probably a better fate than Sal Albanese's. Sal's dot is not even on the graph.

The "underlying battleground for the election" is to move into the upper right-hand corner of effective, compassionate leaders—political Nirvana. This objective is represented on the graph by two directional vectors. Ruth's vector points to the right, indicating her need to become perceived as more effective. Rudy's points from the bottom up, reflecting his challenge to be seen as more warm. If we can get to a point that's higher and farther to the right than Ferrer and Giuliani, we win.

It's all that easy.

March 1

The first polls of the season offer some signs of hope. The news is mostly good for Giuliani, but not entirely. The Marist Institute of Public Opinion finds that Rudy's approval rating is the highest it's been since he took office. Overall, 55 percent of people approve of his job performance. But the racial disparity in the numbers is striking. Among whites, Giuliani has a 75-percent approval rating, but only 28 percent of blacks approve of his performance as mayor. Giuliani has always had trouble attracting minority votes. Even in his victorious 1993 campaign, Rudy captured just 5 percent of the black vote.

Even with the lag in the minority community, Rudy leads all challengers in head-to-head matchups. Ruth comes closest of the Democrats, but she still trails 49–39. Nevertheless, pollster Lee Miringoff concludes that the race is "competitive" because there is a persistent difference between Rudy's approval rating and his vote. Although a significant plurality approve of his performance, Rudy fails to break 50 percent in one-on-one matchups with Ferrer and Messinger. Pollsters generally regard such a lag as cause for concern by an incumbent. Jim takes great heart in the lag.

The news in the primary is good for us. More than anything else, it demonstrates the power of David Dinkins's endorsement. Marist has Ruth leading Ferrer 36–26. In September, Marist had Ruth in the lead by merely 5 points. And a poll by the television station New York 1 shows Ruth leading Ferrer by 7 points. In February, she trailed Ferrer by 6. Her support among blacks has nearly doubled from 15 to 26 percent in the past month. It's often difficult to draw conclusions about causation in politics because there are so many variables, but in this case, since nothing much of substance has happened in the past month, we can say with great confidence that the change in Ruth's numbers is primarily a result of the strength of David Dinkins.

March 2

Of all the traits valued in politics, none is more prized than an appreciation of *message.* Consultants look to work for candidates who are able to *stay on message.* Campaigns look to hire people who understand the *concept of message.* As best I can figure, *staying on message* means repeating something mindlessly. What is most dreaded in a conversation partner is treasured in a politician.

The theory behind *message* is that it is only through constant repetition that a candidate can become associated with an idea. A corollary of that theory is that, since becoming associated with an idea requires so much effort, the most a candidate can reasonably hope for is to become associated with one or two ideas.

Staying on message requires eternal vigilance. It means saying the same thing over and over. It means responding to questions with the message even if the message has nothing to do with what's being asked.

MEDIA TYPE: Madame Candidate, what do you think of the incumbent's position on gay marriages?

OFF-MESSAGE CANDIDATE: The incumbent is wrong. Gay marriages are good.

ON-MESSAGE CANDIDATE: My position on that issue is well established. The real issue that should be of concern to the voters, Mister Reporter, is why the incumbent has ignored the city's unemployment crisis. We need to rebuild the economy and create jobs for city residents. This city has lost 130,000 jobs since last year . . . [ad nauseam].

No one stays on message quite like Sal Albanese.

Take these two examples. At the *Post* debate two weeks ago, Albanese said, "The New York I grew up in had vital middle and working classes. But, my friends, we are rapidly moving toward a two-tiered city. A small group of very wealthy people and the rest of the city poor and working poor."

Today, in a Sunday morning television interview, Albanese says this in response to a question about how he plans to win: "By maintaining the quality of life in our neighborhoods in this city, we're quickly moving toward a two-tiered city, a small group of very wealthy people and the rest of the city poor and working poor." This response has absolutely nothing to do with the question. In fourteen minutes with Gabe Pressman, Albanese uses the phrases "two-tiered city" and "morally bankrupt" (as in a morally bankrupt political system) two times each. He uses the phrase "living wage" seven times. He even manages to work in that he's from Italy three times. It's quite an admirable performance.

Albanese is an interesting character. He told you a good bit of his story at the debate, but the rest is worth exploring. Forty-seven years old, Albanese immigrated to New York City from Calabria, Italy, at the age of nine. His father, who served in the Italian army and was taken prisoner during the war, was disabled soon after arriving in America, leaving his mother, a garment worker, to support the family, which, as you know, she was able to do by virtue of her membership in a union. Albanese went to John Jay High School and straight through to the City University of New York in the days when CUNY tuition was still free and the education of high quality. After failing a tryout for the New York Yankees, Albanese became a gym teacher in the city's public schools.

Like Ruth, Albanese got involved in politics through his local community school board. He lost his first election for state Assembly in 1980, but after that he went on an impressive hot streak. In 1982, Albanese ran for City Council against Angelo Arculeo, a twenty-nine-year incumbent and the minority leader of the City Council. Albanese won. In 1985, Conservative party leader Michael Long spent $400,000 trying to unseat Albanese, outspending the incumbent by four to one. Albanese won again, this time with 62 percent of the vote. In 1989, Albanese's nominating petitions were challenged, and he was bumped off the ballot. He ran as an Independent and won again with a still impressive 56 percent of the vote. In 1992, he lost his first election in a decade, a congressional campaign against Susan Molinari. Along the way, Albanese somehow found time to earn a law degree from Brooklyn Law School.

He's regarded as something of a maverick on the City Council. His living-wage bill, passed last year over Rudy Giuliani's veto, requires some city contractors to pay a higher minimum wage to their employees. He voted in favor of the city's gay-rights bill despite the fact that his district disfavored the bill. Albanese is pro-choice, but also favors the death penalty. And, some would say to his credit, he is not in the good graces of the City Council Speaker, Peter Vallone, because he regularly voted against budgets (sometimes, for the ostensibly good reason that the budgets cut too much from the schools). Albanese is one of the only veteran council members who doesn't collect a stipend, a kind word for City Council sinecures.

A self-described populist, Albanese is running on two main issues: campaign-finance reform and the increasing income disparity. Mike Tomasky of *New York* magazine has dubbed him Sal Quixote. I like him.

March 3

A half million *Daily News* readers woke up this morning to the most disturbing sight imaginable: Rudy Giuliani in drag. The occasion was the annual Inner Circle dinner, an event at which current and former political journalists lampoon city, state, and national politicians. Mayors present a rebuttal, traditionally accompanied by a Broadway show cast. Rudy, resplendent in "a peach gown with sequined chiffon overlay, gold high heels, blond bouffant wig and garish makeup," took the stage with the cast of *Victor/Victoria*, a musical about a woman playing a man playing a woman.

Julie Andrews, the star of *Victor/Victoria,* appeared on stage with "Rudia" and issued a challenge: "Can you play a woman playing a man playing a woman?"

"Haven't you seen my act?" Rudia retorted. "I already play a Republican playing a Democrat playing a Republican." It's reminiscent of what *Spy* magazine said about Rudy's hair in 1993: "It's real hair in an incredible simulation of a toupee."

Deputy Mayor Rudy Washington, the only African American member of Rudy's cabinet, has the best line of the night. "Rudy has got to go to a place he's never been before," Giuliani campaign manager Fran Reiter said during a mock brainstorming session.

"Harlem?" asked Washington.

• • •

After his election, Rudy Giuliani discontinued an affirmative-action program created by David Dinkins to award more city contracts to businesses owned by minorities and women. Under the program, a minority- or female-owned business was awarded a contract even if its bid was as much as 10 percent higher than the lowest bid. During the program's first year, the percentage of contracts awarded to minority- and women-owned companies increased from 9 to 17.5 percent.

The city no longer even keeps statistics about the number and value of contracts awarded to minority- and women-owned businesses. "Data gathering is just not a priority right now," said Rudy Washington. The mayor says the program was illegal. "Had I gone ahead with the program I inherited and awarded contracts on that basis," Giuliani says, "the City of New York would now be paying hundreds of millions of dollars in damages for unconstitutionally and illegally used race-based criteria as a way of helping people." Could Rudy be tweaking the truth? Other classes of lawsuits do not cost the city anywhere near the amounts Rudy is suggesting. Last year, for example, the city paid out $27.3 million to settle lawsuits against city police officers—and there are lots of those.

March 4

My first hires are a pair of campaign veterans. Art, who is about my age, worked last year on Bob Torricelli's winning senatorial campaign in New Jersey. He set up a computerized database of seventy thousand news articles for the Torricelli campaign and offers to do the same for us. That means we'll be able to access any newspaper article we want by keying in a subject code. Art seems to have a great attitude and, best of all, has a grandmother who lives nearby, which means he's willing to consider the meager salary we're offering. I envision him as my deputy.

The other hire is a Californian who somehow by the age of twenty-four has worked on seven campaigns. He's lost them all—including a teenage friend's race for school board—but that's no concern to me. I hire him without a personal meeting. He has experience and is willing to work for less than minimum wage. Though I'm pleased with these two additions to the staff, the fact of the matter is I'm desperate. Jim has been hounding me mercilessly about getting a staff together. I feel fortunate to have landed two people who have actually been through a campaign before. The interviewing had not been going well. Low pay, a long-shot candidate, and a difficult boss don't sell very well. Before Art, the only person who expressed enthusiastic interest in the job was a young, obviously unstable man who was doing computer programming from his home in Long Island.

This background makes the pressure that's coming from the borough president's office all the more frustrating. Over the past two weeks, the fund-raising director and I have hired a total of six people. Ruth's staff is concerned that all of the six are white. I share the concern, but there aren't a lot of places to find people willing to work for $2,000 a month. I've called the Democratic National Campaign Committee, the Democratic Congressional Campaign Committee, the Democratic Senatorial Campaign Committee, Emily's List (a group that promotes women candidates), and a few college students I know. I've even thought about calling the Republican National Campaign Committee. There are just not that many people to choose from. My agenda is simple: If they're smart and willing to do the job, they're hired. We have so very much to do. There just doesn't seem to be time to run an aggressive diversification campaign.

But the people in the borough president's office don't see it that way. For the first time in my life, I'm accused of racism, though not to my face. The charge doesn't bother me as much as what it says about what the people on the government side think about what we on the campaign side do. They view the campaign as symbolic. When Jim was hired, Ruth's aide said the decision was based in part on "his work with black candidates." To them, hiring Jim was an act of constituency politics, or at least an act that should be milked for its value in the constituency. They, indeed, see the campaign as symbolic. We see it as an entity that will work around the clock for the next eight months to raise $10 million and develop an argument that Ruth is better for the city than the popular incumbent.

I wonder whether the two views can ever be reconciled.

• • •

In a sickening column in the *Post*, Andrea Peyser calls Ruth's daughter's bearing of an artificially inseminated child an act of "boundless ego." Peyser does not "categorically oppose the concept of gay adoption," but this, she says, is "quite different." "Little Amani," she says, was given less choice in being used by Miriam Messinger to show people another picture of family life "than a child who's abandoned on the street. That child, at least, can try to trace her parentage, if she so wishes." Amani, writes Peyser, is a child "who was given life expressly to satisfy the desires of two women who have something political to prove."

March 5

The worst kept secret in New York is that Rudy Giuliani's marriage is on the rocks. The second worst kept secret is that the press is afraid to say so. The first fact doesn't have serious implications for the campaign. Voters have shown time and again across the country in elections at every level that they don't care very much about the sexual exploits of their electeds. But the second fact is of very serious concern. We've already seen signs that getting favorable coverage in the press is going to be an uphill battle. Yesterday's article by Andrea Peyser suggests that the *Post* is downright hostile to Ruth. This difficult battle will be impossible if the press is unwilling to take on Giuliani. Jim calls it a *fucking hostile press environment.*

I have mixed feelings about whether marital problems or philandering is within the legitimate scope of news coverage. When Gary Hart defied the press to prove his infidelity, he made the issue fair game. But Rudy Giuliani hasn't done that. Rudy has consistently said that his family life isn't anyone's business. (An understatement, really. When a television reporter asked Rudy whether his wife's absence from the Inner Circle press revue meant his marriage was on the rocks, Giuliani said with typical restraint, "You have no right to ask that. You should be ashamed that you asked it. And asking that question is outrageous, and it's a shame that you've stooped to reaching into people's lives to that extent.")

On the other hand, some factors seem to make coverage more legitimate in this case. Rudy's wife, Donna Hanover, is a public figure in her own right. As First Lady, she has a staff of four that costs city taxpayers about $200,000 a year. And the woman Giuliani is said to be having an affair with is a member of his staff. These things seem to make it a somewhat more legitimate subject.

But whether it's theoretically ethical to write about, I'm quite sure that in any other *press environment* the story would be all over the news. The *Los Angeles Times* says as much today. "In New York," the *Times* writes, "the competition for news may be more ferocious than in any other city. Yet for some, the Giuliani-Hanover case spells trouble, and it may be that the press corps' private obsession will never become public fact."

Unfortunately, it's the *Los Angeles Times* that is saying what everyone knows to be true. Can we legitimately be outraged that the press has not only failed to cover the fact of Rudy's marital problems, but has also failed to cover its failure to cover the problems? Or is this metanews? Imagine the story:

> *Daily News,* New York, March 10: Once again, the *Daily News* is not covering Rudy Giuliani's alleged extramarital affair despite significant evidence substantiating the relationship. *News* owner Mortimer Zuckerman said, "We'd like to cover it, but I have too much of a financial interest in Rudy's reelection and, besides, I'm a little scared of the guy. He's kind of wacky."

The Giuliani-Hanover marriage is sort of an interesting story. Donna Hanover is an accomplished woman. A Stanford graduate, Hanover, forty-seven, worked for several years in cable TV programming. After receiving a master's degree in journalism from Columbia, Hanover held radio and TV jobs in several cities including Miami, where she met Rudy in 1982 while he was still the number-three official in the Reagan Justice Department. Rudy had his secretary call Donna to set up their first meeting. After a month of dating, Rudy proposed and the two were married in 1984.

Hanover followed Rudy to New York and got a reporting job at WPIX. Today, she is anchor of Fox television's early morning news program and hosts a program of her own on The Food Network. She also has a burgeoning acting career. She appeared in the television show *Law and Order* in January and made her film debut in *The People Versus Larry Flynt* to critical acclaim.

During Rudy's first two runs for mayor, Hanover made significant personal sacrifices. In 1989, she gave up her news anchor job at WPIX to avoid political conflict with Rudy's first campaign against Dinkins. In 1993, she was a constant presence at Rudy's side and made a campaign commercial defending his record on abortion, an issue that was a liability for Giuliani both in 1989 and 1993.

But this year, Hanover is conspicuously absent from the scene. When the Yankees won the World Series last year, Hanover and Giuliani rode in separate floats during the victory parade. She publicly dropped Giuliani from her surname and failed to make an appearance at the Inner Circle dinner. (She's probably doubly happy she missed that one.) For that matter, Hanover is rarely seen in public with the mayor at all anymore. During an appearance on *Late Night with Conan O'Brien,* Donna never so much as mentioned Rudy's name.

But no one says anything about it. That's great for Giuliani and his family, but if the press is treating Rudy with kid gloves on this one, how receptive will they be when we start to make our arguments about him?

March 6

Jim believes that Ruth needs *to move toward the center.* Today that concept gets a real-life application.

The police department revealed yesterday that it is switching to a new type of bullet that is (allegedly) deadlier, more efficient, and potentially safer to bystanders of police shoot-outs. The traditional full-metal jacket has nothing to stop it once it hits a target, so it can continue flying through its intended object and put bystanders at risk. The hollow-point bullet, by contrast, expands upon impact like an umbrella, stopping the bullet in its tracks. It rips flesh by expansion. Today, two days after a Manhattan woman lost her eye to a cop's stray bullet that tore through her front door, the police department is announcing that it is switching to the hollow points.

The police are offering three arguments in support of the switch. First, because of the bullet's greater potency, criminals are more likely to be severely injured and will be brought down more easily. Second, there's less risk of bystander injury due to the fact that the bullet, by design, will become lodged in the target. In absolute terms, the risk to bystanders from stray bullets is minimal—seven bystanders were wounded and two were killed in 1995; eleven were wounded in 1996—but any unnecessary injury is too much, the police say. Finally, cops will use fewer bullets if the ones they use do more damage. Hollow-point bullets are actually more expensive—they cost $22 per bullet versus $16 per bullet for full-metal jackets—but since they're deadlier, cops will need to use fewer bullets. The switch could save the taxpayers hundreds of dollars each year.

There's some good authority on the side of the police department. Virtually every other major urban police department in the nation uses hollow-point bullets. But the minority community is up in arms, and understandably so. The entire premise of the switch is that the bullets are more deadly and more likely to maim. There's not much uncertainty in the minority community about who the cops will be shooting at. And one study shows that 80 percent of the shots fired in police shoot-outs miss their targets, meaning some innocent people will be more severely injured by the new bullets.

Civil libertarians are up in arms. "The introduction of the hollow-point bullet may very well exceed the bounds of reason and necessity, especially if massive internal injury is the risk," says Norman Siegel, executive director of the New York Civil Liberties Union. Even Giuliani says the issue needs to be looked at more carefully, though one wonders whether he is acting on conviction or out of anger over the fact that he was apparently left out of the loop on the announcement.

All of the Democratic candidates have been asked for comment. Ruth worries about how the switch will be perceived in the minority community and thinks the evidence of increased safety isn't sufficiently convincing to justify the damage the switch will cause with minorities. But Jim believes we need to "cede" the issue of crime to Giuliani. Among the many uphill battles that Ruth faces is convincing voters that she is tough enough to maintain the gains that the city has made against crime. Jim believes opposing the new bullets will be perceived as attacking Rudy on crime and will ultimately weaken us.

Here's what we actually say: "It makes sense to be sure that police officers are able to protect themselves and the public against people who generally outarm them." The statement is so ambiguous that it's not clear whether we're calling for further study of the subject or expressing outright support. Are we to the right of Rudy? Ruth's deputy borough president wants to issue a more strongly worded statement to a black newspaper, but Jim nixes the idea. He wants to put an end to the idea of dealing differently with different constituencies. If we're going to do this, it has to be full bore.

The strategy is successful in one respect. Although Albanese says the issue should be studied further, Ferrer and Sharpton both oppose the switch. "What we're really saying to bystanders," Sharpton says, "is you won't have a problem with a ricocheting bullet, but if you're hit by a bullet, we hope you have life insurance. It's a walking death penalty."

We're in the "center."

March 8

The much awaited reviews of Rudia's performance are filtering in. "The wig was pro," says the Lady Bunny, the noted New York drag queen.

"The voice was quite effective," said Queen Allyson Allante of the Imperial Queens and Kings of New York. "He does it better than I do."

Even the legendary Lypsinka had words of praise for the mayor. "I thought the makeup was well applied," says the diva.

March 9

The hollow-point-bullets controversy is ancient history already as far as the campaign is concerned, but one aspect of Wednesday's events continues to trouble Jim: Ruth's deputy's proposal to send a more strongly worded statement about hollow points to the black newspaper that asked for comment. It hardly registered a blip on my screen. Even if someone had noticed the quote in the black press, it's quite possible they would not have noticed the difference between the two quotes. But to Jim it is symbolic of a larger problem. When he's in a bad mood, he scrunches his face, curls up his nose, and snarls, "They're panderers," and repeats it a few times. When he's in a good mood, he shakes his head, looks down at the floor, and sadly says, "They're not ready for the big time."

Though the hollow-point-bullets case may not be important on its own, it demonstrates a larger difference between the way Jim thinks and goes about things and the way the borough president's office does its business. Jim thinks solely in terms of the message, which must be one or two basic points articulated in the simplest possible manner to every possible audience.

The borough president's office is organized in a manner that is not readily compatible with message politics. There is a black liaison in Ruth's office as well as a Latino liaison, a gay liaison, an Asian American liaison, and about a dozen other liaisons for every other imaginable racial or ethnic group. It is a bureaucracy of constituencies and the bureaucrats are used to saying and doing what their individual constituency group requires, without much thought about the bigger picture.

The mind-set across the street is that if you can get a few votes by changing a few words in a statement, you may as well go ahead and change those few words. They want the campaign to produce literature for every constituency group. Jim wants to produce a single piece that will state the campaign's message to everyone. The existing literature is bizarre. The general piece quotes "a diamond merchant" saying that Ruth is "very capable." Another piece designed for blacks emphasizes moonlight basketball in east Harlem, the issuance of a black family report, and the appointment of a black family task force as Ruth's accomplishments as borough president.

Even the way Ruth's staff marketed Jim's hiring was driven by constituency politics. In December, Ruth's aides told the *Times* that Jim was "selected because of his work with black candidates," noting that Jim had worked for Harold Washington and Harvey Gantt, both black. Ruth's aides noted that Ruth "has made a particular effort to court New York's black voters."

The statement about Jim's hiring is especially interesting. If Jim was hired because of his work with black candidates, it was at most a tangential consideration that was an added plus on his side of the ledger. Jim was hired because he was the smartest person out there. And even if he was hired because of his work with black politicians, there seems little point to advertising his hiring. No one will vote for a candidate because of who his or her campaign consultant is. The consultant's work might make a difference, but the consultant as a person is unknown to voters, especially one such as Jim with no New York ties. And even if you make the decision to exploit the hiring to score points with blacks, why advertise it to the *New York Times*, which does not have a large black readership? The answer is that the world across the street thinks of the electorate piecemeal, as constituencies, and not as a whole. Its instinct is to modify the message when it suits particular needs.

Emphasizing different agenda items to different constituencies is pretty harmless, but the risk of saying substantively different things to different groups is far greater. The altered statement might cost you more votes than it gets you. Until now that trade-off didn't seem very real to the borough president's staff because Ruth wasn't in the limelight as much. Now, everything she does is going to be scrutinized. Jim's challenge is to change the mind-set over there to accept this new reality.

In the interim, I have a new job. I am to read through every single piece of paper that anyone at the borough president's office puts out.

March 10

In this morning at 6:45. Art is already here, which is a good sign. He's already proving himself a hard worker. It takes us approximately ninety minutes to read through the day's articles and summarize them in a briefing, which Jim is now requiring on a daily basis. Soon there will be evening briefings summarizing the daily television news coverage of the campaign. We fax out the morning briefing at 8:45. Jim says it is "not bad," which I take to be a great compliment.

Jim's interest is piqued by a short piece about an increase in the incidence of domestic violence. This is a subject of great interest to voters, he explains. I am only not aware of it because of my provincial upbringing. "Domestic violence doesn't strike a chord for you because it's not a part of your life. You don't abuse your girlfriend . . . except when you use those manacles. Eh? Eh?"

Fortunately, Jim is off in Chicago for the day.

March 12

Another troubling item in the paper this morning. It is again not substantively disturbing, but of concern, rather, for the additional insight it offers into what Jim would call "where the press is at." More precisely, it offers disheartening insight into where one particularly influential member of the press is at: Adam Nagourney, the *New York Times* reporter who covered the Dole campaign last year and who will cover the mayoral race on a day-to-day basis.

The article reports the results of a *Times* survey of voter attitudes about New York City and Mayor Giuliani. Consistent with the other polls this month, there's much good news in it for the incumbent. Fifty-four percent of the respondents approve of the job Rudy Giuliani is doing as mayor, compared with only 32 percent who disapprove. Forty-three percent say the city is safer compared with four years ago; only 16 percent say it is less safe. People approve of how Giuliani is handling crime 74 to 18 percent.

But as with the other polls, there's substantial bad news, too. People say, 30–18, city public schools are worse than they were four years ago. Forty-six percent of people think Giuliani deserves reelection, versus 48 percent who say it's time to give a new person a chance. Forty-three percent of the respondents think Giuliani doesn't care about average New Yorkers. People say race relations in New York City are bad, 54–35. The mayor's standing among minorities is shaky at best. Blacks disapprove of his job performance 48–34. Latinos and blacks say it's time to give someone new a chance to be mayor two to one.

The poll's basic question is whether life has gotten better or worse in New York City over the past four years. Overall, 34 percent of people say better; 33 percent say worse. Blacks say worse, 43–23; Latinos also, 40–27. In May 1993, when asked the same question about quality of life in the city, New Yorkers said, 60–10, that life had gotten worse over the past four years. The 1997 numbers are a remarkable relative shift, but in absolute terms the results are hardly a ringing endorsement of Rudy Giuliani's performance.

Nagourney virtually ignores the bad news. "New Yorkers are more upbeat about their city than they have been in a decade, with their views on crime, the economy and the future suggesting that many have discarded the grim self-image that gripped them just four years ago," he writes. The title of the article is "Poll Finds Optimism in New York, but Race and Class Affect Views."

At least as the paper reports the results, there is nothing in the poll that indicates either the presence or absence of optimism among New Yorkers. The *Times* has asked only one arguably prospective question (whether Rudy deserves reelection); the rest are backward-looking evaluations of the city and Giuliani's performance over the past four years. Nothing indicates people think things will get better in the immediate future. Nagourney is drawing an inference, and it's a stretch at best. Here's a lead to the story that would have been factually sustainable by the poll: "By a slim margin, New Yorkers think Rudy Giuliani has been a competent caretaker mayor who has not exacerbated the considerable damage done to the city by his predecessor, David Dinkins."

Nagourney's is only one article, but this is shaping up as a critical battleground. The *Times* has influence disproportionate to its considerable readership. The *Times* shapes the fundamental views other members of the press have about the campaign. News is understood in context, and in New York, the *New York Times* provides the context. If the press believes that people are optimistic, regardless of whether they really are, the already daunting task of beating the incumbent will become even more difficult. Jim and Lee are on the phone with Nagourney daily trying to change the tone of his coverage.

Of course, so are Rudy's people.

March 13

I am working late with Jim on the draft of our first poll. In addition to assessing where we stand in the race, this poll will be the first step in shaping our *message*. We will ask voters how they feel about several things that Ruth might say and about some criticisms that have been made and might be made about Rudy Giuliani. The things that score well for Ruth will become the elements of her positive message, and the things that cause people to have doubts about Rudy will become our negative television commercials. My deputy, Art, and I have spent the past two days brainstorming about things we might say.

There's a scientific feel to all this—Jim speaks in terms of *testing* ideas as if they are hypotheses and the poll will produce lots of numbers—but it's pseudoscience at best. For one thing, some of the concepts we're testing are so unrelated I doubt anyone could develop a coherent theory to explain them all. Take two propositions that we are testing:

1. Ruth Messinger is the only Democratic candidate who sided with the police when they wanted hollow-point bullets, because she believes that the police should be at least as well armed as the criminals they are fighting.
2. Even if you don't always agree with Ruth Messinger, she is widely respected as someone with the guts to speak her mind and stand

> up for her convictions—whether that means fighting for a woman's right to choose or opposing the death penalty.

What if it turns out that both of these propositions *test* well? Would we then advertise Ruth's position on hollow-point bullets or not advertise it because it might be construed as a retreat from a career-long commitment to civil rights?

Another concern is that some of the ideas we're testing about Rudy are characterizations of evidence rather than factual statements. For example, I expect many voters will find this statement a very convincing reason for replacing Rudy Giuliani with someone new as mayor:

> Mayor Giuliani has a poor record in dealing with the issue of domestic violence, and has helped create a huge backlog in dealing with these cases by failing to appoint judges to the Family Court.

The last part of that statement might be provable, but I doubt Rudy Giuliani would agree with the conclusion that he has a poor record in dealing with domestic violence. Our saying it won't make it true.

At the same time, I'm anxious to see the results. Many of the things we're asking about Rudy are objectively provable. The Giuliani administration *has* proposed leasing the city's hospitals to private health-care corporations, which would deny care to New Yorkers who are either uninsured or underinsured. New York's unemployment rate *is* the highest among the nation's twenty largest cities. And even though the city cut funds for education and the jobless rate grew, Mayor Giuliani *did* give himself a $35,000 raise. It will be interesting to see which of these voters find most disturbing.

It will also be interesting to see whether more voters have major doubts about supporting Ruth Messinger for mayor because she is "a '60s-style liberal who opposes the death penalty and favors civil-liberties measures that give criminals more rights than victims" or because "she has shown she is out of step with mainstream values by supporting gay marriages and allowing demonstrations in schools on how to use a condom." There's some characterization in these two statements, but there's quite a bit of fact too.

March 15

Spin is another jargon word that gets tossed around all the time in political circles without a precise definition. Here's mine:

spin (v.), to state an argument in a manner that maximizes the significance of the evidence in support of your position and minimizes the significance of the evidence contrary to your position; contrast with "honest reaction."

Spinning is a lot like lawyering. Good spinners are thorough—they know all of the evidence both in support of and against their position and are ready with responses to counterarguments. All of a lawyer's tricks are fair game. The ideal response to an unfavorable argument is direct evidence that disproves the argument. Next best are all of the techniques of cross-examination: Undermine the credibility of the speaker by showing bias or a vested interest in the outcome (Rudy Giuliani's favored technique), prove a prior contradictory statement, or, when all else fails, just call it a lie. The best spinner does what Winston Smith was paid to do in Orwell's *1984*—rewrite history to conform to what those in power say it is. Not only are things as we say they are, they never were any different. Today Randy Mastro, one of Giuliani's deputy mayors, is spinning the city's unemployment problem.

Unemployment in New York City is hovering at about 10 percent—a significant blemish on Rudy Giuliani's record. A Pathmark store in Brooklyn's Atlantic Center recently had 7,000 people apply for 400 jobs. Twelve thousand people applied for 350 jobs at Price Costco in Astoria, Queens. Twenty thousand people applied for 250 jobs at Price Costco in Brooklyn's Sunset Park. Just this week, 4,000 people lined up for 700 jobs at the Roosevelt Hotel in midtown, which is reopening after eighteen months of renovation. New York City ranks first in unemployment and fifteenth in job growth among the twenty largest metropolitan areas in the country. Although the city has added 120,000 jobs since 1994, over 300,000 New Yorkers are still unemployed at the top of a national economic boom.

Moreover, the disparity between unemployment in the city and the nation has increased over the past four years. Unemployment in New York City always runs ahead of national unemployment, but the difference is increasing. In 1993, national unemployment was 6.4, while city unemployment was just over 9 percent. In other terms, the city's unemployment rate was one and a half times the national rate. Today, national unemployment has dropped to 4.6 percent, while the city unemployment rate has increased. According to the latest figures, unemployment in New York City is at 9.6 percent, about twice the national average.

To the extent there has been an economic recovery in New York (in Rudy's defense, in the five years before Giuliani became mayor, New York City, which is home to 3 percent of all Americans, accounted for more than a third of the country's net job losses), it has belonged almost entirely to the rich. Last year, the gross city product grew by 1.9 percent, compared with a national increase of 2.4 percent, and the 1-percent increase in the number of jobs over the past year was half the national nonfarm rate. Over the past six years, real wages in the security industry grew by 42 percent, compared with a 4-percent increase for all other workers. High unemployment is on the short list of Rudy Giuliani's political liabilities.

In an op-ed in today's *Times* titled "New York's Job Market Is Alive and Well," Deputy Mayor Mastro claims that the sudden upturn in unemployment is good news for the city. He writes: "As for the recent rise in our unemployment rate—from 8.8 percent in December to 9.9 percent in January—it actually reflects increased optimism about the city's future: Job growth has encouraged many New Yorkers who took themselves out of the job market to seek employment again."

It is really quite an amazing piece. Mastro has no authority to advance the argument himself—he is not an economist, he is a lawyer who rose through the ranks of the U.S. Attorney's office with Rudy Giuliani—and he cites no authority in support of it. There are thousands of economists out there, but apparently not one could be persuaded to advance Mastro's novel argument on behalf of the Giuliani administration. Nevertheless, the piece serves an important purpose. It legitimates a response. And Rudy needs one.

I leave it to the reader to determine whether or not I am spinning now myself. I am not conscious that I am, and I certainly have no intention to do so, but the possibility exists that I myself have been spun or, worse still, that participating in a political campaign has left me incapable of perceiving the world objectively.

March 16

One conspicuous omission from our poll is a question dealing with the issue of police brutality. Complaints of police misconduct have more than doubled on Rudy Giuliani's watch, and one could make a credible argument that he hasn't taken the problem very seriously.

As a candidate in 1993, Rudy Giuliani spoke at a police rally outside City Hall protesting a proposed Civilian Complaint Review Board (CCRB), an independent agency that now monitors police misconduct. It was an angry rally; the assembled officers shouted epithets against then-mayor Dinkins. Giuliani fed the fever himself by screaming "Bullshit" for no apparent reason.

According to a former senior litigator in the Corporation Counsel's office, money paid by the city to victims of police misconduct is the fastest-growing category of personal injury payments—growing faster than cases arising from defective roads and highways or medical malpractice in the city's hospitals. Last year, the city paid out $27.3 million in settlements of lawsuits against city police officers, up from $19 million over the previous year.

In absolute terms, complaints of police brutality have tripled over the last decade. About one out of every five complaints investigated by the CCRB is deemed credible, but Giuliani has tried to cut the budget of the CCRB each year he has been in office.

After a city commission reported widespread police corruption, the City Council passed legislation in 1994 setting up an independent body to monitor corruption. Giuliani successfully challenged the legislation in court on the grounds that it infringed upon his power as mayor under the city charter. Less than 1 percent of cases substantiated by the CCRB over the past four years have resulted in discipline of an officer.

Giuliani's reaction to a horrifying incident of police brutality highlighted his lack of commitment to the issue. On December 22, 1994, a young man named Anthony Baez was playing catch with some friends when the football they were using struck a police car. An officer named Francis Livoti, who had a record that included eleven civilian complaints, some involving excessive force and four involving use of choke holds, approached Baez. A scuffle ensued. A few minutes later Baez was dead, apparently the result of the use of an illegal choke hold.

The mayor said nothing about Baez's death until Livoti was acquitted of criminal charges nearly two years later. On that day, October 7, 1996, Rudy Giuliani called the decision of acting Bronx state Supreme Court judge Gerald Shendlin "a careful, well-thought-out, legally reasoned opinion."

Five police officers testified that they saw the entire scuffle between Livoti and Baez. All five said they did not see Livoti use the fatal choke hold—despite the fact that the city's medical examiner, Charles Hirsch, said the choke hold lasted more than a minute. Police commissioner Howard Safir declined to pursue perjury charges. Giuliani called Safir's decision "courageous."

If all of that left any doubt about where the mayor stood on the issue of police brutality, it was removed late in 1996 when Amnesty International released a report showing that in thirty-five fatal police shootings, thirty-two of the victims were black, Hispanic, or Asian. Mayor Giuliani responded, "I think a lot of the information in it is exaggerated. Many of the descriptions are totally one-sided." No one asked him precisely how one exaggerates a fatal shooting.

But the issue of police brutality is not in our poll. We're in the *center.*

March 17

Spring begins in only four days, but today marks the start of a season of far greater significance to New York City politicians than any period of time set apart by mere solstices.

Parade season, the longest and dreariest of seasons, runs from now though Columbus Day in October. Aside from a few weeks in August when things are at their stickiest, the schedule is packed from now through the election with parade after parade. Every group is represented. There is a Puerto Rican Day Parade, a Hispanic Day Parade, a Greek Independence Day Parade, and a Gay Pride Parade, among many, many others. People will march in honor of every holiday, regardless of its significance. Labor Day is to be honored no less than five times.

The schedule coincides precisely with the short period of the year when weather in the city is bearable and all but ensures that no candidate will get so much as a day away from the campaign trail, even though everyone pretty much agrees that it would be a good thing for the city if they did. Politicians are expected to be workaholics. Rudy prides himself on the fact that he has not taken a vacation in four years, though there's not a person around City Hall who doesn't think Rudy's bilious disposition would benefit from a day out of the office. Ruth's husband forced her to spend a day skiing last month, but she insisted on rushing back to New York to have an evening meeting. The members of this subspecies of human being are incapable of relaxing. They must watch every news program, attend every meeting, and march in every parade.

Except this one.

The St. Patrick's Day Parade (the Manhattan one, that is—perhaps you have not heard of the somewhat lesser known Brooklyn St. Patrick's Day Parade) is one of the great city spectacles. By organizers' estimates, more than one million people descend on the city each year and line Fifth Avenue with green hats, scarves, and jackets. Everyone is Irish for a day, and everyone marches.

Except for the gays. The parade organizers, the Ancient Order of Hibernians, bar an organization of gay and lesbian Irish Americans from marching under their own banner.

As a result, Ruth, who marched proudly yesterday in Brooklyn's lesser-known event, is not marching in the Manhattan parade. Ferrer skips the event too. Sharpton joins the Irish Lesbian and Gay Organization for a protest in front of the New York Public Library and calls Ruth a coward for skipping the protest, an event she had joined in years past.

For Rudy, the morality of the situation is clear:

> If you want to be mayor of this city, you have to learn to respect all of the groups of the city, and not have political correctness direct what you do. This is a great parade, it's a great tradition. You don't have to agree with everything about this tradition if you don't want to. But you march to show your respect for Irish-Americans, for Catholics, and for the people who have this view and this tradition.

The parade, the mayor argues, should be above politics.

The same man who says the parade should be above politics marches the parade route three times wearing a thick layer of pancake makeup, with his media consultant, Adam Goodman, a few steps in front of him, directing two camera operators taping film of Rudy for a campaign commercial.

All of the papers will show pictures of Rudy giving the thumbs-up to the crowd and shaking hands. The media believes the parade is of political significance. "The St. Patrick's Day Parade provided something of a political windfall for Mr. Giuliani, as three of the four Democratic candidates for mayor chose to skip it," writes Adam Nagourney in the early edition of the *Times*, which we pull off the Internet. I'd pay good money to see a picture in the paper of Rudy marching with his media consultant pointing cameras at his powdered face and using a million Irish New Yorkers as a backdrop for a campaign ad.

That's real politics.

March 18

The preliminary results of our poll are in. The data confirm that Ruth looks strong in the primary. Our numbers show Ruth leading Ferrer 37–22 in a four-way race, with Albanese and Sharpton each getting 6 percent of the vote. In a head-to-head runoff with Ferrer, she leads 42–33. Better still, our supporters are slightly more committed than his. Forty-eight percent of Ruth's supporters say their mind is pretty much made up, as opposed to 42 percent of Ferrer's. All in all, it's good news.

But the general election news is worse than what the Marist and New York 1 polls found. Our poll shows Rudy leading Ruth 53–32 in a head-to-head matchup. And the mayor's vote is solid. Seventy-seven percent of his supporters say they support him strongly. Fully 70 percent of New Yorkers approve of the job Rudy Giuliani is doing as mayor. Maureen Dowd, the *Times* columnist, may be right. Perhaps we are fighting for the privilege of getting our heads kicked in.

• • •

Ruth is in her element tonight. I'm not allowed out of the office much, so I don't get to see her speak all that often, but even I can tell that this is an exceptional performance. She's relaxed and smart and witty and warmly received by the Gay and Lesbian Independent Democrats (GLID). All of the beat reporters note that she gets a standing ovation from the group. Jim was worried about this appearance for political reasons, but it's hard to see why after a performance like this.

March 19

After a day of reflection about the full results of the poll, Jim is encouraged. Explaining why will require a bit of background. It's a good excuse to explain some of the premises and methodology of "scientific" polling.

A poll is a snapshot of a small part of a universe—an invention of necessity to finesse a vicious problem. Imagine that you wanted to determine the average height of all the trees in the Green Mountains of Vermont. One way to do it would be to measure each and every tree and report the mean. There are two problems with this approach. One is obvious, one is not so apparent. Measuring every tree would be enormously costly and time consuming. That's obvious. What's not obvious is that it might take so long that some of the trees you measured early in the study would have grown by the time you got around to measuring the last ones.

If you think about it for a moment, you'll see that there's a limit to what you could ever accurately say about the forest. Asked what the average height of the trees in the forest was at a given moment, the best you could say would be what the height of the particular tree you were measuring was. The rest would be guesswork. Since trees don't grow especially quickly, it might not be bad guesswork, but it would be guesswork all the same, and not everything grows as slowly as trees.

A better approach would be to measure as many trees as possible at the same time. Instead of spending your entire summer climbing up and down trees, you could get fifty of your friends to climb up trees all at once and report their measurements. You won't get to personally visit every tree, as you did under the first method, but the results will be much more useful. Now, instead of being able to report the height of one tree at a given moment, you can report the height of fifty. Any prediction you might make about the average height of trees in the forest generally on the basis of those fifty measurements will be more accurate than a prediction based on a single measurement. And the more trees you measured, the more accurate the prediction would become.

Short of sending two million of your forestry friends up all the trees in the forest at the same time, any statement you made about the average height of trees would still be a prediction (or a guess, if you will), but the more trees you measured, the more confidence you could have in your result. To think about it another way, one randomly selected person may look very different from another, but two different groups of fifty randomly selected persons are likely to look pretty much the same.

Polls follow the same logic. A pollster goes out in the *field* (again, not unlike the forester) and, as close to simultaneously as possible, surveys the attitudes of citizens. The more voters polled, the more accurate the prediction. There are obvious limitations—for one, the pollster can never truly survey the attitudes of voters simultaneously. That's a serious limitation, since voters' attitudes change much more quickly than trees—the 5:00 news can have a dramatic impact. The pollster simply does the best he or she can in an imperfect world. She surveys as many people as she can (exactly how many depends on what the client is willing to pay) over a short time.

The *margin of error* is an expression of the degree of confidence that can be had in the results of the poll. A poll that shows two candidates in a 50 to 50 dead heat with a margin of error of 4 percent means that there is a 95-percent probability that a poll of all of the electorate on that day would have produced a result between 52 and 48 in favor of one candidate and 52 to 48 in favor of the other. The more people surveyed, the smaller the margin of error.

Poll results can be broken down. Just as our foresters might make a prediction about what the average heights of oaks and elms are, pollsters can make statements about subgroups of the sample. The margin of error for these statements is greater, since each subgroup is definitionally smaller than the entire survey group.

I have never seen a political poll before, and I am shocked at the level of specificity. For each question we asked, the results are broken down on three pages of "banners." We have results for whites, blacks, Latinos, white Catholics, Jews, strong Democrats, weak Democrats, residents of the Bronx, Brooklyn, Queens, and Manhattan, men, women, people under forty, people over sixty, the upscale, the downscale, the middle class, people who read the *New York Times*, people who read the *Daily News*, college women, renters, homeowners, union members, people who ideologically classify themselves as liberal, and a category that is the source of Jim's optimism, voters who are *movable to Messinger.*

As I read the poll, no matter how you break it down, the results are discouraging. Rudy is virtually tied with Ruth among likely Democratic voters. He leads among Jews 61–25. He leads among the lower middle class (*downscale* voters) 67–18. He's even leading in Ruth's home borough of Manhattan by a significant margin. Out of forty-eight subgroups, Ruth is ahead in only two. Blacks prefer her 61 to 21 percent. Liberals who identify themselves as likely primary voters prefer her 47–38. Even those numbers seem like bad news, though, when compared with the meager 5 percent of the black vote that Giuliani captured in 1993. And the liberal number is hardly a mandate.

But Jim is fixated on one number: There are enough voters movable to Messinger to win the race. Identifying a *movable,* or *swing,* voter is sketchy business. One way to do it is to simply ask voters whether or not they might be persuaded to vote for someone other than their candidate. To some extent, that's what asking voters about the strength of their support for a candidate accomplishes. But voters' subjective view of their own malleability is generally regarded as less valuable than an objective assessment of malleability. The recipe for making this preferred sort of assessment is to ask voters at the outset of the poll whom they prefer, ask them how they feel about lots of different things they might find out about each of the candidates, and then ask them again whom they prefer. The people who change their minds, whether they admit it to themselves or not, are the movable voters.

Campaigns target movable voters to maximize efficiency. There is no point to tailoring a message to people who would not vote for the candidate under any circumstances. The idea is to identify a group of persuadable voters and then make strategic decisions based on the issues most important to these voters.

That's what we've done. At the outset of the poll, only 32 percent supported Ruth. When asked the same question at the end, 43 percent supported Ruth, versus 41 percent for Rudy. We've identified a group of 179 voters out of 861 polled who can be classified as movable to Messinger. Who are they? They're slightly younger than the response group; 35 percent are under thirty-five, versus 26 percent of the entire sampling pool. They're slightly less educated, make less money, are more likely to rent an apartment, and are more likely to describe themselves as liberal or moderate than the average respondent. Between the beginning and end of the poll, Ruth makes her biggest inroads among Latinos and women. These are Ruth's swing voters.

Three issues seem likely to form the core of our message: education, the economy, and domestic violence. When asked to single out the one or two issues they feel are most important for the mayor to address, 60 percent of the respondents say improving education and the schools, 40 percent say fighting crime, and 28 percent say strengthening the economy. Nothing else breaks double digits. Although voters give Giuliani high marks for fighting crime and reducing corruption, he does less well on the economy and education. Thirty-five percent rate him poor or very poor on dealing with the schools, while only 24 percent give him good marks. He scores low, too, on dealing with health care. Education is clearly his weak spot.

Among the individual proposals we tested, none scores nearly as well as strengthening efforts to protect victims of domestic violence, which appeals to 95 percent of all voters. A proposal to audit every city agency scores extremely well and is also likely to be part of our message. A proposal to ban the sale and possession of guns within New York City borders surprisingly comes in only slightly behind the domestic violence platform, but it's *polarizing*. Although the few people who have a negative reaction to the domestic violence proposal are evenly distributed among the four negative ratings one could give ("1" being the most negative and "4" being only slightly disfavored), those who react negatively to the gun proposal do so quite strongly. It's not likely to be part of our platform both because of the visceral negativity it evokes and because it might be used to argue further that Ruth is weak on crime.

At the other end of the spectrum, a proposal to raise cigarette taxes to fund the city's hospitals scores more negatively than any other. Twenty-five percent of voters strongly disfavor the idea. Since a good number of people scored Giuliani low on health care, it seems safe to conclude that what people are reacting to in this idea is raising taxes, not the idea of giving more money to the city hospitals. Jim concludes that there is high tax sensitivity among the electorate. As a result, he is considering the idea of having Ruth take a pledge not to raise taxes, à la George Bush.

A strikingly odd thing about formulating a message on the basis of a poll is that the resulting platform is governed by no overriding philosophy. It's the process that no doubt led Bob Dole to propose a tax cut just a few weeks before Election Day in 1996, when he hadn't said anything remotely related to cutting taxes during the preceding months. Issue polling seems better suited to student-council elections, where nobody expects ideology ("We want chocolate milk and quicker turnaround on our test papers").

Issue polling produces a disjointed message. Fighting government waste didn't poll well generally, but the specific proposal scored so well that we have almost no choice but to throw it into our message. On the other hand, although education polled strongly as a general proposition, none of the individual proposals we tested on education scored well at all. An idea to forgive the student loans of City University of New York (CUNY) students who agree to teach in the public schools barely scored a majority. An idea to require students to wear uniforms was slightly unpopular. As a result, education will be the key plank of our platform, but the specific reforms we advance will be a mishmash of marginally popular ideas. Holding students to high standards and creating master teachers are likely to be the key ideas. Keeping schools open until 6:00 P.M. also polled well, though that is really more of a crime-fighting idea than a way to improve education.

Another odd thing that strikes me is that we're making strategic decisions on the basis of a small group of people. Though the total interview pool is 861 people, we're really making our decisions in response to what the 179 voters who are movable to Messinger have to say. That hardly seems like much to go on.

And Jim's optimism seems to be based on a razor-thin premise: that we will be able to get our message out in at least approximately the same form that we've presented it in the poll. The arguments we've laid out in the poll are all true. Rudy Giuliani did propose leasing the city's hospitals to private health-care corporations, which would deny care to New Yorkers who are either uninsured or underinsured. Forty-five percent of the overall sample said they viewed this as a very convincing reason for replacing Rudy Giuliani with someone new as mayor. But the fact is individual voters will never hear as much information about the candidates as they heard in this poll. And even if they could hear our argument in such a clear form again, would they conclude that Ruth should be the person to replace him? Seventy-one percent of the sample say the fact that Ruth is a '60s-style liberal who opposes the death penalty gives them major doubts about supporting her for mayor.

• • •

Not a single reporter writes about the GLIA speech.

March 20

Yesterday, Ruth sent a letter to Rudy urging him to allow children between the ages of five and eleven to ride city subways and buses for fifty cents during off-peak hours. Right now, children can ride the Metro-North Commuter Railroad and the Long Island Rail Road for fifty cents during off-hours. Ruth argues that the Metropolitan Transit Authority (MTA), which has jurisdiction over Metro-North, the LIRR, and the subways, is discriminating against city kids. "The MTA calls this good marketing," Ruth writes in her letter to Rudy, "I call this a double standard. A kid is a kid is a kid, after all, whether they live in Stamford or Stuyvesant Town."

Ruth's advisers at the borough president's office have been pushing this idea for months as a "wedge" issue, but I'm not very interested in the substance of the debate, which I expect will not excite many voters one way or the other. I'm more interested in the notion of writing a letter to our bitter political rival.

Politicians do this all the time. I wonder if Rudy will write back.

Dear Ruth,

I appreciate the sincerity of your interest in fare equity for children between the tender ages of five and eleven. Though the policy that creates the disparity has been in place for seven years, it is, I agree, far better to address in this election year when the maximum attention can be directed to it. I will take the policy under advisement. I suggest, though, that the third "kid" in your litany is superfluous.

Humbly yours,
Rudy

Rudy would have a point. Lee thinks things work better rhetorically in threes, but I'm still not convinced we needed that last "kid." I'm more concerned, though, about a vote Ruth's school-board appointee cast last night. The Board of Education voted by six to one to expel any student from the school system who brings a gun to school or injures someone with any other weapon. Ruth's appointee was the sole dissenter. The decision is a major shift for the Board of Education, which has always abided by a commitment to providing a free education for all children, and may violate a state constitution provision that guarantees access to public schools for anyone under twenty-one who has not received a high-school diploma. I might have voted the same way. But the political risk seems obvious. No one reading the papers will draw the link to Ruth, but it's something Rudy could use as another prong in his argument that Ruth is not tough on crime.

Ruth sends a tepid letter to her appointee, Luis Reyes, telling him she would have voted the other way. Perhaps that will be enough to insulate us from a future attack.

• • •

Yesterday the police arrested a young *New York Times* reporter who was covering the funeral procession of rapper Biggie Smalls. According to the police report, the *Times* reporter urged people in the crowd not to follow police directions and then pushed a lieutenant in the chest while trying to get past him. An unedited New York 1 videotape of the incident neither shows the reporter inciting the crowd nor pushing an officer nor cursing, as the police also claimed. Rather, it shows the reporter shielding her eyes from pepper spray that was discharged into the crowd.

It seems fair to say that press–police relations are not at their best. The police commissioner, Howard Safir, has not held a news conference with the reporters based at Police Plaza in more than a year. And going against two decades of practice, the department spokesperson, Marilyn Mode, refused to give reporters either her home number or her beeper number. (I wish I could pull that one off.) Last month, when the arrested *Times* reporter started covering Police Plaza, she raised Mode's ire by asking whether Safir had been summoned to City Hall after announcing the hollow-point bullets without telling Rudy. Days later, when Safir went in for bypass surgery, Mode refused to give the reporter information even as she prepared a press release on the subject. "Don't you have any respect for the man's family?" Mode shouted at her; Mode also told another reporter that she didn't think the reporter would "work out here."

Giuliani defended the arrest and promised a full review of the incident by the police department, which, he reiterated, is fully capable of policing itself. Today the *Post* weighs in on Rudy's side. Despite overwhelming evidence that the *Times* reporter had done nothing intrusive, the *Post* editorial board denounces her as having "set herself up as a one-woman civilian complaint review board . . . at a moment when the gathering—already marred by sporadic lawlessness—threatened to break into a full-scale riot."

In the eyes of the *Post*, Giuliani and his administration can do no wrong.

March 21

Among the many things that Ruth will have to answer about her past is the fact the she was a member of a group called the Democratic Socialists of America (DSA). Today, Jim and Lee are preparing Ruth for a television interview with Marcia Kramer of Channel 2 by firing tough questions at her.

"Are you still a member of the Socialist party?" Jim asks.

Ruth is indignant. "I have never been a member of the Socialist party. I was a member of the Democratic Socialists of America, which was founded by Michael Harrington, who as you recall worked for Hubert Humphrey."

The answer conjures a vivid image in my mind of two elderly women sitting at home watching television. One exclaims to the other, "Oh, it's okay. It was Michael Harrington!"

March 22

Of the many things Rudy Giuliani gives himself credit for, he is perhaps proudest of the fact that on his watch the city has cut three hundred thousand people from the welfare rolls. This would be a fine accomplishment if all of those people had been shifted from welfare to work, but that's not the case at all. The city keeps no statistics whatsoever on what happens to people after they go off welfare.

Moreover, the city is keeping the welfare numbers down by treating applicants like criminals. The city isn't trying to help people—it's trying to prove that people don't need help. Caseworkers have been replaced by fraud investigators. The Giuliani administration allowed a historic agreement that created housing for thousands of the city's homeless mentally ill to expire. Turhan Butler, a nineteen-year-old Bronx high-school student, had to quit school and work a day job to keep getting welfare benefits. Serving as his own attorney, he sued the city and won. Rudy's appointee as commissioner of the Human Resources Administration says that her goal is to "go down in history as the least-known commissioner of all time."

A predictable consequence of the policy is an increase in homelessness. But the growing number of homeless are getting the cold shoulder too. Giuliani cut the homeless services budget by 75 percent. Applicants for aid at the city's Emergency Assistance Unit (EAU) are now required to prove that there is no other place where they can go to get shelter. A thirty-three-year-old woman who was seven months pregnant spent two nights on the floor of the EAU office as a result of the screening policy. A study by Public Advocate Mark Green's office shows that large numbers of people are being improperly denied welfare. Social-service programs are being gutted. Over the last six months, more than a thousand kids have spent at least one night on the floor of the city's foster-care placement office.

But Rudy won't even acknowledge the problem. When a study by the New York Coalition Against Hunger shows a 70 percent rise in the number of meals served in soup kitchens over the past two and a half years, Rudy accuses the advocates of "trying to create an argument for some political point of view." The report shows that more than sixty thousand people were turned away from shelters in 1996. "Maybe they're doing a better job of outreach," the mayor says.

March 23

Freddie Ferrer is the first to take the media plunge. He is running a one-minute spot on two Spanish radio stations. "A son of our community has never been elected mayor of New York. Register and vote for Fernando Ferrer for mayor of New York. Together we can make history." Ferrer then asks listeners to call a 900 number to make a twenty-five-dollar contribution to the campaign. By calling the number, the donation is automatically tacked onto the caller's phone bill.

Our campaign is in the modern age too. Call our office and you can become a Messinger investor. We'll bill your credit card each month for any amount of money you like.

March 25

New York City schools are badly overcrowded. As Ruth pointed out at the *Post* debate, nearly a hundred thousand kids do not have regular classroom seats. High schools average thirty-five students per class. The schools are in need of billions of dollars of repairs. Two-thirds of city schools have substandard facilities, such as deteriorating roofs, floors, and plumbing. Half of all schools lack adequate lighting, heating, or ventilation. According to a study by representative Nita Lowey, a quarter of city schools hold classes in bathrooms, offices, cafeterias, or hallways.

• • •

A picture in the *Daily News* shows students attending class in a bathroom. Seeing the picture, our finance director, who at twenty-six is a veteran of five campaigns, says the image of kids in bathrooms will be in our ads.

"You're nuts," I say, laughing.

"I'm telling you," he says, "it's going to be in one of our ads."

"You've been in politics too long," I say, shaking my head. He's the first to admit he has been in politics too long. The question is whether the damage is irreversible.

March 26

Like any other business, political campaigns are a world of the rich and the poor, the exploiters and the exploited. At one end of the spectrum are high-salaried consultants who set their own hours and work out of their homes. At the other are junior-level campaign staffers who work hundred-hour weeks for subsistence wages.

The magnitude of the salary disparity in our campaign is shocking. Jim will be paid approximately $250,000 for his work on the campaign and is reimbursed for all of his expenses. His rent ($2,200 a month for an apartment in TriBeCa), transportation both within the city and to his home in Chicago, and incidental expenses (including laundry) are all picked up by the campaign. Mandy Grunwald arguably does a bit better. She will be paid

$400,000 for her work in an unconventional deal that pays her based on a projected amount of airtime. Ordinarily, media consultants are paid a percentage of the cost of airtime actually purchased by a campaign. In addition, if things go according to plan, we will bring Lee Jones over from the borough president's office and hire a day-to-day campaign manager, both of whom will be paid something on the order of $10,000 a month.

To put that in perspective, Mandy and Jim make more, by far, than all of the other staffers on the campaign combined. At the other end of the spectrum are Bill Franks and a dozen or so others like him. Bill, a fund-raising staffer, takes Ruth's calls, writes thank-yous and follow-up letters to everyone Ruth meets or speaks to, tracks the results of Ruth's fund-raising calls in a database, and pitches in at events and with mailings whenever the need arises. On an average weekday, he's in at 8:00 in the morning and out at 10:00 at night. On weekends, the days are slightly shorter. For his efforts, Bill, a 1996 Rutgers graduate, makes $1,800 a month. That's not enough for him to afford a place of his own, so Bill lives at home with his parents in Queens, commuting an hour each way to work. The budgets of junior staffers who do have their own places are stretched to the limit. Jim's assistant, who has a modest $600-a-month studio apartment, is only able to budget $5 a day for food. She has a bagel and coffee for breakfast, a $1 hot dog for lunch, and Cup-a-Soup for dinner.

Today, if it's possible to imagine, the poor got a bit poorer in our little universe. Although the degree of disparity between rich and poor is appalling, it's common in campaigns. Campaigns survive by leveraging young, cheap labor to pay for more experienced, expensive talent. Before Jim arrived on the scene, Ruth's small campaign staff, which consisted almost exclusively of fund-raisers, was managed by Ruth's assistant at the borough president's office. Used to dealing with unionized employees who refuse to be treated like chattel, Ruth's assistant made the mistake of treating the original campaign staffers as human beings. They weren't paid well, but they were given a generous health plan that included dental benefits and two weeks' vacation.

Jim was outraged. The health-care plan is far more generous than what campaigns generally offer. Cutting it could save the campaign several hundred dollars a month per employee. Today, Jim cut it. And the vacations too.

It wouldn't exactly be right to say that people are indignant about the decision. For my part, I'm paid fairly, if not generously, and all of us who were hired by Jim understood that the benefits would be minimal and vacations out of the question. But it's a tough blow for the small group of people who have been working for Ruth for as long as a year while struggling to get by. And the fact that their boss gets his dry-cleaning bill paid for by the campaign doesn't make it any easier to take.

March 27

Rudy apparently believes that he can be anything he wants to be. As a member of the Reagan Justice Department, Rudy Giuliani traveled to Haiti in 1980 and reported that there was no evidence of human-rights violations. Today, he is announcing that the city will sue to overturn a provision in the new federal welfare law that will deny cash benefits and food stamps to elderly and disabled immigrants. The suit, which is being brought on behalf of four city residents who face losing food stamps and Supplemental Security Income support, alleges that the welfare law unconstitutionally discriminates against legal permanent residents. "It is inherently unfair to let people into your country, and ask of them what you ask of anyone else . . . and then when they become disabled or elderly, to treat them differently," said Rudy at a press conference. "It's un-American."

Rudy has nothing to say, though, about a story in today's *Daily News* that the city Health Department forfeited $2.3 million in federal AIDS funding because it didn't spend the money by the end of the year.

March 28

Jim, Ruth, and I are in Washington to meet with our pollster, Geoff Garin, and media consultant, Mandy Grunwald. It's not entirely clear why we need to do this in person—it's costing the campaign over a thousand dollars to send us all here. I guess the idea is to soften the bad news.

The modest offices of the polling firm of Garin Hart Yang are located in a brownstone on Connecticut Avenue. We are ushered into a small conference room decorated with several framed Ellsworth Kelly posters. Three diet soft drinks have been placed on a small tray table. There is nothing at all to eat. Garin was one of Bill Clinton's pollsters for the 1996 election, and I wonder whether Clinton has ever been in these offices. If he was, I bet he at least got some cheese doodles.

Geoff arrives a minute later and greets Ruth with a kiss. He is obviously uncomfortable.

"Well, we always knew this wouldn't be easy," he smiles. Geoff explains the results of the poll. Ruth looks strong in the primary, but the *arithmetic* for the general election does not look promising. The campaign will need to attract large numbers of young, downscale white women to have any

chance at all. Geoff explains that it does not make much sense to regard the primary as a significant event. We need to do whatever positions us best for the general election. (Read: Don't worry too much about black votes, I think.) Chances are that won't cost us in the primary, but if it does, it only means that we would not have ultimately won the general anyway.

Ruth takes the news stoically. I am vastly impressed by her composure. "I knew there would be plenty of bad polls along the way. I agree with your conclusion—we should focus on education—but I don't see how that entails forgetting the base." (Translation: We should worry very much about black votes, I think.)

• • •

I am running madly through National Airport trying to make a 6:30 U.S. Air shuttle. We are scheduled on the 7:00 Delta, but Jim and Ruth have decided that we may as well rush and try to get to New York half an hour earlier. Ruth and I are through the gate at 6:30, but Jim is being held for a moment as the inspector checks his laptop computer. Jim screams ahead to me, "I am being held here!" I am no more than fifteen feet away. The inspector stumbles for a second closing Jim's bag. It is a minor slip, but the delay is enough to cost us the flight. Jim attacks the man with invective. "You cost us the fucking plane!" As we head over to the Delta shuttle, he explains to me that sometimes you just have to yell like that. "It's the only way to get your point across," he says.

March 29

A new poll has some good news for Ruth. Ruth is leading Ferrer 37–24 (with Al and Sal at 10 and 4 percent, respectively) and is trailing Giuliani in the general by only 12 points, 50–38.

But the poll has even better news for Rudia. The Quinnipiac College survey shows that 52 percent of New Yorkers liked the mayor's cross-dressing.

Rudia is more popular than Rudy.

April 1

Around 1:00 this morning, Rudy Giuliani called Ruth Messinger, one insomniac to another.

"Ruth," he said, "I've been giving this a lot of thought. Each of us has strengths. I think I'm a better manager and a more effective leader fighting crime, but you're better on some other things. You know the city schools better. And City Hall needs your manner. Your demeanor is softer, and you're instinctively more inclusive."

"Where are you going with this, Rudy?"

"I think the city needs us both. I have a plan. If you'll support my reelection bid, I'll appoint you First Deputy Mayor. Halfway through my term, I'll step down and you can be in command for the last two years. I'll keep working on the areas that are within my expertise."

Ruth was immediately suspicious. Surely this was a sign that Rudy's internal polling had shown weakness. This was a desperate ploy to save his campaign. But after a moment's reflection, she realized that what Rudy was saying was true. The city did need them both. Yin and yang. She put her ambition aside and accepted the deal.

At the crack of dawn the pair called Freddie Ferrer, Sal Albanese, and Al Sharpton. All three agreed that the idea was in the city's best interest. Ferrer would run for borough president again. Albanese would step in as commissioner of consumer affairs. Sharpton would head a new office of minority relations.

At noon, the five held a joint news conference to announce their decision and implored the remaining politicians in the city to respect the pact. The papers called each and every plausible contender for mayor, sure that one would seize upon the obvious opportunity, but none did.

"It's time to put ego aside," said Comptroller Alan Hevesi. "This is best for the city. For once, we will have a government that will operate by consensus."

Early in the evening, Rudy Giuliani, Ruth Messinger, Fernando Ferrer, Al Sharpton, Sal Albanese, and a dozen other prominent city politicians sat down for dinner together at Bouley, the finest restaurant in New York, and toasted the new peace.

"To a government by the people and for the people," Rudy Giuliani said, and everyone drank heartily.

• • •

Happy April 1.

April 2

Even in a press environment that is favorably predisposed in favor of Rudy Giuliani, the coverage of the *New York Post* stands out. On balance, the other major dailies have favored the mayor, but they've also taken him to task in certain instances. Not so with the *Post*. Rudy Giuliani is infallible in its eyes.

Since we've done so poorly with all of the papers, it is hard to make the case that the *Post* lacks objectivity, but it seems fair to say that Rudy's relationship with the *Post* is unique. Australian media mogul Rupert Murdoch owns the *Post*. He also owns Fox News, which employs Donna Hanover. Rudy Giuliani has been one of Fox's staunchest advocates.

When Rupert Murdoch conceived the Fox News Channel in 1995, he offered Time Warner Cable a financial stake in the channel as an inducement to carry Fox News nationwide. Time Warner lost interest after it acquired a 20-percent interest in Turner Broadcasting, CNN's parent corporation. Thereafter, Time Warner refused to carry any cable news network other than CNN. But when Time Warner and Turner Broadcasting merged in 1996, the Federal Trade Commission required the new company to offer cable subscribers a second twenty-four-hour news channel, one in which it held no financial interest. Time Warner chose MSNBC, supposedly because Ted Turner hates Rupert Murdoch.

Murdoch hired former Giuliani campaign strategist Roger Ailes to help develop Fox News. Ailes asked Giuliani, among other Republican allies of Murdoch's, to intervene on Fox's behalf. State Attorney General Dennis Vacco issued a twenty-page subpoena on antitrust issues, though the merger had been announced more than a year earlier. Vacco's backing was trivial in comparison to what Giuliani was to do. Rudy turned the matter into his "personal jihad."

Though Giuliani's attorneys had told the new company that the merger would be no problem, he now threatened to revoke Time Warner Cable's cable franchise. The city's Franchise and Concession Review Committee said renewal of the franchise, set to expire in 1998, would be contingent on offering Fox News a cable channel. Then–Deputy Mayor Fran Reiter proposed that Time Warner move either the Discovery Channel or the History Channel to one of the city channels reserved for educational use. When Time Warner refused, Reiter said the city would give Fox Channel one of the educational channels, even though thirty other cable stations had been waiting longer for cable space to open up. Giuliani said he was protecting the several hundred jobs Fox News would create, though Time Warner is New York's seventh-largest employer, with eleven thousand jobs.

Time Warner said the city was infringing its First Amendment rights. Fox said Time Warner was infringing its First Amendment rights. When Michael Bloomberg of Bloomberg Information Television said his First Amendment rights were being violated, the city said he could have a channel too. Time Warner sued and won. The judge said the city was violating the federal Cable Act and the First Amendment and admonished Giuliani for abusing his power. The battle is ongoing, but Rupert Murdoch already owes a significant debt to Rudy Giuliani, and he is repaying it on a daily basis.

April 4

The *Times* reports this morning that at a midtown breakfast meeting yesterday with lawyers and business executives, Al Sharpton was asked if he would "denounce" Minister Louis Farrakhan, the head of the Nation of Islam.

"I don't publicly denounce anybody," Sharpton said.

The same man then asked Sharpton whether he considered Farrakhan to be anti-Semitic. Farrakhan once called Judaism a "gutter religion," and from time to time has been known to call Jews "bloodsuckers."

"No, I do not," Sharpton said.

It's an interesting opportunity for us. There is no pressure on us to respond. The other candidates will almost certainly leave the matter alone. No one has called us to ask for comment. But Jim, mindful of Geoff Garin's advice to look past the primary, thinks we need to attack. Attacking Sharpton, who had a 64-percent disapproval rating in our poll, has some obvious benefits, including strengthening Ruth in the Jewish community, where she is struggling for votes and money. The attack may cost us a few black votes in the primary, but we'll have no problem with black support if we make it through to the general. If you accept the premise that we should look past the primary, it is an easy decision. Ruth agrees and we engage a fellow Democrat for the first time.

In the afternoon, Ruth sends a letter to Sharpton's campaign, and Lee releases it to the press. We're writing lots of letters these days.

Dear Reverend Sharpton:
This morning's New York Times reported that you were asked at a meeting of New York business executives yesterday whether you considered Minister Louis Farrakhan to be anti-Semitic. Your answer, as reported in the paper, was, "No. I do not."

Reverend, you are wrong—terribly wrong.

When someone calls Judaism a "gutter religion," and calls Jews "bloodsuckers," there really isn't any other word for it: that person is an anti-Semite.

Haven't we—all of us—had enough of intolerance, hate, and division?

What are we saying to the children and families of New York, Reverend, when we close our eyes to racial and religious hate, whether from Mr. Farrakhan or anyone else? We don't tolerate David Duke's racism or Jesse Helms' gay-bashing. Why, then, should we tolerate Mr. Farrakhan's blatant anti-Semitism?

For generations, New York has opened its arms and its heart to people of every color, of every creed. We know there is work to be done to make this a city where those people respect each other. If we New Yorkers don't condemn views such as Mr. Farrakhan's, what kind of city are we?

Our schools, Reverend, are falling apart. Our students face an increasing threat of violence in their classrooms and hallways. And, in the end, they are not learning. One out of every ten New Yorkers is out of a job. The Mayor has put our health-care system up for sale to the highest bidder. Lobbyists and cronies of the Mayor are setting policy in City Hall at the expense of the taxpayer. Cops are vanishing from the beat.

Families and kids—black, white, Latino, and Asian—Jew, Gentile, and Moslem—are getting the short end of the stick in Rudy Giuliani's New York. And *they*—their lives, their future, all of them—are what this campaign should be about.

These problems are not easy ones, and they will only be solved by New Yorkers working together.

Your statements, Reverend, only serve to tear us apart.

Sincerely yours,
Ruth W. Messinger

The letter is a painful reminder of the lesson that you never miss an opportunity to get out your message. It also seems a bit unfair. By restating so much of our message, the letter seems to imply that Sharpton tried to make Louis

Farrakhan a campaign issue. He simply answered a question. It wasn't an answer that I especially like, but it was hardly a plank in his platform.

April 5

Sharpton's reply is here, and it's priceless.

April 5, 1997
Ms. Messinger,
I write to respond to your public missive of April 4, 1997. In a meeting of business leaders, I was asked about my personal opinion of the Minister Louis Farrakhan, I stated that I am not a representative or a member of Minister Farrakhan's group, but I have conversed and spent time with him down through the years. Though I don't agree with everything that he has said, and I'm sure he doesn't agree with all that I have said. I don't condemn him an anti-Semite. I grew up in the civil rights movement. At the age of 14, I was appointed, Youth Director of the New York Chapter of the Southern Christian Leadership Conference, [founded by, the Rev. Dr. Martin Luther King, Jr.], by the Rev. Jesse L. Jackson, (my lifetime mentor). Dr. King never personally denounced Malcolm X, Rev. Jesse Jackson never denounced the person of Minister Louis Farrakhan. I am in that tradition and spirit.

Your public attack is nothing but a cheap political ploy to gain votes at the expense of racial sensitivities in this city. How do I know it is political? You have supporters who have much closer ties to Minister Farrakhan than I do. The Rev. Calvin Butts and New York State Assemblyman Al Vann, to name a few. Have you attacked their public view of Minister Farrakhan?, of course not. This glaring inconsistency of yours is similar to Rudy Guliani Ed Koch tried to use Farrakhan to destroy Rev. Jesse Jackson's 1988 New York primary, it back fired then, and so will your act of political duplicity backfire now.

I have met over the last several years with John Cardinal O'Connor. We have stood together against black church bombings, Haitian Refugees, the Rwandan Crisis, and against budget cuts. I, however, disagree with the Cardinal's view on gays and lesbians, should I denounce him as a *homophobe*? Have you denounced him as a *homophobe*? Maybe it's because you have respect for Catholic voters and take black voters for granted.

I've conducted my campaign for better education, job development and training, the freezing of tax cuts, and anti-police brutality, in a manner not to engage in personal attacks. I will continue to do so. I choose to respond to you in public, because you have raised this issue publicly. I must however, challenge you since you have raised the issue of race, to endorse City Councilwoman C. Virginia Fields to replace you as Manhattan Borough President and to prove that you want to end black exclusion at high ranking levels of municipal government. Your lack of endorsement in this area, shows a gap between your rhetoric and your record, (you refused to endorse Rev. Jesse Jackson in 1988). It is time for you to put up or shut up. It's easy to attack a non-New York black, who is a buzz word in some circles of New Yorkers. It is more difficult to support inclusion at home. I've noticed, Mr. Fernando Ferrer's joining you in this attack of me. I'm confused by his standards for bigotry. His (Mr. Ferrer) campaign is being run by Shienkoff and Alston, who represented the Los Angeles policeman (Stacey Koontz) who beat Rodney King. Mr. Ferrer's first campaign manager was Dick Morris who had represented Jesse Helms and Trent Lott. These are people in his campaign, but he wants to question me on my opinion of people not in my campaign, or even in New York.

Lastly, I personally resent your lecturing me on hate. Every morning when I look in the mirror, I see a scar on my chest, which was the result of me being stabbed, by a white man in Bensonhurst. I forgave him and I now communicate with him. I could have just condemned and denounced him as you apparently prefer me to do so. I chose to try to heal him and help him. I know in doing that, I would heal myself of any ill feelings. That is why I should be Mayor of the City of New York. I can talk to all kinds of people, so that I can try and lift them up and then bring about reconciliation. Any shrill voice can just call people names.

Yours in Progress;
the Rev. AL Sharpton

We have a little contest in the office to count the grammar and punctuation errors in the letter (depending upon whether you count the use of brackets as a mistake, we come up with either twenty-two or twenty-three). Still, with the Cardinal O'Connor example Sharpton has a strong point. It's difficult to differentiate our tolerance of O'Connor's intolerance of gays from our intolerance of Sharpton's tolerance of Farrakhan's intolerance of Jews.

And besides, anyone who can find a way to use three consecutive punctuation marks in a letter can't be entirely wrong.

• • •

Seeing a political opportunity, Rudy Giuliani weighs in today with a legitimate and interesting question. In light of the Farrakhan controversy, Rudy is asking all of the candidates whether they will continue to stand by their pledge to support the winner of the Democratic primary. "I think Ruth, Freddie and Sal have to face up to the fact that a lot of New Yorkers will find it rather incredible that they would say that they would support Al Sharpton over me should that be the choice." Ruth has finessed the question to this point by saying that she intends to win the primary. Rudy is asking it for the wrong reasons, but the question is a valid one. Would we really support Al Sharpton over Rudy Giuliani if it came to that? Will the lasting legacy of this campaign be to legitimate Al Sharpton?

April 6

Early this morning, a sixteen-year-old high-school student was shot in the back and killed by a police officer.

A few hours after midnight, Officer Anthony Pelligrini responded to a call that shots had been fired at a party in Washington Heights. On his way to the scene, Officer Pelligrini saw Kevin Cedeno running up Amsterdam Avenue and tried to apprehend him. Pelligrini said that Cedeno turned to attack him and that Cedeno was carrying a machete. Fearing for his own life, Pelligrini fired the fatal shot.

Pelligrini's version of the story is contradicted by several other witnesses who say that Cedeno was running away from the officer, not toward him. Their version is supported by the fact that Cedeno was shot in the back, not the chest, where one might expect a shot to land in a charging attacker.

Rudy immediately credited the officer's version of the story. "This person came at them," the mayor said. "He was told to stop. He continued to lunge forward and they had to protect themselves." It's a quick reaction by Rudy. There's no evidence to support the officer's story one way or the other. But we're paralyzed. There's too close a parallel between this and another situation in which Ruth Messinger sided with a victim. That decision is widely recognized within the campaign as one of her strong liabilities.

On July 3, 1992, Jose (Kiko) Garcia was shot by Officer Michael O'Keefe in the lobby of 505 West 162nd Street in Washington Heights. O'Keefe said that Garcia was concealing a weapon, but two days after the shooting, a conflicting story of a witness, Juana Madera, began circulating through the press. According to Madera, O'Keefe and two other police officers approached Garcia while he was trying to put a piece of cardboard on the door to his building. The officers asked Garcia why he was trying to fix the door and shortly thereafter began hitting him on the head without provocation. Madera then heard three shots.

Needless to say, tensions in Washington Heights heightened. On the fourth day after the shooting, Messinger and then-mayor David Dinkins met with the Garcia family. Later that same day, violence erupted. The police succeeded in coaxing the crowd into a peaceful march. Ruth joined in. The march began at the site of the shooting and continued peacefully for approximately ten blocks until the protesters reached 184th Street, where a wall of police officers had assembled in riot gear to protect the precinct house. Further rioting broke out and another Washington Heights resident, Dagoberto Pichardo, died.

Sometime late in the afternoon the next day, between one and two thousand people marched peacefully to the 34th Precinct to protest the deaths of Garcia and Pichardo. Ruth again joined the march. She and Al Sharpton were the only politicians allowed to address the crowd. None other than civilian Rudy Giuliani criticized Dinkins and Messinger for their handling of the affair. In an op-ed in the *New York Times*, Rudy Giuliani said Dinkins and Messinger portrayed Kiko Garcia as a martyr without bothering to check his criminal record. Garcia, as it turns out, was a drug dealer, and Officer O'Keefe was later cleared of any wrongdoing. Ruth has always explained her involvement in the march by saying that she was asked to join in by the chief of patrol.

Events clearly moved quickly in those days in the summer of 1992 and I have no doubt that Ruth was motivated by nothing more than a desire to help keep the peace. But the lasting impression of those events for most New Yorkers is a mayor and borough president who marched with an army of blacks to protest the death of a drug dealer. There's too much of a parallel between the Cedeno shooting and the Garcia affair for Ruth to take any chances. This mayor has acted too quickly, but if Ruth were to side with Cedeno and be wrong, it would be devastating. We issue a quiet statement calling for an investigation.

Over at the borough president's office, they view this as a critical opportunity to consolidate our base and solidify support in the black community. Even across several blocks of traffic, we can hear them banging their heads against the wall.

April 7

Jim is doing the question thing with a woman I am desperately trying to recruit for our research staff. She asks the best question ever.

"Have you ever thought of running for office?" she asks.

"I'm an asshole," he answers. "I couldn't get elected dogcatcher in Tuscaloosa."

She doesn't take the job.

Wyatt Tee Walker, minister of the Canaan Baptist Church of Christ in Harlem, writes Ruth to scold her for having conducted her dialogue with Al Sharpton in the press. One of Ruth's advisers apparently told Walker that Ruth would not release the Farrakhan letter to the press. "It is evident," Walker writes, that Ruth and her "political cadre lack the judgment and integrity that are prerequisites for having the responsibility of running the City of New York."

Walker adds that he does not consider Farrakhan an anti-Semite and refers Ruth to a statement he made in response to Farrakhan's appearance at Madison Square Garden in 1985:

> Friday's New York *Post* carried the phrase *gutter religion* despite no evidence yet produced that is what Mr. Farrakhan said. Farrakhan admits to *dirty religion* which was his conclusion in reference to the use of violence, war and death to achieve a nation's goal. Whatever rhetoric one chooses, soft or hard, a nation, religion, people, leave themselves morally and spiritually suspect when they declare over and over again, *We will never forgive . . . and never forget!*

Walker urges Ruth to read the statement "carefully, especially, the last sentence." "You are on notice," he concludes, "that you have little viability as a candidate to attract Black voters without a public apology to Mr. Sharpton for your intemperate outburst. I will use every ounce of energy of my individual and collective influence to see to it that you are not elected."

April 8

With the papers reporting this week that crime dropped still further in New York during the past three months ("Crime's Been Arrested!" trumpets the *News*), our hopes are turning increasingly to a crisis in rent-control laws to give us some momentum.

Rent-control laws, which restrict what landlords may charge for lease renewals and vacant apartments, protect more than 2.6 million New York City residents and another 150,000 tenants across the state. To my mind, the laws are difficult to defend. They are not targeted to the needy. Raoul Felder, Mia Farrow, and Dick Cavett all either have lived or live in rent-controlled apartments. The laws create a black market that offsets a portion of whatever reductions in the cost of living the laws may achieve. And the laws are expensive to administer. Even tenant advocates seem to concede that the laws aren't defensible from an economic standpoint. Their primary defense now is that rent control serves the important purpose of maintaining diversity in the city. Without rent protection, artists and the lower middle class would be forced to leave Manhattan, turning it into an island of the affluent.

Joe Bruno, a Republican state senator from Rensselaer and the majority leader, has vowed to eliminate the laws. The regulations are due to expire on June 15, and Bruno is saying that he will let the laws lapse then unless lawmakers agree to a two-year transition to a free-market system.

The 2.6 million people who benefit from the laws have the moral standing of lottery winners (a generous lottery, I should say) who claim they shouldn't have to pay taxes on their winnings. But they're not about to give up the laws quietly. Rent control is a powerful political issue. Seventy percent of city voters think rent regulation is necessary to provide affordable housing. Among regulated-apartment renters, the figure is 81 percent. Cardinal O'Connor went so far as to call rent control a moral issue that is imperative for Roman Catholics to address.

For the most part, rent control is a matter of state law, but the mayor is an obvious candidate to lead the fight to protect the legislation. Rudy's been pretty quiet about this one. He claims that he has been fighting the battle behind the scenes and lobbying Bruno personally during a recent trip to the state capitol. But he's been equivocal in his position. After a recent vote in the state Senate, Rudy called the actions of two senators who voted in favor of the laws "courageous" and the position of a senator who voted the other way "sensible." His campaign has also accepted $7,700 contributions—the maximum permitted by law—from the two leading landlord associations, including the creatively named Rent Stabilization Association.

As a challenger to a powerful incumbent, we're interested in the introduction of as many variables as possible to the election. A lapse in the rent laws would be especially useful. It's a powerful enough issue that it might stir up anti-incumbent sentiment. And if the laws did lapse, we would be able to tie Giuliani to the failure by virtue of his status as a Republican and by the campaign contributions he accepted. Hoping for something that will bring hardship to millions of people is perverse, I know, but we need for the pot to be stirred up a bit.

April 9

For weeks, the mayor has been defending new rules he imposed that force United Nations diplomats to pay their parking tickets. Diplomatic immunity is a nuisance for New Yorkers. Ambassadors from around the world park wherever they like with impunity, while the few New Yorkers who are lucky enough to find a parking space in the city have to move their cars every two hours to avoid alternate side of the street parking regulations. "The mayor's order couldn't arrive too soon," says the *Post*.

But foreign officials hold the parking privileges dear. Today, the UN Committee on Relations with the Host Country voted 13–1–1 to convene the General Assembly to consider New York's plan to crack down on parking violations by diplomats. Mali and Cyprus voted in favor. The United States voted against. Britain, ever loyal, abstained.

Rudy says we should call the UN's bluff. "If they'd like to leave New York over parking tickets, then we can find another use for that area of town. It happens to be just about the most valuable real estate in the world, not just the United States. That is enormously valuable real estate, and with the vacancy rates that exist in the city of New York, can you imagine what we could do with that?"

The most valuable real estate in the world, not just in the United States, you see.

April 10

Rudy's little spat with the United Nations reminds me that I have been remiss in not formally introducing the 107th mayor of New York City to you sooner. If you're from New York, you already either love or hate the man, but perhaps the rest of you don't have such a strong impression. My team is dividing its time now between researching Freddie Ferrer and Rudy Giuliani. I'll tell you the basics of what we know so far, and you can decide for yourself in the event that you are not predisposed one way or the other.

Rudolph William Louis Giuliani III was something of a miracle. His parents, Harold and Helen, tried for six years to have a baby before Rudy was born in 1944. He was to be their only child. Harold and Helen lived in the Flatbush section of Brooklyn, near a bar and pizzeria Harold owned on Nostrand Avenue.

When Rudy was seven years old, his father moved the family to Garden City in Long Island. Rudy attended St. Anne's, a nearby parochial school, excelling enough to win an academic scholarship to Bishop Loughlin Memorial High School, an all-boys school in Brooklyn run by a French order of Christian Brothers. Rudy had to travel two hours a day to get to Bishop Loughlin from his home in the suburbs, but the commute did not keep him from doing well at school. He was appointed to the sixty-member student council, earned honors grades in his classes, and developed a passion for John Kennedy, delivering the nominating speech for Kennedy at a mock Democratic convention. Though his classmates named him "Class Politician," Giuliani believed he would become a priest.

At Manhattan College in the Bronx, another all-male school, Giuliani ventured into elective politics for the first time as a candidate for sophomore class president. He lost the election by seventy-five votes and showed his incipient vindictive side. When the winning candidate ran for student-council president the following year, Rudy's friend Alan Placa, the editor of the school newspaper, ran a false letter accusing candidate Jon Farrell of cooking the books on the freshman ball. Farrell had had nothing to do with the freshman ball. In the next issue of the paper, Placa ran a clarification: "The substance of the rumor in the letter was, almost to the word, a complete lie." In 1994, Giuliani and his college running mate and lifelong friend Peter Powers ran into Farrell at a fund-raiser. Powers greeted Farrell warmly. Giuliani ignored him.

While at Manhattan, Giuliani decided against the priesthood. He liked dating. He later said that he would have chosen life as a missionary "if the priesthood had encompassed marriage." Instead of becoming a man of the cloth, Rudy became a lawyer. At New York University Law School, Giuliani again excelled. He made *Law Review* during his first year and ultimately graduated magna cum laude. Though he cried at the news of John Kennedy's assassination, Giuliani interned after his second year at Richard Nixon's law firm, Mudge, Rose, Guthrie, Alexander & Mitchell. The highlight of the summer was a two-hour lunch for the interns with Nixon, then considering a second presidential bid. Unlike his high-school and college classmates, Rudy's law-school colleagues didn't regard him as a young politician. One classmate said, "If you looked at our class and said, 'Make a list of the thirty students most likely to run for mayor of New York, one to thirty,' no one would even put [Rudy] on the list." Another classmate thought the future mayor thin-skinned. "He could give a joke but not take one. When he thought he was right, he'd become arrogant and call the other guy a crybaby," said Peter McKenna, Giuliani's classmate and the editor-in-chief of the *NYU Law Review.*

Despite his classmates' reservations, Giuliani prospered as a young lawyer. After graduating from NYU, Giuliani clerked for two years with federal district judge Lloyd McMahon. McMahon, a Republican and former U.S. Attorney, became Giuliani's guardian angel. He urged Giuliani to become a federal prosecutor, helped him land a job at the U.S. Attorney's Office, and wrote a letter to the local draft board securing an uncommon occupational deferment for Giuliani by virtue of his status as a law clerk.

Giuliani thrived at the U.S. Attorney's Office. He won all forty of his trials and earned a legendary reputation as a master of cross-examination. The story goes that former congressman Bertram Podell pleaded guilty of corruption rather than face further cross-examination by Giuliani. In 1973, at the age of twenty-nine, he was named chief of the narcotics unit. Soon thereafter, he became Executive U.S. Attorney. In 1975, at McMahon's urging, Deputy U.S. Attorney General Harold Tyler recruited Giuliani to be his associate at the Justice Department. Giuliani went to Washington and switched parties "more through philosophical analysis and discussion and reading than through some political process." When the Republicans fell out of power in 1976, Giuliani returned to the private sector and practiced at the law firm of Patterson, Belknap, Webb and Tyler.

In 1981, Giuliani was named Associate Attorney General, the third highest position in the Department of Justice. He supervised all of the U.S. Attorney's Office's federal law enforcement agencies, the Bureau of Correction, the Drug Enforcement Agency, and the U.S. Marshals. He was also the Reagan administration's point person on a lawsuit that accused the federal government of racism in its policy of interning illegal Haitian immigrants in the infamous Krome detention center outside of Miami. Giuliani flew to Haiti and determined that Haitians were economic rather than political refugees. "There is not a problem," Giuliani said, "a major problem, a systematic problem, of political repression in Haiti." This was during the reign of President-for-Life Baby Doc Duvalier and the Tonton Macoutes.

In 1983, Giuliani again returned to New York to become the U.S. Attorney for the Southern District of New York. During his six-year tenure, the office enjoyed some colossal successes. Rudy directed several major anticorruption prosecutions, including Wedtech and a case that broke up a racketeering ring in the New York City Parking Violations Bureau. He successfully indicted the entire leadership of the Colombo organized-crime family. And he secured guilty pleas from insider traders Ivan Boesky and Michael Milken.

But Rudy also began to acquire a reputation for spotlight hogging and overzealousness. Some charged that the press conferences he held as a matter of course were unethical and jeopardized defendants' rights to a fair trial. As time passed, he seemed to grow more desperate for attention. He unsuccessfully and bizarrely tried to prosecute a seventy-four-year-old judge named Hortense Gabel for being influenced in a divorce case by former City Council Speaker Bess Myerson. The main witness against Judge Gabel was her less-than-stable daughter. In a decision that symbolized the excesses of his office, Giuliani ordered investment banker Richard Wigton arrested in the middle of the trading floor. Wigton was never convicted. Several judges and colleagues accused Rudy of grandstanding.

Rudy toyed with the idea of running for the Senate in 1987 as an activist candidate against Daniel Patrick Moynihan, but eventually begged out of the race, claiming he had unfinished business as U.S. Attorney and that he would not leave his post unless he were allowed to choose his own successor. But in 1989, he finally plunged into politics. He left the U.S. Attorney's Office, joined the white-shoe law firm of White & Case, and announced his plans to run for mayor.

By most accounts, Rudy was an unpolished candidate in 1989. He was cold and uncomfortable with people. His campaign suffered several public gaffes. Giuliani's supporter and sidekick Jackie Mason called David Dinkins a "fancy schvartze." Giuliani-for-Mayor sent Bess Myerson a fundraising letter. With a campaign slogan of "Rudy . . . he'll clean up New York," Giuliani withstood a primary challenge from cosmetics tycoon Ronald Lauder, who ran millions of dollars of negative ads against Giuliani, which were not without considerable effect. Giuliani lost the general election to David Dinkins by 50,000 votes. On election night, Rudy's supporters refused to believe that he had lost. "Shut the hell up!" he screamed and urged the city to unite behind Dinkins. At home, he crumbled at Donna's bedside and asked, "Do they really think I'm mean?"

Soon after the election, Giuliani began plotting his comeback. White & Case, which represented Panama's Manuel Noriega, had proved to be a liability during the 1989 election, so Rudy jumped ship and joined the law firm of Anderson Kill Olick and Oshinsky, where he spent four years studying the city and polishing his image. He shed a few pounds, bought new glasses, and shortened his combover.

In 1993, Rudy and his campaign were tightly focused. His new slogan, "One City, One Standard," drew attention to David Dinkins's perceived delay in subduing rioting in Crown Heights (and arguably appealed to white voters generally). Giuliani recalled images of Washington Heights. He had the continued backing of the Liberal party, which provided a dependable 50,000-vote base. Giuliani reversed the 1989 result and won in 1993 by 50,000 votes.

Rudy's record as mayor has been one of impressive accomplishment tarnished by a childish capacity for vindictiveness. He has made impressive strides against crime, but when his police commissioner, William Bratton, was featured on the cover of *Time* magazine, Rudy forced him out of his job. When a popular schools chancellor, Ramon Cortines, asserted independence, Giuliani began a campaign to drive him too out of town. He used words like "whiny," "little victim," and "precious" to describe Cortines, who is gay. According to Pulitzer prize–winning columnist Sidney Schanberg, City Hall aides asked whether "you would want him alone with your family." Cortines left.

Some examples are downright petty. A member of Giuliani's public-relations staff failed to notify City Hall that Princess Diana was in town, denying Rudy a photo opportunity; she got the boot. So too with another publicist who mishandled a snow removal photo-op, forcing Giuliani to walk a hundred yards in the snow.

He is, depending on your view, a driven man of action who allows nothing to get in his way or a deeply flawed person who has managed to get some things done in spite of himself.

• • •

There's not much in all of this that will likely be useful to us. Rudy's past—his record as a U.S. Attorney, his affiliation with Ronald Reagan—was aired extensively during the past two elections.

Reviving old attacks will have no offensive value. Rudy has a record now, and our challenge is to attack that record. But some of the things in his past may be useful defensively at some point to rebut charges the Giuliani campaign may make about Ruth's past. "Well, if you want to talk about what Ruth Messinger was doing twenty years ago, let's talk about what Rudy Giuliani was doing fifteen and ten years ago." We need to have this stuff in the can, but we don't expect to use it.

There's one thing in Rudy's past, though, that I can't get over. In 1968, Giuliani married Regina Peruggi, a brunette from the Bronx whom he had known since childhood. Peruggi's father, Salvatore, was Harold Giuliani's first cousin. Alan Placa, the culpable newspaper editor, who had once dated Peruggi, was Giuliani's best man.

In 1982, Peruggi and Giuliani divorced. He attributed their breakup to his workaholic tendencies and marrying too young. The divorce was a trivial matter until two years later when Rudy wanted to marry again. When Rudy proposed after his six-week courtship of Donna Hanover, he wanted a Catholic ceremony. But to have one, he needed to get an annulment, and annulments were difficult to get. Giuliani again turned to the ever reliable Placa, by then a priest and a lawyer for the Rockville Center Diocese. Placa secured an annulment for Giuliani and Peruggi on the grounds that they had not secured special dispensation from the church for their marriage. Second cousins and closer relations require leave of the church to be married. Explaining the annulment, Giuliani said in 1989 that he had not known he and Peruggi were second cousins. He had assumed they were third cousins. Placa recently explained it slightly differently. He said Giuliani and Peruggi had understood their relation, but had not known that special dispensation was required.

The notion that Giuliani did not know that the woman he was marrying was his second cousin seems laughably implausible. I mention it, though, not because I think there's anything scandalous about the substance of what happened, but rather because it's the best of countless examples of Rudy's way of subtly manipulating the truth to his benefit. The wonderful thing about Rudy's version of his annulment is that whatever the truth is—one of Peruggi's bridesmaids recently said that the couple always knew they were second cousins—no one can ever prove that Rudy was lying. Only he knows what he believed at the time.

Rudy, it seems, *likes* to tweak the truth. It is as if he does so just because he can. Even if Rudy knows the answer to a question and knows the answer suits his purposes well, he'll still twist it slightly in his favor. His hyperboles are always specific, to give them an air of credibility, and they always have the same cadence. "New York City has replaced 150, 160, 180,000 jobs over the past year." "*Very, very* few societies, for instance, have thought that murder was good." "Nobody, no place, celebrates Christmas as well as New York City."

Rudy pops his eyes when he exaggerates (the bigger the number, the bigger the pop), which has a suspicious feel to it, but it doesn't really feel like lying. It feels more like a six-year-old boy stealing something he doesn't need, like bobby pins, just because he knows he can get away with it. He doesn't even really want the pins, but why shouldn't he take them?

Even Rudy's assessment of his own candor has an overreaching, hand-in-the-cookie-jar sense to it. Asked by *New York* magazine in 1987 what his strengths are, Giuliani responded, "I'm honest *and* intellectually honest."

Who knew there was a difference?

April 11

Money is a campaign's single most valuable commodity. Some thoughtful people might argue that a charismatic candidate is of equal or greater value, but if so, it's only because the charisma can attract money.

Money can make up for all sorts of deficiencies. A smart candidate may be able to think of a quick, witty rejoinder to an opponent's attack, but at best people will hear it one time on the evening news. A dim, well-funded candidate can pay a group of people to think of a response, test it in front of a focus group, and broadcast it over the television airwaves so that every voter hears it ten times. Given a choice between a smart candidate with a million-dollar budget and an ordinary candidate with a ten-million-dollar budget, most consultants would opt for the latter and take their chances.

Because of its great power, money dictates many campaign decisions. If you are ever confused about why a candidate is acting a particular way or taking a certain position on an issue that doesn't appear obvious, figure out how the action in question will help the candidate raise money and you'll have the answer. City campaign-finance laws and Ruth's honor mitigate the influence of money on policy in our campaign, but it is still a powerful shaping force. It has a daily effect on decisions about Ruth's schedule. An afternoon touring Hindu temples in Queens may not advance the message of the campaign much, but if it can lead to connections that will generate a few thousand dollars, we go. Money has a profound effect on how the candidate spends her time.

Of all of the functions in the campaign, fund-raising is the most scientific. It's still far from science, but given equivalent amounts of information, a fund-raiser is able to make more accurate predictions than any pollster. A good fund-raising consultant can say with surprising precision how much income each hour of fund-raising time will generate for the campaign.

There are three main sources of revenue for a campaign: mailings, events, and direct solicitations by the candidate. As a general proposition, mailings and events are less preferred than direct calls, because they are more labor- and capital-intensive. Direct-mail solicitations require lots of envelopes and stamps and, most important, people to lick them. Special events require a host, a venue, an attraction, and lots of planning. Our January fund-raiser raised about $450,000 for the campaign, but cost more than $100,000, excluding labor costs. It's good money, but still far from an ideal margin. Events are an important way of giving the campaign a public face, but fund-raising consultants don't embrace these events; they tolerate them.

Consultants are most interested in candidate call time. Right now, Ruth's telephone solicitations are bringing in about $1,500 an hour. (That is slightly overstated, since it includes the considerable staff time that goes into producing an hour of call time, but only slightly, given the piddling salaries young staffers are paid.) The candidate is far and away our most valuable asset. There's great concern in the campaign that Ruth's call rate has slipped to 4.75 calls per hour, substantially below the 6.0 calls per hour she needs to make to meet our income projections. Our fund-raising consultant thinks we may already have fallen too far behind where we need to be to meet our goal of raising to the cap (that is, raising the full amount the city campaign-finance laws permit us to spend). He is saying we may fall $1 or $2 million short of our goal, which could have a profound effect on our ability to remain competitive.

The problem is that calling is difficult, time-intensive work. Ruth is attended to by a staff of eight fund-raisers (the largest department in the campaign), who lay an intricate groundwork for her calls. Each has a different specialty area—there is a gay-money person, a minority person, someone who specializes in professionals, and someone who specializes in women—in which they literally prospect for potential donors. The process can begin in several ways. Something as simple as handing Ruth a business card at a party leads to a call from one of our fund-raisers, who asks to sit down for a *rolodexing* meeting. At the meeting the fund-raiser asks the rolodexee who he or she knows who might be willing to give money to the campaign and, quite forwardly, how much those persons might be willing to give. If the prospect is fertile enough, the staff member makes up *call sheets* for

Ruth, telling her who the persons are, what they do, how much they have given to other candidates in the recent past, how much she should solicit (the *ask*), and what she should say to try to persuade them to give money (the *pitch*).

A separate staff attends to the call sheets. Their goal is to maximize the amount of time Ruth spends actually talking to people on the phone. Since people will often hang up if they hear they are getting a call from Ruth Messinger's campaign—as opposed to a call from the candidate herself—the fund-raising team uses a variety of deceptive tactics to get prospective donors to the phone *(pre-calling)*. One staffer, whose voice is uncannily similar to Ruth's, simply identifies herself as the candidate and then hands the phone over to Ruth when the prospective donor is on the line. Another tactic is to call to see whether a prospect is home, hang up if the person answers, and then have Ruth call back.

Direct-phone soliciting by the candidate is far and away the most productive way for the campaign to raise money, but it has one regrettable side effect. It leaves Ruth locked in a room for six hours a day. That might not be so bad if the calls could be made early in the morning or late at night, but donors don't much like being called at home, and calling during lunch isn't a high-yield proposition. So Ruth is sequestered between 9:00 A.M. and noon and again between 2:00 and 5:00 P.M. The calculus is simple: If we schedule a press event during peak hours, it costs the campaign money. If Jim or Lee speaks with Ruth during peak hours, it costs the campaign money. If Ruth goes to the bathroom, it costs the campaign money. This kind of pressure is maddening for the candidate. Robert Abrams, a former New York state attorney general who lost a Senate campaign to Al D'Amato in 1992, says he once threw a phone at a consultant who told him he was falling behind on his calling.

It's mind-numbing work. Message is out the window. If the prospect's main issue of concern is contingency-fee restrictions on lawyers, then for five minutes contingency fees become the key issue in the campaign even if they're something the mayor has no power over. Guilt is a fair tactic. Groveling is appropriate when required by circumstances.

Ruth is stoical about the work, though she resisted it for a while. Back in January she wrote a memo to our deputy fund-raising director saying, "I am more than ready to make calls myself. However, I cannot use every minute of call time for calls." "That was wrong then and is even more wrong now, given our current situation," our fund-raising consultant explains this week in a state-of-the-campaign memo. Ruth is as converted as she ever will be.

She now accepts the time in the phone closet as part of the job, a necessary evil.

Every nineteen year old who dreams of running for office should spend a week watching a candidate on the phone. For every hour the candidate spends doing something that might be regarded as glamorous—attending a press conference or delivering a speech—she spends ten on the phone. And the people on the other end don't feel honored to be called by a candidate for the second most difficult job in the United States. All they hear is another person asking for money.

April 14

Bad as April 15 is for ordinary Americans, it's even worse for politicians. Their tax returns are open to the public (by convention, not by law) and scrutinized by the press.

We're set to release Ruth's return, when it occurs to us to that there may be a problem. Ruth makes a big deal of the fact that she does not accept a $28,000 raise that was part of a 1996 package signed by Giuliani increasing his own salary by $35,000 and raising the salaries of City Council members and most high-level city officials. We've tested the impact of Rudy's pay raise in a poll and are considering using it in an ad. "Rudy Giuliani cut a billion dollars from our city's schools, but gave himself a $35,000 pay raise."

Looking at Ruth's tax returns, it turns out that Ruth does get the pay raise, but donates the after-tax portion to charity. That means Ruth gets a $17,000 deduction against her old salary that she would not have but for the raise. It's not the same as pocketing the money, but it's not the same as refusing to accept it either. Only one reporter thinks to ask about it. Lee truthfully states that the money "either went to charity or it went to Uncle Sam." But on this occasion, it seems to me, we benefit from superficial scrutiny.

Our rivals have their own problems. Al Sharpton, who pleaded guilty to a misdemeanor charge of failing to file a tax return in 1990, files for an extension because, according to his attorney, important financial records were destroyed in a fire at his campaign headquarters last week.

Freddie Ferrer checked "no" in the box for providing $3 to the presidential campaign fund.

April 15

Cunningly disguised in an oxford shirt and khaki Dockers as an Upper West Side yuppie, I am standing next to Freddie Ferrer on the steps of City Hall as he holds a press conference about the Cedeno shooting.

Last week, an autopsy revealed that Kevin Cedeno was shot in the back, supporting the version of the story put forward by friends and relatives. Rudy has retreated a bit from his earlier position. "There's no possible way to judge this event without knowing all of the facts," he says. "We know he was carrying a machete. We know he was shot in the back. So that gives you two facts that could go in either direction, and at this point people of good will and of neutrality in a situation like this will keep an open mind."

On safer ground now, Ruth is attacking the mayor for not having been more restrained in his earlier comments. "When a killing has occurred, I think a mayor should understand by now that the facts are often cloudy and there are usually lots of different perspectives on what happened. If indeed you don't want people to rush to judgment, you shouldn't rush to judgment yourself." Dinkins echoes Ruth's sentiment. It's an especially sensitive point for him, since Giuliani repeatedly blasted Dinkins during the 1993 campaign for reaching premature conclusions on police-community relations (often not in favor of the police). But our coordinated attack is a tepid criticism, really. We're still not saying anything about the problem of police brutality substantively. This is a procedural argument, an argument about the mayor's temperament and management style. The meat of the issue is still too hot for Ruth to handle.

Freddie Ferrer is not so constrained. He is denouncing the shooting as an execution. "It runs against the grain of the American psyche to shoot someone in the back," he says. "To shoot someone in the back is an execution. And that's precisely what occurred here."

For weeks, Jim has been asking me during our morning calls what we can do to nail Ferrer on his waffle on the death penalty. This morning, I suggested an idea.

"Why don't we ask Freddie whether he would support the death penalty for Officer Pelligrini if it turns out that he murdered Cedeno."

"Brilliant!" Jim screamed. "You're really starting to get this!"

Later in the day, Lee suggests the question to a reporter. I'm at a press conference Ferrer is holding on the steps of City Hall to see whether it gets asked. Fifteen minutes into the press conference, the reporter with whom we've placed the question has asked his share of questions and shows no signs of asking mine. The thought occurs to me that I could ask the question. No one knows who I am. I could easily sneak away from the conference unnoticed. And I am so close to Ferrer that he could not help but hear me. I'd never be able to show my face again at an enemy press conference, but the price might be worth it.

Ferrer will be damned no matter what answer he gives. He will either look like a fool or be caught in a waffle. In my exaggerated view of my own importance in the world, I envision that this question could be Ferrer's undoing. A career-ender.

Standing as close to him as I am, Fernando Ferrer doesn't seem like a political commodity. He looks like a human being. I can't pull the trigger.

"I was afraid they would have been able to figure out who I was," I explain back at the office. "There weren't that many people there."

No one questions my actions, but privately I wonder whether I'm cut out for this business.

April 16

I haven't been getting out much, so I am happy for the opportunity to tape Rudy's town hall meeting. Rudy holds one of these a month at different places around the city. This one is on the Upper West Side and it's jam-packed.

The average age in the room is about seventy, and as far as I can tell I am the only person in the room under thirty. The woman seated in front of me is reading the same article I am reading in the *New Republic* about the rise of medical ethicists. This is not exactly a representative cross-section of society.

The main concern among the audience is to see and hear everything, though no one seems to care very much about what it is they are seeing and hearing. The woman next to me strains her neck to see everyone from the mayor's office who comes in, though she doesn't recognize a single face.

"Who is that?" she asks.

"Christopher Lynn, the Commissioner of Transportation."

She nods her head.

"Who is that?"

"Lillian Barrios-Paoli, the Commissioner of the Human Resources Administration. She wants to be the least remembered commissioner in the city's history."

She nods her head in deep understanding. She clearly has no idea what any of these people do, but I don't have the heart to say anything. She so desperately wants to be involved. When a member of the mayor's staff announces that people should take their seats so that they can take a head count, my friend asks whether we are supposed to count.

"No," I say. "But the woman making the announcement is Carol Mosley-Braun."

"Oh," she says, in deeper understanding still.

The mayor's entire staff is here. John Doherty, the sanitation commissioner, is here. So too Earl Andrews, the commissioner of the Department of Business Services, who ran against Ruth for borough president in 1993 and lost by 70 points. Howard Safir, the police commissioner, is back from bypass surgery. Randy Mastro is here, no doubt reveling in the presence of so many optimistic New Yorkers. Deputy Mayor Rudy Washington is wearing the worst tie I have ever seen. The mayor, holding a wireless microphone, introduces all nineteen of them. Surely, there must be a better use of the time of nineteen city commissioners.

Though it is a fixation of Jim's, I haven't paid much attention to Rudy's hair before this. It is pasted down with enormous care, as if great thought had been given to where each strand should go. Even still, it barely covers his scalp. There's a distracting bit of a shine on the front of his head. If Rudy were a junior-high-school teacher instead of a politician, he would be a laughingstock.

People are surprisingly nuanced in their reactions to the different commissioners. Nicholas Scopetta, the director of the Administration of Children Services, receives big applause. He is recognized among insiders for doing a good job. Ruth likes him a lot, but I'm surprised that anyone else is aware of him. The commissioner for the United Nations gets big laughs. For the past month, he has been caught in the middle of Rudy's assault against parking privileges for foreign diplomats. My friend is less discriminating. She gasps in amazement at each introduction and cheers wildly for everyone.

Without any introductory remarks, Rudy solicits questions from the crowd. My neighbor strains to see who is asking. She must know who is asking each question.

"Mr. Mayor, I noticed that property crime is up in our precinct by 2 percent over the past month. Why is this?"

"Why don't I have you step outside with Commander Safir and you can ask him personally."

The process is repeated a few times. Rudy doesn't answer questions; he's the emcee, it seems. There's a gestapo feeling to the whole thing. Whenever someone asks a difficult question, the person is ushered out of the room with the appropriate commissioner, never to be heard from again.

Interests are disturbingly parochial. Here is an opportunity to ask a man with one of the most important jobs in the United States what he thinks about schools and jobs and what direction the city should be taking. But nobody asks him any of these things. One person is having difficulty securing a license for his store. Another is concerned about people rollerblading on sidewalks. A representative from the International Noise Awareness Day organizing committee asks for a meeting with Rudy a bit testily. Rudy has apparently refused to meet with them before and stands firm. He will not meet with them despite the fact that communities from all over the world have come together for this important cause.

The whole thing is maddening. Each questioner seems more deranged and self-absorbed than the last. An obviously paranoid schizophrenic woman asks an unintelligible question about welfare policy. She is ushered off for a meeting with the commissioner of the Human Resources Administration.

The next questioner follows up. "As Mary Figueroa just asked . . . "

Nearly an hour into the evening, someone finally asks a serious question: Was Rudy too quick to reach judgment in the Kevin Cedeno case?

No, the mayor says. He will await the results of the investigation like everyone else, but he will always initially give police officers the benefit of the doubt and urges the audience members to do the same. Officer Pelligrini, Rudy points out, had received eighteen commendations while "saving the lives of other human beings." A heckler mocks Giuliani's answer.

To demonstrate how shooting someone in the back might be justified, Rudy turns his back to the audience and points his finger at Deputy Mayor Randy Mastro as though aiming a gun.

"Suppose I was about to shoot him and you shot me in the back? You think the police officer would be justified in doing that? Or are you so against police officers that you can't possibly assume a situation in which they might have acted properly?"

I have no idea what happened to Kevin Cedeno, but Rudy is being manipulative in discussing the case. Rudy Giuliani, the lawyer, is ignoring the evidence and speaking only to the credibility of the parties. He notes that Cedeno had been arrested five times and was on probation on the night of the shooting. So what? The only question is whether the police officer had reason to believe he was in danger. This is all smoke, an appeal to an all-white audience's worst fears about blacks.

"You know if you run around at 3:00 in the morning with a machete, it might be dangerous to you," Rudy says. "You don't use it to cut cake."

For the first time I have a visceral reaction to the mayor—revulsion.

April 17

Rudy Giuliani, who, like Ruth, has not formally declared that he is running for mayor, whatever that means, is asked today by a nine-year-old schoolgirl whether he will be running for mayor again.

"Will I be running? Well, I think I am running," the mayor replied. "It feels like I am running. You could say that I am running."

The visit to Public School 232 in Howard Beach is the mayor's seventeenth visit to a school in the past five months. From November 1995 through April 1996, the mayor visited public schools a total of four times.

April 20

For the past week, Jim's beautiful assistant, Janine, has been working on a critical assignment. She is overseeing the construction of a wall that will divide our office in half. It is no easy task. As with many things, Jim wanted it done the day before he asked, and he wants it to cost less than $500.

The end product is the sort of wall one might imagine $500 would buy. It's nothing more than some plasterboard slapped on top of a couple of cheap beams. One member of the campaign from Ruth's office travels with a dart board. He mounted it for a time on the new wall so the board would be accessible to everyone, but when people played, the force of the darts seemed to be too much for the wall to handle. After a few close calls, he moved it back to his office.

To the casual observer, it might not be clear what is being walled in and what is being walled out. The walls are so thin, they keep out no sound. The door has no lock, and even if it did, one good blow would take it down. But the wall is symbolically important. It represents the first victory in an ongoing battle for the very soul of the campaign. Ruth and her staff from the borough president's office want to run an aggressive field campaign. Jim wants to save the money for television ads.

Field refers to a campaign's efforts to stimulate friendly voter turnout. In contrast to the message-delivery functions of a campaign (press and research), a field staff does not seek to advance an argument. They identify voters who are predisposed to their candidate and try to get them to the polls. There can be some overlap between field functions and message functions. A postcard reminding people to vote in the primary might include something that advances the message of the campaign like "Rudy Giuliani cut $6 billion from our schools. Remember to vote September 9." But there are lots of things field staffs do that have no bearing whatsoever on the message. They put up posters, leave answering-machine messages reminding people to vote, and make arrangements to drive people to the polls, none of which tell people *why* to vote for someone.

No one disputes that message delivery is, in relative terms, more important than field operations. But there are widely different views on how important field is in absolute terms. Back in the original budget, drawn up by a member of the borough president's staff, when the campaign expected to raise $10.3 million, $6.6 million was budgeted for message delivery and $1.2 million for field. The $6.6-million figure included a considerable amount of money for voter mail ($1 million), which is not a pure message-delivery activity, and for voter phoning ($300,000), which is not a message-delivery activity at all.

Given infinite resources, no one questions the worth of running a strong field campaign. It certainly can't hurt, and in a tight race it might make a difference. But we don't have infinite resources. And as it becomes increasingly clear that we will not meet the original optimistic fund-raising projections, a battle of priorities is stirring. Jim's priorities are clearly different from Ruth's and her advisers' at the borough president's office. One glaring indication of this is that in the original budget, a total of $20,000 was allocated for research. We'll ultimately exceed that by fivefold. That's trivial in comparison to the magnitude of this debate.

As it is shaping up, the constraints of the budget will mean that anything we spend on field will come directly out of our television budget. Jim's inclination is to spend nothing, or virtually nothing, on field at all. As it is, we are going to be badly outspent on television. Ruth feels differently. In a memo to Jim on January 20, Ruth wrote that she understood that the campaign is "constrained by both the budget cap and by the money already spent," but nevertheless wanted "to ensure that from the top (now) we set aside enough money to have a real field operation in both the primary and the general election."

Field, she wrote, is important for several reasons:

> We will need an operation to make use of a very large number of volunteers who will come to this campaign wanting to help in their local areas. This is all of particular importance in very large communities of color where we already have active supporters, where the vote is most likely ours, where we may be able to make the difference by grassroots work. . . . We will need a solid field operation precisely because we have a reputation for having same, which is already attracting some people to us against our primary opponents.

It's hard to imagine two people more at odds with each other on an issue. Ruth wants to solicit volunteers. Jim built a wall to keep them out. It's not clear how the issue will resolve itself, especially since the two seem to avoid talking about it as much as possible. To avoid the uncomfortable situation of telling his client something she doesn't want to hear, Jim has one of our staff members working full-time deflecting field-related calls from Ruth and the borough president's office. They yell at him about why things aren't getting done. And Jim yells at him because he thinks they're crazy for even asking. It's a wonderful job.

To me, it seems an easy choice. I don't believe a single voter will switch his or her vote as a result of seeing a "Vote for Ruth Messinger" sign. I don't believe a single voter will vote for us because we have a large staff of volunteers. Neither of these things advances an argument. Neither of these things gives people a reason to vote for Ruth. And even if there are a few peculiar people in the world who will switch their votes because they like our signs, no one can ever convince me that posters or palm cards will ever move voters in the mass numbers needed to win an election. The public image of a campaign—and the perception of what an effective campaign should be—as a grassroots organization teeming with volunteers and literature is an anachronistic vestige from a time before radio and television and big money in campaigns, when having lots of your friends go door to door was the only way to sway voters. The interesting question is why the image that field is important persists to such an extent that even politicians themselves are deceived into believing in its value.

In part, the image persists because it serves a social function. Thousands of people want to *do something* for their candidate. Though the truth may be that a campaign only needs a dozen or so people to do the critical work of getting out the candidate's message, it would hardly be proper for a politician to stand at the door turning away people who want to help. "Thanks, Saul, but really the only thing you can do to help is tell your friends to watch my ads on television."

To some extent, the image persists because it serves a political function. The public and the press expect a campaign to be teeming with activity. Campaigns and politicians, like businesses, need to project an image of Calvinistic industriousness in seeking votes, even if the most important work on a given day may be the editing of an advertisement by a media consultant sitting in a studio. That just doesn't project the same image as a phalanx of people pounding the pavement with palm cards and posters. The image of industriousness is especially important for Ruth. Ruth rose through city politics, at a level where effort matters, by outworking her colleagues. In 1989, Ruth raised more than $500,000, the overwhelming majority of which was in donations of less than $10. Ruth made her name as a grassroots politician. It isn't easy to ask her and the people who came to revere her to toss that image aside.

And, dishearteningly, the image persists because there are people in the world who profit by its endurance. There's no subtlety or elegance to this process. Local leaders come to the campaign and ask for funds (Jim calls it *street money*) to organize local voter drives.

None of the people give any specifics about how they will spend the money. I don't mean to imply that they all solicit and use the money for personal financial gain. Some may. Others may use the money in a systematic, constructive way. But it seems that, on average, the money gets spent haphazardly. Spending money haphazardly is a luxury we can't afford.

The problem is that while some of the people are easily brushed aside, others have considerable influence. If we refuse their requests, either out of economy or sincere conviction, they will tell the press that the campaign is disorganized or lethargic. And some people, shaped by an outdated conception of how campaigns work, will believe them.

County leaders are already impatient with us, and many of Ruth's closest advisers who have ties to these people and honestly believe that field operations are important are losing confidence in the campaign and growing impatient. Jim is winning this battle, but at some cost.

April 21

Rudy Giuliani's characteristically restrained answer to charges of improper lobbying by advisers Herman Badillo and Ray Harding is that his is the fairest administration in the history of the city. Rudy can say that, but he isn't as different from other politicians as he would like people to believe. Rudy once declared, "There will be no patronage in my administration." But the press has only scratched the surface of the Badillo-Harding story.

Today's news reports that Ray Harding interviewed and approved a candidate for a job at the Economic Development Corporation (EDC). Harding met with Maury Satin two weeks ago apparently to ratify him as the new chief of staff at the EDC. The EDC is the city agency charged with helping businesses locate to or expand in the city. It controls hundreds of millions of dollars in tax exemptions. Harding's law firm, Fischbein Badillo, has more than a dozen lobbying clients with issues before the EDC. Rudy Giuliani acknowledges that the meeting occurred. He says that it was not an interview, though, given the sequence of events, it's hard to imagine what else the meeting could have been if not an interview. Rudy offers no alternatives.

The EDC is a depository for Giuliani patronage beneficiaries. At least a dozen former Giuliani campaign workers have been hired by the EDC, often at the expense of older, well-respected EDC employees (though the

EDC has refused requests under the Freedom of Information Law for the salaries, titles, and résumés of its employees). EDC employees used to have graduate degrees in business or urban planning. The new hires have neither. One of the new EDC workers baby-sat the Giuliani children during the 1993 campaign. Much of the patronage is dispensed through Tony Carbonetti, twenty-eight, whose father was a childhood friend of the mayor's. Carbonetti dropped out of college and once defaulted on $11,000 in college loans. EDC senior vice president Russell Harding, thirty-two, is the son of none other than Ray Harding himself.

The EDC recently passed out $600,000 in employee bonuses. Russell Harding received a $3,375 bonus on top of his $105,000 salary, even though he worked at the agency for only six months. Former Giuliani campaign staffers received bonuses up to $5,500. The Giuliani baby-sitter did not do well in comparison. His bonus was a mere $1,729.

Despite the overwhelming evidence to the contrary, Rudy Giuliani continues to perpetuate the myth that he is somehow different from ordinary politicians. Explaining his hiring philosophy to Gabe Pressman last year, he said, "I had to hire people that were different from the people that were in city government and people who agreed with my agenda. Where was I going to find them except among the people—not all and not exclusively—among the people who campaigned for me?"

He is not only different from other politicians, Giuliani explains to Pressman, he is better. "I've hired more people on merit than any mayor that you can find."

April 22

Kenny Kramer, former jewelry maker, reggae band manager, and the real-life inspiration for the namesake Seinfeld character, is seeking the Democratic nomination for mayor. "When I look at the field of candidates, I realize what a bleak primary race we are in for," he says. "As a New Yorker, I am appalled. As a Democrat, I am appalled. As an entrepreneur and media slut, I'm inspired."

April 23

Over the past three years, the Giuliani administration has denied press requests under the Freedom of Information Law for information about employees at a scandalized battered women's shelter, pension abuse by police officers, and investigations by the Department of Investigation, the city agency charged with monitoring corruption by government officials. The administration forced the Public Advocate, whose job is to monitor city agencies, to sue the city for access to the records of the Civilian Complaint Review Board (CCRB). Only half the complaints of brutality substantiated by the CCRB result in the discipline of an officer. When auditors from the office of the state comptroller, a Democrat, tried to audit certain city programs, Giuliani had them physically kicked out. In May, the police department removed a photographer who was trying to take a picture of a crime scene. The administration is the defendant in four lawsuits over access to information. It even turned down a request by a woman from Staten Island for a list of people who had passed the test for master plumber.

The *New York Times*, *Newsday*, and the *Daily News* have all condemned the secrecy of the administration generally and specifically on the issues of restricting access to crime data and expelling the comptroller's auditors. (The *Post* said the mayor was "correct to resist" the audits.) Gabe Pressman, who has covered New York politics since 1955, said press secretary Cristyne Lategano and others have "grossly restricted media access" to city commissioners and information. Jerry Nachman, a former director of WNBC-TV and WCBS-TV said, "I've covered New York mayors going back to John Lindsay, and there has been no commensurate era when reporters have either been provoked, ignored, or manhandled as they have in this administration."

Today, the *Daily News* won a lawsuit against the city over one of the countless Freedom of Information Law requests the city has denied. The *News* wanted "closing memoranda" from the Department of Investigation. Closing memoranda are filed upon the completion of an investigation. The city gave the memoranda to the *News*, but redacted virtually all of the contents. Today, a state Supreme Court judge found that the city broke the law by refusing to turn over the documents. "The law provides for maximum access to government information, not maximum withholding."

Asked for reaction, Giuliani said, "Although the press will undoubtedly report this story unfairly, we believe the judge has reached the right decision."

Damn press.

April 24

Message politics can reduce intellectual discourse to a third-grade level. A few weeks ago, law professor Derrick Bell wrote Ruth a letter responding to her thank-you for his contribution to the campaign. Bell resigned from Harvard Law School to protest the school's lack of aggressiveness in recruiting and attracting minority faculty. He expressed his hope that Ruth was developing more specific positions than planning for a "vibrant New York into the twenty-first century." He also expressed some reservations about honoring Ruth's request that he write a letter in support of her candidacy. For Bell's taste, Ruth has not yet said enough about police brutality and the "continuing paucity of minority officers." It's an open, honest letter. It is no threat. It is simply a statement of Bell's agenda and what Ruth must do and say to earn his vote and support, the sort of letter that every citizen has a right to write.

As with all letters, our response passes my desk. There's nothing to change. It's on message. Given what we're doing, there's not much more to say. "I was surprised," the letter goes, "that you are waiting for me to 'take very strong and specific stands on issues of concern to the black community.' Indeed, I believe that every issue of importance in this City is important to the black community."

I can imagine Bell laughing, tossing it and Ruth's candidacy in the trash, and thinking to himself, "She used to stand for something."

April 25

Last week, Public Advocate Mark Green wrote a letter to the mayor urging the city to investigate evidence of a link between the ownership of a homeless shelter in Brooklyn and the Lucchese Mafia crime family. On Tuesday, the mayor said the Department of Investigation did not have enough evidence to sever ties with the shelter.

Today, *60 Minutes* announced that it will be airing a story about the shelter's mob ties tomorrow night. This afternoon, the mayor issued a statement halting the referral of homeless people to the shelter.

To be sure, there were no political considerations in the handling of the case.

April 26

Déjà vu.

Back in early February, a horrifying story emerged of a sex and corruption scandal at a battered women's shelter in the Bronx. Residents at the shelter, the only city-run facility for battered women, reported that security guards slept on the job while shelter workers assaulted and raped residents.

Workers routinely took home food and clothing intended for residents. In several cases, the guards allowed the batterers to enter the facility.

On Tuesday, the Department of Homeless Services reported that it was renewing one of the contracts for the security company that provided the guards at the facility. Mayor Giuliani had promised to have the Department of Investigation review all of the company's contracts, but no report had yet been issued. On Thursday, after the story of the renewal broke in the *Post*, Lillian Barrios-Paoli announced that there was no evidence to support the most serious charges against the guards. She said the Giuliani administration went public with the story and suspended the shelter employees only because Freddie Ferrer was planning to break the story himself. Today, Edward Kuriansky, a former colleague of Giuliani's at the U.S. Attorney's Office and the head of the Department of Investigation, whose report is still pending, says Barrios-Paoli's story is "ludicrous, false, and ruinous to the reputation of our department." Barrios-Paoli now says she was misquoted and taken out of context. The Giuliani people are changing the story so quickly they cannot keep up with it themselves.

Whatever the precise truth is, this is an enormously powerful story, and it may be our hook into the issue of domestic violence. The trick is to get Ruth involved. One option is for Ruth to hold hearings on the subject under her contract-review power as borough president. It would be an unusual and clearly political thing for her to do and, what's more, depending on your reading of the city charter, may require the participation of the Public Advocate and the comptroller. Mark Green won't be a problem, but Alan Hevesi may not be so quick to help out.

Late last year, Hevesi, who has admitted designs on the mayoralty, approached Ruth with a deal. If Ruth would step aside, Hevesi would run for mayor himself and endorse Ruth to be comptroller. Many believe that Hevesi would have been a stronger candidate than Ruth, but he had less money and as late as October 1996 was running third behind Messinger and Ferrer in a five-way with Albanese and Sharpton. Ruth turned the deal down, and Hevesi decided to run for reelection as comptroller. He's expected to endorse Ruth, but many within the campaign have doubts about his true loyalties. Some think he has a tacit nonaggression pact with Giuliani, whose support would be invaluable to him in 2001, when term limits force Giuliani to vacate the mayoralty.

Whether Hevesi will join us or not, we will devote considerable resources to investigating this story and making it an issue in the campaign. To my mind, it's the most powerful indictment of the Giuliani administration we've seen so far, and my gut tells me that there must be some connection between that security firm and the mayor. We just have to prove it.

April 27

I want very much to go to the Mets game tonight, so I do what anybody who works a hundred hours a week would do—lie. At 6:30, I say I'm going out for dinner. Once out of the office, I break into a run and head for the train. It's a beautiful spring night at Shea. The Mets are beating the Padres, but I can't enjoy the game. I look at my beeper in dread after every pitch. In the sixth inning, it vibrates. I switched the setting to "vibrate" a few weeks ago, because I hated the sound of the beep, but the vibration isn't much better. It has a sickening sound, like a dental drill, that grates against my very soul. The page says "911," the office code for an emergency. My colleagues use it quite liberally, and indeed when I call in, the emergency is that Jim was mad because he couldn't find me.

"Does he want anything?" I ask.

"No," the staffer says, "he just wants to know where you are."

Trying to have fun isn't worth the trouble. From here on in, I think I won't even try.

April 28

After three months, we've yet to receive a favorable editorial in any paper. The closest we've come is a signed editorial in today's *Times* calling Giuliani a vulnerable front-runner. "Mr. Giuliani won in 1993 by a tiny margin," writes Steven Weisman. "But now, a lot of older whites have moved out of the city, his support among Hispanics has dwindled, voters are upset about schools, and there will not be such a high turnout in Staten Island."

Of course, the editorial would not be complete without a slight against us. Despite Giuliani's vulnerability, Weisman concludes that "political experts agree that the Rev. Al Sharpton has little chance of broadening his support, and that Fernando Ferrer, the Bronx Borough President, and Ruth Messinger, the Manhattan Borough President, have not yet found their voices."

• • •

Weisman's point about Staten Island is not lost on the Giuliani campaign. Staten Island is a stronghold for Rudy. He carried the borough by an overwhelming 82–15 margin in 1993, and there's no reason to think that the numbers will be any worse this time around. But turnout is not likely to be as high this November as it was in 1993, when a secession referendum was on the ballot. Rudy is doing what he can to make sure Staten Islanders turn out. Today he eliminated the fifty-cent fare on the Staten Island Ferry.

Rudy's act prompts my friend Ira to suggest that our campaign consider the daring idea of passing out cash instead of running ads on television. The $7 million or so we figure to raise wouldn't go very far across the city—it would amount to less than a dollar a person if we gave some to everyone—but there are more creative ways we might use it. We could hold a lottery among people who cast ballots or among an even smaller group. Since we know the demographics of our likely voters, we could pass out the tickets to people with whom we do poorly, like white men and Jews. Ensuring compliance would be difficult. One way to do it would be to say that the lottery money would only be paid if Ruth won. That way, everyone holding a ticket would have an incentive to vote for her.

It's a crazy idea, of course, not to mention illegal, but is it really all that different from what Rudy is doing? At least we'd be doing it with privately raised money. It's the taxpayers who are buying votes for Giuliani in Staten Island.

April 29

The battle is fought on every front. When Ruth appears on a New York 1 call-in show this evening, one caller prefaces his question by saying, "It's good to see someone from the extreme left" running for mayor. Another shouts, "Go, DSA!" as Ruth finishes her answer to his question. The questions have obviously been planted by one of our opponents. There probably aren't ten people in the city who know what the DSA is (though if there are, they're virtually certain to be watching New York 1). From now on, we'll throw in a few questions of our own when our opponents appear on call-in shows.

April 30

Some days it feels as if we're running against the stiffest of headwinds. For the past several months, Rudy Giuliani, who ruled the city like a miser for his first three years in office, has been passing out money like candy apples. He allocated $250 million for a reading project in the schools after saying for years that the Board of Education could not be trusted to spend a dime. He eliminated the fare on the Staten Island Ferry, though he stood by idly two years ago when the MTA hiked the subway and bus fare by twenty-five cents. Now it appears the city will end the year with an $800 million surplus, leaving Giuliani with the difficult election-year choice of choosing between offering tax cuts or increased spending for education and law enforcement.

There is probably some element of truth to the Giuliani administration's claim that this surplus is an unexpected result of the boom on Wall Street and that they are genuinely surprised by the news, but more and more this just seems like a game. Holding back money until an election year may not be sound public policy, but it's good politics. And the way the press analyzes it, all that matters is that it's good politics.

May 1

State assemblyman Jules Polonetsky, a thirty-one-year-old Orthodox Jew from Coney Island, will run for Public Advocate on the Republican and Liberal lines. The move serves two purposes for the Giuliani campaign. It will give party balance to the ticket of a man who claims to be unmotivated by party ideology (it's not a ticket in the strict sense of the word; voters make independent selections for mayor, comptroller, and Public Advocate). Giuliani has used the strategy before. In 1993, he tapped another Democrat, City Council member Susan Alter, to be his running mate.

Having Polonetsky on the ticket has the added benefit of giving Giuliani contributors an outlet to give money in excess of the limit on personal contributions imposed by the city campaign-finance laws. Technically, Polonetsky cannot spend money to aid Giuliani without the money being charged against Rudy's campaign, but there are some obvious opportunities for fudging. We plan to keep an eye on it, but even if Rudy violates the law, he will likely, at worst, be forced to pay a fine after the election. Coordinating the campaigns is a costless gamble.

Although Giuliani has arranged for a challenger against popular incumbent Mark Green, he will not run a candidate against equally popular Comptroller Alan Hevesi. Mr. Hevesi's consultant, Hank Morris, says that Comptroller Hevesi will nevertheless "work hard" to elect the winner of the Democratic primary.

May 3

Mornings are always the worst. Jim is full of energy early in the day, and when he calls, as he always does, at 8:30, he has a hundred things he wants done immediately. The fact of the matter is that the world will not end if we don't produce a press release within the next half hour, but I sometimes find that hard to remember. The calls often send me into a panic. Once I found myself growing angry at one of my deputies because he wasn't doing something Jim wanted. I got angrier and angrier until I realized that I hadn't told him what to do. The problem with the conversations, monologues really, is that Jim demands complete attention, which he ensures by repeatedly saying "Hello."

"We're dead, Evan. Hello?"

"Ruth is going to lose by 30 points. Hello."

"I thought you were going to have that done yesterday. Hello."

When we first started talking on the phone, I thought that Jim was hard of hearing or had a bad connection with the cell phone he often uses. I know now that he says it for effect (to the extent he is conscious of saying it at all). I've still never figured out how to respond to the "Hellos." Mostly I just say "I'm here." Lee likes to say "Hello" back. It's really a matter of taste.

I've gotten better at dealing with Jim's calls. I bought a telephone headset, which is a great help. It makes me look like I'm taking magazine subscriptions, but it also frees my hands so that I can write instructions to my deputies while Jim rambles on. I feel a bit ogreish snapping my fingers and writing people notes telling them what to do, but it's better than waiting to start until I get off the phone at 9:30, which is usually past the time Jim wants things done. Even on good days, the mornings are frenzied.

Afternoons are better. By 5:00 or so the day's work is usually done. Most reporters have their stories written by then. And though we all stick around for several hours to watch the news and work on long-term projects, the day's crisis has usually been dealt with. Late afternoon is a good time for Jim too. He usually eats a huge late lunch (three quarter-pounders today) and then dozes off on the couch in his office for an hour or two. When he awakes, he's generally in a good mood and sometimes inclined to reflective conversation about the campaign, moments I relish. Today is one of those days.

"What do you think they will go with first?" Jim asks. We have all agreed that the Ferrer campaign will have to turn to negative ads. Jim is asking my thoughts on which of the several possible attacks they will choose to make first.

I see four major ones.

The most obvious is that Ruth is a tax-and-spend liberal. We've reviewed every one of Ruth's City Council votes, and by our count she voted to raise taxes more than a dozen times. She voted to increase, among other taxes, the commuter tax and the property tax on homeowners and to create a tax on security transactions. Depending on whether you count bridge tolls as a tax, the number potentially goes up by a few. The charge is unfair to some extent, as most political attacks are. Most of the votes on these taxes were unanimous, and Ruth voted against many other taxes, but there is at least a basis for the charge and that is all a campaign really needs. It's certainly something that will be in the arsenal. The Giuliani people have already been using a version of it as part of their attempt to link Ruth to David Dinkins.

The second main potential line of attack is that Ruth is soft on crime. In addition to Ruth's well-publicized opposition to the death penalty, there are two troubling matters in her City Council record. She missed voting on a bill that would have made possession of drug paraphernalia a crime and, more disturbing, twice voted against setting mandatory prison terms for possessors of crack cocaine.

There's an even more threatening item in a 1977 *New York Times* society-page blurb: Ruth hosted a party at her apartment to celebrate the release from prison of John Hill, who was convicted of murdering a prison guard during the Attica riots. We view this one as so bad that we leave it out of our own profile of Ruth and try not to speak about it in the office, as if by so doing it will make it less likely that the Ferrer and Giuliani campaigns will find out about it. I have some small hope that they may not, since the incident is mentioned in only a single short article, written at a time that predates the period when the computer database NEXIS started collecting full *Times* articles. All that's there is an abstract of the article, which was short to begin with. Jim thinks they'll find it. If the article were just a year older, it would predate NEXIS entirely. Bad luck there.

The third possible attack, related to the soft-on-crime attack, is that Ruth has the wrong priorities. I have in mind an ad that combines, say, Ruth's decision to march on the side of the drug dealer in the Washington Heights incident with, say, her school-board appointee's vote against expelling violent students.

The fourth major line of attack that I see is one on, for want of a better word, Ruth's lifestyle. In addition to her membership in the Democratic Socialists of America, Ruth worked for the Women's Strike for Peace and Turn Toward Peace and was the founder and director of the Bronx Draft Information and Counseling Service. We haven't been able to figure out what those entities are yet, but they don't sound helpful to the record. There's a reference in one article to Ruth and Eli having gone to Oklahoma to avoid the draft. It's an inference, I think, and not a fact, but one could make an argument from it. Back in New York, they shared their living space with other couples. One article described the Messinger home as "a nonstop carnival, a de facto community center and informal political salon where social crusaders huddled over the dining room table and the phone rang incessantly." And to top it off, as you know, Ruth's daughter Miriam is a lesbian mom.

No doubt the Ferrer and Giuliani campaigns are out testing each of these ideas in their own polls. Using polls to formulate a positive message produces a result that's a bit awkward, but there's no such problem when it comes to the negative message. No one expects attacks to be linked together by a common denominator. You just poll them all and throw every one that works on the air. The only limitations are money and how nasty a candidate is willing to get. Ferrer has limitations. Giuliani has a lot of money, and my guess is he's willing to get pretty nasty. Between the two of them, we'll likely see all of these ideas and more.

Of the lot I've described, we're best prepared on a factual basis to deal with the soft-on-crime attack. Whatever the reason for those two troubling votes, they're not representative of Ruth's record. Like any other rational human being, Ruth is against crime and cast dozens of votes to toughen laws. But the crime angle also seems to me to be the most likely attack. Calling Ruth soft on crime plays into the fears that led people to elect Rudy four years ago and makes her gender an issue without raising it explicitly.

Jim thinks the issue will either be crime or liberalism. "The Attica attack is the most devastating," Jim says. "I don't need to test that one in a poll." If the attack comes from Ferrer, who has less money than Giuliani, it's likely to be Attica, because he needs to maximize his "bang per buck." Because Giuliani has enough money to run high levels of television ads for several months, he can make all of these arguments. But Jim thinks if the attacks are coming from Giuliani, there will be an emphasis on the liberal charge.

"She's Dinkins," he growls, gnashing his teeth. "Dinkins. Dinkins. Arrr."

May 5

Ruth makes five public appearances a day, and we spend countless hours trying to get the most favorable coverage in the print media we can, but the fact is that the overwhelming majority of voters form their impression of the campaign by a series of short bits on the evening news. These pieces are the province of *advance* people, who do everything within their power to shape the best possible *shot*. The ideal shot has the candidate at the center, surrounded by legions of supporters, with a majestic scene in the background.

On Sunday, Ruth, who insists on booking her weekend days solid, arose at the crack of dawn and donned Spandex biking gear to bike the start of the Five Borough Bike Tour. She went from there to several churches around the city, attended a meeting on the Upper West Side, and finally, nine appearances later, made her way to a Holocaust memorial service at Temple Emanuel, where she proceeded to fall asleep in her front-row seat.

The Giuliani campaign seized on the opportunity. They encouraged a rabbi to go public with his outrage. “It’s a disgrace to the dead and every Jew of New York City that she fell asleep,” said Rabbi Schulim Rubin, of Young Israel in the Bronx. “No New Yorker who did a thing like that should be mayor.” An unnamed adviser to the Giuliani campaign suggested that Ruth perhaps lacked the stamina to be mayor. The *Post* said Ruth couldn’t keep up with Giuliani’s “crushing schedule.”

We, in turn, seized the new opportunity and challenged the mayor—by letter, of course (“Dear Rudy: I hope you are well,” it begins)—to a bike race around the city. Giuliani declined the challenge. (A good thing, too, as far as I’m concerned. I’m none too anxious to see him in Spandex.) “I think Ruth is embarrassed,” he said. “Ruth will have to apologize for what she did. I also think it would be inappropriate to turn that kind of thing—falling asleep during a Holocaust ceremony—into a publicity stunt.” But we were undeterred. Ruth, who insists she is a fine cyclist, went over to City Hall on a bike to give footage to one of the television stations and draw attention to the challenge.

Our shot is not so good tonight. A few hundred thousand people see footage of the borough president of Manhattan wearing a dress and an oversized helmet, stumbling along on a borrowed bicycle two sizes too small for her and nearly falling over as she tries to ride slowly enough for the cameras to catch her, all the while with a bizarrely inappropriate smile pasted on her face. No one smiles while riding a bike. If we do in fact go on to lose the campaign badly, today’s shot will perhaps be a lasting symbol of our ineptitude.

May 7

Since the first poll, Geoff Garin has been pushing for us to find a way to pay for some of the proposals we tested. Jim found a pot of money today, but it’s a Pandora’s box.

It’s a brilliant idea, really. President Clinton has pledged to turn Governors Island over to New York City for one dollar if the city can come up with an acceptable plan for using it. The 174-acre island, which was home to a Coast Guard base until last year, is one of the most spectacular properties in the region. It has panoramic views of the city, several early American forts, and a nine-hole golf course. So far, the city hasn’t made any plans at all for reclaiming the island. There's some talk of turning it into a colonial theme park. Jim wants Ruth to propose to turn it into a casino and use all of the money for education.

The genius of the idea lies in the fact that the site is an island. Many of the familiar arguments against gambling would not apply. Zoning and traffic would not be a problem. The seedy underside of casinos would be confined to a small area, removed entirely from residential neighborhoods.

There are still problems, of course. If the results of the poll are any indication, people are skeptical about the idea of earmarking money for education. One of the strongest issues in the March poll is the idea of Ruth suing the state to demand that lottery money be used for education. That means that people believe the state is using the lottery money for general tax purposes. If people believe the state improperly uses lottery revenue for general purposes, they might be inclined to think the city would do the same.

And Ruth opposed gambling as recently as 1994. When the city discussed the idea of authorizing some riverboat casinos, Messinger spoke out against the idea. "A great deal of money is raised on the backs of poor people, and people—rich or poor—with gambling addictions," she said at the time. "And a lot of money will be made by a small number of people who run the business. It's not a rational way of paying for city services or stimulating the economy."

But the uniqueness of the opportunity offers a possible answer for Ruth. This is a one-time-only opportunity for the city, and the financial situation in the schools is worse than ever. I do some quick research on how much revenue gambling in the city would generate. Conservatively, it's about $500 million a year. That's enough money to hire a thousand new teachers and have money left over.

From a political standpoint, the idea cannot be dismissed lightly.

May 8

It should be noted that ours is not the only campaign struggling to make its way. New York 1 and Elizabeth Kolbert of the *Times* both give extensive coverage to a lackluster Ferrer fund-raiser. Kolbert writes, "Not even Jimmy Smits, the actor, whose arrival produced the evening's one brief frisson of promise, seemed to be able to muster more than the most openly forced sort of optimism."

Money may be a concern for Ferrer. His finance director says that the fund-raiser grossed more than $400,000, despite the fact the room was half empty (or half full). And Ferrer, who had raised just over $2 million at the time of the last filing with the city in January, is said to be up around the $3 million mark. That may sound like a lot, but it's not nearly as much as it seems. For one thing, when campaigns announce the amount of money they've raised, they don't deduct the amount of money they've spent along the way. Ferrer may have grossed $400,000 at last night's fund-raiser, but the event probably cost him at least half that amount. Ferrer may indeed raise $3 million by the next filing, but he certainly doesn't have $3 million in the bank. We've already spent more than $1 million, and we haven't yet put a single ad on television.

And even if Ferrer did have most of his $3 million at his disposal, he'd still be behind Ruth, and far behind Rudy, who has already raised $9.4 million, the full amount he can spend under the city's campaign-finance laws.

• • •

A *Daily News* poll has nothing but bad news: The primary is tightening and the general is widening. The *News* has Ruth leading Ferrer in the primary by only 4 percent, which is within the margin of error of the poll. And in the general, Rudy's lead has expanded to 15. The lag isn't there anymore, either. He's leading both Ferrer and Messinger by an identical 54–39 margin.

May 9

Betty Shabazz, widow of Malcolm X and a leader in the national black community, tragically died yesterday as the result of a fire set by her own grandson. Ruth is among many city leaders and prominent blacks at the funeral, including Louis Farrakhan, who is delivering one of the eulogies.

The news station New York 1 cycles a newsreel every half hour. This evening's reel has a rather disturbing image: a shot of Farrakhan speaking at the funeral followed by a slow pan over to an applauding Ruth Messinger. There's no cut here or splicing of shots. Though it may be proper under the circumstances, Ruth is applauding for the same man we demanded Al Sharpton denounce.

Jim calls in to me at 10:00 this evening and says the race is over.

"Hello."

May 10

If we go with the Governors Island idea, it will not be the first time that Jim Andrews has made gambling an issue in one of his campaigns. In 1994, Jim singled out Zell Miller's championing of the then year-old Georgia state lottery as the first example of the strength of Miller's record. One of the main planks of Babbage's platform in the Kentucky race was a proposal to use lottery money to fund scholarships for high-school graduates and to pay for prescriptions for senior citizens who earn a little too much to qualify for Medicaid. The idea had previously been raised in gubernatorial races in Georgia and Pennsylvania. Two of Babbage's other main planks were also imports from other states. His call for a constitutional amendment to require voter approval of tax increases that raise state revenue by more than 1 percent echoed an identical proposal by Missouri governor Mel Carnahan. His call for longer sentences for violent criminals had been kicked around the country like a tin can.

Pollsters and consultants put a tremendous amount of thought into whether it makes sense to make a particular move, but the fact is that there aren't all that many moves to make. Politicians, Republican and Democrat alike, recirculate a handful of ideas that make better sense at different times (the death penalty, work for welfare, charter schools). When a good idea does arise (take minor crimes seriously), it cycles around the country in a political heartbeat (the "broken windows" philosophy that is the core of Giuliani's crime strategy has made the rounds of campaigns across the country). Consultants may like to pretend that they're playing a game of chess, but it's a lot more like a sophisticated game of checkers. Everyone knows all the moves.

May 11

A member of the borough president's staff bursts into Jim's office, obviously quite pleased with himself. He's a board member of the city chapter of the Democratic Socialists of America (Michael Harrington's group), which made its endorsement in the mayoral race late last night. "They were all set to go the other way and endorse Sal," he says, "but I saved the day. The vote was tied eight-eight. I broke it for Ruth."

"Hooray!" Jim cries after the aide leaves the room. "We got the DSA!" We dance a little jig.

The endorsement is only a minor matter, but it's another vivid illustration of the differences between the worldview of the campaign and that of Ruth's government staff across the street. Ruth's aide sees the endorsement as an asset. Each endorsement is like a little trophy. Collect enough little trophies and you earn the big trophy. In their mind, it's as if there is a tally sheet for the mayor's race and the trick is to record enough marks on your side of the ledger. They view campaigning as a process of aggregating votes.

It's the same worldview that informed Ruth's deputy's desire to send a differently worded message to the black newspaper during the hollow-point-bullets controversy. Aggregate enough support among different constituency groups and you win.

In Jim's worldview, the endorsement is at best irrelevant and potentially a liability. Most endorsements add nothing to the message. They do not advance an argument that might make someone more likely to vote for a candidate. Only a few endorsements carry enough weight to have message value. An endorsement from the *New York Times* is pretty useful. It, in essence, vouches for the competency of the candidate. Endorsements by Ed Koch and Bill Clinton, because they are both popular enough, are assets. No one will vote for Ruth because she is endorsed by the DSA. (As it appears, half the people in the DSA may not even vote for her.) But more than a few people may vote against Ruth, though perhaps indirectly, precisely because of the DSA endorsement. The DSA endorsement is a nice piece to add to the argument that Ruth is liberal and out of touch. All things considered, it would have been better if our friend had voted for Sal.

May 12

Early in the evening, a rumor begins to circulate around the office that Ferrer is withdrawing. Some say it's because his fund-raising isn't going well; others say there's a health problem. Whatever the reason, at 10:00 the rumor is confirmed. Ferrer will withdraw tomorrow and endorse Ruth. Ruth calls Ferrer and asks whether he would like her to appear with him, but the borough president declines.

He wants to do this one alone.

May 13

A few months in this business has made me increasingly cynical about politicians, but Ferrer's withdrawal seems remarkably sincere and honorable. Standing on the steps of City Hall, Ferrer says that he feared that a "bruising primary fight" would unnecessarily divide the Democratic primary. "There is still a dream," he says, "but this dream will be deferred." He will run for reelection as Bronx borough president, a job he claims to enjoy. "I get a chance to return to my hometown and the job I love," he says.

The cynical interpretation for Ferrer's withdrawal is that he is passing on the race to hold onto his job as Bronx borough president, so he will be better positioned for the 2001 mayoral race. One of his aides says off the record that "Freddie thinks he is the most formidable Democrat, and he's pulled out of the race. Draw your own conclusion." The conclusion, of course, is that Ferrer thinks Giuliani cannot be beaten. Either way, Ferrer obviously dearly wanted to be mayor now, not in four years. And he had at least a fighter's chance to do it. It seems magnanimous.

An hour later, Ruth walks over to a nearby school to accept Ferrer's endorsement and face the largest group of reporters we've seen so far. "My mom and dad used to tell me that you can't solve a problem you don't see. And Rudy doesn't see the problems New Yorkers face." She elaborates about the overcrowding crisis, unemployment, and the looming specter of a lapse in rent-control laws.

This will be our message: Rudy Giuliani does not care about the average New Yorker.

• • •

Even as Ferrer gracefully withdraws, Rudy's campaign manager, Fran Reiter, is standing on the steps of City Hall spinning the consequences of his withdrawal.

Back in March, Reiter left her post as deputy mayor for economic development to take over the Giuliani campaign. She's an interesting study in contradictions. A 1972 graduate of the High School of Performing Arts, Reiter worked in theater and film for five years after leaving Boston University following her sophomore year. Though she ultimately concluded that the theater was not a "terribly stable way of life," she still has the bug. She had a walk-on last month in *La Boheme* at Lincoln Center and recently played a jury forewoman on the television series *Law and Order*. In 1978, she joined Allied Entertainment as a sales executive and for the next few years moved around in different jobs in television sales. During the 1980s, she became increasingly involved in the Liberal Party. In 1989, she volunteered on Guiliani's first mayoral campaign. In 1993, she was his deputy campaign manager. In 1990, she ran for Congress herself as a Democrat and Liberal, losing to Bill Green.

Reiter is an effective advocate for Giuliani. She is consistently on message and is aggressive in getting it out. Today is no exception. The Democrats, she says, are now faced with a dilemma. "They are faced with a situation where you have two out of the three candidates left—Al Sharpton, truly an extreme candidate representing the narrowest possible constituency. And you have Ruth Messinger with now a twenty-year history of evoking a Manhattan-centric view of life, not to mention really representing the ex-

treme wing of the Democratic Party."

When asked what precisely is extreme about Ruth Messinger, Reiter is less than specific. "All of Ruth's positions," she says, "whether it's on welfare reform, whether it's on . . . that's assuming she has positions, by the way." Asked how long she has felt this way, Reiter replies, "I have felt that on a citywide basis Ruth Messinger has never had the answer to the problems of this city."

Back in 1989, though, when Reiter was head of the Liberal party, she had some rather nice things to say about Ruth. On endorsing Ruth for borough president that year, she said, "There are many people who are on the correct side of issues. But there are not that many who are effective. We think Ruth has been a force for good government, a force for moderation because she thinks about how decisions affect not one segment of the population but everyone."

Reiter is entitled to change her position for any reason she likes. Whether it is out of sincere conviction or for political or pecuniary gain makes no difference. As a lawyer, I appreciate that people are often forced to defend positions they do not necessarily agree with entirely. But what does it say that Reiter can stand on the steps of City Hall and claim with impunity that the position she holds now is the same position she has always held?

If truth is here at all, it's lying deep at the bottom of some pit.

PART TWO

Polled in Every Direction

"I KNOW I'M RIGHT FOR THE PART, BUT, TELL ME AGAIN, WHAT'S MY MOTIVATION?"

May 14

Ferrer's withdrawal makes the front page of the *Times*. "With Ferrer Out, Messinger Focuses on Giuliani" is the headline. An accompanying picture is even better. It shows Ruth warmly clasping hands with Rabbi Ronald Sobel at the opening of a Judaica museum at Temple Emanuel in Manhattan yesterday. Jim says the picture is worth about $100,000.

• • •

We think we may have a hook into the rent-control debate. The idea is for Ruth to call on the state to make rent control a home-rule issue, that is, to allow the city to decide the matter for itself. That done, a referendum would be held to determine whether the laws should continue. It's not a monumental idea, but we need to do *something* to get Ruth involved in the debate.

Last week we were all but set to go with a press conference attacking Giuliani for having accepted money from the landlord lobby, when Ruth's chief of staff recalled an interview on New York 1 in which Ruth implied that she might do the same. We consulted the tape and, indeed, Ruth had said that she would accept money from any organization that had not been indicted. That's hardly the same as specifically saying she'd take money from the landlord lobby (she hasn't), but Jim's inclination in these situations is to err on the conservative side. His philosophy is to refrain from making attacks that are obviously flawed, even if they may nevertheless be powerful. All that said, we still need some way into the rent-control debate, which is rapidly coming to a head. Though Ruth has talked about rent control on a daily basis, she hasn't been able to get her name associated with the fight. Our hope is that the referendum idea can get us some *traction,* a broad term describing the process of getting a candidate associated with an idea.

• • •

Among newspapers, we pay a degree of attention to the *New York Times* that is disproportionate to its share of the market. Among television stations, we pay disproportionate attention to New York 1, the city's only all-news station. It's on all the time in the campaign office. Even though the news is repeated throughout the day, we watch. In City Hall, they watch. The two campaigns probably represent half the viewership of the station.

We pay special attention to a program called the *Road to City Hall* (called *Inside City Hall* during nonelection years). The station's political reporters Dominic Carter, Andrew Kirtzman, and Melissa Russo host the program on a rotating basis. They are our television family; we know trivia about their lives.

Kirtzman, thirty-five, is from the Lower East Side, graduated from the University of Pennsylvania, and got his start as a reporter at the *Hudson Dispatch* in New Jersey. Carter grew up in public housing in the city. Russo, twenty-nine, had an opinion piece published by the *New York Times* when she was a junior at Tufts. Kirtzman, who is tall and has a preppy look, is a favorite among the women in the office. Russo, who is not as tall, but also has a preppy look, is a favorite among the men in the office. Lee thinks she is the best television reporter in the city, one of very few who do investigative research instead of merely reporting competing spins.

Filling five hours of television a week with news about city politics is no easy task. It is not an inherently interesting subject, and the players are less than compelling. Liberal party chairman Ray Harding is perhaps the least telegenic person in the history of politics. He is a gargantuan man with a prodigious second chin that seems to move independently of the rest of his body. His voice is nearly inaudible and gravelly from years of chain-smoking. When he uses the word "gravitas" to describe the mayor, as he often does, he sounds like a sinister figure in a bad science-fiction movie speaking of a new weapon to destroy humanity: "Rudy Giuliani has the gravitas to be mayor." And Harding is one of the more interesting guests.

Some nights are better than others on *Road*. Tonight, Andrew Kirtzman is interviewing Gerry Austin, one of Freddie Ferrer's political consultants. Austin says that Freddie Ferrer lacked the "fire in his belly" to become mayor. He says it was within Ferrer's grasp, but that Freddie was too scared to reach for the ring. It's a petty, backstabbing performance that makes for better than usual television. It is totally unprofessional. The code among political consultants, as among lawyers, is to never publicly speak ill of a current or former client, which makes Austin's performance all the more entertaining.

The influential *Times* columnist Bob Herbert offers a similar sentiment:

> Some politicians are deceptively tough. They come across as low-keyed, soft-spoken, amiable. But behind the mild façade is an intense and enduring drive, an endlessly competitive spirit, and an unshakable will. Fernando Ferrer is not like that. Mr. Ferrer, the Bronx Borough President and a genuinely nice guy, is

> more apt to embrace the philosophy "When the going gets tough, I'm outta here." . . .
>
> By quitting without putting up much of a fight Mr. Ferrer deprived his supporters and potential supporters of the kind of robust effort they had every right to expect. He encouraged and then quickly extinguished the hope they had in him. New Yorkers deserve better.

May 15

This is a surreal moment. The Democrats have just finished their second major debate, and I am traveling down from the top of the World Trade Center with Al Sharpton, Fran Reiter, and a couple of reporters who are hounding Reiter about the administration's withholding of information. Reiter is here spinning reporters about a story in this morning's *Daily News* about mismanagement at the borough president's office.

A 1995 audit by Comptroller Hevesi, released yesterday by chance, showed that Ruth's office had some costly purchasing practices. They bought ballpoint pens from private vendors for $1.19 a dozen when they were available at the city's central storehouse for $.54 a dozen. They spent $42 per carton of copying paper, when they could have gotten it for $22.80, and $1.51 per gallon of premium gasoline when it was available for just $1.04 from the city. And in 1993, Ruth paid $375 a night for a hotel room during a stay in Orlando for a conference of the National League of Cities. The cap for city officials is $125 a night. Ruth wrote the city personal checks for $940, which also included the cost of a nice breakfast improperly charged to the city. It's really quite a damning report, and Reiter is using it to her candidate's full advantage.

Unknown to Reiter, Messinger staffer Evan Mandery is one of several undercover operatives sent to the debate to track what Reiter has to say to the press. I am armed with a tape recorder.

Reiter is being grilled by a *Newsday* reporter—about the sale of city hospitals, as far as I can tell—and does not want to give an answer, but she can't walk away and has over a hundred floors to travel.

"It's a long way to go, Fran!" says Sharpton, who is suing Reiter for slander. Reiter said Sharpton "incites riots and engages in criminal conduct."

A few more floors go by.

"Forty-four to go, Fran."

"You're right, Reverend," says Reiter.

"Thirty-eight," replies Sharpton. "Come on, try a long 'Noooo comment'—you might get there."

I run back to the office holding the tape recorder in triumph. Jim loves it. "We have to get this to the press!" he says. An hour later we publish a transcript of the entire conversation. It seems like just the thing to graphically demonstrate the Giuliani administration's relentless obfuscation.

• • •

My elation is short-lived. Seems I've made a big mistake. Never use brackets! It wasn't city hospitals the *Newsday* reporter asked Reiter about. It was municipal garages. It makes a big difference. No one cares very much about the sale of municipal garages, but people care a lot about the sale of city hospitals. It makes it appear as if we've tweaked the exchange to make it seem more outrageous than it was.

Lee and Jim tell me not to feel bad and that I'll make lots of mistakes over the next few months. Lee tells reporters that the mistake was his and sends not the slightest bit of guilt my way. But I feel guilty all the same. I've compromised the credibility the campaign is working so hard to establish.

May 16

Rudy Giuliani doesn't know my name, but he is calling for me to be fired. I still feel dreadful about the mistake, but it is sort of exciting.

"It's really like almost illegal," the mayor says of my actions, and the *Daily News* picks it up. An editorial derides Ruth and Lee for playing "fast and loose with privacy laws" and putting "dirty tricks on the table." Of the many liberties Rudy takes with the truth, he is freest of all with the law. Recording a public conversation is perfectly legal. But the *News* just takes his word for it. He is a lawyer, after all.

May 17

On a daily basis, the research team, which is still all white despite the protestations and best recruiting efforts of the borough president's staff, reads, clips, and summarizes the *Post, Daily News, Times, Staten Island Advance, Village Voice, Observer,* and a small black paper called the *Amsterdam News*. We pay very little attention to the *Amsterdam News*. According to our poll, it's read by less than one in twenty people in New York. It's not that we don't take black voters seriously; it's just that we don't take the black press seriously.

We should. The readership of the paper is loyal and not trivial in terms of numbers. And there are a hundred thousand people or so living an entirely different campaign than we are in our Broadway office. An editorial this morning discussed the impact of Ferrer's withdrawal:

> The white press in New York City is treating the news of Ferrer's withdrawal from the Democratic primary for Mayor as a godsend. Now they believe that Ruth Messinger is going to walk away with the primary victory, then on to the conquest of Rudy Giuliani. They dream.
>
> Sharpton cannot be dismissed here, as so much of the white media suggests that he will be. Even now as we speak, an accurate poll would conclude that Sharpton is the front-runner, who might just win the Democratic primary for mayor.

May 18

A *flash poll* by the *Post* makes us the prohibitive favorite to win the primary after Ferrer's withdrawal. The poll shows Ruth with 50 percent of the vote versus 13 and 11 percent for Sal and Al, respectively.

May 19

Much to his professed dismay, Jim is the subject today of a profile in the *New York Observer*, a weekly paper that caters to politicos and the intellectual elite. With the exception of a few notes about his chain-smoking, foul language, and inability to sit in the same place for more than a minute, it's a glowing portrait. To his friends, at least, Jim is different from the ordinary political consultant. Mandy rightly points out that Jim "really believes that campaigns are a battle of ideas." Some of his friends note Jim's practice of e-mailing and telephoning friends with messages espousing his populist, working-class view of the world. Paul Begala, James Carville's old partner, says, "In a business whose poster boy is Dickie Morris, he's a true believer." He also adds that Jim is "legendary for punching holes in walls, kicking walls, throwing chairs through walls." "He's hell on walls," Begala reiterates.

Ruth emphasizes Jim's experience in Chicago in describing why she picked him. "'I know what he did for Harold Washington,' said Ms. Messinger, crunching a treetop of raw broccoli at a small fund-raising house party. 'He knows what the ingredients are of winning large-city races with a heterogeneous constituency.'" The comment drives Jim absolutely nuts. He interprets it as a sign that Ruth is still viewing him as an asset to be exploited for its value in constituency politics and wonders whether we have made any progress at all since the forestalled attempt at sending different press releases during the hollow-point-bullets controversy.

Though the article profiles Jim, Jim manages to get out the message quite effectively. "Crime-fighting versus family-friendly," he says. He describes Ruth as "just one of those really dedicated people that you run across in life. There's no way to stop Ruth Messinger from caring about people who don't have anybody else to care about them."

The message comes through, but Jim does too. Asked his thoughts on Senator Rick Santorum, the Pennsylvania conservative, he replies, "Hitler youth." His words for the mayor are equally intemperate. "They have turned lying into such an art form over at City Hall, they ought to build a Lying Wing at the Metropolitan. It can be interactive for kids—a statue of Rudy, and you press the button and hear the best of them. They're liars. They wouldn't know the truth if it came up and bit them on the ass. *End quote*."

May 20

My friend Matt Moore has graciously invited me to his thirtieth birthday, and I'm more than happy to attend. His hip loft-style one-bedroom in the Lower East Side (coming back since Rudy bulldozed the drug dealers out of Tompkins Park) should be Messinger Country. Matt is gay and so are most of his friends. They're sure to be Messinger voters, I figure.

They're not. One gay man after another tells me he's voting for the mayor.

"But she, like, wrote the city's gay civil-rights law," I tell one man.

It doesn't persuade him. He likes what Giuliani is doing on crime.

I try to pander a bit more directly. "She'll perform gay marriages at City Hall," I tell another party-goer. To no avail. He feels safer and, what's more, he feels personally slighted by Ruth's delay in endorsing Deborah Glick, a state assemblyperson from Manhattan who is lesbian, to succeed her as Manhattan borough president.

For weeks, Ruth has been postponing the decision about whom to endorse for borough president. It's a no-win situation. Glick's main rival is C. Virginia Fields, a City Councilwoman from Harlem, who is black. If Ruth endorses Glick, she'll offend blacks. If she endorses Fields, she'll offend gays.

You should dissuade yourself of any notion that principle is turned to as a useful guide in a situation like this. Ruth likes both Glick and Fields well, but although the borough presidency is an important position, this endorsement is important purely for political purposes. As Ruth puts it, it's a trade-off between the additional money endorsing Glick might earn her in the small, but wealthy, gay community versus the additional votes a Fields endorsement might earn her in the large, but less wealthy, black community.

As it is, it may already be too late. The Gay and Lesbian Victory Fund, a political action committee based in Washington, D.C., recently issued an "election action alert" to a thousand supporters telling them "to warn Messinger she could lose money and support if she endorsed Fields." The Empire State Pride Agenda is said to be leaning toward no endorsement. We've already lost this room. If Ruth Messinger, who has advocated for civil rights all of her life, cannot carry a room of gay men, she's in big trouble.

May 21

As if it's not enough that we're having trouble in the gay community, today the leader of a major tenants' organization criticizes Ruth's proposal for a referendum on rent control. It seems as if every liberal group in the city is turning against us. Michael McKee, the head of the New York State Tenants and Neighbors Coalition, criticizes Ruth's plan as a diversion from the more important efforts to protect existing rent-control laws.

We may have better success with a proposal Ruth mentioned briefly last week to hold a referendum on the question of whether taxpayer money should be used to build a new Yankee Stadium. The common perception is that Rudy Giuliani and George Steinbrenner have a secret deal to move Yankee Stadium to the West Side of Manhattan, at a cost of about $1 billion, following the election. According to the recent *Post* poll, voters favor the idea of a Yankee Stadium referendum 68–15.

Who would have ever thought that Ruth Messinger would do better with Yankee fans than gay tenants?

May 22

Ruth won the endorsement of the Queens Democratic party today, which is good, but the Queens borough president, Claire Shulman, who also won endorsement for reelection, was conspicuously quiet about Ruth. Speculation grows that she will cross party lines and endorse Giuliani. Shulman's endorsement is not of consequence by itself, but if enough Democrats join her it could create a damaging image. We need the local party organizations to keep their members in line, but we don't seem to be getting much help. Congressman Tom Manton, the Queens County chairman of the Democratic party, said that he understood why people might defect and endorse Giuliani. "The city is in pretty decent shape, some people think."

• • •

Rudy's even spinning the kids. Asked by a class of fifth-grade students, writing for the *Newsday* column "Kidsday," how he changed the city, Rudy says, "We are focusing on education and services for children. We have allocated $1.4 billion to be spent over the next five years on needed school renovations. New programs, such as Project Smart School, will put computers in every classroom. Project Read will help encourage reading and improve reading scores." Never miss an opportunity to get the message out. I wonder whether the kids are buying it.

May 23

George Spitz, a retired state auditor and one of the founders of the New York City marathon, is running for Manhattan borough president on an unusual platform: If elected, he'll abolish "this ineffectual attachment to city government." Spitz says the $27 million the city spends collectively on the five borough presidents' offices is a pure waste of money, since the borough presidents were stripped of virtually all of their powers by a 1989 charter revision. If he wins, Spitz says, he'll campaign for a referendum to abolish the office. In the meantime, he says, "my first act as borough president will be to reduce my salary to $70,000, the same as each City Council member receives, from the current $114,000. From that $70,000, I'll deduct the roughly $25,000 I now receive in Social Security and government pensions—and I'll still be overpaid." Spitz says that he'll transfer eighty of the eighty-eight staff members to the public library system, lease out the two chauffeur-driven limousines provided by the city, and buy his own newspapers, which cost taxpayers $4,600 in 1996.

"I know I'm a long shot for the job," he says. "But I also know the job is useless."

May 24

Like everyone else on the campaign, I awoke this morning with a sense of dread. Yesterday, while being interviewed for a profile by the *Daily News*, Ruth admitted that she used marijuana during the 1960s. She said, "It was a couple of occasions with other people who were also not what you would call serious smokers, but who did a little recreational smoking."

It was a helpless feeling. Campaigns have the compulsive need to do something, but there was nothing to do. Lee expressed his hope to the reporter that the campaign would not be run on what the candidates were doing during the 1960s. Beyond that, all there was to do was to wait and see the article.

It's not nearly as bad as we feared. The headline, "Mayoral Hopeful's a Token," is a bit confusing (they mean she's a token toker, I think, but it could just as easily be taken to mean a token Jew or a token woman). And the Giuliani team does not seem to be making a big deal of it. Fran Reiter said, "I don't care if she smoked pot in the '60s. But that's no excuse for her politics still being from the '60s." Reiter admitted that she too smoked pot "many years ago," which is good to know.

May 25

Most people think that a campaign is synonymous with its candidate, but that's not in fact true. A candidate is the campaign's chief spokesperson, exercises veto power on key decisions, and is its most important asset, but a well-functioning campaign is a great deal more than its candidate. Like any other large organization, it is a bureaucracy filled with people who try to affect decisions based upon their own parochial view of the political world and to accomplish whatever they are charged with doing. The press secretary tries to maximize coverage. The advance director worries about the *shot* for the evening news. If a campaign is to be successful, the candidate cannot be involved in each of these things. The candidate needs to be out at events. The candidate needs to be raising money.

That's not a truth that Ruth is willing to accept without a fight. She's a brilliant person and has been a micromanager all her life, involved in the smallest details of what goes on in her office and her home, and she's not about to stop now. Today, Ruth is talking to Jim about the placement of desks in the fund-raising office and the logistics of getting signatures on the ballot.

"I've never spent a second worrying about that in my life," Jim says.

May 26

Rudy Giuliani's temper is his Achilles' heel, and we're banking on its causing him to say at least a thing or two over the next few months that might do him some damage. He makes his first slip today. Defending his record on minorities to the *Washington Post*, Giuliani says, "They're alive, how about we start with that. You can't help people more directly than to save lives." It's the sort of quote out of which we can easily make an effective negative ad. It's also the sort of problem Giuliani could clear up in two minutes with a clarification. But he can't bring himself to do it, and once David Dinkins enters the picture, he becomes intractable.

Dinkins, among others, suggests the remark demonstrates Giuliani's insensitivity to minority concerns. His comments strengthen the mayor's resolve. With characteristic temperance, he says Dinkins's observation represents a "warped philosophy." "I think the old-fashioned incendiary politicians of this city will try to turn that around. It ain't going to work." So we have a nice ad.

May 27

Perhaps my testimony on the subject is not credible, but I nevertheless will tell you that the Giuliani administration's practice of withholding information is not an academic matter. Our research team has filed dozens of requests under the Freedom of Information Law with city agencies over the past few months. Perhaps in some cases the agency receiving the request could suspect that it comes from the campaign (though even that would not be a justification for withholding the information), but we go to some trouble to keep that from being obvious. One of our friends, unassociated with the campaign, files the requests in his name, and we keep a separate phone with an unlisted number to field calls dealing with information requests. None have been answered so far.

To draw attention to the problem, Ruth filed a request under the Freedom of Information Law for a list of all Freedom of Information Law requests denied by the city. The city's attorney denied the request on the theory that it falls outside of the borough president's jurisdiction. Ruth is suing to get the information, though it appears likely she will have to represent herself in the case. The borough president would ordinarily be represented by the city's attorney, but that won't work in this case for obvious reasons. Under the city charter, the borough president requires the permission of the city attorney to retain independent representation, which doesn't seem likely to come any time soon either. The only remaining option is for Ruth to do the case herself. It's not a bad option. It is hard to imagine anyone better qualified to explain what the borough president does and why this information is important.

One of Giuliani's spokespeople implies that Ruth is filing the request to divert attention from the fact that she missed Memorial Day parades in the outer boroughs.

City attorney Paul Crotty, who ostensibly also represents Ruth, makes the bizarre argument that public officials are not entitled to the same information as the public. He says the lawsuit "is like a temper tantrum." Giuliani dismisses the lawsuit as "politics." That response carries some weight for Giuliani, whose image is that of a reformer who is above partisan politics.

On the same afternoon, Giuliani, who is above politics, praised Al D'Amato as "probably the toughest, scrappiest politician in the history of the State of New York." (Not certainly, but probably.) In 1994, Giuliani said "ethics would be trashed" in a D'Amato-Pataki state administration.

May 28

You are either with Rudy Giuliani, or you are the enemy.

At one of Rudy's monthly town hall meetings at the Hebrew Institute of Riverdale in the Bronx, a woman complains about hospital cuts.

"What cuts specifically?" asks the mayor.

"Aren't there million-dollar cuts proposed?" She has shown weakness. She is lost.

"For you to say we've cut the budget is unfair. And I take some offense at your suggestion that cuts have affected the quality of care at these hospitals."

"But—"

"Please! I didn't interrupt you. Don't interrupt me!"

Later in the evening, a sad-looking downtrodden woman complains of being illegally evicted from her apartment. She becomes confused in the details as the story goes on. Rudy says he can't figure out whether the city can help her.

"Well, sir," the woman says, "you can help me get help. What I understand when we talk about rent decontrol is we're talking about greed. Because we're not hearing about all the money that the governor has gotten or perhaps that you have gotten."

Bad idea there.

"Thank you," the mayor says. "I'm glad to hear from you. And that was an enormously insulting thing to say. I listened to you very carefully, and for you to suggest I would make a decision because I got money was enormously insulting. My integrity is important to me, as yours should be to you. Our conversation has ended."

The woman keeps talking.

"This conversation has ended!"

Undaunted, she continues, rising now, "Good evening, ladies and gentlemen. Good night!" With much ado, she starts to make her way to the door.

"I pride myself in displaying good judgment about people," Giuliani says graciously as the woman makes her way out. "Thank you for proving I was right. And I'm glad we didn't help you."

It's all very sensible. Surely this evicted tenant was with the enemy. She wasn't with Rudy, so she must be the enemy.

May 29

Times reporter Adam Nagourney generally pays Lee the courtesy of telling him when a bad story is coming. "You're not going to like this one," he said last night.

Nagourney's argument, in a "political memo" this morning, is that Freddie Ferrer's withdrawal hurt Ruth by denying her the opportunity to hone her skills in a tough primary and forcing her to prematurely send her campaign up against the mayor's. No doubt Ruth would have grown from the experience of facing Ferrer, but Nagourney's logic is hard to follow. It's hard to conceive how being spared the fight with Ferrer could have hurt Ruth, even if you accept the premise that Ruth isn't the mayor's equal. But the fact that Nagourney accepts this premise is very disturbing, and he clearly does. He refers to the "impressive and aggressive re-election apparatus that Mr. Giuliani has created" and at the same time calls Ruth a "relatively inexperienced candidate embarking on [a] difficult challenge."

A metabattle is being fought here. The Giuliani team is trying to convince anyone who will listen that our campaign is not ready for the big leagues. It's a difficult battle for us to fight. To win it we would have to prove to the press that its fundamental view of what wins votes is wrong. The press believes that field events and campaign stops are the indicia of a campaign's aggressiveness; Jim believes that a tight, well-crafted argument is what makes the difference. The press thinks commercials are a part of the campaign; we think they are the campaign. Unless we wage and win a metawar to prove the philosophical point that endorsements and field events don't matter, we're doomed to lose the war of who has the more aggressive campaign. The demands that fund-raising place on Ruth's time mean that she will never be able to match the mayor's schedule.

Nobody votes for a candidate because he or she had a better campaign, but there is a substantive message that the Giuliani team is getting out there: How can Ruth run the city if she can't run her own campaign?

May 30

In an op-ed piece in the *Daily News* today, Sal Albanese identifies campaign-finance reform as the most important issue facing New York City today. From a strategic standpoint, it's an odd choice. Ruth has a strong record on campaign finance (she helped write the city's law, widely praised as one of the best in the nation) and, if our data and ample anecdotal evidence from national elections are to be believed, people don't care very much about campaign-finance reform. Of the seventeen positive issues we polled in our March survey, "Ruth Messinger has a strong commitment to campaign reform and supports a new law to require any candidates for Mayor or city office to release their income taxes to the public" did the worst. Twenty-eight percent of voters said that fact appealed to them a great deal. That's in comparison to the 64 percent who liked the fact that Ruth was planning to sue the state to use lottery money for education.

Albanese's proposal would limit all campaign contributions to $10 and reduce the aggregate amount a campaign could spend on an election to $3.5 million. To get on the ballot, a candidate would have to collect $10 contributions from 7,500 city residents. Once the candidate met that requirement, he or she would be given a "Clean Elections Credit Card" to spend up to $3.5 million on both the primary and, if necessary, the general election.

Albanese's plan is different in degree, but not in kind, from the existing system that Ruth helped develop. Both plans involve public matching of private contributions. The current law matches private contributions dollar for dollar up to $1,000. Since corporate contributions are not matched and since individual contributions are capped at $7,700, but matched only for the first $1,000, the match rate is less than one to one. So far, our match rate is about 42 percent, which is the highest in the short history of the system. Albanese's plan would theoretically result in a match rate of $3,425,000 to $75,000, or about fifty to one. But since Albanese would lower the total cap on campaign spending, the increased ratio doesn't necessarily translate into a higher cost per candidate. The real risk, from a cost standpoint, is that lots of people will be able to collect the 7,500 contributions and qualify for matching funds. Today if they collect 7,500 $10 contributions, they would qualify for $75,000 in matching funds. Under the Albanese Clean Elections Act they'd get $3.5 million.

That may or may not be a bad thing. Under different circumstances, I imagine Ruth would be open to the idea. Sal's numbers on the qualifying end are probably too low, but the idea has some merit. It would certainly reduce the influence of corporations in elections. But our reaction won't be so nuanced. Jim asks me to calculate how much more Sal's plan would cost for the five candidates on the ballot. The answer: $15 million. Our conclusion: Sal Albanese is for higher taxes.

May 31

To my surprise, it turns out that the campaign has accepted $1,000 from Bob Guccione, the editor of *Penthouse*. Friend of pornographers is probably not the ideal image for Ruth to be portraying, but returning the money would probably only serve to draw more attention to the story. We'll keep the money, but from here on in we will be *vetting* all people who contribute $1,000 or more. That means we'll check to see whether they have any convictions and look for negative stories in the press about them. If Al Goldstein hasn't gotten in under the wire, he's out of luck.

June 1

"How many kids go to school in bathrooms?" Jim asks this morning.

I don't know.

"Find out," he says. "And get pictures."

June 2

Our campaign office is short on amenities. The air conditioning works poorly, if at all. The lighting is bad. The toilet still struggles to flush. The fungus in the shower continues to make advances.

We have a water bubbler, but no water to fill it. The cold water tap in our sink doesn't work. The soda machine, which is filled once a month, is emptied within a day of all desirable beverages. The choice of drinks is scalding hot water or Fresca. Most go with the hot water.

We lack even basic office supplies. To save a few cents, there is an edict that no pens are to be purchased with campaign money. The cumulative savings will enable us to buy an additional five seconds of radio time in October. The copying machine in the finance department can only make two or three copies before overheating. And the summer has not yet started.

The amount of garbage in the office is reminiscent of a fraternity house. Garbage cans are not receptacles in our office; they merely mark the target at which to aim waste. There is a free-rider problem with the trash. It is no one's specific responsibility to collect the trash, so no one does. Every few weeks or so, when the garbage starts to ferment, it becomes so oppressive that someone proposes to clean the office on a Sunday. A two-hour frenzy makes the office livable for an hour, and then the pizza boxes start to pile up again.

We have one perquisite, though, an amenity so grand it nearly offsets all of the other deficiencies in the campaign: the Nap Room.

Like everything else in the campaign, the Nap Room is a modest place. It is a closet, really, a six-by-six space without windows or ventilation tucked away in the far corner of the office. It was originally going to be used as an office for not one, but two fund-raisers, but the office manager decided that there was too great a risk of suffocation. He stuck a bookcase and some files in there, and the office lay fallow until one glorious day when Art brought in an old army cot and transformed the useless space into the most treasured spot in the office. The one benefit of working sixteen hours a day is that you can take a twenty-minute nap without guilt. Everyone does it at different times throughout the day. I prefer mine immediately after lunch.

Sleeping in the Nap Room is an unusual experience. It is a ratty cot, sunken in the middle from two campaigns of overuse. In the beginning, Art outfitted the cot rather nattily with a nice cotton sheet. But the sheet itself has become a symbol of the excesses of our decadent life. It is unspeakably mephitic, with suspicious stains. The alternative is to sleep on the thin mattress directly, which doesn't smell all that good either.

No air circulates in the room, which tends to induce a sounder than usual sleep for an afternoon nap. I often dream vividly. Many others report the same phenomenon. But nothing can compare to the experience of arising in the Nap Room. With no windows or ventilation, it feels like awakening in a coffin. On more than one occasion, I have sincerely felt that I was dead.

But it is a great place. Everyone understands its value and treats it with accordant respect. It is sacrilegious to wake someone in the Nap Room, which means for twenty minutes a day you can pretend to be anywhere you want, which for most of us means somewhere far away from here. Like I said, it's a great place.

June 3

After weeks of agonizing, Ruth took the plunge yesterday and endorsed Virginia Fields for borough president. As far as anyone can tell, though, Fields didn't return the favor. When asked whether Fields was endorsing Ruth, Fields's campaign manager said, "Um, um, that's a good question." Another Fields spokesperson said, "She will not come out at this time and endorse." Fields corrects the error later in the day. "I fully endorse Ruth Messinger's candidacy for mayor and have taken no position regarding any other candidate," she says. But it's another embarrassing mistake, especially hard to swallow given the price we're going to pay for forsaking Glick.

Albanese calls Ruth a "a pretty weak individual," saying Ruth caved in to pressure from black leaders. It's an odd argument since Albanese endorsed Fields too.

A *Post* editorial, "Pander Politics," denounces the endorsement. It's not, the *Post* says, that Fields is a better or worse choice than any of the other candidates. The problem, as the *Post* sees it, is that there is no evidence of a debate in our camp over which candidate would do better with the schools. "Nor did there seem to be even a pretense of a discussion about which candidate was temperamentally more suited to a significant office."

In any other circle, the absence of such a debate would be a tacit recognition that the borough presidents have extremely limited power on policy matters, but Ruth and her people believe in the borough presidency. So their silence on policy can only mean the *Post*, for once, is right.

"In a broader sense, the idea of addressing New Yorkers as citizens with potentially common public interests, rather than as members of various constituencies (blacks, gays, Latinos), seems to have been vacuumed out of today's Democratic Party in the city."

The *Post* is only wrong, I suspect, in implying that we've gone about it differently than anyone else.

June 4

The rent-control debate is going down to the wire. Over the past month, Ruth has marched with tenants' leaders in Albany and at City Hall, given ten speeches, and appeared on television ten other times advocating extension of the rent-control laws in their current form. But we still have not been able to get any *traction* on the issue. The press is questioning why Ruth hasn't been more vocal on the issue. The referendum idea was a bust. The tenants' lobby didn't rally behind it and it even earned us the ridicule of one columnist. "Messinger," wrote Mark Kriegel of the *Daily News*, "wants to put the rent regulations to a referendum. That's what passes for her position."

This is an issue that should be absolutely killing Republicans. Governor George Pataki's approval rating has dropped by 10 points statewide, surely far more than that in New York City, where the overwhelming number of rent-control tenants live. But Rudy Giuliani's approval rating has remained steady. He has suffered no discernible political damage so far.

Television ads would be a fine way to link Rudy to the issue, but as usual, we're not getting any help from outside. For the past two weeks, the Tenants and Neighbors Coalition has been running television and radio commercials blasting Republicans for their scare tactics on rent control. Set against a backdrop of a ticking clock and a picture of Al D'Amato and George Pataki, the ad says that the Pataki-D'Amato decontrol plan will lead to tenant harassment and the hiring of "goon squads to force tenants out." There's no mention of Rudy.

The justification for Pataki's presence in the ads is obvious, but why Al D'Amato's? D'Amato has publicly said that he is staying out of the rent-control debate, and there's no evidence that he's done anything to the contrary. He may be guilty of failing to do all that he could, but by that logic Rudy is culpable too. He did once call a Republican state senator's vote against rent control a "sensible position." That would be great fodder for an ad. Why aren't the commercials advertising the "Pataki-D'Amato-Giuliani Plan"?

One answer is that the phrase is awkward. A more powerful explanation is that the ads were prepared by media consultant Hank Morris, one of several consultants in the city with tangled alliances. Jim's nomadic life is unusual among consultants. Many travel, but most have a base that forms the core of their business. Hank Morris and Ferrer's consultant, Hank Sheinkopf, are the two most influential consultants in the city. Each has clients at all levels of city politics. Morris advises Brooklyn representative Charles Schumer, which explains the incentive to link D'Amato to the ad. Schumer is planning to run for the Senate next year. And Morris also advises Comptroller Alan Hevesi, which makes it easier to understand why the mayor is being left out.

June 5

Battle stations! Battle stations! Messinger campaign under attack!

12:00 P.M.: While preparing for the annual Gay Pride reception, one of Ruth's staffers is paged to the front desk of the borough president's office. There he notices two men wandering through the hallways. One is carrying a camera on his shoulder (similar to the type used by *commercial* film companies!) and actively filming in the office. They hoist their camera over some partitions to take pictures of where people should be working. On the way out, they take a shot of the Manhattan borough president's office sign that hangs atop the main entrance.

12:05 P.M.: The same staff member trails the cameraman to a car parked in front of City Hall. We impose upon a friendly police officer to trace the license plate.

12:10 P.M.: The car is registered to a New Jersey rental agency, but someone has identified one of the two intruders as an employee of the Department of Citywide Administrative Services, the agency that provides custodial support for city offices.

12:11 P.M.: With overwhelming circumstantial evidence that the Giuliani campaign is engaged in illegal covert filming, Lee hits the phones.

1:00 P.M.: The Giuliani campaign confesses. It was indeed a campaign cameraman walking up and down hallways shooting pictures of offices. And it was also, in fact, a city employee, Martin Preston, a manager at the Municipal Building, accompanying the campaign worker on his tour of the office.

1:01 P.M.: I call for Mayor Giuliani to be fired. "This is kind of like illegal," I say.

1:15 P.M.: We file a trespassing complaint with the Fifth Precinct.

1:30 P.M.: Fran Reiter says Ruth is overreacting. "I think Ruth has lost her mind," she says. "The offices are in a public building. A municipal building—you don't get more public than that. This is utterly dopey."

1:35 P.M.: Reiter refuses a request for access to the mayor's private offices.

June 6

The results of the Governors Island poll are in, and I've lost the office pool badly. People think, 50–28, that the idea of legalizing gambling on Governors Island and putting all of the revenue into a special fund for education is a good idea.

There's some reason to be cautious about the numbers, though. For one thing, the idea is *polarizing*. Of the 28 percent of people who dislike the idea, three-quarters say their reaction is "very unfavorable" as opposed to "somewhat favorable." By contrast, of the 50 percent who like the idea, the "very favorable" versus "somewhat favorable" split is approximately fifty-fifty. This is an idea that evokes strong reactions. And the proposal is not doing as well as we might like among voters with whom we need to score. Minorities like the idea far more than whites. Blacks favor it 63–15 and Latinos 55–19, but whites only endorse it 43–37.

Still, from a strategic standpoint the idea cannot be dismissed lightly. Those elusive voters who are movable to Messinger approve of it 56–22. Giuliani voters approve of it 42–36. And when we ask voters at the end of the poll whom they will vote for given all they have heard in the survey, they vote for Ruth 45–43. It's a dubious number. As with the first poll, it's based on fifteen minutes of touting Ruth and saying damaging things about our opponent like "The city turns away 60,000 people from emergency food shelters, but Rudy Giuliani has given more than a half billion dollars in tax breaks to Fortune 500 companies" (something that gives 47 percent of all voters major doubts about supporting Giuliani for mayor). But even though it may be a fantasy, any scenario we can construct that offers the possibility of coming out ahead has to be considered seriously.

• • •

There are two ironies in the poll. One is that minorities disproportionately endorse an idea that, if history can be believed, will hurt them enormously. Whatever the ethics are of legalized gambling, as a practical matter it has amounted to a huge, hidden regressive tax on the poor. And minorities are disproportionately poor.

The other irony lies in what people think should be done with the money. As part of the poll, we asked people what they think about seven ideas for improving city schools. The most popular response is to "create strict performance standards for teachers and students, and make it easier to fire teachers who are not doing a good job." That wouldn't cost a penny.

June 7

My morning conversations with Jim are always entertaining. Today's is downright fascinating. It's a lecture on Jim's worldview.

"I'm going to let you in on a little secret this morning," he says. "It's the Rosetta Stone to understanding politics. Do you want to know what it is?"

"Sure." Who would refuse the Rosetta Stone?

"Do you know what Rudy Giuliani was saying back in 1993 when he said he was going to get rid of squeegeemen?"

No time to answer.

"He was telling every white person in New York City that he was going to close the sluice gates at 125th Street. Rudy was saying that he was going to make sure that *they* stay where they belong—up in Harlem and the Bronx. And that's exactly what everyone wanted to hear. What do you think he *really* means when he says that he has improved the quality of life in New York City?

"Race isn't just a part of politics. It is politics. Republicans have carved themselves a nice little niche by figuring that out. They're the white people's party. 'Crime,' 'welfare,' and 'taxes' are all code words. When Republicans say they're tough on crime, they're telling whites they'll protect them from blacks. When Republicans say they want welfare reform, they're telling the whites they won't let *them* get their money. And when Republicans say they want tax cuts, they're telling the whites they'll get some of their money back from them.

"Don't let Rudy tell you he's not a Republican. He's got it all figured out."

• • •

On my first day off in three months, I head to Belmont Park with my parents and some friends to watch Silver Charm try for the Triple Crown. Thirty minutes before the Belmont Stakes is set to go off, we head down to the walking ring to see the horses. They are all there. And Rudy Giuliani too. He's there with Al D'Amato. The mayor gives me a big thumbs-up.

It's nice to see him.

June 8

Day after day, the Giuliani campaign continues to try to make the case that our campaign is dysfunctional. Giuliani argued today that our campaign is in "disarray" because of the endorsement he has gotten from leading Hispanic Democrats. Case in point: The mayor was endorsed today by Nellie Santiago, a state senator whose husband is in business with Herman Badillo and who was recently found to have faked the educational credentials needed to work at a nursing home where she was employed as an administrator. The charges were dropped when Santiago's husband agreed to give up his operating certificate for the nursing home. All of which proves, you see, that our campaign is in disarray.

June 9

Sometimes the game is so juvenile it makes me shake my head in wonder.

Yesterday was the Puerto Rican Day Parade, and by news accounts it was a better day for Ruth than the mayor. Ruth traveled the parade route with Freddie Ferrer, who "received the kind of ecstatic reception normally accorded a rock star." The mayor, trailed by a campaign video cameraman shooting everything in sight, was cheered at points and booed at others, which was an improvement over last year's parade, when he was booed along most of the parade route.

We office shut-ins shake our heads in bewilderment that anyone could care about such things, but the press clearly does. One reporter suggests that our failure to place signs along the parade route indicates that we are taking the Latino vote for granted. "Whether it is primarily due to happenstance or to some valid political shortcomings, the fact is that Ms. Messinger seems to be taking an oddly minimalist approach to courting a key constituency."

But no one takes it more seriously than the politicians themselves. One of Giuliani's supporters—a Democrat no less—blames the hecklers along the route on us. "The rumor is," she says, "that Ruth Messinger has some volunteers doing that."

(It's not true.)

June 10

Six days to go and still no rent deal, but Rudy is continuing to position himself. The mayor announced today that the city has set aside money for lawyers to help tenants fight eviction if the rent rules end. That's half of the story. The other half is that Rudy cut funds for the city's anti-eviction programs in his executive budget and only restored the money after negotiations with the City Council. Steven Banks, head of the civil division of the Legal Aid Society, says the money Giuliani is talking about will be barely enough to keep existing programs afloat. City Council Speaker Peter Vallone says the funding for the program, which goes back to the mid-1980s and which Giuliani tried to cut, will be "woefully inadequate to handle the number of evictions we'll see if the governor allows rent regulations to expire."

But Rudy will once again pay no price for tweaking the truth. His purportedly new task force for tenants is lent an air of credibility by Danny Greenberg, the new director of the Legal Aid Society, who joins Giuliani at a press conference. Earlier in his term, Giuliani tried to terminate the contract of the Legal Aid Society. The image of Greenberg standing side by side with the mayor is striking.

• • •

The city standardized reading scores will be released tomorrow. We've been anticipating their release for weeks. They will either legitimate or undermine what Ruth has been saying about the schools.

June 11

The news on the reading scores is mixed for politicians and city kids alike. Scores are up, but not by as much as Chancellor Rudy Crew had predicted and not at the level they should be. Overall, 47.3 percent of students in grades three through eight scored at or above grade level, an increase of 3.6 points from last year. Depending on what newspaper you read, that will either seem good news or bad. The *News* headline trumpets good news, "School Reading Scores Up." The *Post* is more equivocal: "Kids' Reading Scores Are Up, But . . ." The *Times* is more equivocal still: "Despite Slight Rise, Reading Scores Fall Far Short of Goal." *Newsday*'s headline, "Coming Up Short" is downright pessimistic. An editorial in *Newsday* is evenhanded: "Failure or Success? It's both. The city reading scores rose a bit, but the overall trend is flat." A *Daily News* editorial says "Crew's control is showing results."

The differences in the coverage are striking. Part of the problem is that everyone involved seems to lack a basic understanding of what the scores mean (or those who do understand are acting on the premise that everyone else doesn't). "Grade level" is not some objectively defined standard of what a student in a particular grade should be able to read. It is simply the fiftieth percentile on the test, that is, the median score. Based on this definition, one would expect exactly half of the students in a district as large as New York City to read below grade level. Unfortunately for Crew, eighteen months ago he resolved that "no child will leave third grade who cannot read at grade level" and thus set the bar impossibly high. To meet his goal, every New York City third grader would have to beat the national average.

Crew's misstatement leaves him and the mayor on the defensive on a statistic that would likely otherwise have been interpreted as a great success. *Newsday* refers to the mayor's remarks on the subject as "an attempt to put a positive spin on the latest round of figures." *Times* education reporter Jacques Steinberg says Giuliani told him he considered the scores "very good news," then called back minutes later to say "it would be unfortunate if this were painted as a failure." Crew says, "Let's call time out. Let's say that this is good work."

Sitting in Jim's office, Ruth shakes her head in disbelief at the misunderstanding of the statistics. "Let's be clear," she says. "It's statistically impossible to get every student reading at grade level." Her intellectual honesty is what I like most about her.

We all agree. We all also agree that it makes sense to exploit the misunderstanding. It would be an impossible task to make people realize that the problem is more statistically subtle than it is being portrayed. It's striking that a school district of this size is below the mean at all. That means thousands of kids are falling behind. But we don't have the time to explain that to everyone. Our message will be that "more than half the kids in New York City can't read at grade level." In the afternoon we send out a press release mocking Giuliani's statement that "it would be unfortunate if this were painted as a failure."

June 12

For no obvious reason, our campaign employs the son of a prominent politician in the city as a consultant. He's paid $1,200 a month, but he's rarely around the campaign. In fact he's a full-time student at a graduate program out of state. In exchange, from time to time he circulates a memo with his strategic musings to the higher-ups on the campaign. Today's memo is entitled "The Campaign in African-American Communities." "Remember," it begins, "candidate Ruth Messinger sent a clear message to Black elected officials, amongst others, that there would be a strong field operation in the Primary Election and in the General Election; her personal credibility on the matter is at issue."

Three of the recommendations involve direct cash payments. Recommendation 1: "The following amounts should be appropriated to each of the Brooklyn political organizations listed below to facilitate petition collection—and maintain goodwill." The memo then lists seven organizations and individuals with proposed donations between $750 and $2,000. Recommendation 2: "Goodwill must be maintained with the four other county leaders by making an initial petition donation of not less than $10,000 to each of the Bronx and Manhattan, not less than $7,500 to Queens and not less than $3,500 to Staten Island with the stipulation that these amounts are to be used to target the black communities." Recommendation 3: "To assure goodwill, a commitment should be made now to the county leaders and the Brooklyn centers for primary day election resources, specifically street cash. Approximately $300,000 will be needed citywide with special attention paid to Brooklyn."

Street cash refers to money given to supporters to get people to the polls on Election Day. Jim uses the term more broadly to include any monetary payments to constituency groups. He refuses to pay street cash in any form. His view is informed by a story he likes to tell about a candidate in Philadelphia who is approached for street cash by some black leaders. The candidate explains that he is supported by Martin Luther King's family and he expects that their support will be enough to sustain him in the black community. The solicitors respond, "Kings don't sell in Philadelphia."

It seems to me that Jim's position is an honorable one. There may be a legal difference between paying voters $10 each for their votes and giving them $10 to get to the polling booth, but from an ethical standpoint, they're hard to distinguish. And from a political standpoint, it seems that, like most field-oriented efforts, the cash can't possibly do enough to make a significant difference. Better to spend the money on television advertising.

But the decision not to pay has political consequences. Last week, the Brooklyn Democratic Committee announced that it would be backing Sal Albanese for mayor. A source "close" to the committee's controlling chairman, Clarence Norman, called the endorsement "Brooklyn's answer to tough love" against Messinger, who, the source said, "has been dismissing machine backing in the primary." And the attendant rhetoric isn't flattering. "I don't think [Ruth Messinger] knows where the southern tier of Brooklyn is," quipped another Brooklyn leader.

Such comments have been popping up with increased frequency. This week the director of the Institute for Puerto Rican Policy told the *Observer,* "I'm really perplexed by her whole campaign. I would think that they would have a whole Latino strategy by now." The *Observer* column points out that Rudy already has a Latino strategy "in spades." They've hired Joe Wiscovitch, a Puerto Rican political consultant, who estimates that he spends "60 percent, if not more," reaching out to Latino voters.

Distasteful a practice as it may be, street money is an accepted part of the city's political process. Lots of organizations and individuals count on the semiannual cash payments as their entitlement. Some depend on them. The money is clearly not the most efficient way to sway, but I and others know what is between the lines when we read the increasingly frequent comments in the press from unnamed Democratic sources that our campaign is not well organized.

And I have a strong suspicion of what they really mean when they say Jim is an out-of-town consultant who doesn't understand New York City politics.

• • •

It's easy to lose sight of the fact that, although Jim is influential within the campaign, Ruth is still the boss. Today she proposed that new city teachers be required to live in the city. Back in our poll in March, the idea of requiring new employees to live in the city was disfavored 52–46.

June 13

Incumbency is an enormous advantage, and Rudy Giuliani is taking advantage of it to the fullest. By virtue of his position, he is in the public eye almost every day, which is something of great value, but what he's doing goes way beyond that.

Rudy has a weekly radio call-in show on WABC radio. By law, candidates are entitled to equal time, but even though Rudy has had a campaign manager and a consultant since March, WABC won't pull the plug. WABC's program director says the show will continue until Giuliani "announces he's an official candidate. We're just waiting for his call."

It gets better still. Rudy is spending $200,000 in taxpayer money to tout a new free subway-to-bus transfer program.

The city runs neither the trains nor the buses. The city government's role is limited to helping fund the Metropolitan Transit Authority and running the Staten Island Ferry. But that doesn't stop Rudy. He wrote the ad, speaks in the ad, and tags the ad with the line "One City, One Fare," which sounds virtually the same as his 1993 campaign slogan. To top it off, the Economic Development Corporation—headed, you'll recall, by Ray Harding's son Russell—is spending a million dollars on ads touting New York City.

The irony is that in 1993 Giuliani objected to the use of the same tactics by David Dinkins. Dinkins appeared in ads paid for by Prudential Securities touting the sale of city bonds. At the time, Giuliani said, "The question is: If you are supposed to be operating under the campaign finance laws, and you use your incumbency to launch ad campaigns which feature you, how can you be adhering to the campaign finance laws?" The Giuliani campaign sued to stop the ads from going on. The Campaign Finance Board said it didn't have the authority to rule on whether public funds were being properly used. That was a legislative function.

Hypocritical? The Giuliani campaign says no. "If David Dinkins could do it, why shouldn't Giuliani be allowed to do it."

June 14

Even before Ferrer withdrew from the race, Jim made the decision for us to assume the posture of a front-runner. We respond to only the most serious attacks from our opponents, and when we launch an attack of our own, we direct it at Rudy Giuliani. We've only launched one attack against our Democratic rivals (the Sharpton-Farrakhan matter), and that was done with an eye to the general election, rather than the primary.

Today, Sal Albanese announced that he is accepting the nomination of the Independence party, which has about fifty thousand members and occupies the fourth row on the ballot. There's an obvious attack to be made. Some of the founders of the Independence party have made anti-Semitic remarks. Lenora Fulani, one of the party founders and a former presidential candidate, once called Jews "decadent storm troopers of capitalism," and wrote that they "had to sell their souls to acquire Israel." In 1985, she welcomed Louis Farrakhan to New York "with deep respect and the most profound commitment to the liberation of our people." Tom Golisano, the party's 1994 gubernatorial candidate, supported the legalization of drugs and prostitution.

The party is in the midst of some serious changes, though. It formed an alliance with Ross Perot in 1996 for the presidential election. Whether Fulani is representative of the party in 1997 is unclear. Still, it's a viable attack, and the question on the table is whether to launch it during a televised roundtable debate sponsored by the Citizens Union on New York 1 later in the week. Jim believes that Ruth should continue to act as the front-runner, but should also show that she is prepared to fight if necessary.

These are difficult goals to reconcile, and Jim's instruction to Ruth is not a model of clarity. "You don't get into it with Sal unless he gets into it with you," he says. "But if he hits you, hit him hard."

June 15

The rent deal is settled.

Landlords get a 20-percent rent increase on vacant apartments if the old tenant lived there for more than eight years. The ceiling for rent-control protection is lowered from $250,000 to $175,000. Though there are to be new penalties for landlords who harass tenants, tenants are to be required to place rent in escrow during disputes with landlords. It's a good deal for the landlords.

It's a bad deal for us. Our best issue just went out the window.

June 16

I am sitting at dinner with Ruth, her husband, and her chief of staff in a fine French restaurant in Hell's Kitchen with my dinner uneaten and a cellular phone glued to my ear. Jim is screaming at me like he never has before.

• • •

The evening started out with promise. I was allowed out with Ruth and Lee to the New York 1 studio to watch the debate from the green room (it's actually blue, but all the same). I met Sal Albanese for the first time and joined in the speculation as to whether Al Sharpton would ever show. Three minutes before airtime, the Reverend and his entourage strolled in confidently. Ruth seemed composed and focused. The debate was to be hosted by Nat Leventhal, a prominent city businessman with whom she was close. (Not all good news there, though. He is also a contributor to the mayor's campaign.)

Thing started harmlessly enough. Ruth was asked a question about rent control that she handled quite well. All of the candidates focused their attacks on Giuliani, which suited us just fine.

Things heated up a bit when the conversation turned to campaign-finance reform and Albanese engaged Ruth. Turning to Ruth, Albanese said, "Borough President Messinger talks about the issue of rent regulation, but she never addresses the issue of campaign-finance reform. If she really wants to be different than Rudy Giuliani, she should be talking about that issue. I notice you never talk about that issue."

It wasn't much of an attack, but given the staid tone of all the previous debates, it was notable. Ruth was being tested. An ideal answer would have been for Ruth to have said that she talks about campaign finance all the time and that she authored the law that the Giuliani campaign was flouting.

Instead, she went after Sal.

"I beg your pardon," Ruth replied. "I beg your pardon. That's not what I say. What I say is you have a plan that would require the city to put up $98 for every dollar contributed."

"That's not my plan!" Albanese shouted. "That's not my plan!"

"Yes, it is," Ruth replied. "It is. That is your plan."

It sounded about as childish as it reads and left Al Sharpton to play his favored role of peacemaker. "Let's talk civil," he said. "This is the first Democratic live debate. Don't show everybody how divided you are."

But from there it only got worse. Ruth had interpreted the exchange with Sal as an attack and, following Jim's instruction, she shifted into full combat mode. Answering an entirely unrelated question, Ruth tried to raise the issue of Albanese's endorsement by the Independence party, but she fumbled the attack badly. "I find it reprehensible that you can accept the endorsement of a party whose various leaders at various times in the last several years have endorsed positions that are anti-Semitic, that are antigay, that favor the legalization of drugs."

"Are you calling me anti-Semitic?" Albanese screamed. "Are you calling me anti-Semitic? Are you calling Mark Green and Claire Shulman anti-Semitic? Is that what you're doing?"

Ruth clearly did not think that Albanese was anti-Semitic, but there was no turning back. She responded that Independence party leaders Lenora Fulani and Tom Golisano have made "ridiculous statements" about Jews and others that she could not immediately recall. "The people you were negotiating with for the line!" Sal retorted. Not true, said Messinger. She had steered clear of the Independence party. It sounded even sillier than it reads. The exchange allowed Sharpton to win the debate easily.

"I don't believe we're going to spend the evening debating the Independence party," Sharpton said. "If the two of you aren't interested in the Democratic party nomination, pull out and let me have it. . . . I thought I was in the wrong studio."

• • •

Following the debate, Ruth and her support group invited me to join them for dinner. I wondered to them whether it might be better for me to return to the office, but they all assured me that was unnecessary. "You have to eat, don't you?" asked Ruth's husband, and it seemed quite logical. As it is, I haven't had a bite of dinner. Just minutes after I sat down, Jim called for me on Ruth's cell phone.

"Are you enjoying your dinner?" he asks calmly.

"Yes," I say.

"Did you see that?" he asks, still calm. "Hello?"

"Yes."

There's a short pause. And then the rest comes like a tornado.

"That was the worst performance by a political candidate I have ever seen in twenty years! It was terrible! She is going to lose the primary!"

It goes on for half an hour more. There are hundreds of "hellos" and endless screaming and cursing. All the while, I sit and nod my head while my dinner companions clean their plates, wondering to myself how I can make it through five more months of this.

Finally exhausted, Jim hangs up. It's a fascinating aspect of his relationship with Ruth. He'll scream at me about something she does, but won't say a cross word to her.

"What did he think?" Ruth asks, and I realize then that this is a dysfunctional relationship. This was the sort of thing she needed to hear. And she should hear it not from me, but from him. And while they're at it, they should reconcile their differences about the field plan and diversity in the office. They should either work it out or they shouldn't work together. But I didn't have the strength to say so. I hand her back the phone.

"I think you should ask him yourself."

June 17

I'm not getting to see my family enough (or any other human beings for that matter), so I'm very happy to have my mother's company at a fundraiser for women at the Mayflower Hotel on the West Side. Gloria Steinem is here, along with Ellen Malcolm and the Pulitzer prize–winning playwright Wendy Wasserstein. Suzanne Vega, a folksinger who was a student of Ruth's at the Community Workshop School, provides the entertainment.

"The people in charge told me to sing an upbeat song or two," she says, breaking into a song called "Heroes Fall Quietly." With the crowd livened up, she breaks into a few choruses of her most famous song, "Luka." It's about an abused child.

• • •

A story in the *Observer* about the New York 1 debate mentions Messinger supporters looking askance at Albanese in the green room. Since this can only be referring to me, I want to say for the record that I like Sal Albanese very much and do not think he is an anti-Semite.

June 18

Quinnipiac College is out with its latest poll. It shows Rudy leading Ruth 49–39 in a head-to-head race and has Ruth leading the primary 54–13–13.

The news reports polls sequentially because that's the way the news reports life, but the real usefulness of polls is longitudinal, because different pollsters use different techniques. For example, pollsters use different *screens* to determine who is a likely voter. One pollster may ask persons whether they are likely to vote in the upcoming primary in order to determine whether they are likely voters. Another may ask the same pool of people whether they voted in the previous year's primary to decide whether they are likely to vote. Asking those seemingly similar questions will yield vastly different results. (The subjective question "Do you believe you will vote?" is less predictive than the objective question "Did you vote last year?") As a result, it's not always meaningful to compare contemporaneous polls.

The better comparison is between a current poll and a previous survey by the same pollster. Since pollsters are generally internally consistent with their techniques, comparing polls longitudinally offers some insight into the way a race is *trending*. The trends in the new Quinnipiac poll aren't exactly cause for jubilation, but they're not bad news either. Rudy's 10-point lead in the general is down from a 50–38 lead in March. And his approval/disapproval mix, though still an enviable 60–35, is down from 67–29 in March.

The news relative to previous polls is pretty good, but the press isn't interested in relativity; it is interested in absolutes. The most that can be said about any poll in absolute terms is that it provides additional data for the impossible task of assessing what public opinion is at any given moment. Hank Morris says it well: "What this poll says is that if the election were held today, Rudy would probably win, and if things stay the way they are now, he would probably win." Morris's quote points to the two inherent limitations of polls: First, they are estimates, not certainties. The fact that several different polls reach the same conclusion makes it more likely that that conclusion is true (using the old metaphor, they've surveyed more trees). But still, the poll merely shows that it is likely Rudy would win, not certain. And polls are only a snapshot of time. Attitudes are constantly changing. Election Day is months away.

But the press isn't interested in subtleties. The media believes that poll numbers are facts, not estimates. "Poll: Rudy Is Voters' Choice," proclaims *Newsday*. "Giuliani Would Clobber All Comers: Poll," says the *Post*. Each of the dailies quotes Quinnipiac College pollster Maurice Carroll saying Giuliani is headed for "seemingly certain reelection."

Except the *Amsterdam News*. Its headline: "Poll Shows Messinger Closing in on Giuliani."

• • •

In the same issue of the *Amsterdam News*, Lenora Fulani responds to Ruth's charges in a column. "Messinger's disingenuousness knows no bounds," Fulani writes. "Sitting next to her [at the New York 1 debate] was Rev. Al Sharpton, who has been a target of the Anti-Defamation League's venom. But it did not suit Messinger's purposes that night to 'anti-Semite bait' him (though it did several months ago)." Fulani notes that her colleague Fred Newman is Jewish, that Ruth's representatives "negotiated for three months with Black Democrats who were advising Messinger to seek the Independence line," and that Virginia Fields sought the Independence nomination without recrimination from Ruth.

June 19

My favorite person on the campaign is our press secretary, Lee Jones.

Lee is a legend in New York. He was press secretary to both Ed Koch and David Dinkins, which is quite a feat considering that Dinkins beat Koch in 1989. He is experienced and literate in a world where a twenty-four year old with two campaigns under his belt is considered a veteran. He's endlessly entertaining. Lee never begins a conversation with a reporter by saying "Hello." "How are you, you sexual nightmare" is more like it. He talks faster than any other human being I've ever met. And he's intensely loyal to the people on the staff. When I erred with the elevator tapes, Lee took the blame for it with the press and never said so much as a word about it to me.

But Lee has us in a bit of trouble today. Lee's greatest strength is his passion. Unlike me, he does view the campaign as a crusade. He sometimes seems to believe even more than Ruth that this race means something. He thinks Rudy Giuliani is a bad mayor and a bad person. But his greatest strength is also his greatest liability. His passion sometimes leads him to say things that are somewhat out of line.

A year ago, in response to a report showing a drop in the number of blacks holding top city jobs, Lee called the Giuliani administration's hiring practices "the local equivalent of Bosnia." Two weeks ago, Rudy was asked his reaction to our campaign's practice of videotaping his events. The mayor said our campaign could perhaps pick up a few pointers. "On what?" Lee asked. "How to gain weight? How to lie?" Lee is absolutely obsessed with the mayor's weight, which is especially funny since Lee has the diet of a teenager. It's soda and Twinkees every day at 4:00.

This week, Andrew Kirtzman, writing for *New York* magazine, asked Lee to assess Fran Reiter. "I admire the good work a pit bull does in protecting a drug dealer from getting caught," Lee said. "But I think the drug dealer is still poison and a despicable human being. Fran's job is to bark as loud as she can, to intimidate people and to scare people, and I guess she does that pretty well." Recalling that Reiter, who is being sued by Al Sharpton for slander, had been a Messinger supporter in 1989, Lee says, "It basically says she's a liar for hire. Her word is up for, I guess, auction."

June 20

The word in the press is that Rudy's ads are coming next week. A call from our media buyer (who, working in conjunction with Mandy Grunwald, purchases air time) confirms the news. Rudy has purchased approximately $320,000 of air time through July 2. That equates to between 500 and 600 points.

A *point* is a measure of the reach of a commercial. A 100-point buy means that over a given period of time the average person will see the commercial one time. Of course, that doesn't mean that everyone will see the commercial exactly once. Some groups are easier to reach than others. Senior citizens are easy, men twenty-five to fifty-four are relatively hard. A 100-point general-market buy might be seen by the average senior citizen three times and the average middle-aged man not at all.

Since most advertisers have more specific target audiences, media buys are generally broken down by demographic group. A 100-point buy for senior citizens is cheaper than a 100-point buy for women ages twenty-five to fifty-four, which in turn is cheaper than a 100-point buy for women as a whole. Senior citizens pretty much watch television all day long. A media buyer can purchase time on comparatively cheap daytime television shows and be quite confident of reaching lots of senior citizens. A commercial on *Sally Jesse Raphael* won't reach many younger men, though. They, unfortunately, watch popular evening sit-coms and sports, where advertising time is commensurately more expensive.

Reach is a second measure of the impact of an ad. While points measure the number of times the average person in a group sees an ad, reach measures the percentage of people in a group that see an ad at least once. Increasing the reach of an ad becomes increasingly expensive as you go along (for the mathematically inclined, it is an exponential function). Increasing the reach of an ad from 0 (no one sees it, ever) to 25 (25 percent of the target population see it at least once) is quite cheap. Buy some time on *Sally Jesse* and *The Price Is Right* and you reach the quarter of the population that has their television sets on all day long. To reach the next group of people, you may have to spread time over more expensive prime-time shows. Perhaps that gets you up to a reach of 80. It gets trickier the further along you go. Some people only watch news, so if you want to reach them, you'll have to buy time there too. And some people hardly watch television at all. Theoretically, you could buy every advertising second on television over a week and not reach some people. That's why the reach of an ad never gets to 100 (for the math majors, 100 is a horizontal asymptote.)

On virtually any sort of buy, media purchasers spread their money around on different shows. Even if your objective were a 300-point buy for women over sixty-five over a one-week period and you didn't care whether any other demographic group saw the commercial, it still wouldn't make sense to spend all your money on a single show. Hard as it is to believe, some people don't like the *Sally Jesse Raphael* show. By spreading the buy between *Sally Jesse* and a soap opera or two, the media buyer gets the same number of points, but increases the reach of the ad. Some people will see the ad on *Sally Jesse* and the soap instead of twice on *Sally Jesse*. And the buyer may lose a few people who are not religious *Sally Jesse* watchers, but on average, that will be more than offset by the people who watch the soap opera regularly, but not the *Sally Jesse Raphael* show.

All that said, looking at the demographics of a media buy can offer good insight into a campaign's polling and targeting. Rudy, for example, has purchased slots during two Yankees games. Jim says we will never buy on any sporting event, since our target audience is women.

Rudy may very well have no target at all. Since he has so much more money to spend than we do, there's not as much pressure on him to narrow the focus of his target audience. Rudy's buys include time on various news broadcasts, *Oprah Winfrey, Jenny Jones, Ricki Lake, Jeopardy,* and *Access Hollywood.* Democratic consultant, Hank Morris, speculates that Rudy's target may also be women. "They seem to be buying information-oriented shows, which have a disproportionate share of voters. Those audiences also skew towards women," Morris says. If there is a skew toward women, it's not nearly as pronounced as ours will be.

Of course, the real question on everyone's mind isn't who will see the ads, but what they will say. There are three obvious candidates: a positive ad on crime, a positive ad on education, and an attack on Ruth. An attack on Ruth seems the least likely, since it's the most risky. On the best-case scenario, Rudy would drive up Ruth's unfavorable rating and force us to prematurely spend our advertising money on responsive ads. Rudy would either be left with a weakened Ruth to face in the general if she survived, or underfunded Sal Albanese, or, best of all, Al Sharpton, whom Rudy wouldn't need to spend a dollar to beat. The risk is that attacking Ruth will create a backlash of sympathy and reinforce the popular image of Rudy as a boor. Taking Ruth down in favor of Sal Albanese may also be a risk. It doesn't show in the polls yet, but Sal may be right when he says (time and again) that he's Rudy's worst nightmare. Throwing an Italian man in the race instead of a Jewish woman would certainly change the dynamic of the general election and probably not in a way that favors Rudy.

The choice then is crime or education. Jim thinks the choice should be crime. He thinks the first ads will define the issue in the campaign and that, for the Giuliani people, it's critical the campaign be about crime and not education. As a general proposition, he believes you should "lead with your strength." But there's some evidence that Rudy may be going in another direction. The *News* quotes an unnamed source saying the ads are "Rudy reading to kids, Rudy in the schools, that kind of stuff." We'll have to wait and see.

• • •

Amid all the speculation about Rudy's campaign ads, the publicly financed MTA ads featuring Rudy and the Economic Development Corporation ads touting the drop in crime are continuing to run. The ads sound familiar themes.

The EDC ads, which the EDC says are a response to a New Jersey ad campaign, are narrated by actor Tony Roberts: "There's never been a better time to find more motivated workers, to find safe neighborhoods to work and live in, or clean parks to play in—in a city that's the world's banking, arts, entertainment capital, with streets now safer than in any other major city in America."

The mayor narrates the Department of Transportation ads: "New Yorkers have a lot to celebrate these days, and come this Fourth of July, we'll have even more. Independence from two-fare zones. Free transfers. Free ferries. One city, one fare. I'm Rudy Giuliani." The mayor's 1993 campaign slogan was "One City, One Standard," but he says that his ads, unlike David Dinkins's 1993 ads, don't "blatantly lay out campaign themes."

Are they campaign ads? We think so and so do several public-interest groups. The Straphangers Campaign, which represents public transportation users, calls on the mayor to pull the ads or have his campaign reimburse the city for their cost. The leaders of Common Cause New York and the New York Public Interest Group concur. Both organizations write Deputy Mayor Randy Mastro and urge that the ads either be pulled or the city reimbursed.

We don't have a right to be self-righteous about the issue. In December, the borough president's office spent $7,400 in city money on radio ads criticizing the mayor's plan to zone the city for superstores. Of course, there's a big difference of degree between a puny $7,400 radio buy and $1.2 million in television and radio spots. And Giuliani's response to the criticism is downright paranoid.

"The Straphangers," he says, "are part of Ruth Messinger's campaign."

June 21

One of Ruth's staffers is arguing with me about a report the borough president's office wants to release on animal rights. Last week, the Giuliani gestapo removed the commissioner dealing with animal matters after she publicly criticized Rudy.

"Evan, this is really important."

"I'll run it by Jim, but I'm not sure I think it's all that good an idea."

"I don't understand why not."

"Well, it really doesn't advance any of our central arguments." (I take care not to say "message.")

"But the animal rights people are a large, vocal constituency."

"I understand that, but I still don't think the report advances any of our central arguments."

"But the animal rights people are a large, vocal constituency."

The argument goes on and on, but there's nothing more to it. We've had it countless times before about such important documents as the Manhattan Restaurant Industry Survey and the Rat Report. There is no common ground to reach, no consensus to build. This is a conversation between two people with fundamentally different views of the world (or, more accurately, two people working for people with fundamentally different views of the world). Let's call them the traditional and modern views of politics.

In the traditional view, the electorate is an aggregate of constituencies. A candidate's strength is the sum of his or her support in each of the subgroups of a community. Add Ruth's support with blacks, Latinos, Jews, Indians, gays, and so on and you can calculate her total vote. In this view, candidates collect votes. Attend a gay cocktail reception and pick up three votes, shake hands at a subway stop and pick up twelve. This worldview presupposes a notion of the voter as a binary switch. Voters are either for somebody or against somebody and can be turned one way or the other by stands on particular issues. You just need to find the right key.

If the traditional politician sees the voter as a binary switch, the modern politician sees the electorate as an electron cloud, a subatomic entity that is constantly changing form, never in one place at any given time. Each nudge of the cloud has untold consequences. Whispering to the Latino police officers that you will make sure more Latinos are promoted to lieutenant may strengthen support among Latinos, but the counteracting ripple effects will be more damaging. People will see you as a panderer and unwilling to stand tough against labor.

For that very reason, adherents to the modern view don't like to deal in nudges; they prefer bulldozers. Since every action has a reaction of unknown force, it's best to make sure that the predictable effects of the exerted force are as strong as possible. Rather than whispering "Latino lieutenants," scream "Tough on unions!" with all your energy and hundreds of points of television commercials.

The great flaw in the traditional view is that it presumes idyllically that action can be taken in a vacuum. Saying contradictory things to different groups is not a problem since constituencies don't interact. In fairness to the honorable practitioners of traditional politics, the tensions among conflicting messages are never quite this direct. The shrewd traditional politician does not go around to the 33rd Street Business Improvement District and say, if elected, he or she will fight to make sure the new city pool is built in their neighborhood and then tell the Park Slope Community Association that it will be built in theirs. It is never something so obvious as telling the Amnesty International local that one is opposed to the death penalty and then telling the Conservative Club that one is in favor of it.

It is much more subtle in practice. Traditional politicians would have no trouble, for example, saying in a mass forum like a debate that they were in favor of cutting government spending and then telling domestic violence advocates, senior citizens, and a hundred different interest and advocacy groups throughout the city that they would restore funds to each of their individual programs if elected, despite the fact that if the politicians did all of the things they promised for the different groups, they'd never be able to achieve their larger goal of reducing government spending.

At the same time, modern politicians may go too far the other way. At some level politics is played off the radar screen of the press and the public. Perhaps sometimes there is no harm in slightly adjusting your message to appeal just a bit more to the particular group to which you are speaking on a given occasion.

Ruth thinks so. Jim doesn't. Watching the million ways in which that plays itself out is infinitely amusing.

• • •

Ruth is strikingly comfortable in court representing herself in the proceeding to force the city to disclose statistics about denials of Freedom of Information Law requests. "The case," she says, "is aimed not only at upholding my office's powers, but also at empowering those constituents who have been prevented from gaining access to public records."

The city attorney holds to his position that Ruth is not entitled to the information in her capacity as borough president. The city argues that the information is voluminous and that having Ruth's staff review it would be a waste of taxpayer money. Ruth has every right to ask for the information as a private citizen, they say, but not as borough president. The argument has a nice political twist (casting Ruth as wasting taxpayer money), but no basis in law. Judge Paula Omansky seems unimpressed with the city's position. She says, "I do not understand why you're saying the inquiry by the Borough President into responses to [the Freedom of Information Law] isn't legitimate."

June 22

For modern politicians, money is a campaign's most important commodity. It allows the campaign to advertise on television, the form of electioneering that has the greatest impact on the greatest number of people. But the myth persists in the press that other aspects of campaigning are of equal importance. The coverage of the various parades is a good example of a divergence between what the press views as important and the campaign's own internal view. The press views the parades as critical. Jim views them as irrelevant, except for the minor name-recognition benefit to be gained from the candidate's appearing on the evening news.

Fund-raising is another area where the views of the press and the campaign differ. For weeks, Jim has been saying that the downside of devoting so much of Ruth's time to fund-raising (she's still spending six hours a day on the phone) is that the news will begin to question her lack of visibility.

The first of these stories arrives today. In an article titled "Messinger Playing Peekaboo Politics," Joel Siegel of the *Daily News* asks "Where's Ruth?" "The Manhattan Borough President has kept a lower profile [than the Mayor], and some days has no events to attract media interest. Rudy Giuliani, by contrast, has switched to full reelection mode, holding one to two political events a day and reading to children in schools to soften his image." The question is whether Siegel recognizes that Giuliani's schedule would be exactly the same as Ruth's if he hadn't already raised the maximum amount of money permissible by law. Perhaps he does and is merely faulting us for not doing a good job of perpetuating the myth and image of an active campaign. The real trick is to spend all of your time raising money, but make people believe you're out there shaking hands all day.

In fairness to Siegel and the rest of the press, New York City is filled with people who do not buy into the modern campaign model. Many people believe that handshaking matters. "I know there is a problem," says one union leader Siegel quotes. "If you are asking me whether the campaign is off the ground yet, the answer is, 'No.'" Tom Duane, a Democratic City Councilman from Manhattan, says he is concerned that he has not seen enough "focus" in the campaign. I'm not sure what "focus" and "off the ground" mean, but I'm pretty sure they refer to grassroots organizing.

One person seems to get it. Former Dinkins deputy mayor Bill Lynch says, "I know what she's doing now are the right things, raising money and getting support."

If only everyone understood that.

• • •

A profile of Ruth in the *Daily News*, "Ruth Gradually Pads Her Left Hook," quotes a passage Ruth wrote in a fund-raising letter for the Democratic Socialist Organizing Committee: "The bankers, the corporations and the real estate developers have controlled and profited from the decline of urban America. We must reverse their power and replace it with true democratic planning and participation."

Wherever did they get that one from?

The article goes on to note that Ruth supported parent sit-ins over budget cuts, a 1981 broccoli boycott in support of farm workers, a gay-rights bill, and distribution of condoms in schools. She also traveled to Nicaragua several times and appeared with Sandinista leader Daniel Ortega.

The author is kind enough to note that "by 1986, there were signs of change." Not much detail, though.

• • •

It's an open question whether there is sexism in the New York press, but if there is, it manifests itself in subtle ways exemplified in the papers today. *Newsday*'s story on the Freedom of Information Law lawsuit is titled "Messinger Argues Own FOI Lawsuit." The *Post* headline has a different tone: "Ruth Begs Judge: Let Me Foil Rudy's 'Secrecy.'" The *Newsday* lead: "The campaign trail led Manhattan Borough President Ruth Messinger into the courtroom Friday, where the former social worker argued her own case charging that Mayor Rudolph Giuliani illegally withheld information from her." The *Post*: "Non-lawyer Ruth Messinger pleaded her own case yesterday in Manhattan Supreme Court, urging a judge to tip the scales her way in a politically charged lawsuit against Mayor Giuliani." The key noun and verb in the *Newsday* story are "Borough President argued." The *Post* lead reduced is "Non-lawyer pleaded."

• • •

The fallout from Lee's unrestrained pit-bull analogy is less than we feared. An editorial in the *Post* decries "Messinger's malicious mouthpiece," but that's it.

June 23

Rudy Giuliani is on the air with his first ad. It shows him reading to a culturally diverse group of schoolchildren.

> For decades, bureaucrats and career politicians did nothing to stop the abuse of our schools, but not anymore. We gave the chancellor the power to set higher standards. Now student reading scores are up in every district, the highest one-year increase in the past decade. But more needs to be done. We're

launching Project Read so scores continue to rise. We're rebuilding and renovating our schools. If we can cut crime, we can improve education—together.

Each statement is an outrage in its own right. "For decades, bureaucrats and career politicians did nothing to stop the abuse of our schools, but not anymore." Rudy Giuliani cut $1.3 billion from the projected school budget during his first three years in office.

"We gave the chancellor the power to set higher standards." In 1995, Rudy Giuliani proposed eliminating the position of schools chancellor. And he originally opposed the school reorganization plan that vested greater power in the chancellor. Giuliani wanted control over the schools for himself.

"Now student reading scores are up in every district, the highest one-year increase in the past decade." Reading scores are down under Giuliani, and what's more, the Giuliani administration inflated reading scores by changing which students' scores are counted. Until 1995, all limited-English-speaking students who had been in the schools for two years or more were included in the calculation of reading scores. In 1996, the city changed the policy to exclude limited-English speakers for five years.

"But more needs to be done." Well, that one's true.

"We're launching Project Read so scores continue to rise." Giuliani's budget director said that Project Read is a one-year program, essentially admitting that it is an election-year scam.

"We're rebuilding and renovating our schools." This is the most egregious of the lot. Rudy Giuliani cut $4.8 billion from the Board of Education's five-year capital plan before he put a pittance of $275 million back in the budget this year.

Taken together, the ad is almost offensive. This man did not care one whit about the schools during his first three years in office. Now he's taking credit for what little good has happened under his watch and shifting the blame for what went wrong. The problem is we don't have much firepower.

There are two ways to respond to an ad. The best way is to put out a responsive ad. The other is to fight the validity of the ad in the press. We don't have the money for an ad, but within two hours, we put out a point-by-point response and fax it to everyone in the press and everyone in the city who might conceivably speak to the press. For the first time, it feels like our research operation is earning its keep. But our little fax is nothing in comparison to 500 points of television. The notion that Rudy Giuliani cares about the schools and is committed to fixing them is filtering around the city. Some people just may believe it.

• • •

Jim thinks the ad is a mistake from a strategic standpoint. The ad will also contribute to a press environment in which education will be perceived as the main issue. It will give Rudy a short-term boost by favorably changing people's perception of his performance on education. But in the long run, Jim thinks it will prove to be a devastating blunder. Rudy needs to make the campaign about crime, not the schools.

June 24

Earlier in the month, Wayne Barrett of the *Village Voice* advanced the theory that Comptroller Alan Hevesi and Rudy Giuliani have entered into a nonaggression pact. Back in 1996, Giuliani called Hevesi "reckless" and "unfair." Now it appears the two will run together on the Liberal line. Giuliani forcibly removed auditors from State Comptroller Carl McCall's office, but he welcomes audits from Hevesi. One such audit reached the conclusion that the mayor's battered women's hotline was so badly understaffed that 63 percent of callers were "referred nowhere" and that the hotline "provides little more than false hope." Hevesi appeared with Giuliani at a joint press conference announcing steps to "*continue* to improve the City's domestic violence support system." Barrett has lots of other examples of a marked change in Hevesi's and Giuliani's tone toward each other. For example, Hevesi's chief of staff was recently seen having dinner with Peter Powers, Giuliani's campaign chairman. But today Alan Hevesi put an end to all speculation that he had entered into a tacit pact with Rudy Giuliani.

He endorsed Ruth Messinger, once and for all. "Ruth is one of the smartest people I've ever met," he said.

Why, he is asked, should New Yorkers vote against Rudy? "Rudy Giuliani has some successes and some failures, and it is not necessary, in a campaign, in preferring one candidate over another, to bash anybody," said Hevesi. Shortly before the 1993 Democratic primary, a *New York Times* story alleged that Elizabeth Holtzman's campaign had received a $450,000 loan from Fleet Bank in 1992 while she was serving as city comptroller; she then recommended the bank be named as a city bond underwriter. Hevesi ran thousands of dollars in ads in 1993 broadcasting the *Times* headline. An administrative law judge of the Conflicts of Interest Board found no quid pro quo between Holtzman and the bank, though the full board later fined Holtzman $7,500. Of course, Holtzman herself had been accused of catfighting in her Senate campaign a year earlier when she ran an ad broadcasting a *Village Voice* headline accusing Ferraro of ties to the mob. Ferraro lost the primary narrowly to Bob Abrams. Holtzman finished fourth in the four-way race.

Anyway, back to Hevesi.

Mr. Hevesi, would Ms. Messinger be a better mayor than Mr. Giuliani?

"Certainly with respect to the issues that will define the next four years, she has a great potential to be a great mayor."

There. A ringing endorsement. Case closed.

June 25

Newspapers sometimes print *ad-boxes,* which are short descriptions of the content and accuracy of political advertisements. For people in my current line of work, they're like report cards. The opposition's made a claim, we've offered facts undermining the claim, and now a third party assesses the truth or, depending on your level of cynicism, determines the quality of the arguments.

Newsday's box seems quite fair. It points out that Giuliani "restricted the flow of money to the schools more severely than any mayor since the city's fiscal crisis of the mid–1970s, forcing many schools to reduce services." It credits him, though, for imposing fiscal discipline. On the reading score issue, *Newsday* says, "The number of students in grades 3 to 8 reading at grade level jumped 3.6 percent this year, but more than half still cannot read at grade level." (The spin lives!)

The *Post* story quotes the mayor's line on reading scores. "Giuliani's TV commercial seizes on the fact that reading scores went up in every school district by an average of 3.6 percent—*the largest single-year jump in a decade.*" The story does not mention that the increase fell short of Board of Education expectations.

The *Post* is also more sympathetic to the mayor on the funding issue: "After three years of cutting proposed spending on education, the Mayor this year increased the Board of Ed's expense budget by 4.9 percent." That's not nearly as favorable an interpretation as in *Newsday*, but in this case the *Post* may be closer to the truth. Just as we've relied upon a misunderstanding perpetuated in the press that 50 percent of city kids can't read at grade level, so too we've relied on an overstatement of the mayor's actions on the schools. The mayor has not cut $1.2 billion from the schools as is commonly reported; he's cut $1.2 billion in proposed increases. That's not an entirely academic distinction. If the Board of Education had come in last year and proposed an $8 billion increase in spending, and the mayor had only allowed the budget to grow by its normal $300 million, we would hardly be justified in claiming that the mayor had cut $7.7 billion from the budget. But that's the logic we are employing. The difference is that people believe the Board of Education's spending requests were not frivolous, but rather for badly needed funds.

There's a good lesson in all this about the nature of truth in the political press. Once a fact is printed, it carries a certain inherent validity. Reporters regularly cite the fact that Giuliani cut money from the budget, but none independently assess the validity of that statement. The window of opportunity to question a fact opens when a reporter calls to fact-check a claim in a story and closes when that fact is published. After that it becomes ancient history, which is hard to change.

June 26

When I earlier described the fight to spin Adam Nagourney over the quality of the campaign as a *metabattle,* I meant that it was a fight that would not directly influence voters, but might create an impression that would have an indirect impact on the election. No one will change his or her vote because a candidate's campaign is poorly organized. But the impression that a candidate cannot run his or her own campaign may in turn create a perception that the candidate is a poor manager, which may sway some votes. The trick with metabattles is not to lose them too badly.

Another metabattle we're losing badly is the race for endorsements. Yesterday, the firefighters announced that they are going for Rudy. Last week, the principals' union endorsed the mayor. There's even some speculation that the teachers' union may go with Giuliani too.

Some traditional political types would dispute my characterization of union support as a metabattle. Most adherents to the traditional view would probably concede that few people, if any, vote for a particular candidate because the candidate has a particular endorsement. But that, they say, misses the point. Some unions, they point out correctly, have considerable power. Field coordinators covet *phone banks* (lots of phones in a room) above all else. Big unions can provide large phone banks at no cost to the campaign. And they can provide manpower to help make telephone calls, lick envelopes for mailings, and drive people to the polls on Election Day. Many people within our own campaign think these things are important, including Ruth, who is known to make clandestine calls to union leaders whenever she can find a free minute.

Nevertheless, I'll stand by my characterization of the race for endorsements as a metabattle.

Phone banks and envelope lickers are useful, but the magnitude of their impact pales in comparison to the force of a single television ad. Where money is no object, a strong field operation supported by unions is nice to have and may make the difference in a close election. But we're scraping for every dollar to put on television. No union endorsement is nearly as important as raising as much money as we possibly can.

But like all metabattles, it's a skirmish a campaign doesn't want to lose too badly. It's not true, but voters and the press believe that endorsements make a difference. And what truly may make a difference is the perception that a candidate lacks union backing completely. An obvious lack of union support can create the impression that a candidate is not credible or that it isn't worth voting since the candidate has no chance.

That's the perception we're fighting. Stories in this week's *Observer* and *Village Voice* discuss the emerging pattern of city unions aligning with the mayor. The head of the Social Service Employees Union suggests that several unions felt betrayed by David Dinkins, who tried to privatize some city jobs, and are seeking revenge against Ruth. Others suggest unions simply don't believe that Ruth can win. Wayne Barrett has a different theory. In his story "Big Labor Betrayal: Union Bosses in Tank for Mayor, Sell Out the Poor," Barrett suggests that Charlie Hughes's decision to throw his union of Board of Education kitchen workers and school aides behind Giuliani may have had something to do with a little-noticed loophole in the recently negotiated teachers' contract that lets teachers skip cafeteria duty at a cost to the city of $70 million. The policy is a windfall for Hughes's union, whose hourly workers are picking up the duties. "That's what passes for labor relations in the Giuliani era," Barrett says. "A cozy exchange of favors, unnoticed by the tabloid tribunes who would assail a Democratic mayor for less." But even Barrett has a traditional outlook on political matters. He argues that were the leaders of the teachers' union and the 120,000-member District Council 37 willing to take on Giuliani, "the entire campaign could be different."

Barrett is wrong about that, I think, but these are stinging losses all the same. We need to line up *some* union support to make people think the campaign is competitive. But it's beginning to look like we may not even be able to make that modest goal. We've staked our entire campaign on education. If we can't get the teachers' union, what union can we get?

June 27

While Rudy Giuliani is hosting his first ever New York City Literacy Hero Awards for fourth graders outside our window, Geoff Garin is in town to talk business with Ruth and Jim. Jim asks me to bring in a copy of one of the early polls. Geoff pays me a kind compliment.

"You know, Ruth, if you're elected, you really have to make this guy parks commissioner."

Ruth has bigger plans for me.

"Parks commissioner?" she scoffs. "He'll be commissioner of *sports*."

Dare I dream so grandly?

June 28

Geoff Garin makes the important point that there is one union endorsement that is more important than any other: the Patrolmen's Benevolent Association (PBA). An endorsement by the PBA would legitimate Ruth's credibility as a crime-fighter, a benefit that would go far beyond any volunteers or phone banks the PBA may have.

Police officers are furious with Giuliani. Though the city has made large inroads against crime, police officers have been working without a contract for the past two years, and Giuliani is pressuring them to accept a pay freeze for the first two years of a five-year deal. Some officers are distributing flyers that resemble wills saying that, in the event of their death, Giuliani and Police Commissioner Safir should "be denied attendance at any memorial service in my honor as their attendance would only bring disgrace to my memory."

Geoff says we should do whatever we have to to persuade the PBA to endorse, including supporting a more generous contract offer than Rudy's "zero-zero" proposal. Geoff says it more colorfully. He advocates doing whatever is necessary to "buy off the police union."

• • •

In a political memo in the *Times*, "Coop Treats Giuliani with an Air of Reverence," David Firestone describes a Giuliani town meeting in Forest Hills, Queens. "It was beyond friendly, beyond enthusiastic," Firestone writes. "It was—if it is possible to say this about any New York audience outside a teenage rock concert—almost adoring." The pulled quote is "Retirees act as if they are a choir hearing a sermon." Can we possibly compete with that?

• • •

It seems someone at City Hall forgot to clue the *Post* in on the Hevesi-Giuliani deal. They ask, "Now that he's officially aboard the Manhattan borough president's bandwagon, can Hevesi believably critique the performance of City Hall's current occupant?" No need to worry. There's not likely to be much in the way of critique coming anytime soon. Says the *Post*, "We'll never look at a Hevesi audit quite the same way again, and we suspect we're not alone." Indeed they're not.

June 29

We win today's Gay Pride Parade hands down. Ruth marches with her daughter Miriam and Miriam's partner, Felicia. Fran Reiter is handed a cardboard cover with a condom inside. She unsuccessfully tries to hand it back.

June 30

Part of the research team's job is to monitor the media. Two people from our staff are in every morning at 5:30 to clip the daily newspapers and prepare a briefing for the staff. We also have a panel of six television sets and VCRs that are constantly running in case a commercial airs. It's an incredible distraction and makes working in the office as easy as working in a train station, but this morning the practice pays dividends.

At around 7:00, one of our two college interns notices a Giuliani commercial on New York 1. The ad is a surprise. When Rudy went up with his education ad, our media buyer knew well in advance when and on what stations the ad would be airing. There has been no advance warning this time. Nevertheless, the ad is there. It shows footage of the Staten Island Ferry, Ellis Island, and the Statue of Liberty and pictures of commuters. And it sounds a lot like the MetroCard ads. The campaign ad: "Today, the two fare system is a thing of the past, and One City-One Fare is here to stay. Safer neighborhoods, building better schools. One city. One standard. Rudy Giuliani—the Mayor for all New York." The MTA ad: "New Yorkers have a lot to celebrate these days and come this Fourth of July, we'll have even more. Independence from two fare zones. Free transfers. Free ferries. One city. One fare. I'm Rudy Giuliani." The similarity of the texts undermines the Giuliani campaign's claim that they are not "blatantly laying out campaign themes" as the Dinkins team did in 1993.

By 8:30, we're out with a press release written by Jim titled "One Campaign, Two Standards":

> Do you need a way to make those scarce campaign dollars go a lot farther? Do those cumbersome little facts get in the way of the story you're trying to tell? Is that what's getting you down, Rudy? Well, here's what you do . . . One week you use $200,000 of the taxpayers' money to tout the new MTA one-fare plan. You do it while the MTA is spending millions on ads to say the same thing. You get a little criticism. You deny doing what you criticized your opponent for doing in the last election. You go on the record. You tell *Newsday*, ten days ago—definitively—that your taxpayer-funded ads don't *"blatantly lay out campaign themes."* Then what happens? *Your campaign starts running TV ads today saying exactly the same thing.* Yes, folks, it gets worse every week. And so does the lying . . . not just about the ads, where Rudy says they don't lay out campaign themes last week just before they lay out campaign themes this week . . . but also about what's in the ads.
>
> - Like the fact that the MTA one-fare plan was proposed in September 1993—*before Rudy took office.*
> - Or the fact that the MTA said—in 1993—that the reason the plan would take until 1997 to implement was that it couldn't be done until the new fare-card machines were put in place on all New York subways and buses. And guess what? It's 1997. The new fare machines are in place. And so is the one-fare plan.
> - Or the fact that Rudy cut $200 million in city subsidies for the MTA in 1995, which helped cause a system-wide fare hike . . . so now it's one city, one *higher* fare.
>
> There's one standard in Rudy's campaign all right. It's just not a standard that applies to anybody else. And it's not a standard you would teach your kids. It's called lying.

This is a fairly typical campaign press release. I offer it in its entirety to show what one looks like and to make a more important point about audience. Two things stand out to me about campaign press releases. One is that they're written as if morons are reading them. The other is that they're not written for just the press. The "folks," as in "Yes, folks, it gets worse every week," are a broader audience than merely the press. Immediately after faxing a press release around to the press, we fax it to a list of major donors and prospective donors. We do the same with any favorable story about Ruth or unfavorable story about Rudy. The battle for press has monetary consequences.

As for this press release, the lying thing seems a bit heavy-handed, but it gets the point across. And it successfully shifts the burden back to the Giuliani campaign. At first, they deny the commercial even exists. An hour later, Reiter acknowledges and defends it. Our best educated guess is that the ad wasn't supposed to show in Manhattan. Cable television sends different signals to different boroughs. Advertisers can pay to have their ad seen in only Brooklyn if they so choose. It seems that's what the Giuliani campaign intended to do with this ad. The ad's visual images and message are geared toward Staten Island. Our guess is that somehow reels got mixed up and New York 1 ended up broadcasting the wrong ad. Whatever the reason, the Giuliani campaign has to live with the consequences of the ad now.

July 1

Jim has hired a day-to-day manager for the race. He is a master of the lingo who likes going around the country *whacking Republicans* and believes in a *strict chain of command.* We now have 8:00 A.M. staff meetings. Each day, I and the other department heads are to tell the manager *what we have for him.* We are to make sure that our daily *hit* matches our *message of the day.* It worries me that our message is to change as often as the soup in the building cafeteria.

• • •

As best I can tell, there are four sorts of people who work on campaigns: kids, big kids, really big kids with nice cars, and drifters.

Kids are by far the largest group. Typically kids are twenty-three or twenty-four, recently out of college, and not entirely sure what they want to do with their lives. Like any other large organization, campaigns depend upon the people who get paid the least to work the hardest, and ours is no exception. If Jim were to miss a day of work (he never does), the campaign would be none the worse. If Ruth's call manager, Bill Franks, were to miss a day, the campaign would lose about $10,000.

Because so few people are willing to make a career of working on campaigns, anyone who sticks with politics for more than a year or two is pretty well assured of moving up the ladder and becoming a big kid. There is no weeding-out process to speak of. There is no sieve that eliminates people who aren't well qualified from advancing up the ladder. Campaigns are so desperate for cheap labor that they will take pretty much anyone with any sort of brain who is crazy enough to want the job. The filter is self-selection. People who cannot handle the lifestyle move along to other careers. Everyone else moves up the ladder. Since virtually everyone who works in a campaign decides it's not for them, if you have any sort of experience at all, you're a hot commodity on the political market.

What sort of experience it is makes very little difference. My deputy, at the age of twenty-four, has, incredibly, worked on seven races and is well on his way to becoming a big kid, but he's never worked for a winner. Our new campaign manager is highly regarded in Washington, D.C., I'm told, but his record is hardly stellar. He just finished managing the campaign of Rob Andrews, a New Jersey congressman who was overwhelmingly favored to win the Democratic nomination to challenge Christie Todd Whitman for governor. Andrews lost by 12 points and apparently, to make matters worse, our guy and the candidate ended the race on nonspeaking terms. But that doesn't matter in this world. In politics, it's just another race under his belt.

The big kids have important jobs like campaign manager or press secretary (Lee is atypical—press secretaries are usually thirty years old or so) and have the trappings appropriate to offices of that stature. Our new campaign manager is getting the crème de la crème of the offices (concededly a musty, dusty pit, like all the others), a cell phone, and cabs to and from work, and I think would get an apartment too, except for the fact that he's living with relatives. The worst part is the big kids emulate the behavior of the really big kids.

The really big kids have the best deal of all, because they get to have all of the fun without having to work the hours. The really big kids strategize and appear on television from time to time to spin about the race and take weekends in Nantucket. Jim is a really big kid except for the fact, to his credit, that he's still in it day to day, a fact he often laments. He doesn't get to Nantucket very often, a fact he does not often lament.

The worst part is when the big kids act like really big kids. Our new campaign manager is bossing people around the office, which doesn't play too well with the staff. He's an emperor without clothes, a thirty-one-year-old man on his way to pulling off the unusual feat of working on two losing campaigns in a year. At least Jim can back his attitude up with intelligence and a record of accomplishment.

The drifters are far and away the most interesting of the lot. The most compelling character in our office is Leo, one of the drifters. Leo, tall with scraggly hair and a timeless sort of face that might make him anywhere from thirty to fifty, doesn't smell too good. He works as a bicycle messenger by day and then works overnight in our office inputting data into our fund-raising files. He's been seen working as late as four in the morning and as early as five thirty. Leo claims that he sleeps occasionally, but I've never seen it.

As you might expect, he's sort of a legendary character in the office, but no one knows all that much about him. He supposedly likes working for female candidates, and I once heard someone mention that he had served in Vietnam, but the truth is I'm not sure about that. All I know from talking to him is that he is well read, articulate, and has impeccable taste in classical music, which he plays in the early morning hours as he inputs data.

We've all speculated about whether Leo is homeless or not, but if he is, he's not the only person on the campaign without a home. At various times, other members of our field staff have used the campaign headquarters as a home. There's a shower in the office and a room with my deputy's old cot—both among the nastiest places I've ever seen in my life—and people have felt more than free to use them as home from time to time. One of the drifters regularly uses the shower in our office (the fungus is abated, but fighting back valiantly) and makes sure he floods the room so that no one can use it for the next few hours.

I wonder, when patronage is passed out in the Messinger administration, exactly where these loyalists will land.

• • •

The irony of Ruth's fate is far from lost upon the candidate. "Bill," she says to her call manager, "I've been waiting to be mayor all my life and now my fate is in the hands of a crazy chain-smoker and a bunch of kids."

• • •

An article in the *Post* indicates that Giuliani is working overtime to ensure that every child has a seat when schools reopen. According to the *Post*, the mayor and his aides have met thirty or forty times since February to avoid a repeat of last year's "fiasco" when ninety thousand kids had no seats. As with the release of the reading scores, the opening of school will be a media event. Given how much emphasis Ruth has placed on the schools, Rudy will no doubt be pulling out all the stops to make sure it's a good show.

• • •

Donna Hanover says she won't be appearing in any ads for Rudy this year.

• • •

On message! The *Times* reports today that preliminary statistics for 1997 show the murder rate is continuing to fall. "It's good news," Lee says, "that crime has continued to go down under two mayors. We would only hope that the same focus would now be brought on our schools, which deserve better."

July 2

Tensions are running high in Washington Heights. On Tuesday, a grand jury decided not to bring charges against Officer Pelligrini for killing Kevin Cedeno. Al Sharpton flew to Washington today to deliver a letter to Janet Reno asking the Justice Department to open a civil-rights investigation in the case. U.S. representative Charlie Rangel has asked Rudy to visit Washington Heights to help keep the peace.

The mayor won't be going:

> I think that's a mistake. I think that gives the impression that something wrong happened. To create the false impression that this was an unjustifiable homicide is really a terrible mistake, and even some of the news reports last night that gave more emphasis to the statements of Reverend Sharpton and the family rather than the statements of the District Attorney are very unfortunate.

Having ceded the crime issue, we say nothing.

July 3

My hands are trembling. I am about to be on the air live with Rudy Giuliani.

"Let's go out to Eric in Manhattan," the announcer says. I have shrewdly disguised my identity. The mayor will never suspect that I am in fact the director of research for his archrival, Ruth Messinger, calling to ambush him.

"Eric, your question for the mayor."

"Good evening, Mister Mayor," I say. This is undeniably clever of me. First I will strike a rapport with the mayor and gain his confidence.

"How you doin'?" His guard is down. My ploy is working.

"Okay, thanks." Here it comes, Rudy.

"You just appeared during the commercial break narrating an ad touting the upcoming change in the MTA fare structure—"

Rudy cuts me off. "Right and I even got asked a question about the Sohtoa because he was confused about whether the Sohtoa was included." He is trying to change the tenor of this conversation, but I will not allow it. What the hell is Sohtoa anyway?

"My question is slightly different. How do you justify using taxpayer money for that when it's virtually the same as a campaign ad that you're running?" There. Got him.

"Well. Just by what happened. That gentleman was confused about whether or not he could get the benefit of one city, one fare and I had to explain it to him."

He's not answering the question. Of course it's legitimate for the city to run ads about the fares, but why does Rudy have to be in them on the same week his campaign is running a virtually identical ad? I will steer him back to the subject at hand.

"But —"

Rudy won't let me get a word in. "That ad is on because there are going to be about two to three million people ultimately affected by this. They do not know and understand what is going to happen to them."

I try again. "No, but —"

"Would you like an answer or would you just like to ask a question?" The mayor is snapping at me. I will not be bullied, but I do not want to appear unreasonable to the thousands of viewers whose votes will be influenced by this telephone call.

"Sorry, sorry, sorry."

"Good. Then I will give an answer to it," Rudy says patronizingly. "There's a complexity to this that's very important. There are 300,000 people that ride private buses. The MTA literature does not explain to them how they take advantage of One City, One Fare."

Get new literature then!

"They might not realize that they can take advantage of it, because for fifty years nobody thought of doing this for them."

Rudy is going on. He has seized the upper hand. He is not answering the question at all. He's telling people that he is the smartest New Yorker in the last half century, and I can't get a word in edgewise—he won't take a breath.

"We've included $32 million in our budget to include all of the private buses. And if you listen carefully to that ad, that ad was intended to reach them, so that they understand that they too can get a MetroCard and if they ride Command bus or they ride New York bus, they can get a MetroCard, and we've in essence connected the private bus system to the public system, and that's a perfectly legitimate thing to tell people about.

"Now I suspect that if I didn't do it and tomorrow there was like mass confusion, you might very well be the very first person to call me up and say, 'Mr. Mayor, why are you allowing this confusion to happen in the city?'"

Rudy is affecting his voice to make me sound like a crackpot.

"You would be out there holding up signs criticizing me for it, because I have a feeling you have a bias in this matter. Just a feeling."

Rudy and the announcer cackle at the mayor's slight against my objectivity. I try to respond, but the station has cut me off.

The mayor has worked his magic with me. I've been marginalized.

July 4

A small town in Staten Island called Hamlet has thrown a Fourth of July parade for the past eighty-seven years. Staten Island is Giuliani country, and this is its capital. But Ruth's going in.

In a little while, that is. Ruth hits traffic on her way to the parade route and arrives several minutes late. A city police officer orders Ruth to stay on the sidewalk and off the parade route. She isn't on the list of official marchers. Sal Albanese rushes to Ruth's defense. "She should be allowed to march in the parade," he says, "but I really and truly don't believe she's going to get any kind of reception." Ruth clandestinely sneaks into the parade route several blocks later.

The officer denies he acted on orders from the Giuliani administration, but Rudy is on the attack. "You're not going to get a really good reception when you come just on Election Day to march in a parade you've spurned for years and years as a public official. The people of Staten Island, you know, get insulted when you kind of show up late for the very first time when you're running for office," says the mayor, who first marched in the parade as a candidate in 1989. "Like, you got to have been there before."

As always, the diversity of the coverage is fascinating. "Paraders Bounce Ruth Off Rudy's Turf in Staten I.," proclaims the *Post*. "Rudy at Parade: Ruth Out of Step," says the *News*. The *Times* story, "Mayoral Rivals Invade Parade Long the Turf of Giuliani" sounds as if it's from a different universe. "Ruth W. Messinger and Sal F. Albanese, both Democrats," it says, "dove directly into the heart of what many residents call 'Rudy country,' and both found the reception not nearly as chilly as might have been expected."

So many questions. How can different reporters perceive things so differently? Do they sincerely believe that parades are worth covering at all, or do they know better and merely continue to do so because it is what people expect? Why does the *Times* insist on using middle initials for people every reader knows? And how can the mayor of a city of eight million people, a former U.S. Attorney, utter the sentence "Like, you got to have been there before"?

July 5

One thing Jim has repeatedly said to me that makes good sense is that the task for a challenger is not to prove why he or she should be hired for the job, but rather to show why the incumbent should be fired. In addition to the demands of fund-raising, this belief is one of the reasons Ruth is keeping a relatively low profile. As soon as we put ideas out there, they will become fair game for attack. For the time being, it's better for us to have back-and-forths about Giuliani's record than about Ruth's record or proposals.

But pressure for a higher profile is growing. Whether it is pressure we should heed is an interesting question, but it is undeniably growing. Last week, the *Daily News* asked, "Where's Ruth?" Many of our strongest supporters, burdened by adherence to the traditional view of campaigns, have publicly questioned the aggressiveness of the campaign.

Jim has decided that the time is finally right. Later this week Ruth will formally announce her candidacy (or come out, as my friends at the Nathan Lane fund-raiser would say). The event will take place at a school on the Lower East Side. The speech, which Mandy and Marla have been fine-tuning for the past several days, will focus on education, the issue we will emphasize throughout the race. "This is where it starts. At schools like this all around our city, this is where it starts." It's a good speech.

July 6

With the rent issue settled, we've been looking for a hook into another issue. Today is our best opportunity to highlight the city's job crisis. Swingline Staples, based in Queens, is planning to move its operations to Nogales, Mexico, a city on the Arizona border. The company says the move will save it $12 million a year, but it also means that another 450 city residents will be out of work.

Asked for comment, Rudy Giuliani says that the loss of the company is "no big deal" and that the city will easily make up for the loss with continued job growth. "We're better off sending the signal that we're not going to keep an employer that wants to pay inadequate wages and have inadequate conditions at work," the mayor says. At a news conference, the mayor says the city comes out of the closing "quite well."

Rudy argues that it is a mistake to focus on the loss of the Swingline jobs when, on the same day, the city is announcing that the new Mercantile Exchange in the World Financial Center has preserved 8,100 jobs that might have been lost to New Jersey. A reporter asks whether the comparison is fair since the jobs at Swingline and the Mercantile Exchange affect people in different economic classes. The mayor calls the question "ignorant."

We send out a press release, "Rudy Fiddles as Swingline Burns," in the morning, and Ruth blasts Giuliani for his complacency on this issue and his record on job growth generally. Rudy responds that Ruth is in no position to criticize his record: "She was a very big supporter of the prior administration that lost 320,000 jobs and we've gained 150,000 jobs and she probably did the one single act that cost us the most jobs, which is she voted for and supported the increase in the hotel occupancy tax."

You have to hand it to the mayor, he stays on message. His answer to every criticism we make is that things are better on his watch, and certainly better than they were during the Dinkins years. As the *Economist* puts it, "The mayor's reelection plan is simple: if it is good news, embrace it and claim the credit; if it is bad news, ignore it and ridicule anyone who dares to mention it."

July 7

My best friend on the campaign, the fund-raising director, and I are having a disagreement over a letter he wants to send out as a *direct-mail solicitation* to about 55,000 people. The projection is that the letter, which will cost about $100,000 to distribute, will raise about $180,000. I am fulfilling my responsibility of reading every piece of literature sent from the campaign to make sure that it is factual and on message.

The letter is targeted to women and accuses Rudy Giuliani of sexist behavior. It begins by asking "How do you keep a good woman down?" and from there accuses Giuliani of "spitting out insults, innuendos, and labels that play into people's negative stereotypes of strong women." "'You can't count,' he yells at me. To the press, he charges, 'Her ideas are silly.' To his Republican followers he tags me as a 'far left-wing extremist.' I'm just waiting for him to call me shrill."

From my narrow perspective, I don't think we should send the letter. It's not on message, and though it's really an expression of opinion and not fact, I'm not sure it's an opinion I agree with. Rudy Giuliani may be insensitive to women, but if so, it's only because he's insensitive generally. That may not excuse it, but it's probably not sexism in the sense of the word as it is ordinarily used. And the first line seems over the top to me. The fund-raising director and his boss, a fund-raising consultant based in Washington, assure me that the letter will raise lots of money.

We take the dispute all the way to the top. The letter will go out. Money carries the day. It always does.

• • •

The *Daily News* is calling the debate over Swingline Staples "one of the most substantive campaign exchanges so far," which is remarkable because neither Rudy nor Ruth made a single constructive suggestion about how to create jobs in the city.

Having had a day to reflect, Rudy is taking a more aggressive stance on the issue. If Swingline fulfills its threat and leaves, the mayor says the city will boycott Swingline products. I imagine that must have the Swingline people shaking in their boots. If they lose the city staple account, it might nearly offset the annual salary difference for one of the 450 workers they are replacing.

July 8

One week ago, the Giuliani campaign revealed that it hired Gary Maloney, a national Republican "opposition specialist," as my counterpart (not to imply that anyone knows who I am or ever will).

In 1992, the Bush campaign sent Maloney to England to collect pictures of Bill Clinton's antiwar activities. Today, the Giuliani team fired its first direct salvo at us.

At 1:30, Lee received a call from David Lewis of the *Daily News*. The Giuliani campaign is charging that Ruth voted to raise taxes sixty-two times during her twelve-year tenure on the City Council. As a courtesy, Lewis faxes Lee a copy of the list published by the Giuliani campaign. It's an inelegant document. The words "income tax" look rather lonely at the head of the list. So do "hotel tax" and "commuter tax." There is no substantiation or description of the alleged offending votes. They don't even bother to list the dates.

That's not surprising to us, because the list is either a fabrication or based on a meaninglessly broad definition of tax. Our own review of Ruth's record came up with a dozen tax increases that she supported. It hardly seems possible that our review, which I am convinced is at least as thorough as the Giuliani camp's, could have missed fifty votes. But the charge is there, and unless we respond to it by the end of the news cycle, which is in a few hours, it will become truth. Those are the rules, and they don't allow us the luxury of asking Fran Reiter to clarify her charge.

Lee's experience in city government saves the day. Each year, to keep up with inflation, the city budget proposes increases in fees for city services. Since we know Ruth didn't vote for most of the taxes the Giuliani people are saying she did, they must have included fee increases in her budget votes on the list.

Within an hour, we have a list of thirty-five tax and fee increases the mayor imposed during his time in office. Including the subway and bus fare increase, which he did not oppose, increases the total to nearly a billion dollars. It's a preposterously silly argument, but entirely fair by the rules of the day.

July 9

We are all allowed out of the office to see the announcement speech, and the excitement among the campaign staff is palpable. For some of us, it is the first sun we have had in weeks.

The site seems less than ideal. The Lower East Side is gentrifying, but it still bears the wear and tear of decades of overcrowding and neglect. The school, which is barely visible from the street corner where Ruth is standing, seems as likely to collapse during her speech as not. It is not a scene that inspires awe.

Although the crowd will look fine for television, it seems odd that, among the two hundred or so people gathered here, there is not a single person without a pecuniary interest in attending. There are a horde of reporters and a gaggle of politicians. Most of the borough president's office staff is here, as well as Giuliani's campaign *trackers*. (Trackers are unsophisticated spies. We have one taping the mayor's events every day. He has one taping Ruth's. Today, his are cleverly disguised in sunglasses.) I recognize 75 percent of the faces in the crowd, and I hardly know anybody. Jim is standing far away, pacing back and forth, speaking angrily into his cell phone.

Ruth finally arrives, accompanied by Fernando Ferrer, who is proving to be a gracious and loyal ally. I tingle a bit in anticipation of her delivering the first line ("This is where it starts"), but sadly no one gets to hear it. It turns out that we were unable to secure a street permit, so Ruth speaks without amplification. The television cameras, which have set up microphones directly in front of her, pick up her speech fine, but the scene is surreal. Only the people closest to Ruth can hear what she is saying. The kickoff is a made-for-television event.

From there, things get worse still. Ruth is rushed off after the event, refusing to take questions from reporters, into her city limousine. The car creates an unfortunate juxtaposition with a class-based attack inserted into the speech for the first time earlier in the morning. "If you play high in the sky, send your kids to private boarding schools and go to work in big black cars, eat at the finest restaurants, Rudy is your guy. We need a mayor for the rest of us." By this logic, Rudy is Ruth's guy.

• • •

On days like today when there is a *major press hit,* all of the higher-ups gather in front of the panel of television sets to check out the *shot* on the evening news. There's a lot to be nervous about today, and the mood is generally somber.

As it turns out, most of the stations give us a break. The focus of the New York 1 story is the sound system, but, incredibly, they are the only station to mention it. Ruth seems evasive on CBS, the only station to mention the black car, which shows her ducking a question about how she plans to pay for the plans in the speech. "You don't want to do it in the sun right now," Ruth says. The traditionalists at Channel 7 focus on the size of the crowd, which, they say, wasn't bad for a midsummer day, but hardly anything to scare the mayor. They will be paying careful attention to parade turnout throughout the campaign. Two stations pull an awkward quote from the speech: "Who is Rudy Giuliani kidding? It may be that he only sees one city, the one where the powerful and the privileged live, because he's taken good care of them. The rest of us—chopped liver." I think the speechwriters intended for this to be a sound bite, so we can't really complain about the news picking it up, but I didn't like the line from the start. I argued for pickled herring.

The saddest fact of all is that more stations cover a press conference between the mayor and new Yankees pitcher Hideki Irabu than cover Ruth's announcement.

• • •

Amid all of this, a small victory for our team. Our counteraccusation receives equal billing with the Giuliani campaign's allegations in the *Daily News* tax story. Instead of a story about Ruth's tax increases, it's a story about the feistiness of the campaigns. Most important, the claim that Ruth voted for sixty-two taxes has not become a truth.

Still, the Giuliani team deserves full marks for the timing of their attacks. Their release of the comptroller's audit undermined what would have been a good day for Democrats. And if this attack had been successful, it would have undermined what should have been Ruth's most successful press day of the campaign so far. But they get help anyway. On the front page of the *Times* is a story by Adam Nagourney on the "adrift and divided" Democratic party. "Everywhere Senator Daniel Patrick Moynihan goes these days," it begins, "he runs into Democrats who will vote for a Republican for mayor of New York this year. 'Everywhere,' Mr. Moynihan said, emphasizing each syllable." In the next sentence, Ed Koch repeats that he will vote for Giuliani for mayor.

"I've been to those meetings where they discuss why did we lose," says the former mayor. "When Ruth goes down to defeat, there'll be another meeting."

The Giuliani team couldn't have written a better story themselves.

July 11

There's a lot of second-guessing going on today, which isn't good for anybody. Why did we hold the speech in Manhattan, instead of the outer boroughs? On the substantive side, why did we sound a class-based attack? And why, oh why, given that attack, did we allow Ruth to drive off in a big black car?

It's easy to fix blame on the campaign manager or the field director or the candidate herself, but I think that misses the real lesson. Campaigns, like other organizations, are bureaucratic, divided into departments with missions that do not necessarily coincide with the mission of the organization as a whole.

For example, it's a legitimate question to ask why the speech was in Manhattan. The Giuliani campaign has clearly signaled that it's planning to attack Ruth as Manhattan-centric, and our polling shows that Ruth's name recognition outside Manhattan isn't strong. The announcement speech was an important opportunity, whether real or symbolic, to expand our message to the outer boroughs. But the field staff doesn't look at it that way. Their narrow focus is to find the best shot. They need a place where a crowd can stand, that's not too big so the crowd looks bigger than it really is, and that's well framed so it will look good on television. It needs to be near a school, but not a school that's very good. And while it can be outside Manhattan, it can be only slightly so, since the press won't travel very far. By the time you take all of those considerations into account, there aren't too many choices. The field team looked all around the city and had what it felt were three possibilities. Two were in Manhattan.

Even less thought went into the limousine. Ruth's driver was never given a copy of the speech, so we can't blame him. And the rest of us in the office are so far removed from real life, we don't even think about these things. I didn't even realize Ruth had a limousine until yesterday. I thought she took the train to work.

And the speech too is the product of people with different mandates. Jim and Mandy read through it with an eye to content. Lee writes with an eye to what will get on television. My staff reviews it solely to decide whether we can substantiate the claims. One of Lee's lines was the strongest from a coverage standpoint: "You take care of Wall Street, but not your street." It was also the most class-oriented, which was not the main thrust of the speech.

By the time a speech is done, so many cooks have had a hand in it, it's easy to see how things can slip through. Even with someone at the top concentrating on synthesizing details, things like this happen as they do in any bureaucratic entity. And we don't have anyone concentrating on details.

• • •

Sal and Al are trying to drive the limousine story and, by so doing, it seems to me, are demonstrating a lack of insight. Today Al says:

> The limousine liberal Ruth Messinger cannot win this election. . . . She personifies a limousine liberal who takes carefully calculated positions, but does not speak to the issues and to the heart of people that are needed for a serious challenge against Rudy Giuliani. To come down from your Central Park West view and make periodic visits to other parts of the city is not the same as being engaged in labor fights, in fights against police brutality, in fights against discrimination.

Sal Albanese joins the chorus. "I think Al Sharpton is right, a limousine liberal is someone who is out of touch with average voters. She has as much in common with average New Yorkers as the man in the moon."

Sharpton and Albanese may be doing this to just get their names in the news, which is fine, but if they're making this attack for substantive reasons, which I suspect they are, they're missing an important point. Overwhelming evidence shows that no one cares about the contradictions between politicians' private lives and their public positions. Bill Clinton can be an adulterer who supports family values. It's fine for Al D'Amato to be a sleaze, so long as he delivers for New York. The most visible liberal in the

United States, Ted Kennedy, rides in a limousine. People simply don't care about a politician's private life.

The real damage from the black-car mistake is that it contributes to an impression, fed by the Giuliani campaign, that our campaign is sloppy and inept. Voters may not admit their reluctance to elect women, but history shows that they privately believe women are not, all other things being equal, effective managers. Rather than decry her as a limousine liberal, our primary opponents would do better to quietly whisper to reporters off the record, "Geez, if she can't manage her own campaign, how can she manage the city?" Let that one filter out there for a while and see how much damage it does.

• • •

Perhaps we are completely paranoid, but Lee keenly notes that the *Times* has cropped its front-page picture of the announcement speech so that Ruth's head appears in front of the letters "MESS," cutting off the "INGER."

July 12

An absolute barrage of favorable press. On Thursday, Gail Collins of the *New York Times* said that Democrats have been too quick to desert Ruth Messinger:

> The defecting Democrats are right when they say Ms. Messinger has been a terrible candidate so far. Yesterday she announced her candidacy with a speech that contained not a single surprising word, in front of about 100 people, most of them campaign workers, former city officials of the David Dinkins era and other political hostages. . . . The freshest issue the speech raised was why Ms. Messinger, who must continually fight to prove she has a base outside Manhattan, decided to deliver it on the Lower East Side.

But Collins is firmly on our side. "Predictable speeches and bad event planning in July are not crippling defects for a mayoral campaign."

On Friday, the *Post* said that Ruth's "populist chord" is a direct challenge to Wall Street, which can easily pick up and move elsewhere. "So if Messinger wants to tell Wall Streeters—as hard-working and productive a group of individuals as one can find anywhere in the city or the country—that their efforts are not welcome here, she's off to a fine start."

Today, the *News* endorses Ruth for mayor—of Mars. "In a 17 minute yadayadayada on Manhattan's Lower East Side (quick, somebody give her a map to the other four boroughs), Messinger aimed to paint Mayor Giuliani as the protector of the rich. Who wrote her speech, Barnacle Bill? Only a Martian rock could produce blather so trite. And wrong." The *News* abandons the confusing metaphors for a moment, then recounts how wonderful things are in the city.

"In a silly '60s sci-fi movies [*sic*]," the *News* concludes, "a scientist says in a halting staccato that said 'Mars. Needs. Women. [*sic*]' With her mishmash of platitudes and lack of new ideas, Messinger qualifies as the frontrunner. Earth to Ruth."

I guess this is what Jim means by a *fucking hostile press environment.* But I've had my revenge on the *News* today. I sicced them twice. In one paragraph.

July 13

Further bons mots today from our $1,200-a-month consultant:

> BUTTONS/POSTERS: Emphasizing the use of "Ruth" alone is a problem—it is too close to "Rudy." It even "looks" like "Rudy." As presently designed the button from 20 feet away it could be a "Rudy" button. Since part of our problem is getting her to be better known, I have to express concern about emphasizing the first name over "Messinger" (although I do admit I am very biased in favor of using the last name on everything—particularly in the Black community).

Why is "looks" in quotes?

He also recommends that Ruth "lose the city car for campaign appearances/events prior to the primary election." This month our consultant earned his $1,200.

July 14

With the announcement speech behind us, we've stepped up the frequency of Ruth's public appearances. But we're not getting any television coverage, which is a cause for great concern. Yesterday Ruth went to a domestic violence shelter and blasted the mayor's handling of the New Day Battered Women's Shelter crisis. Today, she went to the city's Emergency Assistance Unit in the Bronx where homeless families are often forced to spend the night on the floor. On both days, we only crack New York 1 and even then, only on the *Road to City Hall,* which is seen by fewer people than the hourly news. And there's no indication that this is an aberration. It's not that we're being cut at the last minute; the cameras aren't showing up at all.

July 15

An item in the paper this morning that probably not a single other person in the city cared about: A congressional committee is in town to hold a hearing with businesspeople and city groups to suggest ways to use Governors Island. Privately, we wonder whether the Giuliani campaign is considering the same proposal we are. There's no incentive for the mayor's people to introduce that level of randomness into the campaign, and nothing any of them are saying publicly gives any indication they're thinking in those terms, but then again nothing we're saying publicly would tip anyone off either. It would be a shame if they beat us to the punch. Of course, if they did, we'd come out strong against it. And vice-versa, I imagine.

• • •

Nothing else in the campaign may work well, but our fund-raising is going great. The latest Campaign Finance Board filings show us with an enormous lead over our Democratic rivals. Ruth raised $1.2 million during the first half of the year. She has now raised a total of $3.1 million, of which $1.3 million is in the bank (an additional $1.2 million in matching funds will be arriving shortly). Over the same period, Sal Albanese raised $167,316 for a total of $472,271, of which he has $250,000 in the bank. Al Sharpton is in debt. He has raised $104,000, but spent $166,000.

Giuliani's fund-raising dwarfs us all, of course. He has raised a total of $8.5 million. But is the Giuliani campaign spending the money too early? According to their reports, they've already spent nearly $2 million this year, including $400,000 on ads, $120,000 on polls (we, by contrast, have spent $40,000 on polls) and $110,000 on a Lincoln Center fund-raiser featuring several opera stars.

July 16

We all have our vices. Ruth's is making phone calls to union leaders. She's locked in a closet raising money for six hours a day and scheduled for public appearances another eight, but that does not diminish her enthusiasm at all. In similar circumstances, you or I might burst out of our shackles when the chance arose and dance shirtless in the rain. When Ruth Messinger has a free moment, she telephones labor leaders. As far as I can tell, she delights in it. She keeps a cellular phone tucked away in her bag like a sinful chocolate bar or the Daily Racing Form and returns to it whenever she can. This is her act of defiance. This is her way of playing what she considers real politics in a world where people tell her that money and television are the only things that matter.

Despite her efforts, the union story is not getting any better. District Council 37, the largest local union, with 119,000 city employees, was solidly behind David Dinkins in 1989 and 1993, but they seem likely to remain neutral this year. Some of the individual local municipal unions may even endorse the mayor. The teachers' union is looking more and more like it will remain neutral.

The obvious question is why. City unions have traditionally rallied behind Democrats in mayoral elections. They worked actively for Dinkins in both his elections, so it's clear this isn't a function of their personal affinity for the mayor. Why the change from 1989 to 1993? One answer is that for all of his tough talk during the 1993 campaign, Giuliani has gone to some pains to placate labor. A little-noticed provision in the recent pact with the teachers' union exempts teachers from cafeteria and hallway duty. That change will cost the city about $70 million. It is also a windfall for Local 372, the 19,000-member union of Board of Education kitchen workers and school aides, which recently announced its endorsement of Giuliani.

Charles Hughes, the head of Local 372, is Giuliani's appointee to the Equal Employment Practices Commission (EEPC), which means he earns a city bonus on top of his $224,000 union salary. Hughes has not been diligent in his work, though. The EEPC is charged with auditing city agencies for compliance with affirmative-action laws. Comptroller Hevesi recently concluded that the EEPC had failed to audit 93 percent of the city agencies under its supervision.

Firefighters won a 15.6-percent pay hike and an extra week's vacation in their recently concluded negotiations with the city. Earlier, Giuliani had restored a fifth man to firefighter pumping companies, a practice Ed Koch had reversed, calling it a ruse to increase overtime pay. The firefighters' union strongly supported Giuliani in 1993 and is endorsing him again this year. The former head of the union is now Giuliani's fire commissioner. Ray Horton, the head of the Citizens Budget Commission, says that nothing has changed in the way city services are delivered under Giuliani.

But Giuliani's alleged coziness with unions is at most part of the answer. It might be part of the explanation for the endorsements by unions in a few particular cases, but it can't explain the larger picture, which is that Rudy has the endorsement of just about every major union, and we have none. A more powerful explanation is that no one believes that we have any chance of winning. It's here where our loss of the metabattle on our prospects is really hurting us. My guess is that most people think Ruth has somewhere between a one-in-a-hundred and a one-in-a-million chance of winning. If people believed that she had a one-in-ten chance of winning, which is approximately what we estimate her chances to be, they might be inclined to act somewhat differently. Many union leaders tell Ruth, explicitly or implicitly, that, as they see it, they will have to deal with Giuliani for another four years and that it is in the best interest of their membership not to get on his bad side during the election.

We're losing the battle over expectations so thoroughly that no one even feels a need to hedge bets. People think the mayor will win, and they think they need to stay on his good side. That affects how the press treats the candidates, it dampens our fund-raising, and it scares off unions. It's a vicious cycle. The perception that the race is noncompetitive will become a self-fulfilling prophecy unless we reverse it. It could just as easily work the other way. The trick is for us to find someone who will listen.

July 17

The concept of message is deliberative. All ideas are polled. The ideas that poll well are tested again to find the best formulation. Once the right ideas are stated in the right way, the candidate is charged with repeating the ideal formulation over and over again for months. The concept of message is not one that comes naturally to a human being, especially one who has an independent thought from time to time such as Ruth.

Operating within message is a frustrating constraint, and it is behavior that is not easily reinforced. The benefits of staying on message are incremental and often imperceptible. As with those on a workout program or a diet, on-message candidates know what they are doing is good for them, but don't get to see day-to-day results. At the same time, the downside of going off message is the sort of high-consequence, low-probability risk that human beings tend to discount. Jim often warns that going off message can *blow up a candidacy,* but it's the sort of cataclysmic event not easily comprehended. Today there are examples of the turtlelike progress on-message candidates can make and the near-fatal damage they can do to themselves with a single misstep.

A bizarre little game campaigns play is trying to generate headlines in newspapers that can be used in television ads. A campaign can use its own money to make any argument it wants about itself or its opponent, but the arguments carry a lot more weight when they're substantiated by newspapers. A *New York Times* headline "D'Amato on the Take" is more credible than the same headline in the *Post,* which is, in turn, more credible than a graphic generated by the media consultant saying the same thing. If a candidate racks up enough endorsements, the campaign will sometimes run an ad doing nothing more than broadcasting the headlines of the endorsements to people who may not have read them in the paper. That won't be a possibility for us, so we need favorable headlines all the more.

Today we get a nice headline in the *Daily News*: "Open Schools Till 6—Ruth." It's a short statement of Ruth's idea, announced yesterday, to keep all of the city's public schools open until 6:00 so that children will have a place to go after the end of the school day. The idea tested well in our polls, and we had planned the speech for several weeks. The headline succinctly captures the idea, which is simplified to begin with. It will make one of our ads slightly more credible. That is the inch of progress we made today by staying on message.

We went several miles backward when Ruth suggested to a reporter that she thought there was merit to the idea that city teachers should be paid on par with their suburban counterparts. It's an innocuous statement really. Ruth didn't say she would double pay for teachers if elected. She merely suggested that one way to improve schools would be to pay teachers enough to keep the best ones in the city. It would be especially important to put more money on the table if the expectations of teachers were elevated.

It is clearly an idea that merits discussion, but from a political standpoint one Ruth derives no advantage from being associated with. When we asked voters to rank various ideas to improve the public schools, the idea of raising pay for city teachers came in a distant fifth. And it opens Ruth to the charge that she's just another spendthrift liberal with no concept of how to pay for her noble ideas. And that's just where Fran Reiter goes in response.

"We have a limited budget," Reiter says. "You can't keep going back to the well. You have to make choices. . . . That's called governing. She is trying to present herself as St. Ruth. I see her as the mayor from Mars. This is total fantasyland." It's the logical play, though the whole mayor-from-Mars thing is wearing thin.

July 18

On the heels of her teacher-pay-parity proposal, Ruth is asked whether she favors pay parity for police officers and firefighters, who are also paid far less than their suburban counterparts. I haven't been present for any strategic discussion of the issue, and as far as I know there has been none. Ruth's response shows a great deal about her instincts.

From a message standpoint, the right answer to the question is to say that teachers are an exceptional case and that city schools present an unique problem. The idea of pay parity for teachers didn't poll especially well, but it won't do Ruth any direct harm. School reform is the enterprise of our campaign. Raising teacher pay is defensible as an exceptional response to a dire problem. We never even bothered to poll the idea of parity for other unions. We'll be charged with generating even more costly proposals on matters of no relevance to our message. There will be no offsetting benefit. But from a traditional politician's point of view, the answer should be yes. It's what the union leaders and members want to hear.

Ruth says yes, though it's an equivocal expression of support for the idea of discussing the idea. On one view, Ruth's equivocation means that she wants only to discuss the idea in connection with extracting productivity gains from the union, an unobjectionable idea. On another, it means that she wants the constituency benefit of supporting the idea, but also to be able to claim it shouldn't be charged to her bill.

Adam Nagourney calls it "the latest in a series of costly initiatives [Ruth] has proposed during an intensified week of campaigning for City Hall." The mayor's budget office produces a calculation showing that Ruth's proposed pay increases will cost the city $5 billion. Fran Reiter says, "Add it to the laundry list of the Mayor of Fantasyland."

• • •

According to our polls, there are only three people whose endorsements matter in New York City: Bill Clinton, Bill Bratton, and Ed Koch. Clinton is an overwhelmingly popular figure. His approval mix is 69–18 favorable. Ruth was an early supporter of Clinton, and we're likely to have his help if we make it through the primary. Bill Bratton is less well known than Clinton, but his ratio, 37–7, is even better than the president's. Bratton's endorsement would be especially useful to Ruth to solidify her record on crime.

Ruth has met with the former police commissioner a few times, but he doesn't seem likely to endorse. In spite of his public disagreements with Giuliani and his thought of running for mayor himself, I think Bratton thinks Giuliani is a good mayor.

Ed Koch's endorsement is up for grabs and, though the odds are strongly against Koch endorsing her, Ruth has been pursuing the endorsement vigorously. It would be a huge boost to the campaign. The former mayor lost his bid for a fourth term in 1989, but remains one of the most respected figures in New York. His favorable/unfavorable ratio is 55–22. Twenty-three percent of New Yorkers view him strongly favorably versus 10 percent who view him strongly negatively. David Dinkins, by contrast, is viewed strongly negatively by 21 percent of the people and strongly positively by only 14 percent.

Koch is omnipresent around the city, engaged in a tireless campaign to remain, as he calls it, relevant. He writes a weekly column in the *Post*, reviews movies for a chain of neighborhood newspapers, teaches at New York University, appears regularly on local news programs, and just signed a contract to be the judge on a revival of *The People's Court.* Listening to his daily call-in show on WABC radio is one of the highlights of our day. Koch modestly refers to himself as the "voice of reason" and regularly refers to his callers as "stupid" or "ignorant." It's great radio. Sort of Howard Stern meets politics.

Ruth was one of Ed Koch's harshest critics, and he is accordingly no great fan of Messinger's. But he is no great fan of Giuliani's either. Koch endorsed Giuliani in 1993, but the mayor seriously offended Koch by ending the merit judicial selection system that was one of Koch's proudest accomplishments. Giuliani, Koch says, "is a ruthless control freak who governs by imposing a state of terror on members of his administration and claiming credit for accomplishments he had nothing to do with." Koch even thinks Ruth has a chance, comparing her lackluster start to his own beginning in 1977.

In his column today in the *Post*, Koch outlines ten planks for Messinger's platform that he sees as the keys to her victory. They range from the commonsensical ("state she will continue Giuliani's policies on law enforcement") to the obscure ("request that the City Council adopt 'question time,' like British Parliament") to the parochial (restore the merit-based judicial selection system).

"Can Ruth confound the pundits in '97?" Koch asks. "You bet," he says, citing his own rise from obscurity in 1977 as evidence.

But Koch won't be voting for Ruth. "In choosing between Giuliani's character and some of his policies and Messinger's sterling character but flawed policies and public record as Council member and borough president, there is no contest. Giuliani has done a magnificent job in reducing crime."

July 19

Jim believes the fundamental dynamic at work in a race of this sort is that the challenger must prove why the incumbent should be fired. A corollary of this belief is that it's better to attack than defend. As a result, we've spent a great deal more time criticizing the mayor than offering constructive thoughts as to what a Messinger administration would do differently. That's not Ruth's natural impulse. She's incredibly smart and has nuanced ideas about what she would do differently at levels of remarkable detail. She's able on demand to offer thoughtful suggestions about how to change even small city agencies. But with some notable exceptions, she's lived, if uncomfortably, by Jim's edict because it makes good sense. At the level of generality at which politicians interact with voters, there aren't that many new ideas. Whatever Ruth says, Rudy will either respond that he's done it or that the idea proves yet again how liberal Ruth is.

A candidate has to advance a platform at some point, though, and there's considerable pressure mounting on us to say at the very least how we plan on paying for some of the proposals Ruth has laid out.

That's no small task, especially if you accept the Giuliani camp's estimate that we've already run up a price tag of $5 billion. There's no reason for us to buy into that exaggerated figure, but we can't come up with chump change either. We're going to need to come up with ideas totaling in the billion-dollar range if the speech is going to have any credibility. And we can't simply wave a wand and say we'll eliminate waste, because we're running against a man who has a reputation as a merciless budget cutter. We need new ideas, and it's been my job for the past week to find them. Jim wants Ruth to deliver a major policy address next week outlining her plans to cut the city budget.

There aren't a lot of new ideas out there. The truth, sad for us, is that sound fiscal management doesn't depend on new ideas, but rather the sound implementation of old ideas. The best ideas I find stem from a report by an independent city watchdog group called the Citizens Budget Commission. One idea is to introduce competition into some city services. By allowing private companies to compete against city agencies to provide services like trash collection and road repair, the idea is that market forces will increase efficiency and drive prices down. Several cities have experimented with the idea and realized significant savings. Realistically, it could save the city $450 million a year. I've also outlined some reorganization of city agencies (the details are arcane) that could save about $50 million. These are sound ideas and not too controversial, but they only get us halfway to the $1-billion goal.

The remaining big-ticket items are a little trickier. One idea advocated by the Citizens Budget Commission is to increase the civilian workweek from thirty-five to thirty-seven and a half hours per week. It's a perfectly reasonable idea—most other cities and states require employees to work at least that number of hours—but, unlike the other ideas, it's not something within the mayor's power to do. Work rules are the product of hard bargaining with municipal unions; they're not easily changed.

Most of the other ideas of significant value would have to be bargained with labor. A proposal to eliminate fifteen minutes of what is known as wash-up time for police and corrections officers, the Budget Commission's recommendation to cut down on the prevalent use of police officers for administrative jobs, and a proposal to staff patrol cars with one officer instead of two during daylight hours would all have to be agreed to by unions.

None of the ideas are popular within the office. At a meeting today, the only idea that enjoys consensus is the privatization of city services. Lee thinks the speech will be read as an attack against pattern bargaining (treating different unions similarly), which he regards as a mistake. Ruth doesn't want to attack the corrections officers, who she thinks may still endorse her. They are cut from the wash-up time proposal. Jim and Ruth both veto the single-officer patrol car idea out of fear it would feed the weak-on-crime argument.

But the downside of any of the ideas is dwarfed by the consequences of our not coming up with a serious proposal to pay for programs we've outlined in the past weeks. We have $1.1 billion in budget-cutting ideas and a ton of liabilities.

Jim asks me how the speech will be regarded.

"Soft on crime," I say.

"Forsaking unions," he says.

But it will be worth it just to put an end to those insufferable Mars analogies.

• • •

The pay-parity proposal certainly isn't scoring any points in the press. A *New York Times* editorial says today, "Ideally, everyone would like to see teachers, firefighters, and police receive higher pay. But Ms. Messinger's vague rhetoric is raising false hopes for the workers and setting the campaign off in exactly the wrong direction."

The *Times* "shares Ms. Messinger's concern that the city is losing its best educators to the suburbs, where pay is much higher, classes are smaller and conditions are more pleasant." It also "welcomes her hints that she would expect higher standards and more accountability from the higher-paid teachers of the future." Ruth's sin is that "her blueprint for how to get there has been extremely vague and her language sloppy."

For that reason, the *Times* concludes, "The talk about parity with the suburbs may just be Ms. Messinger's attempt to mend her bridges with a little old-fashioned Democratic pandering. If so, she is playing right into conservative claims that liberals can no longer govern New York City."

The *News* says Ruth's campaign slogan should be "Spare any change?" "That would be a good mantra for a Messinger administration—because that's the only way she will find the money to pay for such raids on the city treasury." Both papers have accepted the Giuliani campaign's claim that Ruth's proposals will cost $5 billion. We didn't challenge the figure within a day, so now it is fact.

July 20

Our decision to base so much of our campaign on criticism of the public schools creates the dilemma of what to say about the chancellor, Rudy Crew. Crew is popular and black, which makes him an unattractive figure to attack, but it would undermine the credibility of our arguments to exempt Crew from criticism. Our strategy is to direct our arguments to the mayor as much as possible, but not to embrace Crew. Last week, Ruth said that she could work with Crew, but would not commit to keeping him on.

The Giuliani campaign tells Nagourney that they regard the decision to distance Messinger from Crew as a mistake. The implication of the statement is that they regard it a mistake from the standpoint of race, but their agenda may be much simpler. Rudy Giuliani needs any help he can get on the schools issue. In a new radio ad, Giuliani is embracing Crew. "When a mother comes up to me and says, 'Thank you Rudy, for fighting back to save our schools,' I tell her you should thank another Rudy—Schools Chancellor Rudy Crew." It's an unremarkable ad except in one respect: Mayor Rudolph W. Giuliani is sharing credit with someone. I will only note the irony that it is in connection with one of the things that works least well in the city.

• • •

A quick check on the alternative reality in the black press. According to the *Amsterdam News*, the Independence party is on its way to unseating incumbents citywide. "Unless this political observer has somehow abandoned his calling completely and 'lost it,'" writes *Amsterdam News* publisher Wilbert A. Tatum, "political sea changes are taking place before our very eyes, and it has hardly been noticed by major or minor media. . . . The Independence Party, of Ross Perot fame, is fielding 50 or so candidates this year in all of the five boroughs. It is highly unlikely that they will lose, or make a miserable showing in all of them."

Topping the Independence party ticket is Abe Hirschfeld, an eccentric seventy-eight-year-old real-estate developer who owned the *New York Post* for two glorious weeks in 1993 (and hired Tatum to edit the paper for the fortnight). Hirschfeld, who is also running on the Republican line, is under a 123-count state indictment alleging he ran a $2.2-million tax-fraud scheme; he entered his plea of not guilty just five days before announcing his candidacy. His adviser is former Whitman campaign manager Ed Rollins.

The occasion of Tatum's article is the Independence party's political season kickoff event. I don't know what its strategists discussed substantively, but there is fascinating insight into their view of what makes politics work. Lenora Fulani, who Tatum says "could teach Politics 101 through 105 to the least of us without working up a sweat," was at the meeting "to organize." Tatum says, "The key to winning in these next few elections is to organize."

Guess they won't be running any television commercials.

July 21

Major Owens, a congressman from Brooklyn, makes the charge that sexism is hurting Ruth's campaign. Though that view is often discussed, Owens is the first to raise it publicly. (Our fund-raising letter won't hit mailboxes for several weeks yet.) In a letter to Assembly Speaker Sheldon Silver and Comptroller Carl McCall, Owens complains of "rampant sexism" in the Democratic party. He warns that the Democrats are "disintegrating into two parties—one male and one female" and that "the subversion and destruction of the Democratic party in New York City will negatively seal the fate of any Democratic candidate for governor or senator."

Owens's remarks implicate politicians, but raise the larger issue of sexism generally. Is the press sexist? Are voters sexist? The only thing that can be conclusively said about women in New York political horse races is that they start out with a twenty-pound handicap. The evidence on this count is overwhelming. An entire generation of women have been driven out of city politics. Former congresswoman Bella Abzug is now president of the non-profit Women's Environmental and Development Organization. Former City Council president Carol Bellamy now directs UNICEF. Geraldine Ferraro is a host on the CNN program *Crossfire*. Liz Holtzman is now a practicing lawyer and radio talk-show host. And they're all much better off than former consumer affairs commissioner Bess Myerson, whose fall from grace was precipitated by Rudy Giuliani.

Liz Holtzman recalls her 1981 campaign to become the first female New York district attorney to the *Village Voice* this week. She says, "They ran this explicitly sexist campaign against me. 'Liz Holtzman is a very nice girl'... and this woman got on saying they might like me for a daughter, but not for a D.A."

• • •

Figuring out what to say is not nearly as hard as finding the opportunities to say it. Television advertising is like a message wild card. The candidate gets to think about what he or she wants to say, tests the idea in polls and focus groups, and packages the statement in the absolutely most favorable light. That is message in its purist form—campaign Nirvana—but bliss doesn't come cheap. So every politician looks for free opportunities to advance his or her own individual message—and those don't come easy. If you're the president of the United States, everything you have to say, no matter how trivial, is news. Everyone else has to make do with opportunities as they come along, and it isn't always clear how to deal with them.

Part of what we've been trying to argue during these past few months is that there is a human cost attached to the gains of the Giuliani administration. "The cuts, the cuts, we need to remind them about the cuts," Jim says from time to time. If it is legitimate for the Giuliani people to paint Ruth as a spendthrift liberal, then it is fair for us to remind the voters that in the process of running nice budget surpluses and reducing crime, they've sold off a little bit of the Big Apple's soul. That's easy to say in the abstract, but hard to illustrate with concrete examples.

Yesterday federal officials uncovered a horrifying story in Queens: More than fifty-seven deaf Mexican immigrants were sleeping toe to toe in a Queens apartment that was being used as the home of a forced labor program. From dawn to dusk, the deaf immigrants sold key chains and trinkets in subways and on streets and gave the money to their captors, who followed them throughout the day and hunted them down if they did not return at night. A city building inspector checked the apartment where the immigrants were being held a few months ago and found nothing wrong with the living conditions.

Like every other human being in New York City, Rudy Giuliani is horrified by the situation. As always, he's there on the spot, expressing outrage at the situation and at the apparent negligence of the Department of Buildings. But there's an argument to be made here. According to the mayor's own statistics, housing and building inspections are down, a result of cuts to the Department of Housing Preservation and Development and the Buildings Department. It's just the tip of the iceberg of diminished social services.

But is it right to blame the mayor for this incident? Not even the most cynical among us believes that the mayor wanted something like this to happen. But, at the same time, that didn't stop Rudy Giuliani from pinning the blame for Crown Heights on David Dinkins, who just as surely did not want anyone to be killed during those fateful days.

We decide that the context and timing aren't right. The mayor has a certain credibility on the immigrant issue. He has been vigorously opposing a federal law that requires city officials to turn in illegal immigrants who seek city services. And if we get into a debate with him on this, it will deflect attention from Ruth's budget speech tomorrow, which is an important opportunity for our campaign to regain some credibility.

July 22

It's good that politicians write speeches, but it's really a waste of everyone's time to read them aloud. Everyone would be better off if the candidates simply copied a speech and handed it out to the press saying, "Here, this is what I believe on this subject." Reading the speeches is tedious and pointless. There is no drama when members of Congress stand in front of an empty chamber after midnight reading things into the Congressional Record. The hundred or so people gathered at the monthly meeting of the Fourteenth Street Business Improvement District seem bored. Fran Reiter seems bored. And they didn't have to work through a dozen drafts of the speech. I'm bored out of my mind.

I spend most of Ruth's speech looking over at Reiter, who is seated at the table next to me. Little does she know that she is only meters away from Ruth Messinger's research director, out this morning on another clandestine field assignment. I feel sad for Reiter. She stares off into space throughout most of the speech without scribbling down so much as a note. My guess is that she's probably wondering, as I am, when she'll next be able to get eight hours sleep.

The aftermath of the speech, however, is anything but calm. When campaigns propose new ideas, it is incumbent upon them to offer *independent verification*—ostensibly objective third parties to attest to the reasonableness of the proposals. We've lined up two prominent people—and advertised their willingness to talk to the press—but neither is coming through. Ray Horton, the head of the Citizens Budget Commission, is on Fire Island and is perturbed when the *New York Times* calls. And Robert Kiley, the chairman of the New York City Partnership, says he won't endorse the ideas. It's not entirely clear where we went wrong. Ruth spoke to both men about the speech, and they both said the ideas were sound. (Horton should. Four-fifths of the speech is based on Citizens Budget Commission proposals.) Ruth relayed Kiley's and Horton's enthusiasm for the ideas to Lee and Jim. Based on their enthusiasm, someone concluded that they would be willing to talk to the press in support of the speech. No one, however, took the important additional step of specifically asking Kiley and Horton whether they would be willing to be called. That was a mistake.

At 5:00, Ruth is on the phone pleading desperately with Robert Kiley to simply say that our ideas are reasonable. Without much exaggeration, she tells Kiley, "The credibility of my campaign depends on it." These are not simply prominent people who have refused to endorse our ideas. These are people to whom we directed the press. Kiley refuses, and for the rest of the day the mood in the office is sullen. Adam Nagourney will not be able to resist writing about a screw-up of this magnitude. All of our good work on the speech will amount to nothing more than another example of our ineptitude, and our best opportunity to regain some credibility will be lost because two men weren't willing to say that our ideas aren't crazy.

July 23

To the great relief of all, the press on the speech is kind. The lead editorial of the *Times* praises Ruth for "a speech on budget issues that dared to state some hard truths about the way New York City delivers its services." It continues, "If she can make her party, which is often captive to special interests, an advocate of government that is compassionate, fair, and efficient at the same time, this campaign could be a valuable one." It is the first favorable editorial our campaign has received from any newspaper in the city.

Adam Nagourney's article is entirely fair. It quotes municipal labor-union leader Stanley Hill saying Ruth is "playing a real divisive game." And the Giuliani people are saying the only way to save money on police is to fire police officers. But that's all fair game. The *Times* gives us two columns on the front page and a nice headline.

The other newspapers don't feature the story as prominently. The *News* and *Newsday* bury it, and the *Post* mentions the speech only in an article reporting results of a New York 1 poll that shows Giuliani carrying a 57–34 lead. (The poll is bad news. Six weeks ago they had the race at 49–41. Rudy's ads are having an effect.) The *Post* questions whether Ruth should drop out of the race. But all in all it's more than we could have asked for. The speech was directed at *Times* readers. The rest is gravy.

But that was this morning. By 2:00, we're on our heels again. Having had a day to think, the Giuliani people have decided that we would have to lay off eight thousand police officers to achieve the savings we're talking about in the police department. They've offered no proof for the charge, and when candidate Giuliani proposed the exact same ideas in 1993, he didn't seem to think they would require firing a single police officer at all. But even still, the press is treating their charge seriously.

Lee is seeking input on how to respond to the press. Jim says to tell the papers unequivocally that the charge is a lie and that Ruth would not have to lay off a single police officer under her plan. But that isn't an entirely accurate answer either. The idea behind the Citizens Budget Commission proposal is to replace police officers at desk jobs with cheaper civilians. Since the plan is to phase the change in over time, no police officers would need to be laid off, but years down the road there would be fewer cops on the force. If police officers at desk jobs were simply shifted to the streets, the city would have a nice big police force, but it wouldn't have saved any money. The city would be paying civilian salaries on top of the police salaries it already pays. The only way to save money is to have the civilians replace police officers. This doesn't reduce the number of officers on the streets, since the civilians are replacing police officers at desk jobs and not on the beat. But it does reduce the total number of police officers on the force. The problem is, we don't have the luxury of making that nuanced distinction to the people. All we get it is a sentence. So Lee tells the papers that the charge is a lie and that Ruth would not have to lay off a single police officer under her plan.

• • •

On the eighth page of the Metro section of the *New York Times* is a four-paragraph blurb in smaller than normal type reporting that the city unemployment rate topped 10 percent in June. In December 1991, when the unemployment rate last crossed into double digits, the *Times* story on it, which ran two pages, was on the front page. None of the other papers even bother to cover it.

The city's economic recovery is not being evenly shared. The boom is a house of cards. But how can we prove that to the voters when the press won't even acknowledge that bad news exists?

July 24

Tonight we are in the trenches of modern political warfare. We are neither leafleting the streets nor negotiating in a smoke-filled back room with political leaders. We are in a posh office building on Madison Avenue. This is where the war is really fought.

The crew is relaxed. Mandy is fresh from a weekend in Martha's Vineyard. Jim is recently back from Chicago. Geoff is just in from D.C. Mandy, Jim, and I are comfortably seated behind a glass window where we will watch twelve men and women react to drafts *(dubs)* of the commercials we are contemplating running. There is chicken Caesar salad, a plate of warm cookies, and soft drinks in abundance. It is deceptively comfortable for what is at stake. It doesn't feel much like politics, but this event, and three others like it, will fundamentally shape our campaign advertising strategy.

This is a focus group. Advertisers use focus groups to test products and see how people react to commercials touting their wares. Political campaigns use them to provide a qualitative supplement to the quantitative information polls supply. Poll data is more important for determining positions on major issues, but focus groups are used by campaigns to make more nuanced decisions. Do people react well to the candidate's image and voice? How receptive are people to negative advertisements? Polls tell you what people believe; focus groups tell you why they believe it.

I am a skeptic on focus groups. Polls seem quasi-scientific to me at best, but at least the data there are based on several hundred people. We're about to make decisions on the basis of what fifty people have to say. And they won't be giving us true individual impressions. Group dynamics can play a huge role. But Geoff Garin, who is one of President Clinton's pollsters and does more than a hundred focus groups a year, tells me that if he only had $10,000 to spend on a campaign, he would rather have a focus group than a poll.

Tonight's focus group is an important one for us. All eleven people are middle- to lower-middle-class whites. One person is a doorman. Two are medical secretaries. Another manages a hardware store. These are the *movable* voters. These are the people with whom we need to make inroads.

Geoff begins by asking the group how they feel about Mayor Giuliani. On a scale of 1 to 100, the marks range from 45 to 80. The average score is

52. "Dictator," "backslapper," and "arrogant" are some of the words that come to mind as these people describe the mayor, all of whom are convinced that he is a former district attorney.

Virtually no one knows anything about Ruth. Julie, a secretary from Queens with two kids, says that on a scale of 1 to 100 of familiarity with Ruth, she is a 3. The average score is 18. The person who claims the best knowledge in the group thinks she is the borough president of Queens. When Geoff asks who everyone would vote for if the election were today, Ruth wins 6 to 5, which is interesting considering that no one knows who she is.

Geoff then shows the group a series of ads. It is a simulation of what the ad campaign might look like. It starts with Rudy's education ad and includes dubs of hypothetical Giuliani ads, including an especially good one linking Ruth with Dinkins ("Don't go back"). Interspersed are several potential Messinger ads. One focuses on Giuliani's education cuts and shows kids attending class in a bathroom. Three others feature insensitive quotes from Giuliani on education, homelessness ("The homeless will eventually figure out it's easier to be homeless where it's warm"), and minorities (good ol' "They're alive, aren't they? How 'bout we start with that"). Three ads show Ruth speaking directly to the camera on domestic violence, poverty, and overcrowding, some of which invite viewers to write in for copies of her plans to make things better. Another ad discusses making city workers work more hours per week. A final ad discusses the Governors Island gambling proposal.

The nine Messinger ads have a significant cumulative effect, but it's not of the magnitude we would have hoped. When Geoff asks people to rate their feelings about Ruth on a scale of 1 to 100 for a second time, four people's ratings remain unchanged after having seen the commercials, which are skewed in our favor. Seven of the remaining eight slide only one number higher in favor of Ruth. When Geoff asks the group to vote again, Ruth wins by the same 6 to 5 vote.

A few things emerge clearly from the focus group. First, the absolute value of a negative ad is far greater than that of a positive ad. The group members unanimously react more to the bathroom ad and the quotes ad than they do to ads with Ruth talking about education and homelessness in a positive manner. When I suggest this general proposition to Mandy, she agrees wholeheartedly. There's a good reason campaigns rely so heavily on negative ads: They get more bang per buck.

Second, the bathroom ad is our strongest commercial by far. It draws an audible gasp from the assembly. The image of kids learning in bathrooms is powerful. As a general proposition, people are receptive to any argument

we make about education. They believe all of the quotes and believe that kids really do go to class in bathrooms. They think, 9–2, that Ruth would do a better job with the schools than Rudy.

Confirming what the polls said, the gambling idea is indeed a winner. Some people like the idea because it will increase money for the schools, but most just seem to like the idea of having casinos nearby. One woman nods vigorously during the Governors Island commercial and says she'll vote for Ruth just so she doesn't have to go to Atlantic City.

The final thing is that Ruth's appearance is a liability. Julie, a bookkeeper from Brooklyn with two children, says, "I don't like to look at her. She irritates me. She's not pleasant to look at." Everyone nods in agreement.

• • •

The second group of the evening goes about the same.

"What words would you use to describe Ruth Messinger?" Geoff asks.

The responses are not encouraging.

"Unattractive. Angular. Tired. Stressed out. Strident. Ultra-liberal."

This group is a bit more upscale than the first, as evidenced by the surprising emergence of the word "angular." Robert, a carpenter from Manhattan, says that he is completely undecided. He approves of Rudy somewhat, but education is his main concern, and he doesn't think that Rudy has done a very good job on the schools.

"Will we get him?" Mandy asks, wondering whether the series of ads will persuade the carpenter to swing to Ruth.

"If we don't, we're dead," Jim says.

We don't get him.

July 25

The Voice of Reason is buying into the mayor's formulation of Ruth's budget proposal, which is not good news. On his radio program this morning, Ed Koch calls Ruth's plan "dumb" and says he "doesn't want to get fewer cops." Not surprisingly, the Giuliani people are staying on the issue for another day. "Frankly," the mayor says at his morning press conference, "I think she just created a whole new campaign issue for us, of major proportions. I would love to have a debate over cutting seven thousand cops."

"She has to accept!" exclaims Jim, when our tracker tells him of the remark. Within an hour, Ruth writes the mayor (yes, another letter) and takes him up on his offer. The mayor, unsurprisingly, retracts the challenge. No sane front-runner would ever give an opponent the free publicity of an extra debate. For some reason, though, it is not legitimate for incumbents to say that they wouldn't be caught dead giving their opponent free exposure. Instead, Giuliani says, "I'm interested in seeing what Sal Albanese and Al Sharpton have to say."

"He's hiding," says Ruth, who on the same day passed on a debate with Albanese and Sharpton, so as to avoid giving them any free exposure.

July 26

The city campaign-finance laws, which, ironically, Ruth helped to write, are trapping us in a strategic dilemma.

The laws are among the toughest in the nation. The most any individual or corporation can give to any candidate is $7,700 (once persons or entities have given that amount, they are considered to have *maxed out*). Wealthy players who want access to candidates can act as *bundlers;* that is, they can solicit contributions on a candidate's behalf, but the most they can legally give themselves is still $7,700.

There are some obvious avenues to skirt the law. It would be illegal for maxed-out donors to give $7,700 to their sons or daughters and direct them to give the money to the candidate of their choice. But it would be difficult to prove the illegality, since it is perfectly legal for people, regardless of relation to a maxed-out donor, to give any amount they want (up to $7,700) to their candidate of choice. The maxed-out parent could avoid the law simply by waiting until after the election to refund the child's money.

But even with the obvious loopholes in the law, big money plays far less of a role in the mayoral election than it does in state and federal elections. That's not to say that the role isn't significant. It is. But the stakes are an order of magnitude smaller than they are in congressional and Senate races. Rudy Giuliani's largest bundler, a man named Bruce Ratner, has collected $120,000 in donations to his campaign. (If you can believe it, he has also given $5,000 to ours.) That's the bar tab for many of Al D'Amato's soft-money contributors.

In addition to the caps on individual and corporate contributions, there's an incentive built into the law to encourage solicitation of small donations. All campaign contributions by city residents are matched by the city up to $1,000. A $1,000 donation by a city resident is actually worth $2,000 to the campaign. A maxed-out $7,700 contribution by a city resident is worth $8,700.

The final element of the scheme is a cap on spending by candidates. In a mayoral election, each candidate is restricted to spending a total of $10.4 million—$5.2 million in the primary and $5.2 million in the general. (The caps are reduced for lower-level citywide races. For example, the cap for the comptroller election is $2 million. Individual and corporate contributions are limited in these elections to $3,300.)

The cap presents no strategic problem for Rudy Giuliani. Since he has, essentially, already raised all of the money he is allowed to raise, there is no choice for him to make. He will spend up to the cap on both the primary and general elections. Our decision is not so clear.

For the past several weeks, it has become increasingly apparent that we are not going to reach our initial fund-raising projections. At the outset, our fund-raising director and consultant predicted that we would raise between $8 and $9 million. Now, it looks like we will struggle to raise $7 million. There are many reasons for this. Lots of the higher-ups in the campaign are not as respectful of call time as they should be. Conversations with Ruth during call time have two negative effects. The conversations themselves take up time she should be spending making calls and, equally important, they take her mind off raising money. The polls haven't helped either. Whatever the reasons are, the fact is that we are behind projections. The budget has to be cut.

We have already spent $3 million on the primary and have another $2 million in the bank. We can spend all of that money now or hold all or any portion of it for the general election. Here is the dilemma: If we hold the money for the general election and end up raising more than the difference between what we've saved and the cap, then some portion of the saved money will have been wasted. That's a serious risk in light of the fact that in the best-case scenario we are going to be outspent by Rudy on television by two to one.

There are two views on what we should do. Our pollster believes, and has believed since March, that we should spend the money early. Geoff feels the polls show that the race is getting away from Ruth and that if we don't act swiftly to try to bolster Ruth and bring Rudy down a bit, then no amount of money will save us in October. Spending money early will also help the fund-raising effort. It will boost Ruth's name recognition, perhaps prop her up a bit in the polls, and give the fund-raisers something to point to in their pitches. If we spend money early, some of the advertising will, in effect, pay for itself. The return won't be a dollar for a dollar, but if we spend early, we will raise some money that we otherwise would not.

The competing view is that money spent late means drastically more than money spent early. Voters only focus on a race during its last two weeks and generally make up their minds three or four days before the election. A dollar spent on advertising in October is worth far more than a dollar spent in June unless, of course, you're down by 25 points in October, in which case neither dollar is very much at all. And there's the risk if we spend the money early that we won't have any left for the general election. In 1992, Democrat Bob Abrams was helpless while Al D'Amato ran ad after ad accusing him of being too liberal. Ruth remembers the Abrams campaign vividly.

Jim also believes that we need to "hold our fire." There's no right or wrong in making a call like this, but it is a conservative approach. The effect, it seems to me, is to reduce our expected margin of defeat (at least we'll be able to respond to attacks during the critical last few weeks), but to also reduce our tiny chance of winning (this way, we're certain not to ever get a good poll and raise more money).

No one asks me, but if they did, I'd say to roll the dice and blow the money now.

• • •

The real-life Kramer is dropping out of the race and endorsing the mayor. Of Giuliani, he says, "He's an honest man doing a good job."

July 27

No good news on this Sunday. We continue to suffer damage on the civilianization issue. The day before yesterday, Ruth said, "There will be at least as many but probably more police officers doing what it is we hire and pay our police officers to do." The *Post* reports that "Ruth refused to say just how many cops would be cut under her plan to civilianize more police jobs and exact productivity gains." That's fair in comparison to the editorial "Messinger's Cop Chop," which argues that "just as New Yorkers have begun to feel it's safe to go out of doors at night, along comes mayoral wannabe Ruth Messinger and her proposal to slash the size of the NYPD." Lest you think that it is the only conclusion to draw from the exchange, here is what *Newsday* had to say: "Messinger said her plan would make the police department more efficient without laying off any officers. Messinger also accused the mayor of criticizing a plan he supported as a candidate in 1993—putting civilians into administrative jobs within the police department."

Even worse news is that, for all intents and purposes, we have lost the most important of the metabattles. Adam Nagourney's political memo addresses concern among Democrats about "indications of haplessness in Ms. Messinger's campaign." Nagourney cites as examples a visit by Ruth to a nut company in the Bronx to highlight the city's unemployment problem. The company's president cited the Giuliani administration's efforts as a reason the company remained in New York instead of moving to North Carolina. And, of course, he mentions the budget-speech problem. Apparently, the head of the Citizens Budget Commission was "flabbergasted" we released his phone number.

Just once, I'd like to know who these "Democrats" are.

July 28

Adam Nagourney's job wouldn't be complete without praising the Giuliani campaign. Whereas our campaign is its own enemy, the Giuliani campaign, Nagourney reports today, is vigorously pursuing "a strategy to keep heat on Messinger." The evidence: "When Ms. Messinger stepped into the executive dining room on the 19th floor of the Con Edison building for the [budget] speech last week, she saw a table surrounded by Mr. Giuliani's senior campaign advisers, all serious and studious, scribbling on note pads and checking their tape recorders as they awaited her words. And when she was done, they silently filed downstairs to call a news conference dismembering her proposals, all before Ms. Messinger had even made it to the elevator."

We videotape every one of Rudy Giuliani's appearances, but Nagourney mentions only that a Giuliani staffer videotapes Ruth. Nagourney notes that the mayor called to respond point by point to Ruth's budget plan and that his campaign faxed to reporters a press release from our loyal friend Robert Kiley distancing himself from Ruth's speech. When Giuliani put out his first ad, we were out within an hour with a point-by-point response to all of the factual claims in the ad. But Nagourney makes no mention of the things we do well, only the mistakes. He even admiringly cites the Giuliani campaign's trespass into Ruth's office as an example of tenacity. It's all because the operative thesis has been established: His campaign is aggressive; ours is inept. And it's a corollary of a larger, more damaging thesis: Ruth cannot win the election.

• • •

Word is that Giuliani is about to go on the air with a new television ad, paid for with several hundred thousand dollars of state transit funds, touting the MetroCard. In the ad, Giuliani stands outside an East Side subway station repeating the familiar "One City, One Fare" slogan. Fran Reiter is defending the new ads. She acknowledges that Giuliani criticized Dinkins and appealed to the Campaign Finance Board in 1993, but says that their campaign will nevertheless go ahead with the new ads. "If you think it is wrong now, then change the rules," she says. "Mayor Giuliani is following the rules."

July 29

The Ragin' Cajun, James Carville, noted political consultant and manager of the 1992 Clinton campaign, is in town to help Ruth raise some money. He's pinch-hitting for George Stephanopolous, who promised to do a fundraiser for us, but backed out after his new employer, ABC News, told him that he was not allowed to do political events. Carville doesn't know Ruth at all—he's in mostly as a favor to Jim—but he still manages to stop the show. He tells a joke that's he's probably told a hundred times at the expense of Republicans around the country, but tonight it works spectacularly well.

Jim Bakker, Jerry Falwell, and Rudy Giuliani are in hell, facing three different doors. Bakker is told to enter the first room, where he faces a hideous monster. A voice booms from below, "Jim Bakker, you will spend eternity behind door number one."

Bakker is reduced to tears.

An even more hideous monster is behind the second door.

"Jerry Falwell, you will spend eternity behind door number two."

Falwell whimpers.

After a few silent moments, Rudy approaches the third door and turns the knob. Supermodel Carol Alt is waiting inside. Rudy rubs his hands in delight and steps inside.

"Carol Alt, you will spend eternity with Rudy Giuliani."

July 30

With a slow day on the schedule, the campaign decides that Ruth should hold Rudy accountable for the Mexican immigrants after all. This is part of our continuing strategy to remind voters about Rudy Giuliani's budget cuts. "The cuts, the cuts! It's about the cuts!" I hear the screaming in my dreams.

We'll get a few articles out of this press conference, it seems, but the event underscores the box into which we've been cornered. A reporter reasonably asks Ruth whether she would commit to rehiring inspectors. If she says yes, it will simply be the latest program Ruth cannot afford. If she says no, her critique will be toothless. Ruth chooses damned if she doesn't. "The only money that I will spend as mayor is money that I know is available out of the budget of the agency. The issue, first of all, is not to spend; it is to get these inspection efforts to work more efficiently." It sounds like hot air.

The "liberal" label is damaging for its effect on voters in the abstract, but that damage is minimal in comparison to what it does to a candidate on a day-to-day basis. Imagine trying to conduct a debate about public policy without being able to advocate any proposal that would require the additional expenditure of money. Ruth Messinger will operate under that constraint for the remainder of the campaign.

• • •

Time Warner and Fox have settled their dispute, and Rupert Murdoch is indeed in the debt of the mayor of New York. The terms of the agreement are far more favorable to Fox than they might have been but for Giuliani's intervention. Fox gets access to Time Warner cable systems across the United States. Murdoch in turn is giving Time Warner access to his worldwide network of satellite television stations.

In an unrelated, but well-timed, story about Rudy Giuliani's domination of the media, the *Observer* quotes Fox executive and *Post* columnist Eric Briendel as saying that he speaks regularly with the mayor on the phone. Briendel often calls Giuliani or his aides while writing an editorial to "try to find out if what I'm arguing makes sense."

• • •

James Carville has weighed in with his impressions. He says Ruth looks tired.

July 31

My research team has always perceived its charge as having two separate phases. For the first several months of the campaign, we focused almost entirely on collecting and assembling data. We've gone through almost every imaginable facet of Rudy Giuliani's and Ruth Messinger's lives—their tax records, draft records, legislative acts, whom they've hired, where they've lived. We've reviewed every public statement that each has ever made. I even have a copy of the note for Rudy Giuliani's condominium.

The second phase of our work is output. The point of all of the preparation is to be able to respond, with facts, to any charges made against our candidate in any forum. To prepare for this next phase, I am putting the research team through a series of drills. Each morning for the next two weeks, we will try to respond to a hypothetical ad within two hours. We'll go through the obvious ones—Washington Heights, Ruth's record on taxes—and some not so obvious ones, too.

I hesitate to create any more work than necessary. All five members of the team are working fifteen-hour days. One of my deputies and another staffer are regularly in at 5:30 in the morning to do the clips and a daily press briefing. I'm amazed they can stay awake, let alone work, until 10:00 at night. They hold the campaign together. More than anything else, I'd like to send them to the beach for a day. But as always, they are enthusiastic about the drill idea. It seems worthwhile for all of us to go through the paces of what things will surely be like in another few weeks.

I pick a slightly offbeat argument to start. In the 1970s, Ruth abstained from a City Council resolution condemning the PLO for a terrorist raid that killed fifty people, including a New York photographer named Gail Rubin. Within an hour my team has an impressive response: every pro-Israel vote Ruth ever cast during her twelve years on the City Council.

My team is ready. Or at least we think we are.

August 1

Rudy is throwing a bit of a hissy-fit. He's been getting some bad press over the past few days for refusing to turn over a promised reward to Fernando Carreira, a Miami caretaker who discovered the corpse of Andrew Cunanan, the man who killed fashion designer Gianni Versace. Giuliani says that the reward was for information leading to the capture of Cunanan. Carreira merely called police when he suspected that an intruder was aboard a houseboat. Dade County, the FBI, the Florida Department of Law Enforcement, and the Greater Miami Convention and Visitors Bureau are all paying, but Rudy is holding firm. "To make an exception on this case would jeopardize our reward program."

Morning radio hosts Penny Crone and Mike Gallagher, who ordinarily fawn over Giuliani (Crone told one newspaper that she's the mayor's "biggest fan"), have been teasing him good-naturedly about welching on the Cunanan deal. Rudy, who usually calls into the show once a week, won't return their calls.

The mayor deals with the press the same way he deals with inferiors: He favors sycophants and scorns critics. WPIX news anchor Jack Cafferty (falling into the former category) once grilled the mayor for his New Year's resolutions. On another occasion, he asked this poser: "You've done a lot of things in your first term as Mayor, the reduction in crime probably being the most outstanding achievement. Can you get the Dodgers back here?"

One outburst last September was typical of the manner in which Giuliani deals with adverse questions. "Let's really stop being stupid, okay?" he said. "I mean, really. I mean it really is really stupid! The level of questions sometimes is, like, at the point of idiocy."

August 2

If we are going to go with the Governors Island proposal, Jim's thought is that we will have to wheel out the idea within a day or two of winning the primary. Otherwise, it may be branded an election-year gimmick. Since it *is* an election-year gimmick, it may be so branded anyway, but the thinking is that the idea will be most credible if made immediately following the primary, when Ruth will be in her position of greatest strength. Candidates often enjoy a *bounce* in the polls following a primary victory. If Ruth makes the proposal while she is enjoying her bounce, the proposal will not seem like an act of desperation. There is an eerie similarity between the Governors Island idea and Bob Dole's eleventh-hour tax-cut proposal in the 1996 presidential campaign. Jim thinks we can avoid the skepticism with which Dole's tax cut was received only by proposing the idea immediately following the primary.

Neither Mandy nor Geoff is enthusiastic about the proposal. The idea polls well, but the numbers are not strong enough for Geoff's taste. Mandy's thinking is slightly different. Since it is inevitable that Ruth will lose, she feels that we should act in a way to preserve her reputation and credibility. But the call will ultimately be Jim's, and he hasn't conceded the election quite yet.

• • •

Rudy's strategy of using taxpayer money to fund commercials associating him with the new one-fare cards is paying dividends. According to a new poll, 25 percent of New Yorkers credit Giuliani with the one-fare program. That compares with 7 percent of New Yorkers who credit Governor George Pataki, who controls the Metropolitan Transit Authority.

• • •

Ruth is concerned about our failure to purchase billboards. There are people in the city who will expect to see our ads on them and others who count on the few hundred dollars they get every election for posting the ads on their walls and lawns. They will be angry if they are not there.

"We spend so much time strategizing about what we will say and what they will say, but hardly any about logistical matters," she tells Jim. "We should spend as much time thinking about how to deal with union leaders."

August 3

On an otherwise sleepy Sunday, we're awakened by the news that *Vanity Fair* will publish an article this Wednesday (we have an advance copy) verifying that Giuliani has been having an extramarital affair with his communications director, Cristyne Lategano, and that he has bullied the press into suppressing the story.

Lategano, thirty-two and a graduate of Rutgers, worked on the 1992 Bush campaign. The following year she was assistant to Richard Breyers, the press secretary for the 1993 Giuliani campaign. When Breyers returned to Washington after the election, Giuliani made Lategano press secretary. In 1994, her salary was $77,000. A year later, Giuliani promoted Lategano to communications director, boosted her salary to $103,000, and gave her an office adjoining his in the basement of City Hall. In 1996, he raised her salary again, to $124,000.

There are some obvious reasons why Lategano and Giuliani get along. For one, she is able to keep up with the mayor's pace. The article reports that Lategano works twenty-hour days. According to the article's author, Jennifer Conant, Lategano "openly idolizes Giuliani," which generally helps one survive at City Hall. And Lategano has an operating style that is similar to the mayor's. She has been known to call reporters at all hours of the night demanding that a headline be changed. In the early days, reporters "howled about her incompetence, ignorance, arrogance, and rudeness." Several people close to Giuliani thought Lategano was not a good choice, including Giuliani's former media consultant, David Garth. Garth's disapproval of Lategano is thought to be one of several possible explanations for the split between the highly respected Garth, who handled Giuliani's ads in 1993, and the mayor. But Lategano endured.

According to Conant, the relationship between Lategano and Giuliani changed during a series of overnight and weekend trips to Georgia, Michigan, and Massachusetts late in 1994. One unnamed Giuliani aide (all of the sources for the story are unnamed) says that Lategano and Giuliani "touched in a way you wouldn't normally touch a co-worker." On one highly publicized occasion, Lategano and Giuliani went clothes shopping together on a Sunday afternoon.

At the least, the mayor appears to have been protective of Lategano. Former police commissioner Bill Bratton is reported in the article as saying Giuliani "went nuts" when Lategano jumped into the arms of John Miller, Bratton's former press secretary, in City Hall one day. Conant suggests that Giuliani punished Donna Hanover for joining Giuliani's lifelong friend and deputy mayor Peter Powers in suggesting that Lategano be replaced.

Whatever the truth may be, we'll be taking no part in the story. Ruth has nothing to gain from joining in this debate. Anything she says will make the story appear political. When the papers call later in the day, Ruth says that she has nothing to say. Sal Albanese, though, says domestic distractions can impair the mayor's ability to do his job.

August 4

Of all the issues that we have polled, the single most powerful is that "Ruth Messinger will sue the state to require that all lottery money be used for education." For the past week, I have returned to being a lawyer to try to devise an argument by which we can claim, as Jim is convinced, that the lottery money is not being used for education.

In one sense, the money really isn't being used for education. Since the lottery's creation in 1967, its proceeds have increasingly been relied upon as a substitute for state aid to education rather than a supplement. Lottery proceeds have essentially been used to reduce the amount of money that the state dedicates from its general budget to support education. In fiscal year 1967, New York State spent $1.5 billion on its public schools, representing 33 percent of its total budget. The state lottery, which was then in its first year, generated revenue of $29 million, approximately 2 percent of the total education expenditure.

By comparison, in 1995 education aid totaled $8.24 billion, representing only 26 percent of the total budget. Revenue from the lottery, by then more than $1.5 billion a year, accounted for 16 percent of the state's education expenditure. The lottery is generating lots of money, but it is not a net gain for schoolchildren. It is only a gain for taxpayers who don't play the lottery (unsurprisingly, the wealthy play less frequently than the poor), since they're relieved of a tax burden to which they would otherwise have to contribute. This year, Governor Pataki is making the scheme explicit. He's proposing to use lottery money to pay for property-tax relief.

The problem is that though the scheme may be regressive, deceptive, and unethical, there's nothing illegal about it. The constitutional amendment that created the lottery says that all proceeds from the lottery "shall be used exclusively to or in aid or support of education in this state." The lottery money *is* going to aid education. It's just not supplementing aid to education. And the legislative history of the act that created the lottery indicates that the state Senate considered and dismissed the fact that the money wouldn't be a net gain for the schools. If they had wanted to make sure that it was, they would have written a provision into the law that required the state to spend a certain minimum percentage of its budget on the schools and use the lottery money as a bonus. They didn't, and there's no getting around that from a legal standpoint. The case is a sure loser.

But we're politicians, not lawyers. Our consideration is not whether we ultimately win the lawsuit. It's whether we can file the suit, get Ruth a few good headlines we can use in an ad, and avoid having the case thrown out before the election. Ruth's general counsel and I meet with a group of lawyers who brought suit against New York to challenge the formula by which state aid is allocated. They all agree that he suit will be quickly dismissed.

Even in light of all that, the issue is so powerful, filing the suit is still worth considering. It's exceedingly unlikely a case could be dismissed before the election. Though they likely won't see the light of day, I draft a complaint and brief. It's a shame to see such a travesty go unaddressed and to see such a powerful issue slip through our fingers.

August 5

Jim often says that his is an honorable profession, but I have my reservations. His is really two different jobs, and it's important to draw a distinction between them. One thing Jim or those like him do is organize. They set up an office and hire people to perform all of the various day-to-day functions of a campaign. One might question whether our campaign has done those things well, and ask generally whether a field campaign makes a significant difference among voters, but the idea of setting up an office for a candidate doesn't seem to raise any ethical issues.

The other part of the consultant's function is more morally ambiguous. The Jim Andrews–style consultant is responsible for the message, which, by its existence as a term of art, is distinct from the full set of beliefs and policy positions that a candidate holds. At their least intrusive, consultants encourage their candidates to strategically emphasize certain positions over others. We've done this with Ruth. For example, Ruth is against the death penalty and in favor of better schools. The campaign has made a decision (perhaps so obvious it has never been articulated) to emphasize the latter over the former. Ruth answers questions about her views on the death penalty honestly, but it's not on the short list of things she emphasizes in her stump speech.

Slightly higher up the scale of intrusiveness is aiding the candidate in responding to new situations. This can be something as innocuous as acting as a sounding board for the candidate and giving some basic feedback ("It might be better, Ruth, for you to call it a contract instead of a collective bargaining agreement"). Or it can be much more. Suggesting to a woman who has spent her life fighting for civil liberties that she should support the idea of arming police officers with new deadly bullets that will inevitably result in the deaths of more minorities is a bit more intrusive than suggesting the emphasis of school reform over other issues.

At his or her most intrusive, a consultant can advocate a change in established positions. Freddie Ferrer's switch on the death penalty is widely perceived as a result of the pernicious influence of Dick Morris, the same man who steered Bill Clinton into balancing the federal budget on the backs of the poor and signing a welfare bill that sent a million children into poverty. I would argue that Governors Island falls into the category of intrusive influences, though Jim could make a reasonable argument that it falls into the category of new situations (indeed, the opportunity to build an island casino does not come around every day). In either case, if Ruth supports the Governors Island idea, it will be a profound change in her public position on gambling.

The consultant's work is incremental. Candidates don't announce their entire set of views on a single day. They deal with issues as they arise. But the cumulative effect is clear. Jim is *moving Ruth to the center,* and this gives me pause. In some sense, Jim has constructed a public persona of Ruth that is different from the real person. Ruth Messinger the candidate is different from Ruth Messinger the individual.

Part of that is a fact of life—everyone has a public persona that differs at some level from his or her private self; and part of that is politics—we don't want politicians to be too honest. But part is something else. Ruth Messinger the human being would have instinctively said that hollow-point bullets were an unjustifiable risk, an unnecessary investment of power in police officers, who too often abuse their authority and fail to take the rights of victims seriously. But Ruth Messinger the candidate takes a cautious, reserved view of the problem of police brutality. It is still deplorable, but not first on the list of things to address.

I doubt whether Jim and other consultants make a moral calculus when they do what they are paid to do, which is to position a candidate so that he or she has the best chance of winning an election. Nevertheless, the calculus exists. Some deviance between the candidate and the real person is clearly tolerable. If changing your view on a particular issue will ensure your election and thereby facilitate the advancement of an otherwise honorable agenda, then the switch seems fine. I think most people would say that changing your view on an issue like residency requirements or school uniforms in order to get elected on a platform that advocates investing in education and job training and raising wages of the lower class is an acceptable trade-off. Many might go so far as to say that it's a trade-off that is morally compelled.

The calculation grows more difficult as the issue on which the transformation is required becomes more significant and the core agenda less clearly laudable. Is it justifiable to change your position on the death penalty in order to get elected on a platform that might make the tax code slightly more progressive? Is progressivity of the tax code the core agenda or is it really fighting the racially discriminatory death penalty?

I don't think we've come anywhere near crossing that line, but I wonder whether anyone has asked those questions. I think Jim would say that the common agenda of the candidates he has worked for over the years is to advance the interests of the middle class. Short of that, I doubt he could find anything in common among the dozens of people for whom he has worked.

Is this all really a game? Ask me what the right response to the hollow-point-bullets issue is and I would say that, were I positioning an amorphous blob to be mayor, the blob should say nothing on the issue. Concede crime. But Ruth Messinger is not an amorphous blob; she is a thinking human being with a history. She should speak out against police brutality. Or is that statement in itself a political calculation—a calculation about the damage a reversal of positions might do to the candidate's credibility?

Ruth can honestly say that she has remained true to her core values—she's still against the death penalty and still pro-choice. But we haven't been above using her commitment to those principles for political gain. Is that right?

And is it right to implicate the consultant in this discussion at all? Ruth hired Jim. She could fire him at any time. And, most of all, she is the person who ultimately takes the positions.

I don't have answers to any of these questions, but I know there's something wrong in a world where they're not even being asked.

August 6

Lock a bunch of twenty-three year olds in a small box for eighteen hours a day, mix in a good dose of tension, and what do you get? The steamiest of soap operas.

So far, and I should make clear that this is certainly an underestimate because I am always the last in the office to know, there have been twenty-three confirmed intra-office romances. Several people in the office are having a competition to see who can be intimate with the most people in the campaign. The leader is at five. Several others are tied for second at four. At least three of the relationships have been between people theoretically at different levels of the campaign power structure. The longest has lasted four weeks and is going strong. Only three people in the office have stable outside relationships.

This is not an environment for the well-adjusted.

August 7

I should say at the outset of this discussion that I don't think many voters care about whether Rudy Giuliani is having an affair with his press secretary. I certainly don't. Unless a politician's private life has some direct bearing on his or her performance, I don't think it's anyone's business. The 1996 presidential election indicates that most Americans feel the same way.

There's no serious claim here that Rudy's alleged affair has anything to do with his job. Lategano is his employee and did receive a quick series of substantial raises, but that's not much of a hook on which to hang the relevance hat. People seem to have mixed feelings about Lategano, but no one disputes that she's a hard worker and extremely loyal to the mayor. Who knows whether a press secretary is worth $120,000 a year, but Lategano is doing the job.

What's interesting to me is how the press has treated the Giuliani team's response to the allegations and what it says about what is perceived as legitimate in political discourse. To my mind, there are only three responses to make to the charges: (1) "We did it" (or "They did it," depending on who is speaking); (2) "We didn't do it"; or (3) "It's none of your business." These are the only answers directly responsive to the question of whether the affair occurred.

But the Giuliani people haven't really said any of those things. Giuliani refuses to answer questions about whether there are tensions in his marriage, and when he is asked about whether he is having an affair with Lategano, he conspicuously answers in the present (peeved) tense, "No, I'm not [having an affair with Lategano], but it's really outrageous that you ask." Earlier today, Giuliani lashed out at New York 1 reporter Dominic Carter when Carter asked the mayor whether he would appear at a press conference with Donna to dispel the rumors that their marriage is falling apart. "That's really a cheap question," the mayor said, "and we will now move on."

Rather than attack the truth of the charges directly, the Giuliani team is attacking them indirectly by questioning *Vanity Fair*'s journalistic methods. Deputy Mayor Randy Levine faults the story for relying exclusively on unnamed sources. "It's the worst kind of scurrilous journalism," he said, "based on anonymous sources and hearsay." "Where are the sources?" he asks.

The mayor and Lategano are now taking the same tack. Giuliani says, "The best thing for me to say about the article is, it's untrue, it's false, it's based on unnamed sources who are malicious, and I'm not going to say anything else about it. I think that to talk about it any more than that gives it a status it surely doesn't deserve." Lategano says, "Allegations by unnamed sources are not true, and there is no need to comment on malicious works of fiction." She throws in a charge of sexism to boot: "When a woman works closely with her male boss, it's called intimate. When a man does the same, it's called loyal."

Rudy's longtime friend and former campaign manager, Peter Powers, questions whether the charges were politically motivated: "Anytime anything comes out during an election campaign," he says, "it has to be suspect."

All of these may be legitimate points, but none proves or disproves whether the affair occurred. If Lategano's response, "Allegations by unnamed sources are not true," were true, Richard Nixon would have finished his second term. Saying "Allegations by unnamed sources are not true" is quite different from saying "These allegations are not true."

There's an unmistakable lawyerly feel to the Giuliani team's response. Giuliani's instincts and training are those of a prosecutor. He responds to charges by attacking the credibility of the other party ("The Straphangers are a pawn of the Messinger campaign"), demonstrating bias ("I think that caller had a bias"), and pointing out inconsistencies in the charges. Giuliani's people point out that the Massachusetts trip lasted only three hours and that Lategano wasn't even on the Michigan trip.

Any good lawyer would do the same thing for a client. But lawyers are part of a process that is vastly inefficient at discovering the truth. Part of the reason people so distrust lawyers is because lawyers live in a world where it is possible to talk about a person's guilt without hearing what the person has to say and where no inference can be drawn from the person's unwillingness to speak. We tolerate such a system only because it vindicates other values.

There aren't any other obvious values being vindicated by the political process. But spokespeople for politicians act as quasi-lawyers speculating about what truths evidence supports rather than just saying what their candidate believes or says is true. This is obfuscation, but the press treats this metadiscussion of the truth as valid. To the press, spinning is politics, which is probably why public opinion of politicians is headed the way of that of lawyers.

• • •

Donna Hanover, for whom we all feel incredibly sorry, issues this statement: "Above all, my family is deeply important to me and will remain so in the years ahead." Translated in the *Post*, the statement is almost unrecognizable. The headline is "Defiant Donna Denies Rudy Marriage Report."

Hanover said it best yesterday. After spending the day holed up in Gracie Mansion and evading reporters in her limousine, Hanover arrives at the television studio late in the afternoon to tape her daily segment on the Food Network.

"We're talking beans today!" she says, starting off the show on a high note.

Indeed we are.

August 8

A caller to Rudy's weekly radio show asks an interesting question. According to columnist Jack Newfield, Giuliani's 1989 campaign leaked thirty letters about David Dinkins's sex life to the press. "So how can you be mad when people are looking at your affair with Cristyne Lategano?" asks "Jesse from Manhattan's Upper West Side."

"Jesse," Giuliani replies, "I've said everything I'm going to say about these allegations. They're scurrilous, and it sounds like you are too. But in any event, I'm not going to say anything else about it, because I think it's just a platform for people to continue repeating false stories."

Scurrilous Jesse skulks away, shamed for asking such a question.

• • •

A friend of mine from law school is on the phone. We haven't spoken in ages.

"Hi, Steven. It's good to hear from you. How's your daughter?"

"They're both fine. I have two of them now."

I am out of touch.

"That's great. What are you doing now?"

"Well, actually, I'm running for Congress, which is why I'm calling. I was wondering whether you could help me out with my campaign . . . "

Steven keeps talking, but I tune him out. *I am being pitched.* I'm excited for a moment—who would have ever thought someone would ask me for money—but now I am panicked. I know how relentless these people are. Once you're on their list, they never give up until they have bled you white.

I appeal for mercy. "You know, Steven, I'm working on a political campaign myself and as much as I'd love to help you generously, things are kind of tight for me right now."

"Anything you could do would really help. Five hundred dollars, two hundred and fifty dollars—"

I cut him off. "Why don't we plan to talk again after my election is over."

"Okay. In the meantime, why don't I fax you some literature."

"Great." My friend has literature.

• • •

The fax machine is ringing. The literature is here. "To fight for working families and their values" Steven has proposed "The Steiner Plan: Fighting for Kentucky Families." It's a ten-point plan. Those are always the best. Point One: "Guarantee Health Coverage for All Children." That's a good goal, a bit ambitious perhaps—I'm not sure Congress is ready to take on health care for Lithuanians. He probably just means children in Kentucky. Fair enough. Point Two: "Promote Discipline, Safety and the Basics in Our Schools." Who could be against that? I'm not sure "our" should be capitalized, though, and shouldn't there be a comma between "safety" and "and"? I've never been clear on that. Point Three: "Hook Up Our School Houses to Computers and the Internet." I thought "schoolhouse" was a single word. Point Four: "Inspire Our Youth Toward Public Service." Now this is getting silly. The rest of the plan is about "Our Workers, Our Markets, and Our Economy."

My friend is one of the smartest people I've ever met. He graduated Harvard College and Harvard Law School, both magna cum laude. He was Deputy Chief of Staff at the Department of Energy when he was twenty-eight. And now he's reduced to speaking in capital letters. Politics is a pernicious leveler.

August 9

With the *Vanity Fair* article still filtering around in the press, Giuliani is on the air with a pair of ads that emphasize his workaholism.

The first ad shows a series of pictures of Rudy ("An Action Mayor Taking Charge") on the job. Viewers hear:

> As quality of life improves for all New Yorkers—more jobs, a cleaner, safer city—we're often reminded how fortunate we are to have a round-the-clock mayor, there for us when we need him most. We've heard all the big stories.

> About Rudy's leadership during the Brooklyn Bridge shooting, about how he protected deaf immigrants from abuse, and his constant vigilance against terrorism. . . . When a building collapses or subway derailment threatens the lives of New Yorkers, Rudy's there. When a water main breaks, or a brutal snowstorm rages, Rudy's there.

The other ad conveys the same message in a lighthearted way:

> Rudy Giuliani can't sleep whenever the lives of New Yorkers are on the line: fighting back when the unexpected happens, when Mother Nature throws us a curve, when terrorism threatens our neighborhoods, when people need help. Some say Rudy works too hard, but we take comfort that in the city that never sleeps, we have a mayor that never sleeps. Well, almost never.

As the announcer says "Well, almost never," the phone slips from between Rudy's neck and shoulder as he falls asleep. It's Rudy's best acting performance since the Inner Circle dinner.

Jim's brilliant press release says Rudy will try to take credit for the sunrise and the good weather.

• • •

According to a New York 1 poll, voters don't care about whether Rudy is cheating on Donna. Eighty-five percent of the respondents say it won't change their vote. A mere 7 percent say they would be less likely to vote for Giuliani; 4 percent have no opinion, and 4 percent say the charges make them more likely to support the mayor.

What must those 4 percent think about the man?

• • •

Surely it is coincidence, but both Graydon Carter, the editor of *Vanity Fair*, and Jennifer Conant have new early morning street repair going on in front of their apartments.

August 10

Two clues as to where the Giuliani campaign will be going against Ruth. One avenue is what we expected; the other is a bit of a surprise.

It has never been in doubt whether the Attica attack would be used; the only question has been where it would surface. Today, *Slate*, Michael Kinsley's on-line magazine, published an article by James Traub of the *New*

Yorker entitled "New York's Loneliest Liberal." (Guess who.) Traub praises Ruth's intelligence and "her belief in the fine distinction," but says that her problem is "a history of beliefs that look rather embarrassing in retrospect." "In 1979," Traub writes, "while a member of the City Council, [Messinger] hosted a coming-out-of-jail cocktail party for John R. Hill, who had murdered a corrections officer on the first day of the Attica riots. In 1984, she returned from a trip to Sandinista-led Nicaragua to assert that women there 'participated in everything' and were 'ready to die for this freedom.'" It will only be a matter of days before that story filters into the New York press.

The second attack is something we missed or, more accurately, did not see the negative value of. According to the *Observer*, Giuliani's latest commercials about being everywhere all the time are substitutes for an ad about sex shops and the morals of the city. The pulled ad is about the mayor's campaign to wipe out pornography stores and theaters. It reportedly takes a swipe at Ruth for opposing a 1995 zoning law that would have limited the areas zoned for sex-related businesses.

We're aware of Ruth's opposition to the zoning law, but never believed an argument could be made out of it. Ruth opposed that plan, but proposed a zoning plan of her own that would have restricted sex shops to an equal or greater extent. A quick review of the relevant articles indicates that our position may not be as strong as we first thought. Ruth is quoted as saying that sex shops are "an integral part of the fabric" of Greenwich Village.

We've been given a reprieve. Apparently, the Giuliani campaign delivered the ads to radio stations, but then retrieved them, concluding that the time wasn't exactly right to promote Rudy Giuliani's image as a paragon of virtue.

They'll be back.

August 11

A consequence of the different worldviews of the modern political types and the traditional political types is a different view of the importance of press. For traditional politicians the trick is to get as much press as possible. For modern politicians, the goal is to get as much press as possible that associates you with the message of the campaign. Traditional politicians use press as a means to boost name recognition. Modern message-oriented politicians use press to associate the candidate with ideas that will increase the favorable-unfavorable ratio.

Lee once described his press philosophy to the *Observer* as issue definition, saying he liked "thumbs-up, thumbs-down issues." Lee said, "You find issues where [people are] either for it or against it instantly and then the interesting part is not whether they're for it or against it, but whether people talk about it. That's what you want. In six months, people won't remember anything but the name."

Lee calls it issue definition, but it is really name recognition, since he doesn't care whether people go thumbs-up or thumbs-down.

Each approach has its appropriate place. In a low-level campaign with little funding, such as a City Council race, it is most important for a candidate to simply get his or her name out there. Races of that sort are generally crowded and few candidates, if any, have the money to go on the air. The challenge there is to get people to know who you are. In a campaign like ours, name recognition isn't as important as association with an issue. With several million dollars being spent on advertising, getting voters to know who a candidate is will not be a problem. The challenge is to get them to like the candidate.

Ruth thinks my typologies are too general. They may be, but at the same time some of Ruth's actions can only be explained by a traditional worldview and accordant press strategy. Case in point: After journalist Joe Klein admitted last year to being the author of *Primary Colors*, the fictional takeoff on Bill Clinton's 1992 presidential primary campaign, Ruth declared publicly that she would never grant an interview to Klein. Though, as far as we can tell, Klein had never interviewed Ruth before, she sent a sharply worded letter to *Newsweek*, which she released to the press. "[Klein's] entire body of prior work," Ruth wrote, "has been tainted and his reputation as a journalist seriously, if not irreparably, damaged. A journalist is only as good as his or her word, and it turns out, Joe Klein's word is not very good at all." Ruth vowed never to speak to Klein again.

Guess who the *New Yorker* assigned to profile the mayoral candidates?

The point of this story isn't to fault Ruth and her staff for not having anticipated that Joe Klein might be in a position to write an important story about her someday. The question is why Ruth would ever have made the public admonition in the first place. Klein, to that point, had had nothing to do with Ruth whatsoever. If Ruth or her staff had strong feelings about the matter, they could have written to Klein or *Newsweek* privately. That they released the letter to the press ("Always with the letters, that one," I can hear my grandmother saying) suggests that they saw the event as an opportunity for cheap press. And it was—the letter got Ruth exactly one day of stories. But it didn't get Ruth stories that associated her with an idea or an issue. Even if Klein was wrong to have denied writing *Primary Colors,* no one will ever vote for or against Ruth because of the stance she took on the Klein issue. She may very well have done the right moral thing. From a political standpoint, it was an irrelevancy. The hour spent writing the letter could have been better spent on the phone raising money.

For once, though, we've caught a break. It seems unlikely that Klein would hold a grudge against Ruth—lots of people slammed him for his misleading denials—but even if he did, he'd probably be inclined to give us a break. Klein's son worked for Jim on the Harvey Gantt campaign last year and thinks the world of Jim. And Klein is one of Mandy's best friends.

• • •

Under the rules of the Campaign Finance Board, all of the candidates who have opted into the matching-funds system will participate in the first debate, which is scheduled for next week. To our great surprise, that means Ruth, Sal, and Al will be joined by an unknown named Eric Ruano-Melendez.

Melendez is one of several fringe candidates who have been operating for the past few months underneath the radar of the press. Olga Rodriguez, a forty-nine-year-old baggage handler for Northwest Airlines, is running on the Socialist line. She wants to abolish the police department and let the working people defend themselves. Peter Gaffney, running on the Right to Life line, wants to overturn *Roe v. Wade*, though he also supports larger welfare benefits. Roland Rogers, fifty, the president of the New York City Birthday Committee, which was organized to celebrate the anniversary of the city's first government, formed in 1653 by the Dutch (the big 344 is this year), is also vying for the Democratic nomination. The centerpiece of Rogers's campaign is a "dramatic 14-point platform and 12-point economic plan for New York City's future." He won't be in the debate, though, since he missed the deadline for the matching-funds program. He was in our office last week looking for a job.

None are quite as entertaining as the "p.c. candidate" (possibly for mayor), who is campaigning on the link between asthma and the allergens carried by cockroaches. His campaign literature carries an intriguing notice: "This candidate prefers to remain anonymous at present. He is not a public figure and has no interest or connection with this publication."

Compared to the others, Melendez is a veteran. He ran for mayor in 1993 and won 7 percent of the vote against David Dinkins in the primary (perhaps proving that even a teddy bear with a Hispanic last name could get 7 percent of the vote in New York City). He ran for City Council in 1994, but was disqualified from the ballot when few of his election petition signatories could be found. The *Village Voice* looked at his signatures this year and noted "questionable similarities in signatures and the same handwriting for many addresses." That will only be a problem for him if someone challenges his petitions, and since no one has any plans to do that, he'll be in the race.

Melendez likes his chances. "The turnout's going to be low, see," he tells the *Times,* "so if I can motivate the Hispanic vote, as the only Hispanic in the race, and if we can hold Messinger under 40 percent and force a runoff, I'm poised."

Despite his political history and being well poised, Melendez is an unknown commodity. A forty-nine-year-old native of Guatemala, he apparently works for the city as a civil engineer. His 1993 campaign platform had three planks as far as we can tell: statehood for Puerto Rico, bringing in the national guard to help fight crime, and building a gambling casino in the Rockaways. This year he seems to have added the idea of a Disneyland-style theme park in the South Bronx. His stand on drugs is a bit confusing: He thinks either they should be legalized or there should be the death penalty for drug dealers. It makes the DisneyBronx idea sound pretty good.

The uncertainty surrounding Melendez makes preparing for the debate a bit difficult. Mandy is in town to help critique a series of run-throughs, but we're really not sure what to do with Melendez. One of Ruth's staffers who claims to remember Melendez from the 1993 campaign plays him in the practices and makes him sound a bit insane.

I moderate the practice sessions, and with Melendez in the race it seems only appropriate to ask each of the candidates what they think about casino gambling. Ruth shoots me an appropriately dirty look.

August 12

My girlfriend called at midnight, but I could not talk. I was busy working on a response to a genuine outrage.

Back in February, the Giuliani administration removed the staff of a city-run battered women's shelter amid allegations that shelter staffers regularly had sex with residents, often took home food and clothing donations intended for residents, and frequently allowed the women's boyfriends from whom they were seeking protection into the shelter. It was a chilling story. The mayor said that he assumed full responsibility for the failings and would change the way the shelter was run.

In April, the Giuliani administration restored the workers and declared that the security firm for the shelter would retain its city contracts. Lillian

Barrios-Paoli, the commissioner of the city's Human Resources Administration, said that the mayor had acted hastily in February out of fear that Fernando Ferrer would publicize and make a campaign issue of wrongdoing at the shelter, but retracted the statement the next day. Deputy Mayor Randy Mastro denied reports that he had struck a deal with municipal union leader Stanley Hill to restore the workers. The details of any investigation were cloudy. Mastro denied having seen any report by the city Department of Investigation, but Giuliani said that the report showed no evidence of rape or other crimes.

Earlier today, the Department of Investigation released a final report to the mayor. The report showed that staff members had sex with residents in exchange for privileges such as extra food or access to the shelter after curfew. The night staff allowed residents with drug problems or who were engaged in prostitution to use the fire escape after hours. And shelter security guards were regularly asleep on the job. The report terms these problems "management issues."

We have a press release summarizing the report out the door at 6:00 this morning and hold a press conference at noon to call again for the firing of the security firm, but hardly anyone shows up. Only the *Daily News* and *Staten Island Advance* will report on the story, and they will portray it as a "he said, she said" story. Deputy Mayor Mastro says we are firing "unfair political shots." The guards who fell asleep have been fired, he says, and that should be the end of it.

August 13

Ruth got almost no press on the battered women's shelter story. The subject of our morning meeting is whether we should stay on the story for another day. Our field and advance teams are offering the option of a press conference with prominent city women to condemn the Department of Investigation report. Jim thinks we should stay on the issue. Domestic violence polled strongly, and the domestic violence ad did very well with the focus groups. The issue is likely to figure prominently in our ad campaign.

Lee thinks the conference is a waste of time. In his opinion, the press has already moved on to another story. Word has been going around the city over the past two days that several police officers may have beaten a Haitian immigrant and sexually assaulted him with a plunger. Thirty-year-old Abner Louima is in and out of consciousness at Coney Island Hospital. His brother, Jonas, said the police attacked Abner early Saturday morning. Police brutality is certainly a legitimate campaign issue. The Civilian Complaint Review Board reports that it has substantiated more cases of alleged police misconduct in the first six months of 1997 than it did in all of 1996. If Louima's allegations are even partially true, it is an appalling story.

Police brutality is a legitimate campaign issue, but I'm with Jim. The Department of Investigation report is an absolute outrage—an obvious cover-up—and we should stick with it for another day. Our strategy all along has been to concede the crime issue to Giuliani, and there's no reason to veer from it now. Attacking him on the corollary issue of brutality would almost certainly be contorted by the Giuliani campaign into an argument that Ruth is anticop and, hence, weak on crime. Lee may be right that we'll attract more press if we focus on the Louima issue, but that's only the end of the analysis if you adhere to the traditional view of campaigns. Our goal isn't to maximize coverage; it's to maximize coverage of the message.

We stay on domestic violence for another day.

• • •

Whether Lee is right about his strategic opinion is one matter, but he's absolutely dead on in his assessment that the press is only interested in the evolving Abner Louima story. Our press conference is one of the better-attended events of the summer. Standing with Ruth are Carolyn Maloney, the congresswoman from the Upper East Side, Catherine Abate, the state senator who figures to run for Attorney General next year, and a dozen other prominent city women. But the reporters don't seem the slightest bit interested. When it comes time for questions, they are single-mindedly focused on Ruth's opinion about the Louima case.

Ruth takes a cautious tone with the reporters' questions. "I see this case right now as a single, isolated, horrible, terrifying story about alleged human brutality against another human being."

August 14

Just weeks before the 1989 mayoral primary, Yusef Hawkins, a young black man, was murdered by a white gang while shopping for a used car in Bensonhurst, New York. Then-mayor Ed Koch denounced the attack, but suggested that a black march though the neighborhood would be counterproductive. According to Koch, Jesse Jackson asked the boy's father, Moses Stewart, to help elect David Dinkins mayor. Moses Stewart refused Jackson's entreaty, but Koch lost the primary to David Dinkins anyway.

No one can say whether Yusef Hawkins caused Ed Koch's defeat, but the last thing Rudy Giuliani needs is anything that will inflame racial tensions during this hot summer. Perhaps with Hawkins in mind, the mayor is treating the evolving Louima situation delicately. Though he usually gives police officers the benefit of the doubt, in this case Rudy Giuliani is siding with the victim. After visiting with Louima, who is hospitalized with a punctured intestine and ruptured bladder, Giuliani denounces the attack in strong words. "The alleged conduct involved is reprehensible, done by anyone at any time. Allegedly done by police officers, it's even more reprehensible."

The charges are horrifying. In an interview with *Daily News* columnist Mike McAlary, Louima alleges that four cops, using racial epithets, kicked and beat him with police radios, and then drove Louima to the 70th Precinct stationhouse in Flatbush, Brooklyn. There, Louima says, he was strip-searched, walked to the bathroom, and sodomized in the anus and mouth with a bathroom plunger. According to Louima, one of the officers said, "You niggers have to learn to respect police officers." Louima's lawyers claim the police officers said, "David Dinkins is no longer in power; it's Giuliani time. You understand? It's Giuliani time." A family member reports a less incendiary, but still disturbing, version of the statement: "You don't have a black mayor anymore."

Officials are dropping the charge of assaulting a police officer that landed Louima in prison in the first place. The police are also investigating prior charges of misconduct against Officers Justin Volpe and Thomas Bruder. And the police are taking one additional important step: Commissioner Safir has ordered all plungers removed from police stationhouses.

August 15

The "Giuliani time" allegation is enormously powerful, though, as so often seems to be the case in these matters, it trivializes a serious issue. No one believes for a second that Rudy Giuliani condones the sort of police behavior alleged by Abner Louima. It's not even obvious why the alleged comment should be of interest to anyone at all. There's no indication that Giuliani has ever even met the officers, let alone told them to say anything so horrible. And the mayor has responded to the situation forcefully. He and Safir have reassigned the precinct supervisory officers and suspended the desk sergeant who was in charge at the time. They've relied on African American politicians and ministers to spread the word that they will come down hard on any police officer implicated in the case. And Rudy is establishing a $15-million task force on police and community relations.

The Giuliani people are suggesting that Louima may be taking the quote from *Clockers*, a Spike Lee joint. In the movie, a white detective frisking

Spike, a young black man, says, "This is a new day, Strike. Dinkins out, Rudy in. Law and order. Cut the budget. Party's over. Crack down on drugs and crime." Whether the quote comes from the movie or life, clearly its power is symbolic at most.

What could legitimately be claimed is that the mayor, through his refusal to appoint an independent police monitor, by cutting the budget of the Civilian Complaint Review Board, and by his emphasis on law and order, has subtly created an environment in which officers act with greater impunity and brutality is more likely to occur. In 1995, for example, Giuliani failed to act on recommendations by the Mollen Commission urging the creation of a civil-rights unit to deal with complaints of brutality twenty-four hours a day. But say something like that, and people's eyes glaze over. The issue now is whether brutality of this sort is something to be associated with "Giuliani time." That's the issue. Take it or leave it.

By the logic we've followed so far, the decision should be to leave it. But it's obvious that there is mounting pressure—on both a strategic level and out of conviction—to seize it. Were we not involved in the mayoral campaign, there's little doubt Ruth would be out there talking about the case. She sincerely believes police brutality is a problem and has spoken out many times in the past about the need to curb police misconduct. She's chomping at the bit. There's pressure from her friends and constituents who expect her to be out in front on the issue. There's pressure from the press. *Newsday* columnist Sheryl McCarthy writes, "If I were Messinger, I would ride the police brutality issue like a racehorse." (Dan Janison of *Newsday* has a different view: "By the odd logic of New York politics," he writes, "the atrocious police abuse of Abner Louima could hurt Ruth Messinger before it harms Mayor Rudolph Giuliani.") And there's pressure on the strategic types too. They want to cede the crime issue, but the opportunity to get Ruth's name out there is temptingly juicy. The issue is perfectly teed up. A front-page story in the *Times* this morning asks whether the mayor, who has linked his name to police successes, should be held accountable for this "very ugly police failure."

Late in the afternoon, CNN calls inviting Ruth to join Bernard Shaw on *Inside Politics* to discuss the Louima case. Jim and Mandy, who is in town for the debate, decide to accept the invitation, and late in the afternoon have a coaching session with Ruth. They want her to draw a distinction between the sort of behavior alleged in this particular case, which no one believes is a pervasive problem, and the general issue of brutality, which is clearly a problem—a problem for which Rudy Giuliani should be held accountable.

That's a hard distinction to draw, and somehow Ruth comes across as not sounding very much like Ruth. Asked to evaluate Rudy Giuliani's handling of the situation, she says she wants "to keep politics out of it." "I think what the mayor has done in the last few days is right on target," she says. "The mayor, the police commissioner and the district attorney have got to do a swift, comprehensive investigation—they have to identify every single police officer in that precinct who had anything to do with this horrific assault and make sure they are in fact prosecuted and held accountable."

August 16

On the same day we've filed a complaint with the Campaign Finance Board arguing that the cost of the MetroCard ads should be charged against the Giuliani campaign, Rudy is on the air with yet another taxpayer-funded commercial. This time, Rudy appears with Yankee manager Joe Torre touting the city's recycling program. Earlier in his term, Rudy went to court to challenge mandatory recycling levels and said recycling advocates were indulging in a "craze." Giuliani's budget cuts have reduced the frequency of recycling collections, and funds for outreach—to teach people about recycling—have also been cut.

Nevertheless, Rudy is appearing in a $500,000 ad campaign in which he tosses an empty bottle into a recycling can.

"Not bad," Joe Torre says.

"I can just hop on the 4 train from City Hall and be at the stadium in no time," says Rudy.

The mayor defends the ad. He's pulling a planned ad on a sales-tax-free week for clothing that he was also going to appear in, but the recycling ads will run.

"I had already done that," Rudy says, referring to the fact that the recycling ad had already been filmed, as if that makes any difference. "That was already done. It's going to be on before the primary is over. And the fact is, it's an area in which I have received a certain level of criticism which I thought was unfair."

Unfair indeed.

August 17

Most people think of Al Sharpton's campaign as strictly ideological, but the fact of the matter is that Reverend Sharpton, like all of the candidates, has been articulating detailed policy positions on all sorts of city issues. Over the past two months, all of the Democratic candidates, including Sharpton, have written op-eds in the *Daily News* offering their views on matters such as education, the city budget, and crime. This week's issue is taxes.

As in so many other cases, we've finessed the issue by using the column to describe what taxes we would cut. The Reverend writes today that a Sharpton administration will seek to raise additional revenue by taxing elite nonprofit groups, including foundations, private universities, and hospitals. He will also reintroduce the stock-transfer tax and increase the commuter income tax. "To sum up, we must make the richer and the stronger pay their share!"

Sharpton's ideas may have merit, but from a political standpoint they're suicidal. Imagine the effect of an ad campaign publicizing Al Sharpton's plan to tax colleges and hospitals. Maybe next time Sharpton runs for mayor, he'll hire an out-of-town consultant who will explain the tax sensitivity evidenced by the polls and keep him on a more moderate message.

Perhaps not.

In any case, Sharpton's campaign picked up some support yesterday. Jesse Jackson was in town to endorse and attend a party for Sharpton with boxing promoter Don King, Malcolm X's daughter Quiballah Shabazz, and Kwesi Mfume, the executive director of the NAACP. And the Sharpton campaign is on the air with its first ads, a $10,000 buy on *urban* (black) radio. "I am the only candidate that can build a movement to defeat Mayor Giuliani. . . . I've been there even when it was not popular. Don't waste your vote on people who stand for nothing."

August 18

Aside from Rudy Giuliani and Fran Reiter, the person we talk about most in the office is Adam Nagourney. Jim has, in his own words, a "fixation" on Adam Nagourney. He has a picture of Adam Nagourney hanging on the front door of his office. In the picture, Nagourney is holding a microphone, apparently belonging to one of the city radio stations, up to Ruth who is speaking from her podium. Nagourney, short, bespectacled, and curly-haired, is turned away from Ruth and appears to be wincing, perhaps comically, in pain. I think the intended joke is that Nagourney is uncomfortable in the role of a radio reporter, but it looks at first glance as if our candidate is causing him dyspepsia.

Most of us are convinced that Nagourney does not like us. It seems clear, at the very least, that he does not think we're an effective group. But it seems to go beyond that. He seems to genuinely dislike Ruth. The majority of our time talking about him is spent speculating as to why this may be so.

This is amateur psychology at its worst. Speculating about the underlying motivations of someone one knows well is an uncertain business, and none of us knows Nagourney well. Jim has dinner with him from time to time, but the two are hardly friends. Lee talks to Nagourney regularly also, but it is, again, a strictly professional relationship. Nevertheless, we speculate. Some think Nagourney is beholden to a thesis of Giuliani invincibility he decided on long ago. Others think Nagourney dislikes women candidates. Still others think Nagourney was alienated by our handling of the Fields-Glick issue.

I wonder whether Adam Nagourney likes politicians. Yesterday Nagourney profiled Sal Albanese. The piece was either tepid or a hatchet job, depending on your view, but in either case comparable to the lukewarm-to-hostile coverage Ruth has been receiving. Sal is pictured on the front page of the Metro Section marching with a single campaign staffer. It surely must be a parade—his staffer is carrying an Albanese poster and Sal is waving his hand—but there is no crowd in the picture or any other marchers as far as one can tell. The premise of the article is that Albanese's campaign began with promise, but has not yet found its "stride." According to Nagourney, a number of things are working against Albanese. First, Albanese "is not a particularly accomplished campaigner." (On the stump, Albanese's "words come out in a quick and mumbled monotone.") Second, Albanese's "lack of campaign funds reinforces his indistinct image." Nagourney cites no evidence or expert opinion for either claim. I wonder whether it would be possible to find support for the second claim. How does one reinforce an indistinct image?

Nagourney seems to believe that all politics is spin. Perhaps disliking or distrusting politicians is the inevitable result of that worldview. He is entitled to believe whatever he likes. Our great frustration with Nagourney—and where we take exception—is that the *Times* reporter does not merely report facts, he imputes motivations underlying facts. When Ruth did endorse Fields, the second line of Nagourney's story was that the decision "was intended to put an end to a growing dispute that had dominated her campaign for mayor in recent days." No one from our campaign said that. It was an inference, not a fact.

We're not the only ones plagued by this. Just yesterday, when Fran Reiter denied having questioned Abner Louima's credibility, Nagourney wrote, "Ms. Reiter's statements were the latest sign of concern at City Hall—and perhaps of some hope among Mr. Giuliani's opponents—that the brutality case could cause political trouble for the mayor." What Fran Reiter said is a fact. What the statement proves is another thing. Someone's opinion as to what the statement proved would also be fact. But a reporter's own inference as to what it proved is an expression of opinion.

A realist would quickly point out that that may be a distinction without a difference. There are hundreds of experts on any given subject in New York, and any reporter with perseverance can find one to offer the desired opinion. It's easier and more honest for a reporter to simply say what he or she believes to be true—that Reiter's statements were a sign of concern at City Hall—than to spend an entire day calling political consultants to get one to say the same thing. But the question is not an entirely academic one. Some readers will not make the distinction between the fact—the act—and the opinion—the motivation.

Nagourney is far from unique is his methodology. His own motivations are simple, I expect. He reports so often on motives because he believes it is good news. It certainly is news. The question is whether why someone said something should be afforded equal coverage as what the person said. There's no easy answer to that one. Perhaps the press is right, and that is what readers are truly interested in.

But I wonder what it must be like to believe that's true, to believe that every person you deal with professionally speaks to you with some ulterior motive in mind and never out of sincere conviction—to live in a world where everyone has an agenda.

It must be a sad, lonely world.

August 19

This business of constructing a candidate who is different from the underlying individual is a bit like building a structure without a foundation. Personal history or moral principles do not dictate decisions. The constructed candidate opposes abortion not out of a conviction, but as the result of a calculation that includes prior opposition as one factor among many. Everything is fair game. Appearance, matters of principle, fundamental political philosophy are all up for grabs. It is a house of cards. The Abner Louima case is putting a great deal of pressure on our house of cards.

At 2:00 in the morning on the day of the first primary debate, Jim e-mails a draft of Ruth's closing remarks. It begins, "I see a city where the name of the mayor is identified with kids and families and neighborhoods and schools, instead of being chanted during acts of unspeakable brutality." We speak only briefly. He says something like, "We have to use the Giuliani time quote, it's just too powerful," but I'm not really sure what's going on in his mind.

My instincts say that there isn't any long-term strategic plotting going on here. Jim is referring to the quote to make a point about the Giuliani administration that we've been trying to make for months: that the mayor has the wrong priorities for the city. But will the press be able to draw a distinction between the rhetorical allusion to the quote and a direct attack on the mayor's record on crime and police brutality?

The debate goes well for Ruth. Sharpton and Albanese focus most of their attacks on Giuliani, which serves us well. Sal makes a reference to Ruth's behavior in Washington Heights and at one point says that Ruth "simply cannot win against Rudy Giuliani because she lacks the credibility on the issue of crime." Our polling suggests he's probably right, but it's not a very damaging attack.

Eric Ruano-Melendez is entertaining, but not nearly as threatening as we feared. He sings "The Star-Spangled Banner" for his closing and urges people to vote for him on September 7. The primary is on September 9.

The story of the debate is that Ruth is no longer giving Rudy a pass on the Louima case. Fran Reiter's first response following the debate is to deny that Louima ever confirmed that the officers said "It's Giuliani time," but she quickly retreats after we make an issue of her questioning the credibility of the sodomized Haitian. Instead, Giuliani relies on a more familiar tactic: He attacks David Dinkins.

Dinkins raised Giuliani's ire this week by penning an article in the *Village Voice,* titled "Giuliani Time," about what the police must do to end brutality. Dinkins wrote, "I charge that our police department, following the lead of this mayoral administration, is dangerously close to adopting a philosophy that the end justifies the means."

Giuliani says Charles Schwarz, one of the officers charged in the Louima attack, received only a fifteen-day suspension for an incident of brutality in 1992. Like everything else wrong in this city, the Louima case too is the fault of the former mayor. And he rails against the Democrats for trying to make a political issue. "All these people are doing—the candidates last night and David Dinkins—is seeking to divide for their own narrow political purposes, with illogical and irrational arguments."

• • •

These are heady days for Rudy Giuliani. *Newsweek* is running a cover feature, "We'll Take Manhattan," on Giuliani and the rebirth of New York City. *Time* has a competing piece on "a new breed of activist mayors" that features Giuliani prominently. Rudy is rumored to be eyeing a run for Daniel Patrick Moynihan's Senate seat in 2000, and no one is laughing. His power is at a peak, and he knows it. No problem is too large for Rudy Giuliani to solve.

At Giuliani's monthly town hall meeting in Staten Island, a young woman defends a local shelter against complaints by local residents. Cassandra Adams has lived at the shelter since her home collapsed six months ago. She is out of work.

"If I find a job for you, would you work?" Rudy asks.

"Yes, sir, I would," says Adams.

"Then we'll take your name and number and call you tomorrow and find you a job."

It is as simple as that in Rudy Giuliani's New York. Everyone who wants a job can have a job. Those three hundred thousand people out of work must just not want to work enough. Because everything is fine in Rudy Giuliani's city.

August 20

An editorial in the *Post* today says what's probably really on people's minds about the Louima case. "It would be naïve," the *Post* writes, "to deny that some cops may have misperceived their new mission as a license to abuse citizens. . . . So maybe it is 'Giuliani time' in New York City regarding public safety and the New York City Police Department. If so, we find it vastly preferable to 'Dinkins time.'"

The conclusion may be objectionable, but the editorial sets up the analysis right, I think. Everyone knows that increased order leads to increased infringement on civil liberties. It is a price most people are willing to pay. Early polling data indicate that most people agree with the *Post*'s conclusion that Giuliani time is preferable to Dinkins time. Thirty-five percent of respondents to a *Post* poll say the mayor's focus on crime allows police brutality, but Giuliani's vote is remaining stable. People believe, 52–30, that he should be reelected. An incredible 69 percent of Jewish respondents think he deserves reelection.

The Louima case is doing little damage. Fifty-two percent of respondents believe the incident is an isolated one, though the question is so vague it's impossible to interpret. Incredibly, 27 percent of people say police relations with city residents are better, as compared with those during previous mayors' tenures, versus 23 percent who say they are worse.

• • •

The *Post* poll offers even worse news for us for the primary. According to the survey, fully 41 percent of voters are undecided. Thirty-three percent express a preference for Ruth, versus 14 and 10 percent for Albanese and Sharpton, respectively. In May, Ruth led 50–12–11, with just 26 percent undecided. Ruth is still capturing more than half of the voters expressing a preference, but Jim cautions that undecideds, who tend to be anomic and disaffected, tend to resolve in favor of challengers. From a longitudinal standpoint, the poll is disastrous.

"It's beyond horrendous," says pollster John Zogby. "It's close to a meltdown." Zogby was the only major pollster to call the 1994 Cuomo-Pataki race. He tells columnist Sidney Zion, who calls Zogby the pollster "who keeps getting it right," that "Messinger has imploded." He says, "Messinger is in a free fall like I've never seen, and Sal is cooking. I give them both about 38 percent and Al Sharpton 24 percent." Zogby also predicts that Sal will win the ensuing runoff. Zogby's data differ so dramatically from our own that it prompts me to raise the issue of whether Zogby may be spinning and the general issue of the use of pollsters and political consultants as spinners.

Zogby is a Republican pollster. Though it's not obvious why, virtually all pollsters affiliate themselves with one party or another. Geoff Garin is a Democratic pollster. Frank Luntz is a Republican pollster. Some pollsters even develop even more refined subspecialties. For example, Celinda Lake is a well-known pollster who specializes in female Democrats.

In the case of political consultants, it's easy to understand the necessity of affiliating with one party or another. Even though what consultants really do is render advice, they are often cast in the position of advancing the message of the campaign, and that would be difficult for them to do credibly if they were associated with candidates of different ideologies. Jim would have a harder time making the case for Ruth and against Rudy if he had been associated with Jesse Helms instead of Harvey Gantt. But Jim's methodology should serve Rudy as well as Ruth. Jim might feel morally ambiguous about working for Rudy, and he might not work as enthusiastically as a result, but to the extent his techniques are scientific, they should, as perhaps Dick Morris has proved, work as well for Republicans as Democrats. If anything, the pollster's craft is more scientific than the consultant's, and since pollsters are not generally in the position of advancing the message of a client's campaign, there's no obvious reason they should affiliate themselves with a party. And yet they do, because they live in a world where the notion of objectivity is laughable.

Perhaps the consultant's disclosure of a party affiliation is an admirable act of honesty, an open declaration of bias when consultants spin for one side or the other, as they often do. Jim's old adversary Ed Rollins has weighed in on the mayoral race from time to time. So too have Joe Mercurio on the Republican side, Hank Sheinkopf and Hank Morris on the Democratic side, and Dick Morris on no discernible side other than his own. None of these consultants have any ostensible connection to either of the candidates, but everyone operates under the assumption that when consultants appear on a talk show, they're spinning for one side or the other.

In speculating about the value of this sort of spinning, we venture into a reality one step removed from the already indecipherable world of metatruth. Spinning consultants are acting in the role of independent verifier (an aspect of spinning, you'll recall, with which our campaign is extremely facile). The underlying fact that they are vouching for is that the strategy of the campaign is well conceived. When Hank Sheinkopf says, for example, as he has recently, "I would do pretty much what she's doing now," noting "the mayor, Sharpton, and Albanese will seize on any opportunity to cut her up,"—or when Jim Chapin, a political scientist, says, "Everybody says, 'Don't just stand there, do something.' Well, in her case the opposite is true: Don't just do something, stand here,"—they are attesting to the credibility of the campaign strategy.

On the other hand, David Garth, the former media adviser to Giuliani and Ed Koch, says, "The Messinger campaign is not a terribly intelligent campaign." Not even the Democratic consultants are unified behind us. In an article in the *News* questioning our strategy of hoarding cash for the last days of the campaign, one Democratic consultant says, "The mayor's race is not a race where you can just wait around to the end to put up ads with nice pictures." But the quality of the campaign is a meta-issue to begin with. No one votes for a candidate because of the quality of his or her campaign. A poor campaign is only relevant if it becomes representative of a candidate's ineptitude. This is spinning for the spinners.

When pollsters spin, they're doing something similarly abstruse. Polls don't matter except to the extent that a pervasive belief that a race is noncompetitive may suppress turnout. So if Zogby is spinning, he's trying to bolster the case that Giuliani is leading by even more than people believe. Presumably this is because the Giuliani campaign has concluded that the subset of citizens who would vote in a race viewed as noncompetitive perceives the mayor more favorably than the set of voters who would show up to the polls in a race viewed as competitive.

Of course, it could also be that Zogby is being absolutely honest (truth and spinning are not mutually exclusive), and we're heading for a devastating and embarrassing defeat on primary day.

August 21

Over the past six months, I've had the chance here and there to play press secretary. I've handed out flyers at subway stations and advanced an event or two. I've met most of the journalists covering the campaign and lots of famous people and politicians. But I've never gotten to play real politics. Today is my first chance, and I don't like it one bit.

For several weeks we've been trying to get Alan Hevesi to take some action on the Bronx battered women's shelter scandal. The city comptroller has the power under the city charter to certify all city contracts. We want Hevesi to refuse to certify the contracts of the security guard company whose employees were asleep at the switch. Contract review is ordinarily a rubber-stamp process, but we are holding out some small hope that Hevesi's office will take our side because it would be the right thing to do. Yesterday, Hevesi's office called to tell our political director that they had reached their final decision. They want to talk to someone from the campaign about it, and I'm the man. I briefly discuss strategy with Ruth's political director, and we both agree that if the news is bad, as it almost surely will be, there is nothing to be gained from a confrontation.

Larry, one of Hevesi's advisers, sits me down and tells me that they have reviewed the Department of Investigation report and decided on the basis of it not to take any action against the company. The contracts will stand.

"I can't say that Ruth will be thrilled by that," I say, "but we understand that your power under the city charter is quite limited. I hope that Mr. Hevesi will understand that Ruth feels very strongly about the matter and is going to continue pressing it as an issue."

"We certainly understand that," Larry says.

It's not the most intellectually honest conversation, but it's entirely palatable. We demonstrate the unspoken mutual understanding shared by all lackeys. For all I know Larry privately fought to cancel the contracts. He and I have no quarrel. I am preparing to leave when one of Hevesi's senior people, whose name and title I don't quite catch, walks into the room.

"Sorry, I'm late," she says. "I'm glad I caught you."

I introduce myself.

"I'm sure you and Larry have agreed that this report clears the security guard company."

I look at Larry. I thought we had an understanding. "Well, I explained that Ruth understands that your powers under the charter are limited. We wish you would reverse your decision, but we respect it, and Ruth won't make an issue of it."

"But it would be irresponsible for us to make any other decision."

I'm not sure where she's going with this.

"I don't see it that way."

"The guards that slept on the job have been fired. You can't punish a company for the negligence of a few of its employees. And besides, even the guards that slept didn't do anything seriously wrong. They didn't have sex with any of the residents. The report clearly shows this."

This is eerily like Mastro's argument. I'm getting red in the face.

She continues. "If we decertified the contract, a judge would throw the decision right out of court. We don't have a leg to stand on."

The politic thing to do would be to nod my head and excuse myself.

"I happen to be a lawyer," I say, "and that's a bunch of nonsense. Of course you can hold a company responsible for how its employees behave. Would you excuse McDonald's if just a few of its stores used rats for meat? Security companies get paid to protect people. If their guards are falling asleep on the job, then they're not protecting people. They're supposed to protect people. That's what they get paid for. They're supposed to make sure that women don't get raped while they're on duty.

"The report says the shelter staff held back food from residents in exchange for sex. The report says that shelter staff routinely let the residents' former boyfriends into the shelter. Those are the people they're seeking shelter from. The report says the guards slept on the job.

"They were really bad guards," I shout. "I think you can fire the company for that."

Larry seems a bit embarrassed. This isn't the first time I wonder whether I'm cut out for this business.

August 22

One small victory: Supreme Court Justice Paula Omansky has ruled in favor of Ruth on her suit to force the city to disclose Freedom of Information Law requests and responses. "It could be that city agencies tended to deny requests that would reveal their own failures, or requests that put the agency in an unfavorable light," writes Justice Omansky. The mayor says he believes the decision is a mistake and will appeal it.

• • •

A study by state comptroller Carl McCall has found that many officers hired under the Safe Streets, Safe Cities program have been placed in desk jobs that could have been filled by civilian employees. McCall says the unnecessary use of police officers has cost the city $132 million over seven years. But the news is too late to make any difference to us. The two-day period for assessing the validity of competing claims by campaigns has come and gone.

The truth doesn't make any difference.

• • •

Eric Ruano-Melendez reports that he is quite pleased with his debate performance. "A lot of people called me today," he says. "They're offering me some financial help. Some of them even own buildings in Manhattan."

August 23

Related to the distinction between traditional and modern campaigns is a distinction between what most consultants call *wholesale* and *retail* politics. Each of these terms, like the words "liberal" and "conservative," means many different things to different people, but the gist is that retail politics is played at the level of the individual constituent or constituency group, while wholesale politics, like the modern campaign, is played out on the electorate as a whole. Pork-barrel legislation, signing a proclamation for Burmese American Day, or adding a bus stop in front of a senior citizen center are all examples of retail politics. Coming out in favor of the death penalty is wholesale politics (or, perhaps, an act of sincere conviction).

For all the mixed things we say about Rudy Giuliani, he is an extraordinary politician. Part of what makes him so extraordinary is that he is the quintessential wholesale politician. I think anyone who watches Rudy Giuliani on any sort of regular basis has the sense that he isn't like other politicians. Rudy repeatedly says he isn't like other politicians, which makes him like other politicians, but he really is different. Part of that might be attributable to his distinctive look and personality, but every politician has his or her own look and personality and yet still seems like a politician. What makes Rudy stand out, I think, is that he's a wholesale politician in a world of retailers—in some ways, a man ahead of his time.

By necessity, the ordinary politician thinks in retail terms. Ordinary politicians don't get their start in multimillion-dollar high-visibility campaigns. They scratch and claw to win a seat on the City Council or in the state Assembly in races in which ten thousand votes might carry the day. Retail politics is all there is at that level. Proclaiming yourself to be in favor of parental notification for abortion won't help you get elected to City Council. The trick is to shake as many hands and earn as many favors as you possibly can.

It's at that level that politicians become wed to the model of traditional campaigns, which, again, is all there is at that level, and to the notion of retail politics. It's only when politicians reach a high-visibility race that wholesale politics matter. That's when the consultants come in and try to persuade them to fundamentally change the way they view voters and do politics—and try to get them to run a campaign unlike any they've run before. Whether they survive or not depends on how quickly they acclimate themselves to the new environment. But the instincts are always there—they don't just go away with a few months of coaching and some television commercials. Politicians are born and bred to be mediators and facilitators. They thrive by learning to play wholesale politics, but they survive on retail.

As a man whose first political campaign was to be mayor of the largest city in the United States, Rudy Giuliani doesn't have a history of running grassroots campaigns and, as a result, doesn't sound like other politicians. Few other politicians would have spoken the way he did about Washington Heights or Crown Heights. Others would have seen both sides of the issues and stepped lightly, trying not to offend any constituency group. Rudy has no such compunction. Retail politicians see grays. Rudy sees blacks and whites. And that's a large part of the reason for his wide, deep support.

But all that said, Rudy does play retail politics. Perhaps he does it as an afterthought, as if he were an Olympic decathalete who thought tap dancing was silly, but learned to do it anyway just to show everybody he could. Or perhaps that first campaign scarred him forever. Perhaps he vowed that, from that day forward, he would wear his belt and suspenders too. These days, the Giuliani retail machine is working overtime.

Cassandra Adams, the woman to whom Rudy Giuliani promised a job at the town hall meeting on Staten Island, is being offered a job as a clerical associate at the Income Support Center of the city's Human Resources Administration. The city is spending millions of dollars to fight rat infestation and $2 million more to improve animal shelters and crack down on dangerous dogs. I dismissed similar proposals from the borough president's office as too retail to be worth doing. And Giuliani is dispensing patronage like any good retail politician. The daughter of Priscilla Wooten, the black City Council member who is endorsing the mayor, was hired to a $74,000-a-year job at the Board of Education three months ago as special assistant to Giuliani appointee Irene Impellizeri.

But a leopard cannot change his spots. Rudy will not be attending the opening of the new Arthur Ashe stadium in Queens. The mayor, who has awarded more than $600 million in tax breaks to Fortune 500 companies and wants to spend another $1 billion to build a stadium for the Yankees in Manhattan, is protesting a clause in the contract that requires the city to pay a fine when airplanes fly over the stadium during matches. From one standpoint nothing could be sillier than disrespecting Arthur Ashe. But a more important principle is at stake—David Dinkins negotiated the contract.

"I'm not going," Giuliani says.

August 24

Then, the house of cards collapsed. At the Evangelical Crusade Church in East Flatbush where Abner Louima is a parishioner, the campaign implodes in self-contradiction. Just two weeks after having praised the mayor for his handling of the Abner Louima case, Ruth makes "Giuliani time" the theme of her speech. She uses the phrase over and over.

"Giuliani time is a time when it's out of fashion to care about the poor and homeless," she says. "Unemployment is at Depression levels in some boroughs and neighborhoods. It's Giuliani time. Some ninety thousand children will be forced to go to school in closets and stairwells and locker rooms and bathrooms. It's Giuliani time. And what did they chant when they beat and brutalized Abner Louima? 'It's Giuliani time.' Why did they chant his name? Why? Because Giuliani time is a time of cold shoulders and hard hearts."

I wish I could offer some insight into where the speech comes from. Clearly, Lee and Jim and Ruth have all signed off on it, but I'm again not sure what the motivation is. Lee probably just thinks it's a good speech that will generate some news. Jim may be drawing a distinction between the rhetorical use of the quote to make valid arguments we have been making throughout the campaign and a direct comment on the Louima affair. Mostly, I think, it is an inevitable surrender to the constant burden of trying to make a person something she is not. This is what Ruth wanted to say all along. But now she has to reconcile her new outrage with her prior restraint.

Sharpton and Giuliani, united for the first time, both call the speech pandering. Giuliani says, "This is, like, misrepresentation of the worst kind, intended to divide people, from a candidate who is probably at this point desperate." According to the mayor, the remarks are "pandering of the worst kind, almost at the verge of really severe irresponsibility." Almost, but just a hair short of the verge of really severe irresponsibility.

From a press standpoint, the speech is a disaster, another symbol of the ineptitude of the campaign. Adam Nagourney contrasts the Democrats' handling of the Louima case with Bill Clinton's handling of the riots in Los Angeles following the Rodney King verdict. The Democrats, he says, "have not shown the aggressiveness or nimbleness that Mr. Clinton displayed when he seized on an episode of racial strife to dramatize what he described as the failures of a popular President." Ruth, he says, "has veered from describing the beating of Abner Louima as an isolated incident, to praising Mayor Giuliani's initial response to it, to finally using it to condemn Mr. Giuliani's entire record." An article in the *Observer* calls the Louima case a "live political grenade that Messinger, frankly, just couldn't handle."

Of course, it's voters and not the press that we're interested in, so at some level it doesn't matter what the newspapers think, but we're not putting hundreds of thousands of dollars behind the speech. Only New York 1 covered the "Giuliani time" speech, so though it earned us a spate of unfavorable articles, we are receiving no discernible offsetting benefit.

• • •

As an aside in his article, Adam Nagourney mentions that Ruth's long record in public life has been thoroughly researched by the Giuliani campaign. My team has known for weeks that the campaign is earning a lousy reputation, but this brings the lesson home. We've thoroughly researched the Giuliani campaign too, but Nagourney is already spun too far on this issue to be brought back. None of my team's hard work will ever be recognized.

August 25

I am with Ruth for an interview with the *Post* editorial board. Editorial-board interviews are a rite of passage in elections. I don't know why the Democrats put themselves through it. There's no doubt the four dailies will endorse Giuliani in the general. Last week Ruth went to the *Daily News*. The *News* spent most of the time trying to get Ruth to say what the unemployment rate would be during her tenure. It's a ridiculous question and Ruth wouldn't answer it.

The next day, the *News* proclaimed in "Ruth Less Than Meets the Eye":

> Ruth Messinger's mayoral campaign has made some important strides in recent weeks. Her speaking style has improved and she is avoiding the embarrassing gaffes that plagued her earlier. Even her fund-raising has picked up. Now for the bad news. She shies away from specific promises as though they are the plague. If God is in the details, Messinger must be an agnostic. She has focused on New York City's 10 percent unemployment, which is about twice the national figure. But on the obvious query—what is her goal for unemployment—she won't offer a number. If 10 percent is too high, what would the rate be under Mayor Messinger? Nine percent? Eight percent? She wouldn't say.

It seems like even more of a waste of time to visit with the *Post*. We could raise $5,000 in the two hours it will take to travel and conduct the interview. But we're going anyway.

Jack Newfield, who once said that most politicians are half human beings, is here. He dislikes Ruth so much that he refuses to even look at her. And here also is Andrea Peyser, who called Ruth's granddaughter the product of an act of "boundless ego." Peyser recently listed Ruth as one of the top sinners. Under "Envy" she wrote "Hands down-winner: Ruth Messinger." Said Peyser, "The Manhattan borough president so badly wants to unseat the mayor, her shame knows no bounds. Recently, she enlisted top aide Lee Jones to accuse Giuliani of gaining weight. Anyone who's ever stood behind Messinger on a buffet line cringed (see Gluttony)."

I think we're going to get a fair shake.

• • •

Sal Albanese is charging that Ruth's two years of experience teaching classes at the Children's Community Workshop School does not qualify her as a teacher. Bizarrely, he refers to himself in the third person. "Albanese charges she's distorting her own occupation!" he says to the *Times*. This isn't a very damaging attack, but the enthusiasm with which it is received raises the question of why Sal hasn't gone after Ruth more throughout the past month. The papers seem to like Sal, and the *Post* and *News* would certainly receive any arguments against Ruth favorably. For the most, though, Sal has remained positive. Jim thinks it is a fundamental mistake on Albanese's part.

August 26

I am more buoyant this morning than I've been in weeks. We are delivering our ads to the television stations today. Our first ad airs tomorrow. (On *Jenny Jones*!) We are up. It may not make any difference in the outcome of the race, but it feels good to be fighting back.

The ad begins with a shot of the New York City skyline and a few notes of music that sound like the beginning to "New York, New York." (It's not the real song—using the original would have meant paying a few extra bucks for the rights.) From there, it shifts to the face of a pitifully unhappy girl. ("Things are looking up, right? Well, not for our kids.") She and other kids are taking class in a school bathroom. ("School overcrowding is so bad, classes are held in bathrooms.") One of the students looks like he may be sitting on a urinal. ("Six billion dollars slashed from our schools. Test scores down.") The music turns upbeat. (Ruth Messinger says it's going to change!) Ruth is shown walking purposefully down the street (she's got a plan!) and in various poses with schoolchildren, at her desk in the borough president's office, and with children. "Her plan: Cut waste in government and invest in our schools. Hire more teachers to lower class size. And set tough standards. Keep schools open till 6:00, so kids have someplace to go. Former teacher, mother, 20-year public servant. A mayor for our kids. Ruth Messinger."

It's an absolutely brilliant ad. It introduces Ruth to the voters and makes a damning argument about Rudy Giuliani's performance on education. If the focus groups are an indication, it is an argument with enormous power.

August 27

Today the *News* editorial board does a shameful hatchet job on Sal Albanese. "The longer you listen [to Sal Albanese], as the *Daily News* Editorial Board did in a meeting with him yesterday, the less sense he makes. It's not that he's not sincere. He is. But while Albanese has focused in solid issues—economic development, education, campaign reform—he is more than a little confused on the facts and shaky on specifics."

Note the message of the editorial is not that the *News* disagrees with a position owned by Albanese; it's that Albanese does not understand the issue well. If he did, Sincere Sal would inevitably agree with the *News*.

The evidence of Sal's confusion: Albanese brands the city workfare program "bankrupt" and "unfair" and questions whether it has channeled "doletakers" into permanent jobs. "Asked where the 300,000 people who have left welfare have gone, Albanese doesn't have a clue." According to the *News*, Albanese concedes that some former welfare recipients may have

gotten jobs, but suspects "most have wound up on breadlines." "Funny," the *News* writes, "soup kitchens aren't reporting vastly increased demand."

Funny, they are. According to the Coalition for the Homeless, seventy thousand people a month are turned away from food pantries and soup kitchens, up sharply from years past. And the reason Albanese cannot say how many people have moved from welfare into jobs is because the city does not keep statistics. According to one estimate by the state Department of Labor, only 10 percent of people who leave workfare are documented as getting jobs.

Even the reduction in welfare rolls is deceptive. Giuliani has reduced the welfare rolls by creating new hurdles for applicants. Under his Eligibility Verification Program, 45 percent of new applicants are rejected. Public Advocate Mark Green says many of those turned away are truly needy.

The *News* stands guilty of the same charge of which it accuses Sal: of being "less interested in the facts than advancing an ideology." Albanese's idea to emphasize job training over work is a serious, meritorious proposal. One could easily disagree with it, but it is quite another matter for the *News* to trivialize Albanese as ignorant.

August 28

The *New York Times* is doing its best to blunt the impact of our commercial. The other dailies cover the ad in a straightforward manner. The *Staten*

Island Advance's story, "Messinger Assails Schools in First TV Campaign Ads," doesn't mention the urinal at all. *Newsday*'s story, "Ruth Launches TV Attack," and the *News*'s story, "Ad Plumbs Schools Issue," each mention the urinal, but in neither case as the central point of the story. But the *Times*, no doubt at the urging of the Giuliani campaign, has fixated on the urinal. Adam Nagourney's story, "Messinger's TV Ad Leads Crew to Charge 'Sordid Duplicity,'" focuses primarily on the alleged misrepresentation, barely mentioning the content of the ad:

> In the first televised advertisement of her campaign, Ruth W. Messinger offered a hard-hitting assault on Mayor Rudolph W. Giuliani's education record yesterday. But the ad, which featured a staged scene of children being taught in a bathroom so crowded that one boy's back was nestled against a urinal, prompted Schools Chancellor Rudy Crew to accuse her of "denigrating the public school system for political gain."

Today in an editorial, "How Not to Run a Campaign," the *Times* says our campaign "manufactured an illustration of school overcrowding that is worse than anything in the city's system. By exaggerating, [Messinger] manages to trivialize the horrific reality." Three pages later in the paper is a story titled "Schools Often Turn Bathrooms into Classrooms" that says: "The issue of whether public school children have received instruction beside urinals suddenly became a shrill point of contention this week in the mayoral campaign. But for years, overcrowded districts throughout the city have used some of the bathrooms in their schools as classrooms and as offices for teachers and guidance counselors."

It's possible, but difficult, to reconcile the article and the editorial. Clearly, it's not the fact of staging the ad that is objectionable—it's illegal to film ads in public schools. Rudy Giuliani's first ad used some footage filmed in a parochial school. The issue must be whether the ad depicts life accurately. As today's *Times* article shows, bathrooms are regularly used as classes. So the key to understanding the *Times*'s disapprobation must be in the second clause of the second line of Nagourney's story, "[the ad] featured a staged scene of children being taught in a bathroom *so* crowded that one boy's back was nestled against a urinal." It's not that the ad was staged, or that it was filmed in a bathroom, or perhaps even that it was filmed with a urinal; the problem is that it depicts an overcrowded bathroom.

There is a distinction to be made there. The deputy schools chancellor for operations is pointing out the difference between bathrooms and "converted bathrooms." A converted bathroom, says Lewis Spence, "has blackboards and it has appropriate furniture and all those kind of things that go with being a classroom." Converted bathrooms, he says, "do not have urinals," and in any event, the use of bathrooms does not "suggest anything about the quality of instruction."

But is the distinction meaningful enough to justify the *Times*'s admonishment? Overcrowding is a legitimate issue. We've demonstrated that bathrooms are regularly used as classroom space. We've demonstrated that some of those bathrooms have operating fixtures. And surely the *Times* doesn't believe that any bathroom, even a converted bathroom, is an appropriate learning space. Ed Koch defends the campaign, saying there is "nothing wrong" with the ad. Every other newspaper reported on the ad without criticism. But somehow, we have not satisfied the *Times*'s burden of factual support to legitimate the ad.

The *Times* could just as easily have written this editorial:

> Ruth Messinger's first campaign ad somewhat overstates the conditions in New York City public schools. That the ad has some basis in reality and only slightly overstates conditions in city schools should give all city residents pause. For two days, the Giuliani campaign and the office of schools chancellor Rudy Crew have been trying to differentiate between the use of real and converted bathrooms for use as classrooms. Bathrooms, in any condition, are inappropriate learning spaces. It is now Ruth Messinger's burden to say specifically what she will do to relieve overcrowding. It's Rudy Giuliani's burden to explain why he hasn't done more.

• • •

Traditionally, and for good reason, city schools chancellors are above politics. But Rudy Crew, the popular schools chancellor, is out in front on this issue. Yesterday, after the *Times* focused on the urinal, we published a photo of a bathroom at Midwood High School with a table placed against a bank of urinals, students around the table, and the urinal tops being used as a bookshelf. Crew first said that the scene was an isolated event. Then his spokesperson said the teachers' union had staged it. Apparently they hadn't checked with the teachers' union. The union says the scene was an "absolutely" real science tutoring session.

The chancellor's action puts us in a terrific bind. It pits us directly against Crew, which couldn't serve Rudy Giuliani better. Giuliani doesn't have the credibility to defend the schools. Crew does. A poll released today by the

Empire State survey shows that even as three-quarters of people give the city schools a D or an F, people think, 50–11, that Crew is doing a good job. (Giuliani's ads are having an effect too. Forty-eight percent gave Rudy Giuliani an A or B, up from 31 percent in 1995, and only 23 percent gave him a D or an F, down from 41 percent in 1995.)

Although its impossible to prove that Crew is taking the lead at Rudy Giuliani's behest, abundant circumstantial evidence suggests that he is. To begin with, his statements are full of Giulianish vigor. Ruth "acted in very, very, very poor taste," the ordinarily reserved Crew says, and committed "gross misrepresentation" by showing kids "routinely being seated in urinals." How can one ad show a routine?

Giuliani claims that he has not spoken with Crew, whose contract is up next year, but how precisely is Crew supposed to interpret Giuliani's statement, "You create an unfair depiction of the system he's running, he's going to fight you"? Crew defends his involvement using language conspicuously similar to the mayor's: "When you attack this system, when you portray our children inaccurately, then you will hear from me."

August 29

Our dilapidated office looks out over City Hall and a small triangular area dotted with benches and trees known as City Hall Park. During warm weather the park hosts occasional protests, which Jim likes to refer to as "Communist Happy Hour." Today, the streets are filled with several thousand marchers chanting "PBA-KKK" and "No justice, no peace." They are protesting the beating of Abner Louima.

The turnout is a bit disappointing to the organizers of the march. Some had predicted that more than twenty-five thousand people would turn out. One police officer stepped forward this week with information substantiating Louima's allegations. The police department's legendary blue wall of silence seems to be cracking. But that hasn't spurred turnout.

It is, nevertheless, a surreal moment. From our view, we can see the marchers come over the Brooklyn Bridge, led by former mayor David Dinkins, resplendently dressed entirely in white, as if on his way to a tennis date. Our campaign stops working and hangs out the window watching the spectacle. Ruth waves up to us in the office as she makes her way onto the stage.

A few black men who are dressed in the manner of the Nation of Islam appear near the stage, and for a moment the buzz in the office is that Louis

Farrakhan may appear. Our field operation is under orders to immediately pull Ruth out if Farrakhan appears, but he never does. It is a false alarm.

Al Sharpton tells the crowd, "Crime has gone down everywhere in New York City except in the Police Department." David Dinkins is savoring the moment. He relishes the irony of turning the tables on Rudy Giuliani, who in 1992 participated in a police rally against the Dinkins administration in which officers shouted racist slogans. But Dinkins is polite as always. He denounces "the dastardly deed that has aroused so many people."

Ruth's remarks are restrained. The negative reaction to the speech at Louima's church has forced us back into our shell. We are reacting now on this one. "We are all Abner Louima's family," Ruth says before reciting a prayer. As she reads the prayer, one can almost feel the real Ruth trying to burst out from inside and scream, "Yes, we have order in this city, but at what cost? At what cost?"

• • •

If the *New York Times* and New York 1 are opinion leaders in the sense that they have influence disproportionate to the size of their audience, then the *New York Times*'s weekly program on New York 1 must be an opinion czar. Every Friday night, several *New York Times* reporters sit around a table and interview themselves about their own articles. It's a masturbatory exercise. I don't want to imagine who is watching the program on a Friday night at 10:00.

Of course, we watch.

Adam Nagourney is a guest tonight. Our ad is first on the agenda for discussion. Clyde Haberman, a senior *Times* reporter, asks Nagourney to define the nature of the alleged exaggeration. Nagourney says: "The question is—this is not as pedantic as it sounds—there's no question that there are students being taught in converted bathrooms, in other words, rooms that were once bathrooms that were rebuilt into classrooms. In this case, it made it look as if kids were literally sitting on urinals in operating bathrooms and learning. The school board said that either that does not happen or it if it happens, it happens rarely."

Even the host can't seem to figure that one out. "I'm a little confused about this myself," says Haberman. "Is the issue whether it's a working toilet that students are learning in or whether it's a toilet at all, or is it whether the room was converted and had once been a bathroom and now has been converted into a classroom?"

Nagourney says, "I think the issue—to simplify it—the issue is did

Messinger or her advertising people unnecessarily sensationalize a real situation in order to get attention."

Hard to imagine a political campaign doing that. Rudy's people would never think of doing anything of the sort. But it gets worse still. Nagourney has been so thoroughly spun that he is discrediting the story in his own paper.

"Later in the week," he says, "Somini Sengupta at our paper found a labor newspaper that had what appeared to be a picture of kids learning in a bathroom with urinals within arm's length. However, the Board of Education suggested that this picture was doctored or either completely fabricated." Nagourney doesn't mention that the *Times* itself reported that the teachers' union maintained the accuracy of the picture.

Haberman continues: "Let's assume for a moment that the long-term goal of the Messinger campaign was to get the conversation away from the reduction of crime by Rudy Giuliani and onto the condition of the schools, which would seem to be advantageous to Democrats. Didn't she succeed, whether inadvertent or not, because all of a sudden now there are days of stories about the condition of the schools. And all of a sudden, the school's chancellor, in a very unusual move, is debating her on this question."

Nagourney has been hopelessly spun against us on the competence of our campaign. "The fact of the matter," he replies, "is that her issue now is being discussed—overcrowding in schools. I think she stumbled into it."

Months of polling and focus groups and half a million dollars' worth of commercials and we stumbled into it inadvertently.

Wonderful.

• • •

Nagourney's comments are maddening, but Jim reminds us all that he is not our audience. Nothing Nagourney or the *Times* does changes the fact that the ad is filtering around out there, reminding people that Rudy Giuliani cut billions of dollars from the schools.

August 30

"Low Turnout Is Ruth's Primary Fear," reports David Seifman of the *New York Post* this morning. "The anticipated low turnout for the Democratic mayoral primary has some Democratic officials thinking the unthinkable—that front-runner Ruth Messinger could be forced into a runoff."

"The evidence," says Seifman, who, unlike his editorial board, has generally been fair throughout the campaign, "is strictly anecdotal."

The source? An unnamed "top Democrat."

The comment? "There's a buzz. Albanese is cooking."

This debate resides somewhere in the fourteenth sphere of banality. It's only in our universe that a debate about pollsters' expectations for the race could be of any interest to anyone. But it seems, yet again, that we're being held to a different evidentiary standard. Seifman acknowledges that "every public poll shows Messinger with a huge lead over main rivals Rev. Al Sharpton and Sal Albanese." Yet we get a bad story because of an unsubstantiated claim by a single person who is not even willing to go on the record.

There's a buzz in the Mandery house about Ruth. Perhaps that's worthy of an article too.

August 31

This, this morning, from Richard Cohen of the *Washington Post:*

> A woman named Ruth Messinger is running for mayor of the City of New York. She is not doing well. The incumbent, Rudy Giuliani, is the beneficiary of a steeply lower crime rate, a booming local economy and a talent for turning up just about anywhere a television camera might. All this might be enough to account for Messinger's poor showing—but not for some people. They think Messinger isn't doing well because she's homely. That she is—although I never would have said so, had not a woman said so first.

Cohen asks whether the refusal to vote for a woman on the basis of looks is equivalent to sexism. He suggests it is not. Both men and women, he says, are judged by their looks. Cohen's own research demonstrates that height in men is often confused with intelligence. (He does not address whether height in women is confused with intelligence.) Voters favor male politicians who are trim. Women must care about different things like fashion, hairstyles, and clothing styles. (He does not address whether men are exempt from the same.)

It's not that looks matter for women; it's simply that looks matter. "All of which," Cohen concludes, "leaves Ruth Messinger with a problem that transcends wardrobe and makeup: She has a radio face in a television era. If she is being penalized for that, it is not because she is a woman, but because she is a politician in an age that has elevated appearance to an importance it never had before."

When I tell my mother about the article, she forcefully responds that Ruth is a nice-looking woman, but we agree that's not the issue. I don't know whether Ruth is a victim of sexism in the sense that voters will vote against her because of how she looks. I do know that no one would ever have written an article about looks costing a man votes. I guarantee you Rudy's hair costs him votes, and I don't see anyone writing about that.

Lee brings the article to the attention of Andrew Kirtzman, who interviews Ruth in the evening.

"Do you feel that you're being discriminated against because you're not a more beautiful woman?" Kirtzman asks.

It's among Ruth's proudest and most impressive moments:

> We've got a lot of people who've heard about this column who are, frankly, outraged. You know, part of this is how people respond, but people have at the top of their list, I promise you, not how a candidate looks, but what a candidate says about the issues that really matters to them. And over and over, as Melissa Russo noted, where I've been, day after day, week after week, is talking to moms and dads in this city who are worried about the opening of school when they shouldn't have to be, who are outside of schools this morning saying, "Look, I know the teachers are trying, but there are twenty-six kids at my son's second grade, and that's too many." Those are the problems that are on the minds of kids, parents, teachers and businesspeople in this city.

Ruth took the question back to message.

September 1

There are parades on holidays I never knew existed. Today is Caribbean Day, time for the annual Brooklyn West Indian–American Day Carnival Parade. Up and down Eastern Parkway the candidates prowl the most important of campaign fora. The mayor's reception is mixed, but he quiets the occasional jeers by tossing autographed soccer balls into the crowd. Al Sharpton receives a hero's welcome ("Looking fit and trim!" according to the *Caribbean News*). Adam Nagourney says Ruth is "so buoyant she did not seem to notice when the sound truck played a reggae version of the theme from *Mission Impossible*."

The comment understandably drives Lee and Jim nuts, but I'm more interested in the fact that Nagourney's writing continues to reflect an antiquated worldview of campaigns. "The presence of the candidates," he writes, "demonstrated the political influence of immigrants from the West Indies who have settled in the New York area." Could he possibly believe that the presence of the candidates demonstrated anything other than their campaigns' belief that a few television cameras would be there? And even if it does, what must he believe about human nature to think that someone would change their vote on the basis of seeing someone at a parade?

"Oh, Carlos, that nice man threw us a miniature soccer ball with his name on it. He must truly care about the Brooklyn West Indian–American community. Let's vote for him."

• • •

The focus of Adam Nagourney's story this morning is Democratic consultants who believe that Ruth may have trouble winning the primary, a notion that was unthinkable months ago. In the best case, Nagourney says, Ruth will squeak by and emerge badly bruised. She will be bruised because "in politics, unlike sports, winning is not the only thing." The argument is that the actual vote for her does not matter, it is how she does relative to how she was expected to do, though, of course, Nagourney doesn't say who sets the expectations. Is it voters? Consultants? His relatives? Ruth's relatives?

Perhaps the *Times* should take the ultimate metapoll. Instead of asking voters whom they plan to vote for, it could ask voters what percentage of the vote they expect each of the candidates to receive. Then it could ask whether it will affect their vote in the general if the candidate does not meet their expectation in the primary.

"So it is," Nagourney says, "that Ms. Messinger's aides are already trying to lower expectations for her performance." He quotes Lee saying, "It's probably difficult to get out of the low 40s." The implication, of course, is that Lee is spinning. Trying to manage expectations about Election Day performance has long been the province of spinners, but in this case it's the truth. It will be difficult, if not impossible, for Ruth get out of the low 40s. Our internal polling has said as much for months, and we've never indicated anything to the contrary. But, of course, in Nagourney's world, there is no truth, only arguments. It matters not one whit to the *Times* reporter that every bit of objective evidence suggests that Lee's opinion is valid. The statement comes from a candidate, so it is inherently laced with ulterior motivation.

Perhaps that's fair. Lee may have been telling the truth in this case, but there's not much doubt he would have offered that opinion even if it were not so well supported by the facts. But the substantive validity of what someone says must count for something.

Not here. The fact that Lee said it matters. What it indicates about our campaign's internal polling matters. What it suggests about our strategy matters. But the truth of what he actually said doesn't matter at all.

I wonder whether Adam Nagourney's head spins when he wakes up in the morning.

September 2

Earlier today, Lee received word that Senator Al D'Amato would be holding a press conference outside of our campaign headquarters. At about 1:00, D'Amato's associates set up a podium in front of our building and pass out a press release (with the name "Messinger" misspelled) assailing Ruth's record on education. "Our problems in our education system are the direct result of people like Ruth Messinger and her allies in the teachers' union."

Jim is incredulous. He paces in the office saying the name "Al D'Amato" over and over again. Though he's in his third term as senator, D'Amato is among the most unpopular figures in the state. In our March poll, 54 percent of voters had a negative view of D'Amato, by far the worst rating of any of the public figures we polled. Jim calls Ruth on the cell phone and tells her to work D'Amato's name into her press conference this afternoon. She's at a new school in Brooklyn that came in $600,000 over budget and is more than a year late. By coincidence, the general contractor gave $13,000 to Giuliani's campaign. Ruth agrees. It's a good day and about to get better.

Our best guess is that this is not an attack coordinated with the Giuliani campaign. Giuliani and D'Amato have had a tumultuous relationship. They were firm allies at one time. D'Amato formally recommended Giuliani to be U.S. Attorney in 1983 and the two were close enough early in Giuliani's tenure to pose together as crack dealers in an undercover drug bust. Shortly thereafter, though, their relationship chilled, and the two hardly spoke for a decade. In 1994, Giuliani endorsed Mario Cuomo over D'Amato's candidate, George Pataki. After the campaign, D'Amato said of the mayor, "He will move to whatever drummer gives him the best beat, the best opportunity. There is no philosophical underpinning to him." But D'Amato, who is pinned under no discernible philosophy himself, reconciled with the popular mayor earlier this year. At a Manhattan fund-raiser for D'Amato's reelection bid, Giuliani and D'Amato hugged like long-lost cousins. D'Amato, who swore in his last election that he would never run again, is running for reelection next year.

It is entirely conceivable that D'Amato would launch an attack for Rudy. But why would Rudy want it? He has access to the same data we do. D'Amato would be a burden on the Giuliani campaign. And Rudy doesn't need any help. Indeed, the senator denies any coordination between the two campaigns. "Oh, this is much more important than a mayoral race. This goes to the essence of the education of our children," D'Amato says.

More to the point, attacking the teachers' union doesn't seem to fit in with the Giuliani strategy of trying to keep the teachers' union at bay. Giuliani has never signaled an attack against the union, though that is clearly the crux of D'Amato's argument. "We have to stand up to the teachers' unions that are more interested in pay and perks than they are in children and classrooms."

On the other hand, D'Amato points out Ruth's school-board appointee's vote against expelling older students who carry guns to school, which suggests coordination between the campaigns. It seems unlikely that such a fine item in Ruth's record is the product of D'Amato's own research.

In any other world, the teachers' union would rush to defend itself and attack D'Amato. In ours, it rushes to distance itself from Ruth. The spokesperson for the union responds to D'Amato's charges later in the day. "I guess Mr. D'Amato has failed to note that the teachers' union has not endorsed Ruth Messinger. At the moment, we're staying neutral."

September 3

We spend so much time lamenting our treatment by the press that I wonder whether we are unreasonable in our expectations. An editorial in a local newspaper, the *Riverdale Press*, mildly reassures me of our sanity. The editorial features a set of photographs of children attending classes in closets, hallways, dressing rooms, and a bathroom.

"The Chancellor seemed particularly upset by the urinals in Ms. Messinger's ad. When have we heard the Chancellor speak so forcefully about the appalling conditions in which thousands of students spend their school day as he spoke about Ms. Messinger's ad?" the editorial asks. "Our pictures of the bathrooms where the children of Riverdale and Kingsbridge have gone to class show no urinals. Does that make them fit places for learning?"

September 4

Sal Albanese came one step short today of violating the time-tested principle that candidates should not back their campaigns with their own money. He took a short-term, high-interest loan of $200,000 from a bank to finance his television commercials on the expectation that he will soon receive matching funds from the Campaign Finance Board.

To qualify for matching funds, a candidate must raise $250,000 in match-eligible contributions; that is, $250,000 in contributions of $1,000 or less from New York City residents. Albanese submitted records last week showing $250,023 in matchable contributions. Before releasing the funds, the Campaign Finance Board verifies the identities and addresses of the contributors. If more than $23 of Albanese's contributions are invalidated, virtually an inevitability, he won't qualify for matching funds until after the primary. He'll certainly reach the threshold eventually, but the money won't do any good after the primary, so his only choice was to borrow the money on a personal guarantee.

All in all, it hasn't been a good day for Sal. The 1,300-member union representing parking, traffic, and sanitation enforcement ticket agents dropped their endorsement of him and went with the mayor. "It's just a commonsense decision," said Robert Cassar, the president of Communication Workers of America Local 1182. With typical class, Albanese refuses to bash his former endorsers. He has other things to worry about anyway.

• • •

Under the campaign-finance law, costs incurred by a campaign to comply with the law are exempt from the cap. That means that the costs of employee time spent on things like finding the address of a contributor or checking to make sure that a contributing company or individual has not exceeded the cap do not themselves count against the cap. In theory, this should be only a trivial exception, since no aspect of compliance is expensive or time-consuming. In practice, it's a gaping loophole, because it's difficult to define precisely what compliance work is, and even more difficult for the Campaign Finance Board to determine whether a campaign is telling the truth in accounting for employee time.

We've been testing the law. We charged about 2 percent of our expenses to compliance. It's likely an exaggeration. We claimed, for example, that one of my deputies spends about a quarter of his time on compliance-related work. In truth it's less than that. Our aggregate total is probably less than 2 percent.

But if our claimed exemption is exaggerated, it is trivial in comparison to that of the Giuliani campaign, which is claiming exempt expenses at more than ten times our rate. In its latest filing, the Giuliani campaign reported that it has already spent more than $1 million on compliance, more than a fifth of the total spending cap for the primary. Of course, Rudy's campaign has greater incentive than we do to inflate compliance expenses, since it has raised to the cap and we neither have nor will. Extra dollars charged to compliance mean extra money that can be spent on television. For us, it frees up money we do not have. All the same, Giuliani's team seems to have gone a bit overboard. They list bills for water, coffee, pagers, locksmiths, and rent as compliance expenses. And they mysteriously list thousands of dollars for "compliance consulting" as exempt. There is an innocent explanation for each of these charges, but how much water can a twenty-two year old drink? What sort of compliance emergency could require a pager? And what could compliance consulting be? Even in an age in which there are consultants for everything, it's hard to imagine needing a consultant to teach a campaign how to verify addresses.

In 1993, the Campaign Finance Board labeled David Dinkins's compliance expenses "inordinately high" and hit his campaign with a $320,000 fine. Dinkins '93 claimed about one-quarter of its expenses were exempt. At the time, Randy Mastro, then one of Giuliani's lawyers, called the decision "a vindication of what we have been saying all along: that the Dinkins campaign has been doing everything in its power to try to get around the campaign finance law." Giuliani testified at a 1993 public hearing in favor of limiting compliance costs to 10 percent of a campaign's total spending. He said 10 percent "should more than accommodate the needs of the law." Giuliani was praised by public-interest groups after both the 1989 and 1993 campaigns as a friend of the campaign-finance system.

Now the mayor is exploiting the same system he once defended. If we were locked in a competitive campaign where every cent would make a difference, I could understand his behavior as an act of survival. But this is gratuitous exploitation, not political strategy, eerily similar to what Giuliani has been doing with taxpayer-funded commercials. It's almost as if he has been going out of his way to do the same things he felt Dinkins got away with in 1993, as if somehow by so doing he might exact one more bit of revenge on the former mayor.

September 5

Four days to go.

Our internally controversial direct-mail solicitation to women, which begins "How do you keep a good woman down?" is the news of the day. The press got its hands on the letter, and the Giuliani campaign is defending the mayor against its charges of sexism. Not surprisingly, Fran Reiter is out front on the issue. "For someone who has throughout her career been a leading feminist to now characterize as sexist legitimate criticism in the middle of a political campaign is something she should be ashamed of," she says. Giuliani says he's not going to comment on it. "It would make no sense for me to give more attention to her paid advertisements."

Nagourney's story on the letter is front page on the Metro Section. A full quarter of the story is speculation about the motives behind the letter. Nagourney's elusive "several Democrats" say that the letter "could serve to rally women in the final days of the primary." The letter, he writes, "also underscored a dynamic that politicians of both major parties contend is potentially significant: in the 1993 mayoral election, 57 percent of the voters were women, so Ms. Messinger's sex could give her an advantage with some women."

His analysis underscores another fundamental misunderstanding of the operation of modern political campaigns—he resists the valid premise that campaigns are bureaucracies. The starting point in examining the letter should not be what it says, but rather what it is. Recognizing it as a fund-raising letter is the critical step. The core message of a campaign is one or two basic themes, but campaigns will say virtually anything in remote settings to raise money. If Nagourney accepted this truth, he would be asking a different question: If the mayor's sexism is not part of the central message, did the campaign make yet another blunder by sending the letter knowing that it would inevitably end up in the hands of the press?

In this case it's better that he holds on to his outdated notions of campaigns.

• • •

The *Post* ridicules Ruth for charging Giuliani with sexism, saying she has "at least contributed some comic relief" to a campaign season otherwise free of political drama. It questions the political expediency of making the charge: "Perhaps enough Democrats in a low-turnout primary will respond in Pavlovian fashion to words like 'racism' and 'sexism' and give Messinger a substantial victory." And the *Post* raises the important issue of whether there is sufficient factual evidence to back up the charge. "To be sure, Giuliani's campaign has been critical of Messinger for her irresponsible approach to the school-crowding issue, and curious about how she would finance the various municipal pay raises she has advocated. The *Post* has on several occasions been compelled to note her dismaying tendency to resort to divisive and demagogic language. But 'sexism'? Not a trace."

The insidious evil of the *Post* editorial is not that its opinion of Ruth is without objectivity, but rather that it has passed off an element of its opinion as fact. It's amusing to think that the editorial board of the *Post* associates Ruth with demagogic language, but it's wrong to speak of her "irresponsible approach to the school-crowding issue" as fact. That is an expression of opinion passed off as fact. It requires at least some substantiation.

• • •

The endorsements for the primary have been funneling in over the last few days. The *Post* leaves "registered Democratic voters to sort through the muddle on their own" and makes no endorsement. So too the *News* endorses "none of the above." (For borough president, the *News* endorses George Spitz, whose only campaign issue is to abolish the office.) The *News* trivializes the candidates' positions. "To them, crime is not an issue. They harp only on police brutality, as though it is the single measurement of the NYPD. They are wrong."

The *Caribbean News* endorses Al Sharpton, who it says "has fashioned the most sensible and sensitive platform" and faults Ruth for painting "an unfortunate and distorted picture of conditions in the City schools." It isn't that conditions in many schools, especially those in black and Hispanic neighborhoods, aren't in deplorable shape. "Far from it," it says, "but by staging the commercial in a private school with a girl studying near a urinal, Messinger reduced a potent campaign issue to a farce." Ruth is paying dearly for missing the editorial board meeting with the *Caribbean News*.

The *Amsterdam News* also endorses Al Sharpton, "as comfortable in a Brooks Brothers suit as the dirt farmer's striped overalls of the Civil Rights Movement." And it too has kind words for Sal Albanese, who, it says, "has been decent, polite, and caring, playing by the rules with the healthiest respect for process, his opponents, and the party." "Messinger is a different story. Even as this is being written, she is under attack, legitimately, by many who once wished her well, but who see in her performance as a candidate the opportunism, inconsistency and pandering that make for a self-destructive candidacy."

Only *Newsday* endorses Ruth with some nice words. "Messinger shows a strong grasp of city government and offers nuanced criticisms of Giuliani's programs."

• • •

Even if what I've said about the lack of objectivity in polling is true, polling remains, in the eyes of most, a legitimate, quasi-scientific enterprise. Over the past few weeks, however, there have been charges of polling that is somewhat less respectable. Two candidates to succeed Ruth as borough president, City Council member C. Virginia Fields and state Assemblywoman Deborah Glick, have exchanged charges that each other's campaign is *push polling,* calling voters under the pretense of a survey and then providing negative information about the opposing candidate. Push polling is generally frowned upon by legitimate pollsters as compromising the basic integrity of the profession.

There's some evidence that other candidates may be engaging in *pull polling,* a process by which campaigns identify voters they want to target to call or drive to the polls on Election Day. A reporter from Brooklyn was called last week, asked his opinion of Jules Polonetsky and Rudy Giuliani, and then asked "Who's more likely to work twenty-four hours a day, seven days a week for the city—Messinger or Giuliani?" In the arbitrary moral universe in which we live, pull polling is regarded as more legitimate than push polling. But it's not exactly condoned, so Jules Polonetsky suggests it's our poll. "It could be a Ruth poll, it could be a Rudy poll, there are lots of polls going on."

It's not our poll, but Polonetsky's argument makes good sense. Even as he says it, we're planning to go in the field with a new survey that asks other provocative questions such as "Who do you think is more likely to defeat the Lucchese crime family, Rudy Giuliani or Ruth Messinger?" It had not occurred to us before, but once Polonetsky said it, we realized just how important data on that question is for us to have.

• • •

Last week, the Citizens Budget Commission (CBC) released a report that was critical of the mayor and his administration. Today the mayor says that the new CBC report is wrong and that the commission is in cahoots with our campaign. "I don't think there's any doubt about it," Giuliani says. "Largely they've been very critical of almost anything we do or say. I think there's a pretty partisan nature to this that is pretty obvious."

Ray Horton, head of the CBC, as you will recall, is the same person who refused to comment on our behalf after the budget speech, leaving us all sleepless as we waited to see just how devastating the following day's articles would be. Deputy Mayor Mastro cites our reference to the CBC chief in our press release following the budget speech as evidence of collaboration.

The culture of paranoia in City Hall runs deep. Even Ed Koch thinks the charge is ludicrous. "The CBC in league with Ruth Messinger? It's ridiculous!" he says. "They would leave town if she were elected."

September 6

One of the things Rudy often says about Ruth is that she is, like, praying for failure. Over the past few days that has been essentially true. While parents and kids have been out shopping for books and new clothes for back-to-school, our team has been hard at work. Our research staff has targeted the schools most likely to have overcrowding problems on the first day of school. Our field staff has scouted them all out to see which ones might produce the most depressing shots for television. Having done that, we sat back and, like, prayed for failure.

There is good news and bad (or bad news and good, if you view the world through the lens of a sane person). Several students were turned away from Newtown High School in Elmhurst, given a number, and told to come back the next week to register for classes. A newly converted dry-cleaning plant opened its doors to three hundred students, despite a test showing high levels of the dry-cleaning chemical perchloroethylene, which causes bladder and liver cancer. At the same time, there's considerable evidence that the opening is smoother than usual. Rudy, who spent opening day meeting with Michael J. Fox and the New York Liberty women's basketball team, is spreading the word that his administration has created more seats than any administration in some period of time.

As usual, it's hard to figure out the truth. The news is useless. "It Was Nearly a Textbook Job," proclaims the *News*. "1 Is 'Sold Out'" is the more solemn *Newsday* headline. The press is reporting politicians' accounts of the opening of school, rather than investigating independently. "There hasn't been a chancellor making this kind of progress in at least the last decade," says the mayor. "Smoothest in decades," says the Board of Education spokesperson, echoing the mayor's time frame by chance. Once again, it is what "they said" that's the story rather than "what is." And, as so often is the case, the "they said" in "they said these are the facts" somehow gets lost in the translation.

• • •

I wish I could have been in the meeting where they came up with that idea to put a school in a laundry.

"Let's turn the old dry-cleaning plant into a school."

"Good thinking, Stan. That way the kids will have lots of places to hang their coats."

• • •

Alan Hevesi is barely bothering to keep up the image of independence anymore. As Giuliani revives his charge that Ruth lacks the objectivity to say that Sharpton is not qualified to be mayor, Comptroller Hevesi criticizes Sharpton as too tolerant of bigoted remarks by Farrakhan and professor Leonard Jeffries. Hevesi's comments catch us in a pincer move that we only evade by virtue of the fact that no one is taking Sharpton's campaign seriously.

• • •

With the primary upon us, the air war is being waged night and day. Even though Giuliani is not facing a primary, he is still dominating the market. Between September 1 and September 9, the mayor is spending about $350,000 on television ads, about 540 general-market gross rating points. We're running ads at just slightly under that level.

It's interesting to speculate whether Giuliani would have chosen to run ads at this level during the Democratic primary if he had been faced with scarce resources; that is, if money spent during the primary meant that he could spend less during the general election. Since, as things are, he is not faced with the scarcity problem, there is no strategic choice for him to make. He enjoys the luxury of dominating the air war even at the point when attention is most closely focused on the Democratic primary.

My assertion that Giuliani faces no strategic dilemma may seem counterintuitive. Surely, one would say, Giuliani could put aside the $350,000 he is spending this week to buy even more commercials during the general election. In point of fact, there would be little or no marginal benefit to him from spending still more on commercials during the general-election campaign. Just as it is exponentially harder to reach those last few voters who hardly ever watch television, so too there are diminishing returns in airing a commercial over and over. The thought is that there is a saturation point beyond which there is no marginal benefit to running a commercial again. Once everybody has seen the Bugs Bunny–Michael Jordan commercial a dozen times or so, they've pretty much gotten the point. Common belief is that 1,000 points or so over a short period of time is enough to saturate the market. The Giuliani campaign has enough money to saturate the market for the entire general-election campaign. So having the extra $350,000 at the end wouldn't buy them much, if anything.

Giuliani is currently running a combination of two different ads. The first vindicates yet another prediction Jim made about the advertising—that one of the mayor's commercials would prominently feature a woman. In past campaigns, Donna Hanover was featured prominently in Giuliani campaigns and was regarded as being especially effective in rebutting charges that Giuliani had waffled on abortion. Donna's unavailable this season, but Rudy has an able stand-in. Vivian Drennan, whose husband died fighting a fire in SoHo in 1994, is the focus of one of Giuliani's new ads praising the mayor for securing bunker gear for city firefighters. "The Mayor provided a tribute to my husband, John, and to every firefighter who made the ultimate sacrifice," she says to the camera. "Leaving us a whole lot safer."

The other ad compares Giuliani to legendary mayor Fiorello LaGuardia. Rudy says in the voice-over:

> For me, he's always been a role model. New Yorkers admired Mayor LaGuardia's hands-on style, and that he was there when it mattered most. His example inspires me every day. To move quickly when the unexpected happens, when Mother Nature throws us a curve, when terrorism threatens our neighborhoods, when a city worker is seriously injured or people need help. Some say I work too hard. But when the lives of people are on the line, how can I do anything less?

How indeed?

Sal Albanese is finally on the air with two 30-second ads and a third 10-second spot that feature him speaking directly to the camera, highlighting, as he has throughout the campaign, his personal background and his image as a straight shooter. Seated in front of a blue curtain, Albanese says:

> I was a teacher in New York City public schools for eleven years. But what's important is not what I taught, but what I learned. I learned that you can make a difference. On the City Council I fought and passed a living-wage bill for working families. I'm Sal Albanese. As Mayor, I'll fight to get guns out of the hands of children and to get special-interest dollars out of the hands of politicians. It's time to set our priorities straight. It's time to take a stand.

Muddying the airwaves still further, Al D'Amato is up with a commercial blaming liberals for allowing teachers' unions to put their interests over kids. "Our present system isn't working because liberals have put union demands ahead of our children. Al D'Amato wants to change that. It's time to expel violent, disruptive juveniles, so good kids can learn. It's time for merit pay. And finally, it's time we told the teachers' union to put our children first." The ad is chintzy and unpolished, and D'Amato is accordingly spending a mere $100,000 a week on the spot—a trivial drop in the bucket for the senator—and nearly a third of what we're spending per week.

The question arises in times like these whether any ad can make an impact in all of the clutter. Some think that political ads begin to blend together to voters once they reach an aggregate level. Of the lot, it seems to me—and I can hardly be objective about this—that our education ad is the most effective. Even with all the bad press that surrounded it, I know from seeing the focus groups that it is making an impression on voters.

The Drennan ad is an effective ad for the mayor. It advances, in a poignant way, his core message that the city is safer. Bunker gear isn't likely to be a major issue in the campaign, so the ad likely won't run for very long, but it's effective for what it is. The LaGuardia ad seems like shameless self-promotion and Rudy's own handiwork, but again I cannot be objective.

I'm of two minds on the Albanese ads. I like Sal and think he comes across as honest and likable, so I give Joe Slade White high marks for the decision to put him to the camera. But I don't think the ads put forth an effective message. I agree with almost everything Sal has to say about campaign-finance reform, but I don't think people will shift their votes to him because of his stand on corporate contributions. Having handguns and corporate contributions in the same ad seems the sort of odd juxtaposition that can only be explained by the disjointed linking that issue polls produce, but neither of these is an issue that polls especially well. And more than that, Albanese has again passed up the opportunity to go negative on Ruth, his last, best hope.

September 7

On this, the last Sunday before the primary, the candidates engage in no less than three televised debates. The first, hosted by WABC, is the second of the Campaign Finance Board (CFB) debates and Eric Ruano-Melendez's last opportunity to speak to the people of New York City en masse. Subdued in the first CFB debate, Melendez is sharp on this occasion, his arguments honed by practice, his psyche emboldened by surviving his first skirmish with the more established candidates.

He sounds his themes in his opening statements:

> Good morning. One of the worst problems in the city of New York is the conspiracy that we have in Brooklyn right now. Even though crime is down, we still believe that when we walk out of this building, we'll see a lot of homeless sleeping on Fifth Avenue or Madison Avenue. Everybody, especially the elected officials, is closing their eyes to the real issues in the city. The people are in

> peril in the city of the environment. Day by day, we see children selling drugs on the streets. And after-hours restaurants allowed by our laws. We don't do anything. But the worst thing that we have in the city of New York is the corrupted lawyers that are dealing with corrupted contractors.

Clearly, Melendez's polling has indicated that antilawyer sentiment is running high in the city, and he stays on message throughout the debate. Asked about the Louima case, Melendez responds:

> It is very clear there is a conspiracy to defraud the taxpayers of the city of New York by billions of dollars by creating this chaos intentionally in the city of New York. Police officers, doctors, teachers—they are being holding hostage by those corrupted lawyers that are coming to New York. What I call them, the two-leg rats, that are coming to defraud the city of tax dollars. Who is going to pay for that circus again? We are. We the citizens of New York. We have to acknowledge. I don't know if it was a set-up to make the mayor lose the election. I'm not sure about that, but somebody did it. Somebody caused that and we need a full investigation. But at the same time we cannot accuse anyone of doing any harm to anybody. I respect the idea of protecting the citizens. But at the same time we have to respect the laws. If we don't respect the laws we are in chaos. And I guess we need a full disclosure, a full investigation. And I guess the borough president, the councilman should be the first to come out. And no, not a preacher.

When the candidates are asked what they would do to improve schools, the other candidates take the bait and talk about schools, but Melendez takes it back to message. "I believe that the worst thing in the city of New York is the people are being hostage to corrupted lawyers."

He argues that crooked lawyers are responsible for rising unemployment in the city. "Which crooked lawyers are taking those jobs?" Melendez is asked.

"Paparazzi lawyers," he replies. "Two-legged rats."

Though the other three candidates maintain the détente that has prevailed throughout the primary campaign, Melendez goes on the attack. He accuses Sharpton of violating the Constitution by breaching the separation of church and state and of belonging to organizations that are trying to overthrow the country. "Like the Democratic party?" asks Rev. Sharpton.

Melendez is quick on his feet. When he accuses Sharpton of being a divisive force in the city, Sharpton replies that Martin Luther King was "accused of that before he was killed."

"You're not Dr. King. You're a preacher without a church," Melendez says.

"So was Dr. King," Sharpton replies nimbly, but even he would admit, I think, that he lost the exchange.

Melendez is merciless. Having disposed of Sharpton, he sets his sights on Albanese. "His [Sal's] alliance with the Independence party," Melendez says, "is making me suspicious he is also part of the Communist group that is involved there."

By the end of the debate, Melendez has laid out more proposals than the other three candidates combined. He has restated and defended his idea to bring in the national guard to fight police brutality without undermining crime. He proposes to use the Army Corps of Engineers, his former unit, to build homes to help the housing crunch.

Summing up his qualifications, he says, "I'm an environmental engineer and I know where to place job."

• • •

At a subsequent debate at NBC, Gabe Pressman spends no less than fifteen minutes trying to get the three main candidates to differentiate themselves from one another. Sharpton says he won't entertain the media with that. "I don't want it for entertainment," Pressman says. "I want to know what the difference is between you guys and gals."

But the Dems won't budge. Over the course of seven hours of debate today, Albanese charges Ruth with having a school-board appointee who supported a budget including tax cuts and of running a campaign without core values. Both Sal and Al charge Ruth with trying to balance the budget on the backs of city employees. And that's it.

Jim shakes his head once again, expressing his belief that Sal never understood the power of negative attacks on Ruth.

• • •

Joe Klein's story is finally in the *New Yorker.* The main focus of the story is Rudy Giuliani's personality. He writes extensively about Giuliani's relationship with former police commissioner Bill Bratton. Bratton was forced out after he made the cover of *Time* magazine under the headline "Finally We're Winning the War Against Crime and Here's Why." After he resigned, NYPD detectives were ordered to work overtime finding and deleting all mentions of Bratton on the NYPD Web site.

Bratton, who is writing a book about the drop in crime in New York City, says, "Rudy provided phenomenal leadership, but now he's trying to reinvent history because he can't stand to have anybody onstage with him. It's like a cult he's got there; you can't work with the guy unless you're willing to drink the Kool-Aid." Bratton recently told the *Financial Times*, a British newspaper, Mayor Giuliani is an "asshole, but a successful asshole."

Klein reports that Bratton's people used to speculate that Rudy was "the sort of kid who never made it to school with his lunch" too often and that his adulthood is a "revenge of the nerd." If so, says Klein, "Giuliani came from a distinctly nerdy subgroup—the defiantly self-possessed, messianic kind."

He describes Ruth as "an eat-your-peas Democrat, the sort of person one can imagine carrying a placard at a SANE rally in the old days. Worse, she seems intermittently intent on running a substantive, honorable campaign." Ruth suggests to Klein that schools require the same sort of attention that Giuliani has paid to crime. When Klein repeats the statement to Giuliani, he is shocked by the response. "There was a breathless, feral quality to the assault. The Mayor didn't raise his voice, but the intensity of the attack was startling, and probably unnecessary: Messinger seems a sparrow heading toward a threshing machine."

September 8

It seems only appropriate that the last day of the primary campaign is Labor Day, the last parade day of the season and a perfect occasion for another rash of stories about our lack of labor support.

As always, my first reaction is amazement that people accept on faith the premise that union backing is important. An article in the *News* states matter-of-factly that unions were "instrumental in electing David Dinkins mayor in 1989." That's a useful belief for unions to perpetuate, but there's no evidence to demonstrate its truth. If union support were the only thing that changed between 1989 and 1993, the conclusion would be valid, but a few other little things happened in those years—like Crown Heights—that may have played a small part too.

An even more interesting aspect of the story, I think, is a short quote from teachers' union president Sandra Feldman on why labor unions aren't taking an active role in the campaign. "There isn't an overriding issue," Feldman says, "and the race seems very lopsided." That one goes down hard. The president of the New York City teachers' union says there isn't an overriding issue in the campaign when the Democratic candidate has made schools the centerpiece of her candidacy and the incumbent cut billions of dollars from the schools by anyone's count. That's either an abdication of responsibility or the most forceful statement imaginable about how dim people think Ruth's chances are.

That's only the beginning of the bad press. Bob Herbert fires up our supporters with an op-ed about "Ruth Messinger's disappointing effort." "Her main focus has been schools, but she undermined the legitimate overcrowding issue by running a television ad that gave the incorrect impression that kids were being taught while virtually jammed up against urinals." And Ruth's attack on Giuliani's sexist language is proof, Herbert says, that Ruth "is not ready for the rough and tumble of big-time politics. . . . The truth is that Mr. Giuliani dismisses men and women, fairly or unfairly, with the same kind of rhetoric."

As evidence of the tough time Ruth will have if she wins the primary, Herbert scientifically surveys two black voters outside of a press conference Ruth is holding at a public school in East Flatbush (where she "listlessly offers boilerplate to the small cluster of reporters"). Both are voting for Rudy, prompting Herbert to conclude that the black vote is slipping away from Ruth. "Without an extreme sweep of the African-American vote, all hope of upsetting Mr. Giuliani is lost."

Pulitzer prize winner E. R. Shipp bemoans "Primary Colorless." "The candidates have raised worthy issues," she says, but "are so understated and passionless that it's hard to get too excited about any one of them." Shipp is voting, she says, because she always does, but says it's time to "figure out how to fix this lousy system."

Ed Koch will vote for Ruth in the primary while holding his nose. Conservative *Post* columnist Ray Kerrison, a former sportswriter, says that even he pities "this sorry bunch of losers." And, appropriately, Adam Nagourney tops it all off with a story about two women eating dinner at the Country Club diner on Staten Island as Ruth walked in. One asks the other, "Is that Liz Holtzman?"

• • •

Rudy Giuliani is making the case that "we started it." The mayor is planning to *go negative* after the primary, but only because we've been the aggressors. Of the debate Giuliani says the Democrats were guilty of "massive, repeated, negative campaigning." "When it comes time for us to respond to that," he says, "I don't think there can be anyone that's going to complain that we started it." To the *Post* he says, "I'd like everyone to be clear that each one of these candidates has engaged in massive, repeated negative campaigning, so when it comes time for us to defend ourselves, I don't want anyone to say that we started any kind of negative campaigning."

And the mayor, remarkably, is encouraging people not to vote: "If they want to register their displeasure at the negative way in which each one of them has campaigned, they can not vote. If they feel none of the candidates would make a good candidate, then they have a right not to vote for any of the candidates. That's also American."

• • •

Speculation is that turnout may be as low as 15 percent. That's a pretty pessimistic projection considering that in 1993, 22 percent of eligible Democrats turned out to elect David Dinkins in a noncompetitive primary against Roy Innis, the conservative head of the Congress of Racial Equality. Juan Gonzalez suggests that people may find out tomorrow what it would be like if "they had a primary election and no one showed up to vote."

• • •

All that remains, then, is the important business of booking bets. A last-day poll by New York 1 has Ruth at 40 percent, Sal at 19 percent, and Sharpton at 18 percent, down from 44–12–16 in July. (It also has her losing 51–37 in the general, closer than the 57–34 in July.) Rudy Giuliani has a bet of a bottle of wine with Rafael Martinez Alequin, of a small community paper called the *Free Press,* that Ruth will win the primary outright with 45 percent, which is some indication of where his polling thinks the race is. Our last survey, taken on September 2 and 3, showed Ruth 46–14–11 over Albanese and Sharpton, respectively. That result includes *leaners,* respondents who express a candidate preference only after prompting.

In our office pool most of the predictions fall in the range from 43 to 45 percent. The picks are posted on a bulletin board in our office that Ruth can see, so it's not clear to what degree people are being strategic in their voting. Only one person has the nerve to predict that Ruth won't clear 40. I call 50 percent, which puts me as the second most optimistic prognosticator in the office, behind only Lee. Despite the bad press and the discouraging polls, I cannot bring myself to believe that people will pull the lever for Sal or Al (or Eric) when the chips are down. It seems to me, too, that low turnout will favor Ruth. The most loyal voters, I figure, are likely to be the most liberal and sensible.

All in all, I still like our chances.

September 9

Lee Jones and I are hunched over a toilet bowl in a suite at the Grand Hyatt working on a speech for Ruth acknowledging that there will be a runoff election with Al Sharpton. Things haven't gone exactly according to plan.

All things considered, the bathroom is the best place to be. The small suite outside is like a morgue. David Dinkins, immaculately dressed in a pinstriped suit, is sitting in a chair nodding off and muttering that we needed to do more to energize the black community (read Abner Louima). Freddie Ferrer is in the room with his small entourage staring at the ground. Earlier, he whispered to Mark Green that he could have done better than this. Randy, our field coordinator, is holed up in a corner of the room watching returns come in on laptop computer. Our vote is holding steady at 39.4 percent. Mandy and Ruth aren't saying much. Jim is quiet too, though he snaps at me to get people back to the office so they can fax us the appropriate version of the speech.

Fact is, the appropriate version of the speech was thrown together earlier this evening when Ruth's chief of staff and I thought we should have something "just in case." To that point, the only alternate version of the speech that anyone had thought of was in case we won by a wide margin instead of a narrow one.

Still, Ruth does a great job. This was another body blow to her, but she keeps smiling as always.

"No one ever said this was going to be easy."

• • •

A mere ordinary human being would be exhausted by the events of the day, but Ruth is energized. It is after 1:00 in the morning, and we have all convened at Ruth's apartment to regroup and talk about where we go from here. The group is larger than usual. It includes loyal people from the borough president's office as well as several staffers who are not usually in on strategy sessions. The mood is somber. Ruth's husband offers up a few bags of chips for us to munch on, but the salted products don't do much to improve the atmosphere.

Somehow, though, Ruth appears genuinely buoyant. She says the result is actually good news for us. Her logic is that Sharpton's showing means that the black vote is energized by the Louima case and that after we beat him in the runoff, they will shift to us and carry us over the top. Or something like that. I'm not paying all that much attention, really. I am just in awe that this woman can keep going after all that has happened without taking so much as a minute to feel sorry for herself. She is either the strongest person I have ever met or so totally consumed by a thirst for power that she cannot possibly remain objective. That's the question, really. Can she be objective? Is she honest with herself?

Whatever the answer, Ruth is not letting up. She is planning a subway stop for tomorrow morning at 6:45 A.M. to show the press she's still standing.

That's okay. I'll sleep enough for the both of us.

September 10

The mood in the campaign is so vastly different from what it has been for the past eight months that it seems surreal. Jim, Mandy, and the campaign manager tender their resignations, though Ruth rejects them all. Most people show up late, some not at all. Those who do show up sit around without any sense of what to do. Our research team is in limbo. Sharpton's past is well explored, and it's not as if we need to do anything to boost his negatives. We sit around watching a tape of Sharpton's victory speech. It is, far and away, the best speech of the campaign by any candidate.

"I want to thank the mainstream media for ignoring me, he quips at the outset." The speech rises in a crescendo around his theme, "I got wings and I can fly," from a song by hip-hop artist R. Kelly. "We are going to fly from the outhouse to Gracie Mansion. We're going to fly. This is our date. This is our time. I can fly. I can fly. I can fly." And we believe him.

The mood in the office reflects the feeling that we are no cinch to beat Sharpton in the runoff. I'm no longer making predictions. My forecast of 50 percent wasn't exactly dead on, and turnout, which preliminary figures indicate was 18 percent yesterday, figures to be even lower for the runoff, meaning the result will be even more unpredictable. Only the fund-raising team is energized. Ruth is raising money as never before. Many of the mayor's Jewish contributors have given us $1,000 out of fear that Sharpton may be further legitimized. On top of that, the $7,700 spending cap is bumped up by $3,750 for the runoff, which means we can go after previously maxed-out donors for even more money. And we're already entitled to an additional $325,000 in matching funds as a result of being in the primary.

Late in the afternoon, Jim convenes a meeting of the entire staff. From here on in, he announces, the strategy will be to run an all-out field campaign. We will be targeting likely voters and launching a sizable get-out-the-vote effort. All of our resources are being funneled to our field director, a seasoned pro who to this point had been relegated to the farthest corner of the office. Field, Jim says, is what makes the difference in low-turnout runoffs.

In a day, we've gone from a modern message-oriented campaign to the traditional operation Ruth's people always wanted to run. That's fine if it gets us through the runoff with Sharpton, but I wonder whether the premise is true. What's the difference between a low-turnout runoff and a low-turnout primary? If field makes the difference in one, it must surely be worth doing in the other.

There must be some other agenda. Perhaps the idea is to get through this as cheaply as possible. If we squander our resources now, then it won't make any difference if we survive the runoff since we'll be dead in the water. Or perhaps the idea is a reaction to the prevailing view in the media that our implosion is a result of taking the black vote for granted (evidence cited by the *Post:* "She skipped a debate sponsored by the Urban League and didn't bother posting signs in many black neighborhoods").

Maybe if you read enough of that stuff, you start to believe it yourself.

September 11

The best thing I can say is that we're alive. There isn't much good news, but at least there's life.

From a strategic standpoint, we're in a terrific bind, and it isn't any secret. Adam Nagourney's assessment of our dilemma coincides for once with our own view of the issue: "How to defeat Mr. Sharpton without alienating his black and liberal supporters, whose votes will be critical in the race against Mr. Giuliani in November."

As they have before, the Giuliani campaign is trying to link Ruth with Sharpton. Rudy says Sharpton and Messinger are indistinguishable members of the extreme left wing of the Democratic party. "It does pose for the people of this city a choice, which is Messinger-Sharpton—they're virtually one—or the present Mayor. They're virtually identical. They virtually agree on everything. They were virtually cross-endorsing each other this morning, so they're basically running together." Fran Reiter echoes the message of the day without as many adverbial qualifiers. "Right now," she says, "they are marching hand in hand and that is a story, because Ruth is defining herself when she does that. This is a man who continues to suggest that Tawana Brawley wasn't a hoax." When asked to detail the evidence proving Messinger's and Sharpton's positions are virtually identical, Reiter says, "I am not going to get into an explanation of their policies for you." But the similarities are self-evident to the *Post*, where the lead editorial, by coincidence, echoes the Giuliani campaign theme of the day, arguing that "if nothing else, New Yorkers can fairly conclude that Messinger believes the Rev. Al Sharpton to be a credible, qualified candidate for mayor. On the actual issues, of course, Democrats Messinger and Sharpton are Tweedledee and Tweedledum."

Giuliani's argument that Messinger and Sharpton are indistinguishable still seems overstated—one wonders whether Rudy means "not" when he says "virtually"—but it now has a kernel of credibility that wasn't there when Giuliani first sounded the theme months ago. Asked how she and Sharpton would differ as mayor, Ruth says, "Why don't you listen to what I say I'll do, and then listen to what he says he'll do, and then you'll be able to identify the differences." Ruth calls Al an "eloquent spokesperson" on the issue of police brutality. Al has nary an unkind word in return.

Ruth tells one reporter she's "delighted" with how she did in the primary, but she really should say she's "virtually delighted," because we're in a Catch-22. There's nothing we can do to preserve our already tenuous standing in the Jewish community short of calling Al Sharpton a race-baiter and anti-Semite. (In our most recent poll, Sharpton's approval/disapproval split among Jews was 84–2, negative.) Of course, that would alienate more than a few black voters and do some serious damage to the Democratic party. And Ruth wouldn't do it even if it might pick her up a few votes. The best we can hope for is that we'll trounce Sharpton in the runoff, and voters will understand the position Ruth was in and give her credit for having handled a difficult situation well. But Jim wonders aloud to me what's on everyone's mind: "Will the legacy of this campaign be the legitimization of Al Sharpton?"

• • •

The one nice thing about being in a runoff with one of the few politicians the press reviles more than Ruth is that the press has turned its sights away from us for a change. The *News* reports that Sharpton owes more than $100,000 in overdue taxes, saying the facts "surfaced a day after the Brooklyn preacher rocked the city's political landscape." It's pure coincidence, of course, that the facts "surfaced" on the day after Sharpton's surprising performance in the primary. Sharpton says he is disputing the amount of the debt and that there's a racist pattern of scrutinizing the tax returns of successful black politicians.

The *Post* reports that Sharpton owes the city more than $12,000 for treatment he received at Coney Island Hospital in 1991 for a well-publicized stab wound he suffered at a protest rally in Bensonhurst, Brooklyn. Sharpton forgave the stabber, but he hasn't paid the bill. He says the city owes the bill, because cops were negligent in failing to protect him.

The *Times* and *Staten Island Advance* report that Al Sharpton and his wife renewed their marriage vows at Reverend Sun Myung Moon's Unification Church. Moon, who served time in federal prison for tax evasion, is thought by many to use the church to proselytize young and vulnerable members. Sharpton says that he would not join the group because of its political ideology and that he knows little about its theology, but that he supports the marriage-blessing ceremony that Moon developed in 1960. Sharpton's participation in the blessing ceremony was featured in the *Unification News* in June. Sharpton is scheduled to renew his vows once again at R.F.K. Stadium, in Washington, three weeks after the election at a ceremony to be attended by more than 30,000 couples, with more than 3.6 million couples participating by satellite hookup.

• • •

Although the mainstream press is letting Sharpton have it with both barrels, an editorial in the *Amsterdam News* declares Sharpton the winner of the primary and ridicules the mainstream press for not having a sense of the city. There's real bitterness here:

> Blacks and Hispanics who work for major media in this town are so afraid of losing their jobs by telling white editors—assignment and otherwise—what they do not wish to hear; continue to say to those who cause a paycheck to be written for them, "Yes, boss! Whatever you say, boss. You're right, boss." And under their collective breaths to their white employers: "Run out there with your racist polls that have no one in the Black and Hispanic communities except those who have phones, or those who work as domestics and 'go-fers' in white firms, whether they be called chief engineer, columnist, editorial writer, reporter, scholar, or administrator." The generic term for all of these to you is nigger. Why

don't you use it to express how you really feel? The vaunted *New York Times* columnist Bob Herbert, who on the same day moaned the runoff between "two losers, one meek and essentially devoid of leadership qualities, the other brash, irresponsible and very loud," is a "sick puppy." That is the very best that can be said of him, for his hatred of Blacks, as witnessed by his columns, is palpable.

• • •

Sharpton's vote total in the primary was virtually the same as it was in his two previous Senate tries. In 1992, he received 136,118 votes, 28.5 percent of the total. In 1994, he received 138,197 votes against Daniel Patrick Moynihan, 19 percent of the total. This year, his unofficial vote count is 126,782.

By virtue of doing better on Election Day than in the polls, Sharpton is something of a political anomaly. Many pollsters believe that white voters lie about their intentions, embarrassed to admit that they will vote against a black candidate. In 1989, Dinkins showed a double-digit lead over Giuliani in the polls in the last week of the 1989 campaign, but barely pulled out the race. Jim describes a similar phenomenon from the Gantt campaign.

The evidence is mixed. In 1993, polls showed the Giuliani-Dinkins rematch to be too close to call. Expecting a repeat of the 1989 behavior, some pollsters predicted that Giuliani would win by eight or nine points. As it was, the polls were accurate. The race was too close to call, and Giuliani barely squeaked it out. But as David Moore and Frank Newport point out, the dynamics in the 1989 and 1993 races were very different. In 1989, the undecideds were mostly white Democrats, who predictably broke for Giuliani. In 1993, the undecideds were racially mixed. And a poll is nothing more than a snapshot in time. Voter attitudes are always changing, especially in the final days of a campaign.

But Sharpton is unique. He does better on Election Day.

• • •

Sal Albanese is showing no signs of endorsing. "I think some of my supporters will vote for Sharpton," he says today. "They saw that he conducted an above-board campaign, that he spoke to many of the same issues that I did, like unemployment, things that really matter to working people." He calls our campaign a "fiasco" and says Ruth is "beginning to look more like Giuliani-lite."

• • •

The aftermath of the primary includes some inevitable second-guessing of the strategic types. *News* columnist Juan Gonzalez calls on Ruth to fire her out-of-town advisers who urged her to adopt a Clintonesque move-to-the-center strategy, starting with Mandy Grunwald, "she of the tasteless classrooms-in-bathrooms ad."

Crain's Magazine calls Mandy and Jim the "biggest losers" in last week's primary for recommending that Ruth "hold on to her money for TV ads after the primary and not use any of it for a primary-day field operation."

Adam Nagourney says that by largely ignoring her primary opponents and instead making the case against Giuliani, Ruth violated an "enduring rule of politics: Ask your audience to vote for you. The fact that she didn't certainly helped produce the lowest turnout in a Democratic primary since World War II." (He in passing refers to Sharpton as "one of the smartest politicians in the city.") I haven't figured out why it's not possible to both ignore your opponents and ask your audience to vote for you, but I'm sure Nagourney must be right. It is, after all, an enduring rule of politics.

• • •

And, as if to add insult to injury, Rudy is holding a press conference with a hundred endorsing Democrats in front of the City Hall fountain, no more than fifty yards from the front door of our campaign office. We all take lunch and witness the spectacle. Among the endorsers are Priscilla Wooten, a black City Councilwoman from Brooklyn; Claire Shulman, the borough president of Queens; and Lincoln Center head Nat Leventhal. Leventhal is the ultimate fence-sitter. A former deputy mayor for Koch, Leventhal, whom you may recall as the moderator of the Citizens Union debate in June, has contributed money both to Messinger and to Giuliani. He's endorsing Giuliani, but he's a close friend of Ruth's.

Giuliani is already on the air with an ad featuring Claire Shulman's endorsement. "Great things are happening," Shulman says in the ad. "Even the Mets are doing a little better since he became Mayor." To top it off, Giuliani is expected to pick up the endorsement of Stanley Hill, head of the city's largest municipal union, tomorrow.

We picked up Peter Vallone, the Speaker of the City Council and an all-but-announced candidate for governor.

• • •

After spending nearly $1 million complying with the city's campaign-finance laws, the Giuliani campaign has been suspended by the Campaign

Finance Board for accepting more than $300,000 in illegal contributions. The Giuliani campaign has already acknowledged that $290,000 of the contributions were illegal and is returning the money. Most of the violations result from related corporate entities making combined donations in excess of the limit. The Giuliani campaign says that the errors result from a misinterpretation of the campaign-finance law.

September 12

By a bizarre confluence of cosmic forces, I have just bought George Will a Diet Coke and am chatting with him about baseball. Will, a conservative correspondent on ABC's weekly news program and a syndicated columnist, is here to interview Ruth for some reason that I cannot begin to imagine. The press people think Will may be writing a story about the toppling of King Rudy and, besides, any press is good press. Ruth is running late, so I have been asked to entertain Will.

I have a favorable impression of Will, though I can't ever recall agreeing with him about anything. I've read two of his books. The first, *Statecraft as Soulcraft,* argues (this is a drastic oversimplification) that religion may reasonably inform political judgment. The second, *Men at Work*, makes the case that baseball is played and managed by shrewd intellectual men who are constantly making calculations at all levels of the game of which the fan is entirely unaware. I don't agree with much of either book. Baseball seems like safer turf.

"Your Orioles are doing well," I say. Will is an Orioles fan.

"Yes. We'll see how their pitching holds up down the stretch. I just went to see the Giants try to hold on for first place against the Phillies."

"Everybody beats the Phillies."

"Actually, the Phillies have the third best record in the National League since the All Star break." Most people would say that I have a geekish knowledge of baseball, but I am no match for Will.

"I bet lots more people want to talk to you about politics than baseball," I say.

"Actually, it's about 80–20 the other way."

I'm wrong again.

"What is the campaign's issue?" he asks.

"Education."

"Which way is the teachers' union going?"

"It looks like they're going to stay neutral."

"Why is that?"

"Partially because we're saying some things like toughening standards for teachers that aren't very popular with the union. Partly, because of our standing in the polls."

"That's why I'm here," Will smiles. "Death knell of liberalism and all."

Wonderful. The campaign photographer takes a picture of me and Will. Will tries to prompt a smile by saying, "Everybody say Statecraft as Soulcraft." I never should have told him I read the book.

Come to think of it, I want my seventy-five cents back for the Diet Coke.

• • •

I've been laughing myself silly about this all day.

Jules Polonetsky, Rudy Giuliani's "running mate" and a candidate for Public Advocate, has quite reasonably been making an issue of the stated intention of his opponent, Mark Green, to run for the U.S. Senate even if reelected as Public Advocate. Today Polonetsky, who is trailing by 70 points in the polls, sent Green a letter challenging him to a series of debates, including at least one in each borough. We have a copy of the letter.

> Dear Public Advocate Green,
>
> Congratulations on your primary "victory." I am looking forward to a good, hard campaign that I hope will focus on the issues affecting New York City and what the Public Advocate can do about them. . . . I am sure your official duties, as well as your campaigns for Public Advocate and United States Senate, are keeping you on a very tight schedule. However, I am confident that we can both find the time to speak to the voters. They are, after all, the people we both hope to represent.

At the top of the letter, the words "Public Advocate Green" are crossed out and "Mark" is written in Polonetsky's hand.

For a personal touch.

September 13

"Turn all guns to Sharpton," Jim commands me in our morning call today.

His words make me realize that Jim Andrews is out of his time. Jim would be happiest, I imagine, as a naval commander or an infantry squad leader in some bygone era when wars were fought by men and not by computers. He thinks in military terms and consciously emulates Patton in managerial style. He is smart and nuanced in his thinking, but he instinctively sees the world in black and white. He wants orders obeyed without question and implemented without delay. Political campaigns are among the few places in modern America where Jim's legendary skills are highly valued and his methods tolerated.

All in all, he fits rather uncomfortably in the world of politics. Political campaigns, if it isn't clear already, are not like politics. Politics is deliberative and civil, filled with people who say nice things about everybody, regardless of whether they like them or not. Political campaigns are impulsive and nasty and filled with people who say nasty things about everybody, regardless of whether they like them or not. Politicians look the other way when they hire campaign managers. They are the Smoking Men, the Dirty Harrys, characters like Jack Nicholson's in *A Few Good Men*—men you don't like to believe exist, but want guarding your fence when bad things start to go down.

There's a schizophrenia to the whole enterprise. It's as if politicians hire these people so that their consciences can tolerate acts they could never bring themselves to do. "Accuse my opponent of murder for paroling a criminal who went out and killed somebody? I never did that and never would do that. (I might hire somebody to do that for me, but that's a different story.)"

In another era, political consultants might be honored heroes. In this one, the Jim Andrewses of the world are grudgingly tolerated as a necessary evil during the campaign, then tossed aside, win or lose, never to be spoken of again (unless reelection needs demand it).

All that said, we're turning our modest guns to Sharpton. We're checking his real-estate holdings, corporate affiliations, tax returns, criminal convictions, and anything else we can think of.

We're doing the dirty work.

• • •

In an interview on CBS, Alan Hevesi announces that he will not endorse Al Sharpton if the Reverend wins the runoff:

> A mayor has to be committed to the idea of bringing people together. The behavior of Al Sharpton, as I have perceived it, is the reverse. I do not believe Sharpton is a bigot. But I believe he has occasionally exploited fear, anger, and frustration in a very divisive way. When he's a candidate, he's a very forceful advocate and very mature. But it's in the interim that you get his support of Leonard Jeffries, Farrakhan and the Brawley case.

Asked why he, the comptroller of the city, was the right person to repudiate Sharpton and why he chose this time to do so, Hevesi cites his own less than well known work in civil rights.

By coincidence, Hevesi's remarks coincide with increased rhetoric from the mayor linking Sharpton and Ruth. Rudy says that Sharpton lacks the basic qualifications to be mayor and that Ruth lacks the "guts" and "courage" to say so. "I think he's unqualified to be mayor," Giuliani says. And "I think that Ruth Messinger is afraid to say so."

The mayor continues:

> This is a real job. You have to know how to deal with some of the most complex issues that face governments anywhere. There has to be a background of having worked, having had a job, having distinguished yourself at things before you come to the position of being mayor. Otherwise it becomes a catastrophe and politics becomes a joke. Ruth Messinger doesn't have the independence to say what she really thinks. Or maybe she really thinks that Al Sharpton is qualified to be mayor.

Giuliani praises Hevesi for "talking like a real person, not like a politician."

Sharpton accuses Giuliani of using racist code words, specifically citing the word "qualification" as offensive. Sharpton says "everybody darker than Liz Taylor knows what that code word means when you talk about qualifications." Sharpton's retaliation against Giuliani is nothing new, but the attack from Hevesi is closing the pincer he set up earlier that we evaded only by virtue of the fact that no one was taking Sharpton seriously.

People are taking Al Sharpton seriously now. Sharpton demands that Ruth repudiate Hevesi "for playing the race card and attempting to polarize the campaign." Our sole defender is Sal Albanese, who criticizes Hevesi for doing a "destructive thing" that he calls dangerously polarizing.

What to make of Hevesi's actions? What he says has some validity, but where was Hevesi in May when Ruth stood up to Al Sharpton about his comments on Louis Farrakhan? It's hard not to be cynical. Hevesi's timing is not that of a supporter. He gave us no warning of this attack. He made no effort to signal where he was going.

On this day, Alan Hevesi did more to ensure Rudy Giuliani's reelection that any other person in New York City.

• • •

Hank Sheinkopf tells New York 1 that Stanley Hill's endorsement of Rudy Giuliani heralds the end of *retail* politics in New York City for all time. The distinction between *retail* and *wholesale* politics is akin, as you recall, to the distinction between modern and traditional political campaigns. The retail politician sees voting blocs as aggregates of economic interests and attracts voters by promises of quid pro quos. Vote for me and I'll do something good for your group. Wholesale politicians reject the notion that voters make their decisions on the basis of single issues and campaign by advocating positions that cut across group lines. Retail politics is traditional; wholesale politics is modern. Retail politics is the province of old-time liberal Democrats. Wholesale politics is message, media-oriented politics. Retail politics is pandering.

Hank Sheinkopf's point is that Rudy Giuliani has shown that labor is capable of being attracted by a broad, pragmatic platform that does not directly result in a tangible benefit for the union. As I've pointed out, there's a strong case can be made that Rudy Giuliani plays plenty of retail politics. Rudy has not been the hard-line negotiator with unions that he promised to be in 1993, which has more than a little to do with Hill's remarkable endorsement. But Dick Morris says that when Ruth lost, "white liberalism as a force in New York City politics died as well." If Morris and Sheinkopf are right, Rudy Giuliani has changed the very nature of New York politics.

September 14

One would hardly recognize our campaign office from to the place it was four weeks ago. There are posters and cards and envelopes and stamps and lots and lots of volunteers. Who these people are who have the time to come into a decrepit office at 2:00 in the afternoon and lick envelopes for a woman who has almost no chance of winning, I don't know. But they're here—still outside the wall, of course—but here all the same, because this is a field campaign now. And since it is, you may as well know some of the basics.

A field campaign has two primary objectives: identifying likely voters *(targeting)* and ensuring that they make it to the polls (*get out the vote,* GOTV). Campaigns target voters in a variety of ways. Sometimes they call and ask whether a person is likely to vote. In the best of all worlds, they procure a list of registered voters who turned out in previous elections. The lists contain the 24-karat gold of the field world, the citizens who voted in the past year's general election and primary, the *double-prime* voters. From 5:00 until 11:00, our volunteers telephone double-prime voters reminding them to vote in the runoff next week.

My skepticism about field operations stems from the absence of a few necessary logical steps in the process. Why would we expect that any individual double-prime voter would be more likely to vote for Ruth Messinger than Al Sharpton? And what evidence is there that telephone calls have the desired impact? Do hundreds of hours of telephone calls actually bolster turnout? When we drive people to the polls, are we driving people who are likely to vote for us or our opponent?

Our field coordinator is shrewd and answers some of those questions by coordinating field operations with polling. We may not know whether an individual black voter will vote for Ruth, but we know that black voters generally prefer her, so it is to our advantage to try to bolster black turnout. Of course, we don't know whether an individual voter is black, so the best we can do is try to bolster turnout in areas that contain high percentages of subgroups that are favorable to us. The field director has a computer program that compares lists of voter names with a list of surnames that are likely to belong to minorities. We then can target areas that are likely to disproportionately favor us. It seems like a useful enterprise.

Some aspects of the field campaign advance the message. When we send direct mail reminding people of the primary, it also contains information advancing the message of the campaign ("Rudy Giuliani Cut Six Billion Dollars from Our Schools"). That is useful regardless of whether the target audience is predisposed in our favor. If the message is powerful, then it is persuasive in all forms. A well-constructed field campaign is a valuable asset to a campaign. For a campaign with limitless resources it is well worth doing. The question is whether, for a campaign like ours with quite limited resources, it is more or less valuable than television commercials. I'm quite sure that it is not, but the press certainly thinks it is.

"Campaign Shifts into High Gear," proclaims the *Daily News,* reporting that Ruth has begun "marshaling an all-out blitz for her run against the Rev. Al Sharpton," favorably noting that the campaign began preparing phone banks, organizing volunteers, and printing literature. "We're making a multi-front effort," the *News* reports a Messinger adviser saying. "We are not taking anything for granted." Adam Nagourney picks up on it too. Recalling his prior criticism, Nagourney writes, "Messinger is trying to do in the runoff what she did not do the first time around: set up an operation to get her supporters to the polls." (Nagourney still manages to find fault with Ruth, who, he says, is asking voters to support her without saying precisely why. "'I need your help,' she said yesterday during a Democratic Party breakfast in eastern Queens.")

Why does the notion persist in the press that field operations equate with a vigorous campaign? Why isn't it enough to work hard at polling and focus groups? Why aren't hundreds of hours dialing for cash ample evidence of vigor and persistence? Perhaps the Judeo-Christian ethic requires that candidates prove themselves through sweat rather than thought. Perhaps going door to door and standing at subway stops handing out leaflets are a rite of passage to higher office. Perhaps we're not quite ready to put both feet into the television age. Old-style politics is warm and fuzzy.

• • •

Another sign of the changing times within our campaign: After our highly public squabble with the Brooklyn Democratic organization over street money, it is going to get cash to help with field operations after all. Carl Andrews, party chairman Clarence Norman's close ally, will get $2,250. The same amount will go to Watson Jean-Baptiste, an aide to Brooklyn assemblyman Nick Perry, and to Heather Gayle of the Brooklyn Democrats. Leticia James, counsel to Brooklyn assemblyman Al Vann, is getting $4,000. Brooklyn state senator John Sampson is getting $2,000.

And, oh yeah, the Brooklyn Democrats are going to endorse Ruth.

• • •

A remarkable editorial in the *Times* asks the question where all the women in New York politics have gone. "It cannot have escaped everyone's notice," writes Gail Collins, "that whenever a woman runs in a big election in New York, disasters occur." Collins notes that New York has the second-worst record in the nation for electing women, behind only West Virginia, which does not elect a lieutenant governor.

Collins concludes that the blame lies with the New York Democratic party, which "lost the ability to handle competitive elections right around the time women came of age as a political force." As a result of the party's complacency, women candidates are "untrained in quick response, clumsy at give-and-take and rusty in the [all-important] art of street organizing." Perhaps this assuages the *Times*'s conscience, but it makes no sense. Why do Republican women candidates do poorly and why do some Democratic male candidates, trained by the same complacent party, manage to get elected?

• • •

The polling on the runoff is encouraging. A *Daily News* poll shows Ruth winning the runoff 53–25. Quinnipiac College puts it at 63–19 in Ruth's favor. According to the *News*, Ruth is running a credible 32–52 behind Sharpton among black voters.

In the general election, the *News* poll has Ruth losing to Giuliani 49–38. Giuliani would win a matchup with Sharpton by 34 points. A contemporaneous New York 1 poll shows Rudy with a 51–37 lead over Ruth. Both the *News* and New York 1 polls on the general election are tighter than in August, offering some hope that our bathroom ad has sliced into the mayor's favorables a bit.

The good news for Rudy is that he's maintaining a 63-percent overall job-approval rating, and the polling indicates that the Louima case hasn't caused him the slightest damage. Seventy percent of respondents say the Louima case will make no difference in their vote, though 71 percent say police brutality is a "serious problem in the New York City Police Department." And Quinnipiac has Rudy beating Ruth among Democrats 49–42, perhaps proving, as the mayor has always said was true, that he would win the Democratic primary.

• • •

Jimmy Breslin, for one, hopes the polling is wrong. "More and more," he writes, "it is becoming clear that if there is one thing this city cannot survive, it is an election between Ruth Messinger and Rudolph Giuliani. People would drop dead of boredom right on the sidewalk in front of you. So it is a medical necessity for the city to have a contest between Sharpton and Giuliani."

September 15

I think even the most optimistic among us accepted today the sad truth, that this campaign is cursed.

In the morning, Ruth is kicked out of the American Jewish Congress (AJC) luncheon honoring teachers' union president Sandra Feldman, even though she has attended past luncheons as a member. The AJC says Ruth's presence turns the event into a political one. We produce an invitation to no avail.

In the afternoon, hours before a scheduled debate between Ruth and Al Sharpton, word filters in that after a recanvass by the Board of Elections, Ruth is only 2,500 votes short of 40 percent out of the approximately 400,000 votes cast. With a total of 39.93 percent of all votes counted so far, Ruth needs to capture just slightly more than 40 percent of the absentee and affidavit ballots, which for some reason cannot be counted until one week after the election. The Board of Elections is now saying it's likely Ruth will be the winner.

Though the board never made this clear, election night results are unofficial. Election inspectors record the votes from each voting machine by hand on a standard form that is then delivered to the board's central office by the police. Apparently the police made a few mistakes. In one district where Ruth had more than a hundred votes, they reported her with zero.

A spokesperson for the Board of Elections explains that "nothing is official until our people count the machines back at the warehouse, refreshed and under bright lights." It hardly seems possible, but it's true. The Board of Elections, which works all of two days a year, has a spinner. She's not that good. Back in May, the state comptroller's office conducted an audit and found that 18 percent of the dead people they checked were still on the voting rolls. Twenty-two percent of convicted felons were still registered to vote. The spinner had no comment.

It's easy to understand the discrepancy once you understand the process. "The inspectors have been there sixteen-plus hours," explains board director Daniel DeFrancesco. "A nine looks like a zero. An eight looks like a six." "Sometimes a five can look like an eight," says spokesperson Naomi Bernstein, who is earning her pay this year.

All of this leaves Ruth and Al in the unusual position of debating for an election that likely will not occur. The format of this debate is unusual. The candidates will have approximately thirty minutes to question each other directly. In the waiting room, Ruth Messinger suggests to Al Sharpton that the question time would be a useful opportunity to draw attention to some of Rudy Giuliani's failings. The result is theater of the absurd.

Sharpton, leading off with what will prove to be the toughest question of the exchange, asks Ruth whether she regrets not endorsing Jesse Jackson's Rainbow Coalition in 1988. No, Ruth says, she endorsed the Democrat she thought had the best chance of winning, Michael Dukakis.

Good. Invoking Willie Horton should help fight her image as a liberal.

Ruth asks Sharpton whether the media should pay as much attention to Rudy Giuliani's campaign-finance transgressions as it has to reported Democratic abuses.

Indeed they should, says the Reverend.

But the Giuliani people say the violations stem from a misinterpretation of the law.

"Half the people on Riker's Island say it's a misinterpretation," says the Reverend, quickly replying with his next hardball. "How can you explain to the public and me what is healthy about a 10-percent unemployment rate?"

"There is nothing healthy about 10-percent unemployment," says Ruth. "Have you thought out what steps you would take to make sure lobbyists and insiders do not have the access they have had in this administration?"

Indeed he has, says the Reverend, asking in turn whether Ruth would try to reverse the administration's deplorable record in public housing.

Indeed she would.

• • •

Two moments redeem the debate. Echoing the Giuliani campaign's line that the two candidates are indistinguishable, Ruth is asked what sets them apart. "It's obvious," she says. "I'm taller."

And in a classy, impassioned moment, Ruth says that she will not take Giuliani's bait and denounce Al Sharpton. "I will not divide New York for political gain," she avers. "If this were to cost me the election, so be it."

It's among her most impressive moments of the campaign. What other candidate uses the subjunctive?

• • •

As word filters around the city that the runoff may be off, reaction ranges from disappointment to outrage. Bronx assemblyman Larry Seabrook says cancellation of the runoff will suppress minority turnout by making minorities feel as if they have been "robbed." Sharpton sounds a more ominous warning: "They don't understand that this is a democracy," he says. "If they try to take this away . . . "

• • •

However angry and upset Sharpton may be, I think Ruth has every right to feel worse. Governors Island is out. Our two-day window has come and gone. There will be no election bounce for Ruth Messinger ever. Only a slim, hollow victory gained, minority voters doubtless will conclude, as a result of an unfair process. "She'd win the runoff two to one," says Dick Morris. "Now all that's left is the taste of defeat and the end of her momentum."

September 16

Down at the Board of Elections, inspectors, paid $135 a day, are working in teams of two (one Democrat, one Republican) to count the remaining ballots. Seated at folded tables, the clerks check the ballots against spiral notebooks of registered voters, open ballots by hand, and record them on tally sheets. They count at a rate of approximately one per minute, not including time lost to debating important matters such as whether to disqualify the ballot of a voter who voted for all of the candidates.

The director of the board has a real powder keg on his hands. The media is scrutinizing the voting process closely as the city waits impatiently for the results of the recount. The pressure is taking its toll on the inspectors. "The water cooler's empty!" one cries. "We cannot work under these conditions. We need water!"

DeFrancesco is empathetic. "We're whipping people to death here," he says.

• • •

As it appears more and more likely that Ruth will prevail without a runoff, Al Sharpton is exploring his options, which include a lawsuit. In January, Sharpton said runoffs are no more than a "Dixiecrat trick created to make sure that the party bosses can control the nominee." As recently as the day after the primary, Sharpton's campaign manager, Jacques DeGraff, said that Sharpton was committed to supporting the winner of the primary. But Sharpton isn't endorsing yet.

"I'm determined to make this election happen," Sharpton says today. "We're not going to back down. There will be a runoff. We will not be disenfranchised." The Reverend thinks there has been foul play. "Something doesn't smell right," he tells reporters in the evening. "At best there's been some incompetence," Sharpton says, "at worst, deliberate maneuvering."

The question within the campaign is what posture to adopt with respect to whatever challenge Sharpton ultimately brings. So far, we have not defended our victory vigorously. Campaigns have the right to have representatives present during counting and may challenge particular ballots they find objectionable for one reason or another. We have not done that so far. But making the decision not to challenge ballots in a recount is one thing. Defending a lawsuit is quite another.

Our deputy political director, who is black, says that Sharpton's people are saying that the Reverend's plan is to cause a bit of a stir, but not to disturb the results of the election. Sharpton can either sue in state or federal court, and his choice of venue will say a great deal about his real intentions. The Reverend would have a small but realistic chance for success in state court. There, his burden would be to show that there were sufficient irregularities in the election to call the outcome into doubt. In federal court, Sharpton would carry the additional burden of showing that there was intent to deprive people of the right to vote, something that would be almost impossible to prove in a case of this sort. Either case would be difficult to win—courts are understandably reluctant to set aside the results of an election—but a federal suit would be a charade, a lawsuit for show only.

The main concern among Ruth's braintrust during an evening meeting is that Sharpton could name us as a defendant. It's a meaningless act from a legal standpoint—Sharpton's challenge is against the Board of Elections; we would be named only as an affected third party—but people feel that it would have a public-relations impact and would demonstrate Sharpton's real intentions. The sense of the group is that we can do nothing more than wait and see what Sharpton's next move is.

I advocate a different approach. We should join in the lawsuit and advocate that the runoff be held. It's the only act, I say, that could restore minority faith in the process and in Ruth. The risk, of course, is that we won't win the runoff, but if we don't have the political strength to beat Al Sharpton, then winning the primary, by whatever means, is only postponing an inevitable defeat.

It's not a popular idea.

Ruth would be the first candidate in history, Jim says, to advocate her own defeat.

• • •

If the *Amsterdam News* is any indication, it may already be too late to regenerate confidence in the voting process. The lead editorial is a scathing indictment of the Board of Elections and of Rudy Giuliani, who, according to the *News,* was "running scared" and did not trust polls that put him 70 percent ahead of Sharpton, especially because Giuliani's support among Jews is tenuous. "Rudy is a hater" and "Jews are not exempt from that kind of hatred, for it scars the soul."

There's a wonderful nuance to the editorial, "A Time Beyond Anger, A Time Beyond Giuliani." Its author, Wilbert A. Tatum, "Publisher and Editor in Chief," quotes himself. The lead of the story: "No matter which way the election goes now, everyone has lost—W.A.T."

• • •

Rudy Giuliani doesn't think much of Ruth's victory. "To sort of be the nominee of your party with the lowest turnout in history of the city," he says, "and then to have the bare minimum vote, this is like creeping in rather than winning." And he didn't think much of last night's debate either. "Al Sharpton, do you think Rudy Giuliani was the worst mayor in the history of the city of New York? And Al Sharpton would say, 'No, no, I think he was the worst mayor in the history of the world.'"

• • •

George Will's story about the mayoral race is finally in the paper. As promised, he argues that the end of liberalism is upon us, which is bad enough, but what really hurts is his description of our campaign. He calls it a "jalopy." I suppose Republican campaigns give him twenty-ounce bottles of Diet Coke.

September 17

It is 11:00 at night and I and a few reporters are sitting in Daniel F. DeFrancesco's Broadway office. DeFrancesco is a leviathan of a man. His clothes and chin hang loosely around him, as if to allow himself the luxury of gaining or regaining a few pounds. His government office is spartanly decorated. There are three books on the shelves: *The Civil War*, *The Rice Cake Diet*, and *The Complete Guide to Television*. This is not a man who relishes the spotlight. The Board of Elections was last in the news in May, when the state comptroller released the audit showing that 20 percent of dead people and convicted felons remain registered to vote.

DeFrancesco makes it official. Ruth is the winner with a whopping 40.13 percent of the vote.

September 18

The Board of Elections is in full session to certify the results of the mayoral primary. This body is patronage at its absolute worst. The ten commissioners are appointed directly by the "major political organizations" of each of the five boroughs. There's no pretense of merit. They're paid $12,500 a year to meet once every other week. DeFrancesco, it turns out, is paid more than $90,000. And he gets a driver too.

The board president, Frederic Umane, is explaining some of the reasons that the original vote may have varied from the ultimate vote, but I'm too involved in a fascinating conversation to notice. Eric Ruano-Melendez is sitting directly next to me. This is too good to pass up.

"Hello, Mr. Melendez," I say. "Here for the vote?"

"Yes, you really have to keep an eye on these people. It's a conspiracy."

"Who is the conspiracy by and against?"

"It's everyone. The lawyers. Everyone."

"And they want to see Ruth get nominated."

"Yes, that's right."

Melendez breaks off his conversation with me and makes his way toward the front of the room.

"I want to know why my vote went down by 1,000 votes. Everyone else went up from the first count, but I went down."

Today Frederic Umane will earn his $12,500.

• • •

For the record, Ruth Messinger became the first woman in the history of New York City to carry the nomination of the Democratic party with 165,377 votes, 40.19 percent of the total vote cast and just 793 more than the minimum needed. Al Sharpton earned 131,848 votes (32 percent), Sal Albanese 86,485 (21 percent). Eric Ruano-Melendez collected 17,663 votes (4.2 percent), about 1,000 fewer than he had after the initial canvass.

No explanation was given for this glaring discrepancy.

• • •

Ruth celebrates her victory with a party at the Water Club on Manhattan's East River. She enters to Elton John's "I'm Still Standing" and issues a rousing address. "To my former opponents, I say join me. To their supporters I say, join me and we will win. And to the mayor I say 'The battle has just begun. We will beat you.'" I suppose the truth wouldn't be very inspiring. "Join me and we will lose by less than if you do not join me."

"What a long, strange trip it's been," Ruth says, joined onstage by her husband, David Dinkins, Freddie Ferrer, and a few others.

Somehow the picture of Ruth quoting the Grateful Dead doesn't seem quite right.

PART THREE

Into the Breach

"WHOEVER SAID *POLITICS MAKES STRANGE BEDFELLOWS* DIDN'T KNOW RUTH MESSINGER!"

September 18

Just like that, we're in a real campaign.

Late in the morning, Rudy delivers what his campaign is billing as his first "major" reelection address. We send two people to infiltrate. One is turned away at the door, but the other successfully passes himself off as a reporter. By noon we've received word where Rudy is going against Ruth. It's sex shops.

The venue for the speech is a newly renovated theater in Times Square, and Giuliani devotes most of his half hour to talking about the revival of Times Square. "To a very, very large extent," he says, it "symbolizes the entire turnaround for the city." He claims that his rezoning plan spurred the turnaround and ridicules Ruth for opposing it. "You think it [sex shops] lends character to the city," he says, as if addressing Ruth. "There are people who think that, and they are entitled to think it. I think it destroys the character of the city, and there are people who are entitled to think that. And let's see who thinks that more, people on your side or people on my side." He doesn't stop there, though. Displaying, as Adam Nagourney notes, "the first fruit of months of research into Ms. Messinger's record," Rudy warns ominously that Ruth favored "one sex shop per block."

It's a ridiculous exaggeration. Although Giuliani might reasonably contend that Ruth's plan was less restrictive than his and that her greater willingness to tolerate the sex shops shows a lack of judgment, it's preposterous to claim that she actually favored sex shops. Ruth's plan, like the mayor's, would have reduced the number of sex shops in the city, just in a different way. Shortly after the speech, Giuliani retracts the statement and clarifies. "Her proposal," he says, "was not to have one on every block, but to permit one on every block." The frightening consensus in the campaign is that a majority of people at the speech believed that Ruth favored making sure every block in the city had at least one sex shop, if not more.

We're as prepared for the attack as we can be and respond to Rudy's release of Ruth's unfortunate 1995 letter, by releasing copies of her competing report and plan to restrict adult businesses. The press seems to be leaning in the direction of covering the story as a "he said, she said," but the tone for the next few weeks has been set. It is going to be nasty and bitter or, as Rudy Giuliani says, "like, really issue oriented."

"Since I've been asked all the questions so far," Rudy tells the crowd at the New Victory Theater, "I thought it might be useful to start asking the questions the other way. And to illustrate that the general-election campaign will be very different from the primary. This will not be attacking people. It won't be trying to avoid issues. This is going to be like, really issue oriented."

• • •

Al Sharpton's lawyers, Ron Kuby and Michael Hardy, file a class-action suit on behalf of five Sharpton voters this afternoon in federal court. The complaint alleges that the Board of Elections "led the African-American electorate to believe that an election would take place," causing them to squander "personal and financial resources." What exactly those resources are isn't clear.

At a hearing on the complaint, Judge Denny Chin asks Sharpton's lawyers why they don't file suit in state court. Hardy explains that the same politicians who appoint the election board—who, he says, have a "Boss Tweed attitude"—influence state court judges. "We have come to the point where a strong federal hand is needed."

Chin asks Sharpton's lawyers to produce evidence of irregularities. Even though there is as yet no evidence before the court, Chin comments on the merits of the case. "I don't know if I'd use the word ineptitude," Chin says, "but there appears to be a pattern here." Chin leaves open the question of whether ineptitude can be so pervasive that it becomes intentional conduct of the sort required by federal law.

"It's not over until the fat man sings, and I haven't sung yet," Sharpton says, walking a tightrope between protecting his interests and blaming Ruth. "Something doesn't smell right about this recount," Sharpton says. "Ultimately we will unite for that fight, but we can't unite until we are sure there is a level playing field." So far, this isn't sounding like a man who is just putting on a show.

Our public stance focuses on the legally meaningless fact that Ruth was not named as a defendant in the suit. "I have not been named in this court action and I am not opposing it. I understand what it means to a candidate or his supporters to feel aggrieved with an election result, and I certainly understand how confusing these last few days have been. They have an action in court. I am not opposing it."

• • •

After months of saying that we would not spend money on positive ads or put Ruth to the camera, Jim and Mandy have decided to go up with a positive ad that puts Ruth to camera. There's some basis for deviating from our strategy. Ads take at least a couple of days to produce, and in light of the uncertainty about the runoff, the thought was that—regardless of whether the runoff is held—this is the time to introduce Ruth to the voters and not a time to run negative ads about the mayor. All the same, it's a terrible ad.

In the commercial, Ruth says:

> This campaign's been on and off and up and down, but one thing hasn't changed: That's who I am and why I'm running for mayor. I'm Ruth Messinger—a New Yorker, a wife and mother, a Democrat. I love this city, but I also know we've got problems. A school system that's failing our kids, an unemployment rate twice the national average, rent regulation under assault, and far too much violence in our homes and schools. Those are the problems I'll fight as Mayor, and believe me I know how. Join me.

Ruth stands in front of a chintzy brown curtain that clashes with her bright orange suit. An off-key trumpet plays a song in the background that sounds a little like "Auld Lang Syne." Ruth gesticulates at inappropriate times, like Edith Bunker rehearsing her famous "We welcome you with open arms" speech. At the end of the commercial, the words "Messinger for Mayor" appear in the top right corner in thin white lettering. The ad is a stark contrast to our highly polished first commercial. The first ad managed to generate outrage at the mayor and set forth Ruth's own platform. That ad was the product of months of research and development. This one was thrown together in a couple of days, and it looks it.

• • •

More than halfway through a meeting of the Campaign Finance Board, a man walks in, pulls a chair from the audience, and seats himself at the dais alongside the other board members. The board is meeting to vote on a proposed $220,000 fine against the Giuliani campaign for violating individual contribution limits. Father Joseph O'Hare, the chairman of the board, extends his hand to the stranger and says, "I don't believe we've met."

The newcomer is Joseph Erazo, Giuliani's newest appointee to the board. Erazo was appointed to replace a board member who retired earlier in the year, but hasn't yet been cleared to take his seat by the Department of Investigation. In fact, this is the first attempt he has made to contact the board. Erazo says that Tony Carbonetti suggested to Erazo that he attend this afternoon's meeting. Carbonetti, who dropped out of college and once defaulted on $11,000 in college loans, is Giuliani's patronage czar. His father is a childhood friend of Rudy's. Shortly after the meeting, City Hall distributes copies of a letter stating that Erazo's Department of Investigation check has been completed that day. Rest assured, Deputy Mayor Randy Mastro says, Erazo is clean.

Erazo may be clean, but if he is, it's only by virtue of a recent shower. Erazo, the director of Nassau County Medical Center in Long Island, was charged with serious mismanagement of the hospital. Nassau County comptroller Fred Parola cleared Erazo of the charges, but found that Erazo had an "inappropriate relationship" with the New York Health Plan, a for-profit HMO owned in part and represented by Erazo's longtime friend Herman Badillo. The New York Health Plan was run by Jay Fabrikant. Fabrikant was convicted in 1983 by then U.S. Attorney Rudy Giuliani of tax evasion and for selling quaaludes through diet clinics. To top it off, Erazo attended the September 10 rally in City Hall Park of Democrats for Giuliani. The city charter prohibits members of the Campaign Finance Board from participating in any way in any political campaigns.

And to think Father O'Hare once praised Giuliani for the quality and objectivity of his appointments to the board.

• • •

Although we have tight control of the message that comes from our offices, the fact remains that this is still Ruth's campaign and she can say whatever she wants. Though we've argued time and again that we need to concede the crime issue, word is coming in from the field that Ruth has been unable to resist talking about an increase in subway crime reported in this week's papers. The candidate's instinct is to attack at every opportunity, even if the ensuing victory is a Pyrrhic one.

September 19

For weeks, I've been lobbying for Ruth to appear on the Howard Stern show. Aside from the fact that I'm a fan of the show, I figure the appearance will get us votes. Stern has a simple rule: The first person to call into the show gets his endorsement. His track record is impressive. Christie Todd Whitman and George Pataki both won tough races with his help.

Finally, last week, Lee and Jim gave me approval to make the arrangements. They go smoother than I thought possible. Stern's producer, Gary dell'Abate, reminds me that there is a history between Ruth and Howard. In 1994, Stern was considering a run for governor of New York State on a platform with but three planks: implement the death penalty, shift all road construction to evenings, and put in more toll takers on bridges and tunnels to make traffic flow more quickly. Stern promised to resign after doing those three things. He was searching for a strong running mate and heard that Ruth had a solid reputation. Plus, Stern felt he needed a black running mate to balance the ticket. So he called Ruth and invited her to join him on the Libertarian party line.

She explained that she was against the death penalty and, in any event, she was not black.

"Are you sure you're not black?" Stern asked.

Ruth assured him that she was not. Stern dropped out of the race a few weeks later after learning that he would be forced to make his tax returns public. The two narrowly missed being forever linked in New York history. Gary reminded me of all this.

"I'm looking forward to it," he said.

"Me too," I said. And indeed I have been for weeks. But the headwind is blowing strong against the campaign today. This is not at all what we bargained for.

Stern starts by summing up the situation.

"For those of you listening out of town, we have a mayoral situation going on. We have a mayor, an incumbent, Mayor Giuliani. Mrs. Messinger is running against Mayor Giuliani on the Democratic side. And then there's this rabble-rousing black guy, who has the brain of a pinhead. Who is completely dumb and retarded."

"Now, now," Ruth scolds. "No one said that when you were running for office."

"Oh, believe me, they did," Stern says.

From here, it goes downhill. When Stern asks how Ruth plans on beating Rudy, Ruth says that it will be no problem with Stern's endorsement.

"I gotta tell you something," he says. "I am so in love with our mayor. I've never met the man, I don't know anything about him, but I am completely in love with this guy. Isn't there another office that you could run for?"

Ruth explains that this is where her "interest and passion" lie in the city. She wants to fix the schools. She tries her best to appeal to Stern's prurient interests. "I know one of the things that I've been talking about will interest you. You know that there are schools so overcrowded that there really are kids going to schools in converted closets and in hallways and in bathrooms."

Stern doesn't bite. "Can I tell you what the problem is with the city schools? Let's be honest. It's the parents. They don't give a rat's ass about their children.

"I have a thought," he says. "There's rumors that Rudy's marriage is in trouble. I say you become the next Mrs. Giuliani. Then you could run the city together."

Ruth is way out of familiar territory now. "I'm happily married. I have a wonderful husband, and he is supporting me in this race. And I know I can count on his vote."

"What does he do for a living?" Stern asks. "How does he get a happening woman like you?"

"He works in the public-school system."

"Then blame him!

"There should be a place for you somewhere in government," Stern says. "But I'm just in love with Rudy Giuliani. I would have sex with him. And he's not an attractive man.

"I'll tell you what. I'll vote for you if you legalize prostitution.

"And pot."

Boy, was this a bad idea.

• • •

A. M. Rosenthal, the dean of *Times* editorial writers, has some scathing words for Ruth. He writes: "Faced with a critical political dilemma, Ruth Messinger reviewed her principles, made a firm, important decision, and told New Yorkers what not one of them thought she believed: Al Sharpton would make a better mayor than Rudolph Giuliani. . . . If she had had courage to say that a Mayor Sharpton would have been a disaster for New Yorkers of all colors, all religions, she could have run a decent campaign for the mayoralty."

• • •

In 1993, when the Campaign Finance Board fined the Dinkins campaign $320,000, the *Post* put the news on the front page: "DAVE'S CAMP FINED 320G FOR PRIMARY ERROR." Today, Giuliani's fine is on page 20 of the *Post*. And though every other daily, including the *News*, has condemned the Giuliani campaign for its transgressions, the *Post* editorial board hasn't said a word.

September 20

Federal judge Denny Chin is pandering.

The new federal courthouse in New York City is a scandalously ornate affair. Each judge has his or her own private courtroom. Until today, Chin probably hasn't had more than twenty people in the room at any time, including jurors and lawyers. Today, Chin has about a hundred people, almost all black, packed into the courtroom waiting to hear how he will rule on the case. Ronald Kuby, William Kunstler's old partner, is arguing his position elegantly, but every lawyer in the room knows he doesn't have a case. There's no evidence here of racial bias.

But Chin won't say as much. "I'm really constrained here. Mr. Sharpton's constituency has a lot to be proud of and even more to be outraged by. The evidence of irregularities in the election is significant. But I'm afraid there's nothing I can do about it." Chin, a former Assistant U.S. Attorney under Rudy Giuliani, has all but made out a state court case for the Sharpton camp, without hearing from a single witness.

The crowd disperses chanting "No justice, no peace."

September 21

Rudy is living up to his pledge to launch an attack a day.

After lying in quiescence for several weeks since the *Slate* article, Fred Dicker of the New York *Post* reports that Republican assemblyman Thomas Reynolds from Buffalo (a district that includes Attica) said that Ruth Messinger once hosted a party for prison-guard killer John Hill. According to Reynolds, the egregiousness of Ruth's behavior is increasing over time. "I think it was outrageous, incredible behavior what she did in 1979, and I think it is even more outrageous when looked at today."

Reynolds said that he discussed the party with the Giuliani campaign. "I would hope they will use it against her at the appropriate time," Reynolds says.

Perhaps I'm cynical (well, I'm certainly cynical; perhaps I'm wrong), but my guess is the discussion went in the other direction. My hunch is the Giuliani campaign planted the information with Reynolds and asked him to leak it to the press. If so, it's skillfully done. Coming from upstate, the charge bears no taint from the Giuliani campaign. It will take a day or two longer to circulate in the city press than it might otherwise have, but in this case the Giuliani campaign isn't interested in people reading about the charge in the newspaper. They're laying the foundation for a devastating television ad.

And as if that's not enough. Rudy foreshadows an attack based on Ruth's involvement with the Harlem Urban Development Corporation (HUDC), a city-supported agency that misspent more than $100 million in federal aid. Ruth was a nonvoting member of the board by virtue of being borough president. She had nothing to do with the day-to-day management of the HUDC, but Rudy may try to prove her guilt by association. The mayor calls today's Harlem Day Parade, which he skipped, a reunion of the HUDC.

Perhaps Rudy really can live up to his promise.

To prepare for a direct attack from Rudy, Jim has us assemble all of our research about Giuliani's past. We've concluded that the statute of limitations has expired on Rudy's waffle on abortion rights, his denial of human-rights abuses in Haiti as a Reagan Justice Department official, and the difficult decision to dismiss evidence that he ducked the draft. But if Rudy's going to go bring this campaign into the '70s, we'll fight him on his own turf.

• • •

A poll by the *Observer* and New York 1 shows that Ruth has cut into the mayor's lead significantly and now trails Giuliani by only 49–40 in a head-to-head matchup. In July, they had the spread at 23. This is the third poll in a week that has shown the race tightening, but not a single paper has yet reported the story from that angle.

Instead, the news is focused on the results of the *Observer*'s penetrating inquiry into which candidate New Yorkers would prefer for company if stranded on a desert island.

I suppose I have to give the results.

Twenty-seven percent said Rudy, 23 percent Ruth, and 18 percent Sharpton. A plurality, 32 percent, said none of the above, including one person who said he would kill himself first.

• • •

Forgotten in our discussions of the various subdivisions within the campaign is the political department, which is located in the farthest reaches of our office, outside the wall and behind the water cooler. It has little space—two desks in an office shared with the field staff—and is often displaced by other space-needy functions, like our growing women's desk. The team is headed by the nicest woman on the campaign, recently a grandmother for the first time, a decade-long supporter of Ruth. Her deputy, a Dinkins alum, is a former Columbia student who plays chess and writes poetry in his spare time.

They do all of the things for which I would never have patience. They make sure the right local politicians are invited whenever Ruth goes to a neighborhood, they smooth things over when Ruth accidentally steps on someone's toes, they tell her who has been active on a particular issue Ruth decides to advocate, and they line up endorsements. Today they're dealing with the president.

In 1992, in the midst of the Gennifer Flowers scandal, borough president Ruth Messinger declared her support of and belief in candidate Bill Clinton. Clinton has a reputation for being fiercely loyal politically, but so far he hasn't done anything to help Ruth. In town today for a speech to the United Nations, Clinton invites Ruth to meet Marine One at the Wall Street helipad. It's a good photo opportunity, but Clinton won't take questions from the press with Ruth, saying that there's too much going on in the campaign-finance scandal for him to risk an open encounter with the press. Ruth meets him at midday and the picture of her alone with the president and the First Lady is impressive, though it's quite a bit less than we would have liked from the president.

Clinton is one of a handful of people whose endorsement and support could actually make a difference. He carried 83 percent of the vote in New York City in 1996. In our March poll, he had a 69–18 favorable-unfavorable ratio. The president and the First Lady have been actively campaigning for Jim McGreevey, who is running for governor in New Jersey against Christie Todd Whitman. Today was the first time either showed up for Ruth. We'll need a lot more from the Clintons if we are to have any chance.

September 22

Rudy's hitting hard on Attica. At a press conference this morning, Norman Seabrook, the head of the corrections officers' union, whose endorsement Ruth had been optimistically courting throughout the campaign (she exempted corrections officers from the reforms outlined in the budget speech), declared Ruth "not fit to hold any public office." "What the hell were you thinking?" he cries.

The mayor echoes the sentiment. "I'd like to know if she remembers giving a party to a convicted murderer or not," Rudy says at his daily press availability. His campaign releases a copy of the 1979 *Times* article and several stories about Hill's arrest in 1981 for allegedly stabbing a man (the charges were eventually dropped). The Giuliani campaign press release says Hill is now living in British Columbia and was "a key player in the Gustafsen Lake standoff" and the famous "Oka Blockade in 1990."

No, Rudy, not the Oka Blockade. We've polled the Oka Blockade. We know its power.

Hill, reached by telephone in British Columbia, recalls the party, which he says was a fund-raiser to help him get his life back on track after prison.

He laments that it wasn't a lavish affair and didn't raise all that much money. "It was an apple-juice-and-cheese gathering," he says. "Kind of a low-budget thing."

Apple juice and cheese at the Messingers'! She must have been real popular with the neighborhood kids.

• • •

The research team is taking a closer look at the Attica story, and it's clear it needs a bit of context. Prison conditions at Attica were legendarily deplorable. For some time, prisoners tried to improve conditions there to no avail. On September 9, 1971, the prisoners rioted, in the process bludgeoning guard William Quinn to death. The prisoners held forty guards hostage and demanded to negotiate with people who had over time expressed some level of sympathy for the prisoners, including none other than Herman Badillo, Giuliani's trusted adviser. After four days, Governor Nelson Rockefeller ordered the state police to retake the prison by force, if necessary. Force was necessary. Twenty-nine inmates and ten prison guards were killed in the takeover. Ninety more people were wounded. Autopsies showed that the police were responsible for the carnage. Badillo described the siege as a "willful police riot" and a "bloody massacre." After the dispute, Badillo said that a congressional investigation of the rebellion was "a subterfuge to insure that the [prisoners'] demands are not met."

Hill, then nineteen, was identified by an eyewitness as having participated in the attack on Quinn along with Charles Pernasilice. There was overwhelming evidence that Hill and Pernasilice were only two of many who struck Quinn. Pernasilice was convicted of attempted interference with a police officer, a minor felony, but the jury sentenced Hill to life in prison. Many felt that Hill had been scapegoated. Known by the Indian name of Dacajeweiah, Hill became something of a cause célèbre among liberals. Then-governor Hugh Carey finally commuted Hill's sentence in 1976, as part of an effort to bury Attica in the past. Carey said the state "failed abysmally" in investigating the Attica riot and felt it was unfair for the burden of Attica to fall on a handful of people. "Attica," he said at the time, "lurks as a dark shadow over our system of justice." Ray Harding was Carey's special adviser at the time. Just this past June, a jury awarded a former Attica inmate $4 million for abuse he suffered at Attica. This former inmate was forced to walk barefoot over broken glass and to lie on a picnic table, keeping a football under his chin, under threat of death or castration if the ball came free.

Hosting the party still doesn't seem like a tasteful decision, but in context the decision at least seems comprehensible—certainly, at the least, more complicated than "holding a party for a cop killer," as the event is being summarized. Herman Badillo himself says that the prison revolt "goes back to a very different period of time" and that Messinger's alleged hosting of the party was "perfectly understandable." Ruth continues to say she does not remember the party, and I have a theory how that might be possible, though Fran Reiter would disagree. Reiter says, "If you throw a party or don't throw a party for a killer, you remember it." True enough. I remember many parties for killers I did not throw.

During the 1970s, the Messingers lived an unusual lifestyle. Bits and pieces of old news suggest that the Messingers lived with several other families and shared common areas in the Upper West Side brownstone where they lived. Ruth told us that they simply needed to have tenants to afford their apartment. Whatever the reason, from the news and knowing Ruth, it's clear that the Messinger place was an open forum for ideas and meetings. There probably were lots of meetings and parties there, and it's easy to imagine that Ruth, busy as she always has been, wasn't at every one. Indeed, the 1979 article did not say that Ruth attended the party. It merely said that the party was hosted at her home.

Of course, that isn't a very convincing defense, and reviving the image of Ruth as a product of the 1960s would probably do us more harm than whatever good we might derive from convincing a few people that Ruth was not at the party. Jim urges Ruth to apologize, and later in the day she issues a statement saying that she does not, in fact, remember the party, but if it occurred it was a lapse of judgment.

Ruth adds a serious threat. "I don't think it makes sense to wage this campaign on the far distant past," she says. "Does Rudy really want this campaign to be about his effort to dodge the draft, or his flip-flops on a woman's right to choose, or his action in a past administration to put Haitian immigrants into internment camps?"

The response sets the Giuliani campaign back on its heels. Giuliani press secretary Sunny Mindel explains that Giuliani initially got a student deferment, then an occupational exemption as a law clerk. Of course, no one does any investigative reporting. The *Post* itself noted in 1989 how unusual an occupational exemption for a law clerk was. It doesn't even check its own old articles. But the research served its purpose. Giuliani is off of Attica and doesn't seem likely to go back there anytime soon.

• • •

On the eastern front, Al Sharpton is taking his case to state court. If Sharpton is really merely putting on a show, as he is telling us behind the scenes, he's doing a pretty good job of it. I think we're being taken for rubes. Sharpton is trying to win, I think, and in state court he has a chance. Supreme Court justice Beatrice Shainswit is appointing a referee to investigate irregularities in the election and report back to her by tomorrow.

• • •

The picture of Ruth and the president is featured prominently in all three dailies. The word in our office is that Clinton showed the picture to one of his aides and expressed his hope that it would be a sufficient show of support for Ruth to keep him from having to return to New York.

• • •

At this evening's opening night of the Metropolitan Opera season, a performance of *Carmen* featuring Placido Domingo as Don Jose, all eyes are on Bill Clinton and Rudy Giuliani. Bill and Hillary have the best seats in the house, center stage at the parterre level, just three seats away from Rudy Giuliani. It's a tricky situation for the Clinton political department. Clinton is endorsing Ruth, but has cordial relations with the mayor.

Clinton's people handle the situation with Solomonic wisdom. Though Rudy is nearby, Clinton conspicuously does not speak to him on the way in. Instead, the two chat only during the intermissions.

Opening night at the opera is the place to be.

Giuliani and Clinton are joined in their chats by Henry Kissinger and Brooke Astor.

Dick Morris and his wife are seated in the orchestra.

Eric Ruano-Melendez is on a bench in the lobby.

"I just happened to be in the area and I thought I would stop in and try to buy a ticket."

September 23

Rudy is on the air with an ad about sex shops. An announcer says:

> Ruth Messinger says sex businesses give New York character—that they are an integral part of a neighborhood's fabric. And an important part of our city's economic and tourism industry base. Messinger argued the Mayor's plan to restrict sex shops was unconstitutional. But six judges on two courts have agreed

with the Mayor and upheld his plan. Unanimously. Sex shops in our neighborhoods? Messinger thinks they add character. What do you think?

Superimposed over an aerial shot of New York City is the quote: "Ruth Messinger: 'Sex Businesses Give New York Character.' FOX TV *News* 9/13/95."

Thing is, Ruth never said that.

One of a campaign research department's functions is providing factual backup for claims made by its candidate and its advertising. For positive ads, there often isn't much backup to provide, but for negative ads the burden is greater. When we put out our bathroom ad, we provided fifty pages of backup to reporters detailing the mayor's budget cuts, statistics about overcrowding in the schools, and pictures of classes held in bathrooms. As backup for its ad, the Giuliani campaign is offering a transcript of a Channel 5 news broadcast. At the end of the story about the dispute over the zoning plan, anchor Rosanna Scotto, who did not report the story, says, "Incidentally, Ruth Messinger says sex businesses give New York character." That's the sole basis of the quote the Giuliani campaign is attributing to Ruth. Channel 5 refuses to get involved in the controversy.

Giuliani sounds childish in defending the ad against Ruth's demands that he pull it from the air. "She said it," he says, even though she didn't. "I don't have to defend it. Every single thing that you see in that commercial, she has said. So she is going to have to deal with it."

• • •

The sex-shop quote is not the only thing the Giuliani research team got wrong. CBS's Marcia Kramer finds John Hill in Vancouver, British Columbia, where he is training Canadian Indian militants how to kill Canadian police officers. "Rudolph the Red-Nosed Reindeer put me in a Willie Horton–type advertisement," Hill says. I wonder how he keeps so up on New York politics that he has such strong feelings about the mayor. But Hill has more to say. Ruth was away that summer. A woman named Annette Rubinstein hosted the party.

Wayne Barrett of the *Village Voice* confirms that Rubinstein, in her words, "borrowed the house" and that Ruth was not there. Rubinstein's recollection differs in only one important respect. She says it was a potluck affair, implying that there may have been more on the menu than apple juice and cheese. Barrett personally testifies that he recalls attending at least two get-togethers for progressive causes at the Messinger house that Ruth did not attend.

It may seem like a big deal, but it is only a hollow political victory. Within the campaign it reaffirms our faith in Ruth's integrity, but we won't be able to score any points by taking the Giuliani campaign to task for their overreaching. Doing so would require us to revive the Attica story, which, though not as bad as we had feared, is still hardly a credit for Ruth. There doesn't seem to be anything to be gained from going out there and saying, "Rudy lied again. I wasn't there for the party for the convicted cop killer. It was at my house, but I wasn't there."

The only good news is it means Rudy can't make an ad out of it.

September 24

Drawing an obvious comparison, it seems to me that the level of exaggeration in the sex-shop ad is equal to or greater than the bathroom ad. Ruth never said that sex shops give New York character. What she said, as you may recall, was that the mayor's plan threatened gay neighborhoods like the West Village, where adult stores exist "largely without incident" and form "an integral part of this neighborhood's fabric." If she indeed did say something to a reporter about sex shops contributing character, she was likely talking about the West Village and not New York City in general.

Sex shops seem like a fair subject for an ad. Whether her reasons were valid or not, Ruth did oppose the mayor's zoning plan. Were the roles reversed, I'm sure we would have made an ad on the same subject. But the misquote, which is central to the ad, turns a difference of opinion into a caricature of an argument. Giuliani, it seems, has not paid as dearly for the exaggeration as we did for the bathroom ad, if that ad was an exaggeration. An editorial in the *Times* criticizes Giuliani for the sex-shop ad and for the Erazo fiasco. The *Times* says that Rudy, like Ruth, exaggerated his opponent's position, but implies that Rudy's transgression is worse since Ruth could claim to have been earlier on the learning curve. That's the worst of it. The all-important *Times* ad box is measured. The scorecard says that Giuliani "by exaggerating her position on the subject, risks the same kind of backlash that accompanied Ms. Messinger's first commercial on education, in which she showed classroom conditions that do not exist." Of course, Adam Nagourney generated most of the backlash on our commercial, so the risk isn't too great if the *Times* reporter is convinced of its essential validity. The *News* says the truth lies somewhere between Rudy's overstatement of Ruth's position and Ruth's indignant denials, but on the whole the *News* says "an order of crow seems far more appropriate for the Messinger menu." The bottom line is that the message of the ad is sticking.

Undeterred (perhaps emboldened) by the controversy, the mayor spends another day on sex shops.

Giuliani says that since there are between 5,000 and 7,500 commercial blocks in the city, Ruth's plan would "literally mean opening up all the neighborhoods in the city to sex shops. You would have neighborhoods flooded with sex shops." It's a preposterous, intellectually dishonest argument, akin to arguing that someone who wants R-rated movies restricted from prime time wants R-rated movies to be shown throughout the remainder of the day.

Transportation commissioner Christopher Lynn, who is gay, says Ruth has demeaned homosexuals by implying that sex shops were important to Greenwich Village. Lynn has been in the news some recently. He is feuding with budget director Joseph Lhota over a plan to install low-energy lightbulbs in Queens traffic signals. Lhota said Lynn lacks "prudence and fiscal acumen." Lynn said Lhota, who is bald, was having a bad hair day.

Lee has the goods on Lynn, and lets him have it with both barrels. Lynn, it seems, had a professional relationship with Robin Byrd and supported her bid to become Manhattan borough president. Byrd hosts an adult show on public-access cable that features male and female stripteases, interviews with performers, and a famous "Bang Your Box" segment in which Byrd plays with the genitalia of all guests on the show to the tune of a bizarre song from the turn of the century that Byrd recorded on her own. "I've been playing pianos large and small," the song goes, "but yours is the best piano of all."

Lynn issues an ominous warning in response. "They can attack me, I'm fair game," he says, "but they ought not to attack Robin Byrd, because they will incur the wrath of gay men in this city."

This is strictly first class.

• • •

At a state court hearing on Sharpton's lawsuit, DeFrancesco explains the mistakes in the counting. "The numbers are small. Your eyes get tired. A six can look like an eight."

• • •

The good news on the polling front is fleeting. Marist College has Rudy up 54–36 and shows him with a sky-high approval rating of 66 percent. Education has supplanted crime as the top issue on voters' minds, according to Marist, but voters are split 50–50 on whether Rudy or Ruth would do a better job with the schools. Rudy's first education ad may have ended this campaign before it began.

September 25

Eat your heart out, Rudy! Rudy Giuliani may have Ed Koch, Mario Cuomo, Claire Shulman, and a hundred other Democrats in his corner, but he hasn't got Abe Beame. Former mayor Beame, now ninety-one, presided over New York during the heady days in the 1970s when the city narrowly skirted bankruptcy. We unveil the Beame endorsement at a press conference on the steps of City Hall. It's not entirely clear that Beame knows who Ruth is, but he delivers a rousing endorsement all the same. If Wall Street goes south, Beame warns, the city's finances could suffer.

I'm thinking that about now we'd hold a press conference with just about anyone willing to stand with Ruth on the steps of City Hall.

• • •

Staten Island City Councilman John Fusco is running negative ads about Ruth saying she "doesn't know New Dorp from New Zealand." (New Dorp is a neighborhood in Staten Island; New Zealand is an island country about three hours off the east coast of Australia). Under the campaign-finance laws, the money spent on the ads must count against Giuliani's spending cap if they were coordinated with the mayor's campaign.

Fusco says what seems obvious. "We'd never do anything without their say-so."

"I don't know what Fusco's talking about," Fran Reiter tells *Newsday*.

Later, Fusco calls the reporter back and says the mistake was his. "I got two young guys running my campaign. They thought it was okayed." Perhaps those are different young staffers from the ones who earlier in the day referred *Newsday*'s request for a transcript of the ad to Giuliani campaign headquarters.

September 26

Another key endorsement today. New York's senior senator, the esteemed Daniel Patrick Moynihan, is hopping on board the Messinger steamroller. He endorses today. By press release. At 5:00 in the afternoon. On a Friday.

• • •

Justice Beatrice Shainswit rules that the results of the election will stand. The Sharpton campaign, she says, has not provided enough evidence of voting irregularities to call the outcome of the vote into question. Sharpton's lawyers are publicly advising him not to appeal, but the Reverend says he is considering his options.

Behind the scenes, Sharpton's people have opened negotiations with our political department about a possible endorsement. They want money, which is no surprise. What is a surprise is the amount they're demanding. Emboldened by the Reverend's strong showing in the primary, they're talking about hundreds of thousands of dollars. We're telling them that we don't have that kind of money, which is really a polite way of saying we have the money, but choose to spend it on television ads. They know we have the money and we know they know, but it doesn't really matter. Their bargaining position is not very strong. If he didn't endorse Ruth, Sharpton would undo much of his hard work in legitimating his standing within the party this year. He can bargain with the enthusiasm of his support, but the endorsement itself seems an inevitability. He'll make us sweat a little, though.

• • •

Eric Ruano-Melendez's nominating petitions are being reviewed for fraud. Melendez submitted more than 10,000 signatures—the law requires only 7,500—but many are in the same handwriting with only clumsy attempts at disguise and an occasional change of pen.

Melendez says he has no idea who signed his petitions. "I give it to people. People get it for me. What can I do?" says Melendez.

Melendez speculates that he is being targeted for revenge. It's those paparazzi lawyers, no doubt.

September 27

Two influential black leaders are endorsing the mayor: Congressman Floyd Flake, who is retiring from the House to devote more time to his duties as pastor of the Allen African Methodist Episcopal Church in St. Albans, Queens, and Congressman Edolphus Towns of Brooklyn. Towns first endorsed Freddie Ferrer and then Al Sharpton in the primary.

At a ceremony inside City Hall—the ceremony is inside because a few black protesters are demonstrating outside—Flake praises Giuliani's reduction of crime in the city. "Children were dying on the street corners because of drive-by shootings. I actually walked out to get my newspaper to find a child lying in an alley, and it happened all too often."

Getting the newspaper or the shooting?

Towns explains his switch. "I felt a lot of the things [Sharpton] was saying made a lot of sense, but he's no longer a candidate now and that is not an issue with Ed Towns."

Evan doesn't understand what Ed Towns is talking about. Evan is confused.

Giuliani neglects to ask Towns whether he still thinks Sharpton is qualified to be mayor. When a reporter asks the mayor why he is willing to tolerate Towns's willingness to endorse Sharpton, but not Ruth's, Giuliani snaps back and criticizes the reporter's "excessive desire to criticize."

• • •

The defections of Ed Towns and Floyd Flake are bad news indeed, but the loss that really hurts is Mary Tyler Moore, who has also decided to endorse the mayor. Mary says Rudy is the "top banana of the Big Apple."

Political endorsements are business, but celebrity endorsements are what get the candidate's juices going. In eight months with Ruth, the most excited I've ever seen her was on a day in early summer when Bill Franks walked in on a meeting we were having and told her she had an important fund-raising call. It was not unusual for a fund-raising call to take precedence over other political business—fund-raising takes precedence over virtually everything. What was unusual was that Ruth, who hardly loves fund-raising, was downright gleeful to pick up the phone.

"Hello, Paul," she said. "How's Joanne?"

• • •

Parade season isn't over, after all. Ruth marches today with Freddie Ferrer in the Bronx African-American Caribbean Heritage Day Parade.

Goodness.

September 28

Not only is the Giuliani campaign not retracting the sex-shop ad, they're airing a second version of it that restates the mistaken quote from the first. The commercial opens with a shot of a peep-show house with Ruth's infamous quote superimposed in white block letters: "Sex businesses give New York character." An announcer says, "Ruth Messinger says sex shops are an important part of our city's economic and tourism base, give character to our city, fabric to a neighborhood." From there, the commercial cuts to a series of person-on-the-street interviews with women of various ages and races.

"She said that?" says a young woman.

"That's not the kind of character I want," says a middle-aged woman.

"It's demeaning," says another.

"It degrades women."

A mother carrying a child says, "It contributes to street violence and domestic violence."

The cochairperson of Giuliani's Commission to Combat Family Violence, Eleanor Pam, chimes in, saying, "You build character in neighborhoods with schools and libraries, not sex shops."

Then, back to the announcer (a man). "When did sex shops ever become an important part of any neighborhood?"

And finally back to a young woman. "And she wants to be Mayor?"

A small amount of investigation reveals that all of the speakers in the ad, with the exception of Eleanor Pam, are actresses. But no one is interested in the story. The press, it seems, has collectively forgotten that we were criticized mercilessly for "staging" an ad in a private school.

• • •

Sharpton finally announces that he will support Ruth for mayor, though he plans to continue to pursue his lawsuit. "My inclination is to pursue a Federal civil rights lawsuit and, at the same time, campaign for the Democratic nominee." Sharpton says that he is not seeking help retiring his campaign debt.

• • •

Muslim Day Parade today.

September 29

I imagine the sex-shop ad must play exceptionally well in the focus groups, but by relentlessly remaining on the attack, the mayor is running a risk that he will revive the image of what consultant Hank Morris calls "mean Rudy." There's no moral high ground in the exchange of televised charges between Rudy and Ruth. We've been just as nasty as Rudy and just as liberal in selectively using facts in our favor. But nasty plays differently for Ruth Messinger than it does for Rudy Giuliani. People like Ruth; they just don't think she'd be a good mayor. People don't like Giuliani; they're willing to tolerate his mean-spiritedness because they think he does a good job.

The cover story of the current issue of *Esquire* is headlined "Rudy Giuliani Is a Colossal Asshole." ("Behind his back, they compare him to Mussolini.") The subheading is that being an asshole is "precisely what makes Rudy the best mayor in America," but all the same it's probably not in Rudy's best interest to revive images of himself as a bully.

Rudy could be taking some easy steps to diminish the likelihood or magnitude of a backlash. Candidates, especially front-runners, generally don't take on the burden of getting out the negative message themselves. Rather, they ordinarily rely on supporters or commercials, sparing themselves whatever backlash there may be against the purveyor of a mean, negative message. You'll never see politicians appear or speak in a negative ad about their opponent. During one of the presidential debates in 1996, Bill Clinton said he was personally fond of Bob Dole, even as his campaign ran a relentless negative media campaign.

But Rudy has been on the front lines of this battle. He has defended each of the commercials so far. (Imagine Bill Clinton commenting on one of his advertisements.) And he's stayed true to his word of raising an "issue" a day. Yesterday Rudy suggested that Ruth and her fellow Democrats were responsible for the departure of the Brooklyn Dodgers in 1957, when Ruth was seventeen. People who had run the city "with an attitude and philosophy like Ruth Messinger's, which is very anti-business," Giuliani says, caused the Dodgers, Jets, and the Giants to flee the city. Ruth had dared to suggest that unabashed Yankee fan Giuliani and Yankee owner George Steinbrenner have a secret plan to build a new Yankee Stadium on the West Side of Manhattan after the election. Ruth called for a citywide referendum to decide whether taxpayer money could be used to build a new Yankee Stadium. Rudy went on the attack.

The mayor is beginning to pay a price for his inability to control his combative instincts. The *Times* scorecard on the second sex-shop ad says that the principal message of the commercial "is not supported by [Ruth's] public statements." An editorial in the *Times* questions whether both candidates have violated the statute of limitations for personal mistakes. And in an article about the excessive nastiness of the campaign, Adam Nagourney flatly writes that the evidence for Giuliani's charges against Ruth on Attica and on sex shops is "questionable." Nagourney calls the race "striking for its virulence." Ed Koch says the mayor should run a tough campaign, "but there's a difference between a tough campaign and a vicious campaign. This is a vicious campaign."

It's easy to forget, as Tip O'Neill used to say, that politics is personal. Rudy and Ruth disagree about many issues. But I think if you asked Ruth to single out the single reason she should be mayor instead of Giuliani, she'd say that she's a more level-headed, more inclusive, less vindictive person, which she probably is. If you go back as far as the first debate in February, what Ruth singled out as the thing that made her different was that she would "listen" to New Yorkers. Rudy, whose lack of tolerance for people who disagree with him is well documented, might say that he's a better administrator, which he probably is, and that he resents career politicians who are all talk and no action. Where Ruth says that what sets her apart is that she listens, Rudy would probably say that he gets things done. They are fundamentally different people.

Koch is right. This is a vicious campaign. A nasty, mean-spirited campaign between two people who genuinely dislike each other. One person dislikes the other so intensely that he has not put aside his rage, at least in public, even though it is in his best political interests. That he cannot do so, sadly, is our one ray of hope for pulling this out.

September 30

Giuliani is at the Kennedy School of Government at Harvard to deliver what his campaign is billing as a major address. There is some speculation in the press that the mayor's decision to deliver the speech at Harvard is a signal of his larger political ambitions. Alice Wolf, the former mayor of Cambridge, faxes us a bootleg copy of the speech from an office at the K-School. We listen to Giuliani deliver it on a live Internet feed in Jim's office.

Though the speech is boldly titled "The Resurrection of the American City," this speech is really about the resurrection of New York City. Not a single other city is mentioned by name in the speech. It is simply the mayor's stump speech filled with statistics, many misleading, about the reduction in crime and welfare. Giuliani, though, sounds one new campaign theme. The city must begin a war on drugs. Drug abuse, he says, threatens the city's reductions in crime. It's a logical place for the mayor to go. Though there's no evidence of this in the polling, one could imagine voters thinking that, now that Giuliani has done the job on crime, it's time to let someone else take care of the schools. The mayor's trick is to show that there's a continuing crisis demanding his attention.

As Giuliani speaks, several students hold up signs in protest. One says "Crime Is Down Everywhere but the NYPD." Three students hold up toilet plungers.

October 1

The battle is fought on every front.

At a groundbreaking for a new Pathmark supermarket on 125th Street in Harlem, Ruth, who fought for the project for years, is kept off the dais. The Giuliani administration refused to give final approval to the deal until organizers of the groundbreaking agreed to disinvite Ruth. The mayor says he has no knowledge of the snub. "I think she's a perennial complainer," he says. "I think Ruth Messinger spends most of her time complaining."

In Tottenville, Staten Island, Ruth joins parents at a rally criticizing the Giuliani administration for delay in building an overdue and much needed new elementary school. Minutes later, Deputy Mayor Mastro announces that the city will spend $35 million to build Public School 6. They had not wanted to make the announcement until after the election, Mastro explained, but Ruth forced a change in timing. "We did not want to politicize the issue," says Mastro, but "then Ruth Messinger went to Staten Island and pandered to the crowd."

When Ruth writes parent-teacher associations, encouraging them to invite her to speak at their schools and capitalize on Giuliani's pattern of bestowing gifts on schools at which she appears, Giuliani implies that Ruth has inside information on the Staten Island school and shows up demanding action. "I think the fact is that sometimes she may find out—because of connections that she has with the Board [of Education] about actions that we're taking and she tries to get in front of those politically."

At Joseph Pulitzer Junior High School in Queens, Chancellor Rudy Crew bars the press from entering the school to cover an appearance there by Ruth, though he has allowed cameras to cover Giuliani school events at least fifteen times in the past year. The school principal has a photo on the wall of himself and Rudy Giuliani, who visited the school during the last mayoral campaign. Crew denies a double standard. "Campaign activities typically are not permitted," Crew says. After Ruth teaches a seventh-grade social-studies class, twelve-year-old Alberto Luffi asks Ruth if she thinks sex shops improve a neighborhood's character.

A day later, Ruth's invitation to a scheduled appearance at Kingsborough Community College is rescinded. A CUNY spokesperson says allowing Messinger to speak will jeopardize the college's nonprofit tax status.

On the campaign trail, the Giuliani campaign responds to our events with astonishing speed. Just minutes after a press conference by gay leaders endorsing Ruth yesterday, Giuliani unveils his own endorsement by the board—the full membership of the club has yet to vote—of the gay Stonewall Democratic Club, which includes transportation commissioner Christopher Lynn and three other paid members of the Giuliani administration.

Their attention to detail often produces impressively smooth results. On the same day the Giuliani ad featuring Vivian Dressen first aired, fire commissioner Tom Van Essen announced that civilian deaths from fire are at their lowest mark since 1959. The new bunker gear allows firefighters to penetrate farther into buildings to save trapped residents. Van Essen's announcement lends the commercial an air of credibility.

Today, on a day when Ruth delivers an important, long-promised address on education, Rudy delivers a speech of his own announcing his plan for the war on drugs hinted at in his speech at Harvard. The mayor dominates the evening news coverage.

Two weeks into the general-election campaign, a picture of Rudy the Candidate is emerging that is not unlike Rudy the Mayor: a tireless, smart, message-focused campaigner with an obsessive attention to detail (perhaps thinking our campaign is searching for evidence that the quality of life in the city is not what he says, Giuliani directs his commissioners to call a police hotline should they spot any squeegeemen). And like Rudy the Mayor, the Candidate lacks any capacity to tolerate dissent. One of Giuliani's former aides explains the contradiction within the man: "Even after I'd figured out he was a lunatic, I'd meet with him and think, 'What a brilliant man.' I'd agree with everything he said, and then I'd leave the room, hitting my head."

In some cases, Giuliani's ferocity is a real asset. Countering endorsements and speeches helps control the message of the day. The message of the day influences voters. But other examples seem to be reflections of paranoia rather than measured responses to campaign events, the dark side of a compulsive personality. Kicking Ruth out of a school or a supermarket unveiling won't affect a single voter. The mayor, it seems, rages at the notion that anyone dares to disagree.

Oppose me and pay the price. No matter who you are.

When two members of the board of a nonprofit group that holds the city's animal-services contract criticized the Giuliani administration at a City Council hearing for having blocked the appointment of a new executive director, they were fired hours later.

Three months after saying the city had difficulty punishing landlords who create illegal apartments because they don't have basic information in the files, the head of the Queens office of the Buildings Department is transferred to something called the technical compliance unit.

At a town meeting in Forest Hills about a new retail complex that Giuliani supports but many in the community oppose, an elderly man asks the mayor about the fact that the developer of the complex, Bruce Ratner, is one of Giuliani's largest contributors. "Is it quid pro quo, Mr. Mayor?" the man asks. "You should be ashamed of yourself," the mayor responds.

When James Schillaci videotapes police officers rigging a light near the Bronx Zoo to turn red and trap motorists, the police arrest Schillaci hours later for some unpaid parking tickets from 1984. The police department announces that Schillaci had a lengthy criminal record, including a sodomy conviction. "I'm not going to allow the entire Police Department and police officers who are putting their lives at risk to become a punching bag," the Mayor rages. "Just because you call yourself a whistle-blower doesn't mean that you are. I can see behind things, because I have respect for our police officers and I don't just assume that they're always doing the wrong things." Giuliani faults the *Daily News*, which reported the story, for not mentioning Schillaci's "long record."

Schillaci had been arrested twenty years ago for using drugs and taking his mother's car without permission, but had been clean for decades. The Bronx District Attorney's office cited Schillaci for helping to catch a pair of arsonists. The sodomy charge is a fabrication.

When Mark Green suggests the police department apologize to James Schillaci, Randy Mastro writes him a stinging letter saying that Green fails to mention Schillaci's "lengthy criminal record." "Once again," Mastro writes, "you betray your anticop bias by jumping to unwarranted conclusions and seeking to demonize the Police Department without basis or justification. In short, it is you who owes the police department an apology."

Perhaps, you think, I am the victim of paranoia.

Consider the case of Bronx assemblyman Jeffrey Dinowitz, who refused to endorse the mayor. Dinowitz is no longer invited to ribbon-cuttings for local park projects. When he complains to those in the Parks Department, they tell him he's come to the wrong place. "This doesn't come from us," he's told. "This comes from the top."

Oppose me and pay.

October 2

Jim often says that the value of a research department is not the victories it helps a campaign score, but the mistakes it prevents the campaign from making. Back in May, Jim praised us for doing both parts of our job when we suggested the idea of attacking Rudy for having accepted contributions from the landlords' lobby and for pointing out that Ruth had implied she would do the same. Jim's approach to campaigning is lawyerly. He conceives of arguments and then thinks ahead to what the response will be. At our morning meetings, where we discuss what to *whack the mayor* with, the first question is always what the other side will say in response.

An article in the *Daily News* today makes the case that Rudy Giuliani has used the advantage of incumbency to lure Democrats to his side with pork. As examples, the *News* notes that City Hall allocated $1 million for library expansion, $1 million for a new Boys and Girls Club, and $7 million for a new pumping station in City Councilman Howard Lasher's district in the weeks before he endorsed the mayor. After Lasher came through, the Giuliani administration pledged another $3 million for repairs to public housing in his district.

Councilman Martin Malave-Divan won a new day-care center for his Brooklyn district. Councilman Victor Robles landed funding for a community center. Brooklyn assemblyman Vito Lopez's district received $5 million for a day-care center after he endorsed. Dennis McManus, the brother of legendary West Side Democratic boss Jimmy McManus, landed an $85,000-a-year vice presidency at Off-Track Betting. Giuliani supporter Councilman Noach Dear's father has worked at the Housing Authority since Giuliani took office in 1994. Deputy Mayor Randy Mastro, who is said to be taking the lead on securing Democrats' endorsements, says there is no quid pro quo. "Public officials, both Democrats and Republicans, who have endorsed the mayor, have done so because of his record of achievement," he says, but the attack is there for the making.

The problem is we're vulnerable to the same charge. Our campaign has several people on the payroll as political favors. Ruth fired someone from the borough president's office earlier in the year who was on the payroll of two city agencies. The best argument we could make is that the degree of Giuliani's patronage and abuse of incumbency is objectionable. We decide to pass.

Ed Koch, who shows no bias in forming his opinions, says that Giuliani is the "most political, patronage-dedicated mayor" he has ever known. But Giuliani dismisses it as an election-year story that is "very simplistic," and without Ruth to fuel the fire, the story ends there. Letting the opportunity pass is a great shame because it is an opportunity to draw attention to the fact that, contrary to his repeated assertions, Rudy Giuliani is just a politician. He cuts deals and makes compromises like every other officeholder.

The experience demonstrates why it is that campaigns focus on so few issues and almost no issues of political conduct. Though campaign-finance reform and eliminating patronage are noble ideas, the fact is that all politicians cast stones from glass houses. A self-financed candidate (or an underfunded candidate like Sal Albanese) might be able to credibly raise campaign finance reform as an issue. A political outsider, like Rudy Giuliani in 1989, might be able to credibly decry patronage. But when campaigns look at issues they can raise, they face a cruel process of elimination. In virtually every case, candidates are susceptible to an argument of inconsistency. The best they can do is scratch the most obvious hypocrisies from the list. And so political conduct issues are the first to go.

• • •

Whatever gains we may have made into the mayor's lead appear to have dissipated. The consistent trend in the polling shows Giuliani with approximately a 20-point lead. The latest poll from Quinnipiac shows Rudy beating Ruth 54–33. Sixty-three percent approve of Giuliani's job performance, though a mere 43 percent think he has a likable personality. The only signs of hope are that voters continue to think Ruth would do a better job handling education and race relations. The poll also shows that (surprise!) confidence in police has dropped. Forty-eight percent of New Yorkers approve of the way cops are doing their jobs, compared with 61 percent in February 1996.

• • •

At his forty-third birthday party, attended by Jesse Jackson and Johnnie Cochran, Sharpton gives a rather tepid endorsement of Ruth: "I am going to launch a full-scale anti-Giuliani campaign on our streets and if we have to support Messinger, we will."

October 3

Yet another of the many luxuries the Giuliani campaign enjoys is the ability to run a *two-track campaign.* While media consultant Adam Goodman continues to air the sex-shop ad, driving down Ruth's favorables, he is simultaneous up with a positive ad about the mayor. The ad starts by showing black-and-white footage of a burned-out neighborhood, shifting to color film of children frolicking in a playground in Bushwick, Brooklyn. "In less than four years," the announcer says, "murders in Bushwick have fallen 55 percent. Overall, crime is down 50 percent. Some still want to turn the clock back. With Rudy Giuliani, Bushwick and neighborhoods across the boroughs will keep moving forward. And we're a whole lot safer for it." The bread and butter of the Giuliani advertising campaign will be to remind voters of the mayor's progress on crime and urge them not to "turn the clock back," a not very subtle code for returning to the Dinkins era. It seems only a matter of time before the former mayor appears with Ruth in a negative ad from Giuliani.

We've been beaten thoroughly over the airwaves over the past week. Conventional media strategy is to respond immediately to all negative ads, but partially because of our money restrictions and partially because we don't have an effective response, we've allowed the sex-shop ads to air for five days without a response.

We're up today with a response that shows Messinger shutting off a television showing Giuliani's sex-shop ad:

> Isn't this just what you'd expect from Rudy Giuliani? False quotes. Absurd accusations. Rudy Giuliani may not want to talk about the city's future, but I do. We've got real problems in our city's schools. We've got to get serious about raising standards and reducing overcrowding. I've got a plan to do that. Rudy Giuliani can keep throwing garbage. I'm talking about the future.

It doesn't seem like a strong ad. Responding to the sex-shop charges a week after the fact makes us seem slow and, what's more, this is the second consecutive ad that violates our preestablished principle of not putting Ruth to the camera. The idea is to draw attention to Rudy's bullying of a woman, but it seems to me we've lost this exchange badly.

At least Ruth is in front of a new curtain.

• • •

In an open letter in the *Jewish Press*, Jules Polonetsky writes that there could be grave consequences for Jews if they do not turn out in large numbers on Election Day. Polonetsky says that a Messinger victory would be a disaster for Jews and the city as a whole. It's an extraordinarily charged and risky letter, and Polonetsky's campaign manager at first denies that Jules wrote it. Later in the day, however, he acknowledges that the letter is Polonetsky's doing. We will exploit the divisive nature of the letter and in the process remind voters that Ruth is Jewish, too.

• • •

Sal Albanese is beginning to show some signs of coming around. He has publicly said that he will not actively campaign on the Independence party line and that he will not appear in the debates. He's also beginning to talk about the possibility of endorsing, but wonders to Ruth whether he can credibly endorse in light of the damaging things he said about her during the primary campaign.

"I said you had no moral compass," Albanese reminds Ruth, who tells Sal that reporters will dismiss the comments as made during the heat of battle. Ruth is right to disregard the press as a concern. Since the New York press believes that all politicians speak out of motivation and not conviction, it will simply regard Sal's change of heart as a political necessity.

That Sal even thinks it would be a problem shows again just how different he is. He really meant what he said.

• • •

Giuliani is proposing that the first debate, scheduled for Thursday night, be postponed to accommodate a possible Yankees playoff game. In a letter to Campaign Finance Board chairman Joseph O'Hare, Giuliani proposes that the game be moved to ensure the maximum possible audience for the debate.

The mayor admits to reporters that he'd rather watch the game. "Wouldn't you?" he asks. Giuliani also says it will be difficult for him to concentrate if the debate is held the same time as the game. "That's just the reality of things. I could possibly be distracted by people whispering scores in my ear."

October 4

The ultimate honor for a research department is to place a story in the press that is not attributed to the campaign. If the campaign is recognized as the source, then the story is nothing more than an accusation by one campaign against another. If the story is unattributed, then it has the credibility of the paper behind it. A headline reading "Clinton Campaign Takes Foreign Money" is infinitely more valuable than "Bush Accuses Clinton of Accepting Foreign Money." With the first one, the campaign takes a few hundred thousand dollars and puts it on the air the next day to make sure everyone sees it—eight or nine times. The second one goes in the toilet.

Placing an unattributed story is difficult to do. Since the newspaper that runs the story places its credibility behind it (and assumes liability in the event something turns out not to be true), the evidence needs to meet the newspaper's burden of proof, which is quite strict in the case of reputable periodicals.

The evidence needs to be clear and convincing and cannot be susceptible to multiple interpretations. It cannot be an argument. It must be facts and only facts. And campaigns have little leverage to coerce papers to take stories about which they have reservations. The only bargaining power a campaign has is the threat to take a story to another paper.

So far, the two great story placement successes in the campaign belong to the Giuliani team. They planted the audit story in the *Daily News* and got it to run at a perfect time—the same day as the first Democratic debate. And they artfully handled the Attica story. The charge was so powerful that a newspaper would almost certainly have attributed it to the campaign. Placing it in an out-of-town publication allowed it to filter into the New York press without attribution to the campaign. Moreover, they succeeded in selling the facts as more than they were. Virtually no spinning is allowed in planted stories, but the Giuliani team nevertheless sold James Traub of *Slate* on a factual inference: The *Times* story said the party was in Ruth's apartment; Traub reported that Messinger hosted the party.

For the past two months, our research team has been focusing our energy on trying to find evidence that the Giuliani campaign has taken money from still more donors in excess of the contribution limit or from shady people and organizations. Today, for better or worse, is the culmination of that work.

We've got the Giuliani campaign dead to rights. In addition to the more than $300,000 in illegal contributions already identified by the Campaign Finance Board, we've found another $60,000 by corporations that are over the legal limit. The board has covered the obvious links—contributions made on the same day or contributions from companies at the same address. We've covered the not so obvious. We've checked the principals of these companies from the original corporate filings. The board has missed about thirty linked corporations. We'd find more if there were more time. Some of the contributors are salacious. Bill Fugazy, Giuliani's tax-cheating friend, exceeded the limit by $1,300.

Mostly through on-line research, we've also found an array of contributors to the Giuliani campaign who are less than pillars of the community. The best story is a man named Jay Fabrikant, the former president of the New York Health Plan for Hispanic Americans. In 1993, the company sought a Medicaid contract from the Dinkins administration, but was turned down over questions about how the company was being operated. In 1995, with part-owner Herman Badillo lobbying on the company's behalf, the company landed a multimillion-dollar city contract. Within months, state Medicaid officials began investigating the company. They found that six thousand people had never been assigned doctors and at the same time the company was billing for fictitious clients. The city finally canceled the contract in 1996. The state banned Fabrikant from Medicaid. But Rudy's campaign took $7,700 from Fabrikant and thousands more in bundled contributions despite the fact that, on top of everything else, Giuliani's office prosecuted Fabrikant for selling drugs and tax evasion.

Some of the others are good too. Rudy took money from a company with ties to the mob, even though he had returned a contribution from the same company in 1993. He took money from two trash companies that were cited by a city commission he created for being involved in a mob cartel. His campaign took money from three companies convicted of bribing federal officials.

Neither the illegal contributions nor the shady contributions are damning without some context. The fact that Rudy Giuliani's campaign accepted a few thousand dollars from companies with ties to the mob certainly does not prove that his administration was somehow funneling business to the Mafia. The scandal is in the fact that the Giuliani campaign is claiming about 25 percent of its staff time as related to compliance. If Rudy's spending five times as much time checking his contributors and running what he and his campaign treasurer have repeatedly called "the most ethical campaign in the history of the city," then why couldn't they catch this tainted money, which we found fairly easily?

We give the illegal contribution story to the *New York Times* and the unsavory contributors to the *Daily News*. The negotiation with the *News* reporter, who is light-years more familiar with the world of funny money than we are, is interesting. We will not share the information with anyone else, and he will tell us if he is not going to use any of it. He will also let us know if the story will be anything other than a story about contributions to the Giuliani campaign that does not mention our campaign. Jim has the preliminary discussions with the reporter from the *Times*. Both reporters compliment us on our work. The *Times* will run the story in a few days; the *News* in a week or two.

This is the fruit of $250,000 Ruth Messinger has spent on research.

October 5

The *Times* story on the illegal contributions is a bitter disappointment and, though no one in the press will notice it, a mistake equal in proportion to any we've made so far. The story is not an unattributed report of the acceptance of additional illegal contributions by the Giuliani campaign. Rather, it's a report of Ruth Messinger's accusation that the Giuliani campaign has kept some illegal donations. Politically, it's a powerless story.

The focus of the story is that our campaign will be filing a complaint with the Campaign Finance Board. It was supposed to be that we filed the complaint as a response to the report of the additional transgressions, thereby keeping the unattributed story alive for another few days. It's not clear exactly where the conversations went wrong with the *Times* reporter, Clifford Levy, but somehow we gave the information to the *Times* without condition on its use.

The gaffe leaves the Giuliani campaign an easy response, though the mayor nearly blows it. "We strive very, very hard," he says, "to err on the side of returning money," and he says his campaign is "bending over backwards to remove any question imaginable that somebody could raise about money. And I don't think there has been any campaign that has ever done that before." Ruth, he says, is making a "desperate attempt to get attention." His temper and overstatement trivialize a serious issue, but Fran Reiter saves the day.

All of the so-called illegal contributions, Reiter points out, derive from what the Giuliani campaign has all along called a new interpretation of the law by the Campaign Finance Board. Since their campaign could not have anticipated this change in law, it is only now that they are going through their books and checking for further violations. "I can't swear to you that she may have found something in that moment in time that we haven't found yet," Reiter says. "But to suggest that we aren't making a good-faith effort to comply with a very complex law is a lie." It's a smart, nuanced answer that's consistent with the Giuliani campaign's position. Likely, thanks to Reiter, it's the end of this round of stories.

• • •

Ruth accuses the mayor of orchestrating Jules Polonetsky's attack against her in the *Jewish Press* and decries the letter as appalling. "To talk about the election of a fifty-six-year-old Jewish grandmother as the Jewish community's worst nightmare, to Rudy Giuliani and his mouthpiece I say this is divisive politics at its very worst." Polonetsky calls Ruth a liar. "This is an out-and-out lie, but certainly in keeping with her history of personal, ugly name calling and unsubstantiated attacks on her opponent," Polonetsky says, denying that he ever discussed the letter with Giuliani. Fran Reiter says Ruth is "making ugly, lying statements about the Mayor."

• • •

Rudy is continuing to tout his antidrug program, campaigning today at a Roosevelt Island hospital clinic for drug abusers. His staff kicks out our tracker, present as always to videotape the mayor. They say he lacks proper credentials. Rudy, whose campaign has been tracking Ruth daily since her announcement speech, defends the decision. "Ruth Messinger has a very hard time accepting the rules that apply to everyone," he says.

October 6

Attempting to stanch the perception that every Democrat in the city is behind the mayor, we hold a unity press conference today at a union hall in Manhattan. Ruth is joined by Peter Vallone, Charles Schumer, and Sal Albanese. Sal Albanese drops his third-party bid and endorses Ruth, telling reporters that, yes indeed, his criticism of Ruth for "standing for nothing" and as a "limousine liberal" were merely comments made in the heat of battle. Al Sharpton is conspicuously absent. "When I do it, I want to do my own press conference," Sharpton says. "I'm doing it as my campaign. I'm not going to do it as another part of the lineup."

• • •

Ruth's husband, Andrew Lachman, is a delightfully pleasant man who dislikes public attention as much as Ruth relishes it. Andrew met Ruth twenty years ago at the Children's Community Workshop School on the Upper West Side, where they both worked. Ruth's daughter Miriam was a student in Andrew's kindergarten class. Andrew and Ruth married the day before she took office as borough president, but he hasn't been infected with her passion for public life. Lachman was briefly on the opposite side of an issue from Ruth when, last month, a group of parents raised private money to rehire a teacher fired by the Board of Education. Rudy Crew refused to let the parents pay for the teacher. Ruth sided with the parents. Andrew, who has worked for the past ten years as the executive assistant to the district's superintendent, defended the decision to refuse the aid. He's been unimaginably supportive and patient throughout the campaign, but other than that one example has remained out of the spotlight.

But when asked today by a *Daily News* reporter for his opinion of how the press has treated Ruth, Andrew speaks his mind. "It's like you type the words Ruth Messinger, and then there's a whole string of words in the computer that sort of pop in automatically: incompetent, inept, clearly going to lose. . . . I think the coverage sucks," he says.

• • •

Rudy Giuliani is urging the federal government to modify regulations and require casino cruises to sail twelve instead of three miles from shore before allowing passengers to start gambling. Guess he's not going to spring Governors Island as his own election-year surprise.

October 7

A report by the Board of Education suggests that gang activity is on the rise and calls on the city to respond to the problem swiftly and surely. The mayor will be announcing a major antigang initiative later today.

The newly discovered crisis seems just a little too convenient. Part of the ingenuity of the drug speech was to plant the seed in voters' minds that the crime problem is not over; in other words, that Rudy Giuliani is still relevant. But no one other than Rudy had suggested that the drug problem was any more immediate than always. This feels slightly different. It has an imprimatur of objectivity. And gang violence, unlike drugs, is a direct threat to personal safety.

The author of the report, Edward Stancik, is beyond reproach, universally recognized as an independent voice at the Board of Education. And Brooklyn District Attorney Charles Hynes, a Democrat, recently announced a crackdown on gangs by his office. But all Stancik has done is report that the number of violent incidents on school grounds has risen over time. It's his superiors who are playing it up, and I wonder whether they may have tweaked the timing and tone of the report.

Deputy Chancellor Harry Spence calls the gang problem "pervasive." "It's clear," he says, "that the level of activity is rising significantly and has risen to the point where it requires a strong, clear direction. New York can't rely on the sense that 'It can't happen here.'"

• • •

Giuliani is up with a new ad criticizing Ruth's school-board appointee for voting against expelling students age seventeen and older who are found with guns in school, the same vote that was the subject of Al D'Amato's attack against Ruth in September:

> When a child feels threatened here, learning is replaced by fear, and parents are left dreading the unthinkable. That's why Rudy Giuliani is driving drug dealers off school grounds and away from kids. And Rudy strongly supported Rudy Crew's fight to expel students who carry guns or use weapons in school. Incredibly, on this vote to expel these dangerous students, Ruth Messinger's appointee was the only one to vote "no." For Rudy Giuliani, this is one investment he's going to protect with everything he's got.

It's again an attack that we've anticipated, and within minutes we're out with the letter Ruth wrote to Luis Reyes telling him she disagreed with the vote. "If I were a member of the board," she wrote in February, "I would have voted to support the new policy."

Giuliani dismisses Ruth's reply. "If she believed [Reyes] acted improperly, she should have put enormous pressure on him, because the lives of children are at stake." He says Ruth is running away from her record, just as she did in forgetting that "she had a party for a convicted murderer." (On that charge, the *News* reports that Ruth has no memory of the event, declining to mention that it has been proven that she wasn't there.) But this ad seems like reasonable political discourse and far fairer than the sex-shop ad. First of all, it is factual. Ruth's appointee did vote against the resolution. And even the inference is reasonable. School-board members are tenured, so Ruth could not have dismissed Reyes, but she could have called for his resignation.

Publicly, Jim calls the ad "sly and sleazy" distortion. "They are sleaze peddlers," he tells the *News*. "They wouldn't know the truth if it bit them on the ass."

October 8

The mayor gets the jump on this busy day. At 6:00 A.M., rod in hand, Rudy Giuliani makes the short walk from Gracie Mansion to the East River to do a little fishing. As a result of the Yankees loss to the Cleveland Indians the other night, Rudy Giuliani is free for this evening's debate, but he also owes Cleveland mayor Michael White ten pounds of bass fished out of the East River and a case of Brooklyn Lager. Joined by Yankee general manager Bob Watson and two deputy mayors, Rudy pulls a thirteen-inch bass out of the water in record time.

• • •

At 8:00, Jim joins us on the speaker phone for our morning meeting. The number of people at the morning meetings has been growing over the past few weeks and now includes virtually all the department heads. We review the morning clips as a group and note a disturbing item in Eric Briendel's column in the *New York Post*. Today, Briendel argues that Ruth's standing among Jewish voters is low because of her abstention from the City Council vote condemning the PLO for the terrorist act that led to the death of photographer Gail Rubin. Ruth has always said that she abstained from the resolution because the Rubins were personal friends and felt the resolution was not in their daughter's spirit. Briendel questions the veracity of Ruth's defense. "As it happens," Briendel notes, "Gail Rubin's parents—conveniently—are no longer alive."

We're well prepared with a defense to the charge that Ruth is weak on Jewish issues, but we decide to let the matter pass. If Rudy levies the charge, it's one thing. If it's in a column, we'll only be perpetuating the story by actively defending against it.

Of greater concern is the continuing spate of stories on gang violence. Several more incidents have been reported, and an editorial in this morning's *Times* calls the problem increasingly serious. Rudy's antigang program is getting good press. Last night, he announced a plan to attack gang violence by using the same computerized tracking system now used by the police department to track crime, and to push for legislation making gang recruitment a crime.

The idea on the table is for Ruth to attack the mayor for having cut youth programs and thereby contributing to the growing gang problem. There's no evidence that youth programs reduce gang violence, but the argument is appealing because it draws attention to Ruth's plan to keep all schools open until 6:00 P.M.

Ruth will take five minutes at the beginning of her speech on job creation to address the mayor's plan to fight gangs.

• • •

Around 10:00, word filters in that the mayor's fishing gig was a fix. His thirteen-inch beauty was strung to the line beforehand. Jim cackles maniacally at the story. Rudy says it's good fun, but Jim insists to all of us and anyone in the press who will listen that it's yet another example that he's a liar, further proof that he can never been trusted. Ruth, Lee, and Jim all think the story is hysterically funny, as if, it seems to me, they think it somehow diminishes Rudy's manhood. The press isn't biting on our arguments that this is part of a larger story.

I wonder whether we're becoming just a little too invested in our positions.

• • •

Perhaps we're *all* becoming just a little too invested in our positions. A press release from the Giuliani campaign is saying that some hecklers at the mayor's speech last night on gang violence were "paid political operatives for Ruth Messinger." The objectors were protesting the mayor's treatment of the homeless. The mayor says they are from the advocacy group

ACORN (Association of Community Organizations for Reform Now) and as proof shows that our campaign paid ACORN $14,000 in consulting expenses during the primary. The mayor fails to offer any proof that the protesters were affiliated with ACORN in any way, but then again he lied about the fish.

• • •

At 11:30 or so, Ed Koch tells his radio audience that our campaign is "the worst in history." Hearing of the remark, Jim sends a message to Koch by way of Ruth's friend Peter Aschkenazy, also a friend of Koch's.

"Tell him I said 'Fuck you.'"

Jim turns to me.

"I understand how to deal with politicians."

• • •

At noon, Ruth outlines her economic program to the Fifth Avenue Association, a Manhattan business organization. Ruth isn't happy with the speech. We don't have much in the way of innovative ideas to propose for revving up the city's economy. A report by Ruth's staff last year put forth the idea of requiring businesses contracting with the city to hire city residents for jobs and outlined a few tax breaks that have been kicking around for years. Short on ideas, I've devoted most of the speech to a detailed description of the magnitude of the city's unemployment problem. Ruth wants to devote more of the speech to outlining what she would do to help particular industries. Earlier in the year, the borough president's office issued a report outlining an approach to improving the climate for the retail industry in the city. Ruth thinks attacking economic problems industry by industry is effective. Jim and I think it's parochial and small-minded and cut it out of the speech. Ruth, in turn, cuts out about half of the speech and leaves the Waldorf-Astoria early.

• • •

Jim is angry that Ruth cut her speech short and takes the matter up with Peter Aschkenazy, who is now traveling with Ruth from site to site. Peter says that Ruth said the organizers of the event asked her to keep her remarks short. Jim says it's because she didn't like the speech.

"I'm not a mind reader," Jim says. "I'm just imputing a motivation that makes a great deal of sense."

• • •

At 3:00, Ruth returns to the office for the second of three debate prep sessions with Mandy and Jim. Last night's session did not go especially well. We brought in a lawyer, himself a former federal prosecutor, to play Rudy and try to fluster Ruth, and he succeeded a little too well. Ruth also seemed a bit put off by the presence of yet another third-party candidate, Olga Rodriguez, of the Socialist party. Ruth always starts off slow in these preparation cycles and improves the more she focuses on the event, but we're all concerned nevertheless. The most important potential benefit of a debate for a challenger is to be seen side by side with the incumbent. Ruth needs to look mayoral tomorrow. It's critical that she not be intimidated by Giuliani.

Under the format of the debate, the candidates will be allowed to ask two questions of the other candidates. The consensus in the room is that this round of questioning is the time when Ruth will be at greatest risk, but it will also be our best opportunity to fluster Giuliani. We accordingly spend the entire three hours today peppering Ruth with tough questions and discussing which issues to raise with the mayor.

"Are you still a member of the Democratic Socialists of America?" Jim asks.

Ruth begins to explain that she hasn't paid dues in years, but Mandy cuts her off and tells her not to let Rudy goad her into that stuff. Don't let him dictate the debate, she says. "Remember, this election is about the future."

I fire question after question.

"As a former drug user, do you feel qualified to lead the assault on drug abuse?"

"You've run one of the nastiest campaigns in recent memory. Do you feel this has anything to do with your lack of labor support and your dreadful standing in the polls?"

"The death penalty is the law, Ruth. Will you uphold the law?"

Jim dreads this question, because he thinks the answer disqualifies the candidate either way. The candidate is forced into a position of either not upholding the law or enforcing a law he or she is morally opposed to. We pick the latter poison.

"Why do you think Al Sharpton is more qualified than Rudy Giuliani to be mayor?"

Ruth has a way to wiggle out of this one and does so nicely: "For two weeks, you tried to divide this city by driving a wedge between Reverend Sharpton and me. I wouldn't let you do it then and I won't let you do it now."

But she can't wiggle out of the next one.

"Who do you think is a better mayor, Ms. Messinger, David Dinkins or Rudy Giuliani?"

Ruth thinks a long time about that one and finally talks about the need for a mayor to focus on more than just one issue and ticks off a few of Dinkins's successes. Mostly, we all pray that no one asks.

There are several possible questions to ask the mayor. We will ask one question on his campaign-finance violations and tainted money if the press does not raise it on its own. The other question is up for grabs. We could ask about Giuliani's relations with his supporter limousine tycoon Bill Fugazy, who recently admitted he lied to dodge bankruptcy creditors about transferring his assets into a company owned by his children. Fugazy has also been tied to a kickback scheme involving a company called GTECH, which runs lotteries nationally in New Jersey and is being investigated by federal prosecutors. Alphonse D'Arco, the FBI's most trusted mob informant, identified Fugazy in sworn testimony as an associate of the Genovese crime family. Giuliani wrote a letter to federal judge Deborah Batts, urging leniency in her sentencing of Fugazy. Asked about the letter, Rudy said, "Bill Fugazy's worked tirelessly to improve the standard of living for our nation's immigrants. The legal problems he's experiencing now are a separate matter, and it seems that he's dealing with the problems appropriately."

Rent control is another obvious possibility. So is Jules Polonetsky's letter, though Mandy thinks that Rudy will simply deny any involvement. For that matter, she thinks that virtually any factual question is a dead end. Lee proposes, for example, that we ask the mayor why his chancellor doesn't know how many students study in bathrooms. Mandy thinks he'll simply deny that the condition exists. Moreover, he'll be prepared for any general education question. Instead, she argues, we should ask a question about priorities.

Jim proposes the pay raise as a starting point. The mayor and his staff got large raises while teachers got the shaft. The question is how to phrase it.

"Cristyne Lategano makes $100,000 a year or whatever it is, while a starting teacher makes $30,000." Everyone laughs at the prospect of mentioning Lategano.

"If we say communications director instead of mentioning her by name, I think we're fine," Lee jokes. That won't be the angle, but it will be the question.

Mandy likes it because "anything dealing with his inner circle drives him crazy."

Ruth likes it because she thinks people will be appalled to learn the starting salary for teachers.

Jim likes it because he thinks they won't anticipate it—we haven't used the pay raise attack yet—and because we have a great defense to a counterattack. "If he says, you got the pay raise too, Ruth, you say, 'No, Rudy, you see, I don't take my pay raise.'"

Only one other decision remains to be made. Jim and Mandy are bandying about the idea of having Ruth make a self-deprecating remark about her own looks and the mayor's. She doesn't do well with jokes, but our hunch is it will annoy the mayor to no end. Ultimately, they decide, it has to be Ruth's call.

• • •

On *The Road to City Hall*, Andrew Kirtzman reports that the audience was falling asleep at Ruth's economic development speech. At 8:00, after the end of the show, Lee calls Kirtzman and blasts him with a furious tirade. For those five minutes, Kirtzman becomes the object of all of our frustration with the press. How could Kirtzman possibly trivialize such an important speech by such an irrelevant detail? Perhaps quite reasonably. Adam Nagourney tells Jim that lots of people were falling asleep at the speech.

It's been a long day.

October 9

While dozens of New Yorkers are curling up on their couches with soda and chips to watch the first mayoral debate of the season (New York 1 isn't even seen in half the city), the research team is on high alert. Our goal is to be out with a rapid response to every false statement made by Rudy Giuliani within five minutes of the close of the debate.

This is going to be tricky. We're running four VCRs and two tape recorders. Every time the mayor says something we think is false or needs clarification, one of our interns will take the tape, retire to our press office, transcribe the allegedly false quote, and e-mail it to my deputy. My deputy will then place the false statement in a chart opposite one of dozens of factual statements that we've prepared in advance. Five minutes before the end of the debate, we'll fax the rapid response to the debate site, where it will be copied by Lee's assistant and distributed to the press.

For us, this is the Super Bowl.

• • •

Ruth starts the debate in style. "When you look at the two of us," she grins, "you know this election isn't a beauty contest." It's delivered perfectly. The audience is stunned for a second, but soon they get it and it seems to have the desired effect. Rudy is miffed. The mayor thinks he is handsome.

"It is, seriously," Ruth continues, "a contest between two candidates with different styles and different priorities. You'll see a lot of evidence of that tonight. He bullies. I bring people together. He tears people apart. I care about people. He cares a lot more about himself."

Ruth is seated next to the mayor and stares directly into his eyes as she closes.

"You don't have to be mean to be tough. And a lot of times, Rudy, I don't think you know the difference."

The mayor says he wants to keep the debate on the issues "rather than personal attacks." To us, he seems timid and defensive. It's a great start.

• • •

Rudy seems strangely subdued.

His first question is from Gerson Borrero of the Spanish newspaper *El Diario*. Noting that several public officials, including schools chancellor Ramon Cortines and police commissioner William Bratton, were forced to resign under pressure from the mayor, Borrero says, "Many believe you have an abusive, confrontational style that interferes with some of the good things that you actually do. Does one have to be a bully in order to get this city into the next millennium?"

"That's about the nicest thing he's said about me in two months," Rudy quips, interrupting.

"By the way," Borrero says, "I think you're both cute."

"Gerson, there will be no flirting. Let's keep this on the up and up."

It's an appropriate, lighthearted response that defuses a sensitive situation for Rudy. Prior to the debate, Rudy's campaign tried to have Borrero removed from the panel. The light touch serves the mayor well in this case. One wonders why he doesn't display it more often.

• • •

Beth Fertig of WNYC radio asks Ruth whether she shares a piece of the blame for the failures of Democrats past.

Ruth switches to autopilot. "This election is about the future," she says and goes on to talk about her own agenda. Rudy says that it is "entirely unrealistic" for Ruth to say that her record is not up for examination, but Ruth seems to survive the exchange. Predictably, she does less well when asked a version of the dreaded Dinkins question.

"Do you feel safer walking down the streets of New York than you did four years ago? As an upper-middle-class Manhattan resident, do you feel that your quality of life has improved over the past four years?" asks Andrew Kirtzman.

There's an easy answer. Yes, Ruth's life is better, but that's precisely because she lives on the Upper West Side. Life isn't better for the city's poor and homeless and for the people who aren't lucky enough to live in Manhattan. But she doesn't see it. She argues that the question is whether the city is going to pay attention to other issues over the next four years, but Kirtzman won't let her off the hook.

"The question is whether your quality of life has changed."

"No," she says.

• • •

Giuliani's goal is to link Ruth with David Dinkins. When Ruth is asked whether she shares the blame for Democratic failures of the past, Rudy points to Dinkins and says it's clear that Ruth prefers the policies of the "prior administration." Ruth, he says, represents "a way-out fringe of the Democratic party."

Defending his education policy, he says that at least his administration did not have to be sued twice, as David Dinkins's was, for spending too little on schools. But Giuliani doesn't seem to be landing many punches. He invokes Dinkins's name so many times it seems to demonstrate his obsession with the former mayor rather than show any connection between the two Democrats.

Ruth gains confidence as the debate progresses. When Gerson Borrero asks about police brutality, Ruth says that if Giuliani had adopted the recommendations of the Mollen Commission, the Louima and Baez cases might have turned out differently.

"That's a totally absurd statement," Giuliani says, openly annoyed for the first time.

When Ruth pushes Rudy on his answer to her question of whether it was a mistake to raise his own pay while teachers get nothing, he gets genuinely testy and gives her the full treatment. "I didn't interrupt you, so I think you should give me a chance to answer the question."

And when Ruth asks her campaign-finance question, the mayor looks as if he is about to have an aneurysm. "Why aren't you as tough on criminals who give you illegal contributions?" she asks. "And will you release the Fugazy letter?"

"Sure," Rudy says. He's steaming and never once looks at Ruth. "Absolutely I'll release it. At the same time you can read Cardinal O'Connor's letter and [District Attorney] Bob Morgenthau's. And that really is a pretty outrageous attack on the reputation of a man who had a problem, was convicted, but also is a man who gave a great deal to the city of New York. Kind of a cheap thing to do.

"The fact is," he explains, "you don't investigate every single person who gives to you. If I did, I expect that my political opponent would attack me for being a bully, which she constantly calls me, and then says that I call names."

Giuliani was obviously prepared for the question and, on reflection, it seems like it wasn't a great idea to give him an opening to invoke Cardinal O'Connor's name. At the same time, Ruth isn't backing down to him, which is critically important. And she more than holds her own answering his questions.

When Rudy Giuliani asks her whether she will keep on Rudy Crew as chancellor, she smartly says that "her beef is not with Rudy Crew's performance, it's with Rudy Giuliani's." She looks Giuliani in the eye and says she needs to speak with the chancellor before making a decision, because "you do not allow anyone who works for you to say anything without your permission." Rudy's question about the death penalty goes nowhere.

Ruth's close is strong. "Rudy and I are different in more ways than you can count," she says and seems to have made her case.

Rudy, who has the last word, pops his eyes and says, "I'm not going to let all this negativism get me down."

• • •

At 8:55, we fax out our rapid response, correcting the most glaring inaccuracies by the mayor. Reading scores are down, not up as the mayor says. The Giuliani campaign was alerted about possible campaign violations months ago, not recently, as the mayor claimed. The response goes out without a glitch. Jay DeDapper, the ABC reporter, says the rapid response gave the debate the feeling of a presidential campaign.

• • •

Our deputy press secretary declares us the "hands-down winner." Randy Mastro, out spinning tonight, says Ruth was "personal, nasty and vicious." Giuliani press secretary Sunny Mindel says Ruth "replaced Leona Helmsley as the new queen of mean."

Whether we won hands down or not is one thing, but we're elated. Minutes after 9:00 I tell Ruth on her cellular phone that she did magnificently and that we all are extremely proud. I hold up the receiver as the office gives her a big cheer.

It's impossible for us to be objective on this, but it seems to us that Ruth more than held her own with Rudy Giuliani. It was the sort of performance that might have turned a few voters.

October 10

The reviews of the debate are more tepid than our own assessments. The *Times* says it was "not the kind of debate to drive voters from one candidate to another." David Seifman of the *Post* says Ruth "put up a game fight last night," but didn't "score the knockout she needs." A survey of five high-school debate coaches in the *News* unanimously scores the debate for Giuliani.

In an editorial, the *Post* compares Ruth's support of after-school programs as an answer to the gang problem to the kids' reply to Officer Krupke in *West Side Story.* The *News* says Ruth is "blowing smoke," trying to run from her past—as a "hair shirt to the mainstream elements of her party as fast as she can."

Ed Koch, objective as always, says the subdued mayor we saw last night was trying to hide his true colors. Rudy, he says, "sees everyone as either a sycophant or an enemy. If you're not one, you're the other."

David Dinkins sees the world through his own lens. Giuliani, Dinkins says, made a mistake by attacking him and assuming he is an unpopular person.

• • •

Vice President Al Gore snubs Ruth at a New York state Democratic party fund-raising luncheon. Virginia Fields and Assembly Speaker Sheldon Silver join Gore at the dais. Ruth is seated off to the side at a table with her parents. Gore says a few words in Ruth's behalf, but quickly steps down from the podium, preventing reporters from getting a shot of Ruth and the vice president together. Gore never so much as mentions Rudy Giuliani.

At virtually the same time, President Clinton, who had only five minutes for Ruth on a helicopter pad just two weeks ago, joins Democratic gubernatorial candidate Jim McGreevey for six hours of campaigning in New Jersey. This is the fifth visit by either the president or the First Lady in support of McGreevey. We've had a single photo opportunity with the First Family.

In her time of greatest need, Ruth's party is treating her like a pariah.

Like Ruth, McGreevey is a Democrat in a Democratic state running against a popular Republican incumbent, Christie Todd Whitman. But the similarities end there. Unlike Ruth, McGreevey is having some success. The latest polls have him down by only 6 points, though he started off down by more than 20. And McGreevey is getting traction on a real bread-and-butter issue, car-insurance rates. Car-insurance rates isn't any better or worse an issue than improving schools, and Ruth is every bit McGreevey's intellectual equal, but McGreevey seems to be scoring points with his five-point plan for reducing insurance rates in New Jersey. Individually, they're five piddling little ideas that could never be enough to raise an issue in a gubernatorial race. Together, they're taken seriously. The success of McGreevey's presentation reminds me that one of the most popular ads with the focus groups was one in which Ruth invited voters to write in for a copy of her plan to cut government waste.

Perhaps the lesson of McGreevey's success is never to underestimate the power of charts.

Or perhaps it's a reminder that any woman in politics faces an uphill battle.

October 11

Giuliani's ad attacking Ruth on expelling violent students has cast us once again in a defensive position, but this time we have a more attractive option. Among several callous quotes we tested in front of the focus groups are several relating to education. One is extraordinarily powerful. Some in the focus groups audibly gasped when we played the line, "Most of Rudy Giuliani's constituents don't have kids in public schools." The quote is attributed to Edward Costikiyan. Costikiyan advised Giuliani on education policy for a time, but he's not a partisan character. Costikiyan is more of a public intellectual. His views are widely respected. It seems only slightly fairer to use Costikiyan's quote against Giuliani than it would be to use one of Lee Jones's against Ruth, but citing the quote to a Giuliani education adviser will tie it to the mayor nicely for commercial purposes. Kicking and biting has been part of this game for a long time, though, and no one thinks for more than a second of the ethics of using the quote. The only consideration is whether the press will regard it as legitimate. In light of what Rudy got away with on sex shops, there seems little reason to doubt that they will.

It's a good ad:

> Ruth Messinger believes kids who bring guns to school should be kicked out. Zero tolerance. So what are these attack ads from Rudy Giuliani? Under Rudy Giuliani, school violence is up 30 percent. Giuliani slashed $6 billion from the schools. He said, "Something has to give somewhere." But why our schools? Giuliani's adviser explained, "Most of his constituents don't have kids in public schools." Ready for a mayor who cares about our schools? Ruth Messinger.

As the announcer reads the powerful quote, Mandy cuts to a shot of the mayor wiping his face, to which the focus groups had a strong adverse reaction. We call it Rudy's "tell."

Renewing our emphasis on education seems especially appropriate in light of the teachers' union announcement that it will remain neutral in the campaign.

• • •

In the *Amsterdam News*, Lenora Fulani urges a black boycott of the Democratic party in November. "The party's disrespect for Rev. Sharpton, its inability to hold itself together to re-elect David Dinkins four years ago, and its constant refusal to stand up for us—those most abused in the era of Giuliani—should be enough evidence to convict." Fulani is putting her energies behind indicted millionaire developer Abe Hirschfeld's bid for the Manhattan borough presidency. She is his Harlem coordinator.

Hirschfeld is finding his stride. His message is that the city needs "a builder to rebuild the city's schools." When a *Times* reporter asked Hirschfeld over lunch at Le Cirque 2000 what his other issues were, Hirschfeld turned to his twenty-three-year-old campaign manager and said, "Let's see, what are my other issues? Sometime I forget."

Hirschfeld has got this message thing down. Keep it down to one idea.

Finally, when pressed, Hirschfeld sounded the "tree issue." His idea is "to plant trees on every street and every avenue, every 25 feet, throughout Manhattan." Says Hirschfeld, "Manhattan can look like Paris, Rome."

Fulani's got her money on the right guy.

October 12

Successes for both campaigns on this Columbus Day.

As badly as the campaign-finance story went in the *Times*, our tainted contributors story goes well. The *News* reports that "Giuliani has accepted more than $100,000 in campaign contributions from a rogues' gallery of donors." "Businessmen of firms that have been indicted, convicted or banned from city business or have alleged ties to organized crime have given to Giuliani," records show. Jay Fabrikant is discussed at length. Our campaign is never mentioned.

We launch a well-coordinated attack. At noon, Ruth holds up the *News* article and calls on the mayor to return the funny money. "It appears clear from the record," she says, "that the mayor is practicing what he used to prosecute." In combination with the *News* article, Ruth's charge packs a rare punch. The Giuliani campaign is on the defensive. Fran Reiter says the campaign did not know of Fabrikant's contributions.

The Giuliani campaign continues to enjoy a triumph of equal or greater magnitude.

The thesis of Bob Herbert's column this morning is that "the Messinger campaign was born to be rained on." Maybe true, but his evidence is the interesting part. It's just her luck, he writes, that "the most important topic in the schools is the rising influence of violent Los Angeles–type gangs ["Ex-Blood Reveals Savage Rites" in an exposé in the *Post* today], a development that plays right into the hands of a law and order mayor." It's the sixth consecutive day of gang stories in the press.

But, as Herbert himself acknowledges, there are no reliable estimates of gang activity. And in the same issue that Herbert's column appears, the *Times* reports that police officers and school officials say there is little evidence that gang violence is increasing. The *News* reports that of 170 arrests arising from a well-publicized crackdown on the Bloods, only 40 turned out to be gang members.

Herbert, among many others, has been persuaded that an argument (Rudy believes that gang violence is rising and must be addressed) is a fact (gang violence is rising). The Giuliani campaign has subtly and skillfully created the perception of a crisis with persistent spinning and sometimes amusing attention to detail. In appropriate cases (that is, virtually all cases) the police department issues press releases with the heading NOT GANG RELATED.

• • •

In a Sunday sermon at the Bethel African Methodist Church in Harlem, Al Sharpton delivers his long-awaited endorsement of Ruth. It's a powerful sermon. "I've been stabbed!" he cries. "I've been indicted! But through it all! I'm learning to trust in Jesus!" But the Reverend isn't as effervescent in describing Ruth. He calls her merely "the best alternative of the candidates that are in the field." Sharpton stares at the ceiling while Ruth, not even trying to follow his act, says a few kind words about Reverend Al's candidacy.

Following the service, reporters call the endorsement lukewarm and question its sincerity. Hearing the questions, Sharpton slings his suit jacket over his shoulder, breaks into a full run, and heads for his nearby van.

In an evening sermon at the New Jerusalem Baptist Church in Queens, Sharpton is more enthused. "On the ballot in November there is no one equal to her deserving of support of the city, me and anyone I influence—write that down." After the second speech, he is downright testy over further questions about the earnestness of his endorsement and speculation about matters like the seating arrangement during Sharpton's morning sermon (Ruth is seated off to the side). "What do you want from my life?" Sharpton asks. "I get up there. I introduce her as the next Mayor. I've said five different ways I'm endorsing her.

"I compared her to the biblical character Esther. There is nothing a minister can do more than compare someone to a biblical figure."

October 13

There are, as it turns out, three Columbus Day parades. Two are not held on Columbus Day. The Morris Park Columbus Day Parade in the Bronx and the Hispanic Day Parade in Manhattan step off on the Sunday before the holiday. The main event is the Columbus Day Parade up Fifth Avenue, which has come to be associated with Italian Americans and Roman Catholics. The parade itself is preceded by a celebration. A breakfast sponsored by the City Council and morning Mass at St. Patrick's Cathedral are a traditional part of the day's agenda. Rudy and Ruth are both marching in the parade, but Ruth skipped the morning Mass, using the time to deliver a speech to a Jewish community group in which she essentially explains how her religious belief impelled her to handle the Sharpton situation as she has. ("It is unthinkable to me," she says, "to drive a wedge between the Jewish and the African American communities.")

The parade route is a battleground. Rudy's people trail Ruth with signs calling her the "Queen of Mean." One of the vagrants from our office dressed as a fat green plum follows Rudy. He is none other than Bagman, foe of campaign-finance law violators across the city! Bagman tosses out fake dollar bills with pictures of the mayor, all the while drawing attention to the mayor's double standard.

Actor Paul Sorvino marches behind Rudy, strengthening his front. Good soldier Sal Albanese holds down Ruth's right flank. Joe Franklin remains neutral, but even he cannot impose reason on this madness.

In the heat of battle, Rudy attacks Ruth for skipping the Mass earlier in the day and for not finishing the entire parade route. Rudy says: "This is a community she doesn't care very much about. It's never been a community that she cares about extending herself to. She wasn't at the Mass today. She drops out of the parade at 70th Street [nine blocks short of the end of the thirty-five-block event]. She's like giving away about three-quarters of the city, more than that, in the sense of no outreach to communities other than very, very narrow groups that she tries to appeal to."

Rudy refuses to say what community he is referring to. He says he means "the community that celebrates the parade. This is a big, big celebration. This is one that you should revel in and enjoy. I think you basically see very little regard for it. And it was kind of returned in terms of the cold response she got here.

"You basically have a campaign that is truly falling apart—she dropped out of the parade on 70th Street. You know this is a great parade. I'm going to march it twice."

The mayor sets out to march the route a second time, but only manages to finish two blocks on his encore.

• • •

Incredibly, this is no off-the-cuff attack. Sunny Mindel echoes the mayor's charges later in the day. "She attended four churches, none of which were Catholic," Mindel says of Ruth's Sunday schedule.

We're forced to respond, and we do so in an appropriately juvenile way, with a list of thirteen parades Giuliani missed, including the African American Parade and the Queens Pride Parade. We refrain from pointing out that Jules Polonetsky spent the morning with his grandfather, who was visiting from Miami Beach, and also missed the Mass. ("It wasn't a slight," his spokesperson explains.)

The attack is confusing. Rudy has nothing to gain from it. More than any other example, it demonstrates his near-compulsive need to attack enemies, his view of the world in absolute black and white. He immediately pays a price.

Ed Koch says it shows "extraordinary viciousness. It's unbelievable."

Giuliani cannot even bring himself to admit he made a mistake in accepting money from Jay Fabrikant. "The campaign will decide what to do," he says, "but in my view, they shouldn't return it. There's absolutely no illegality, no impropriety, and it's a great example of how independent we are."

• • •

Walter Brecher, whose wife was Gail Rubin's first cousin, said they "never heard of Ruth Messinger at the time of the vote on the PLO resolution and doubts the Rubins had ever heard of Messinger either." Malcolm Hoenlein, who also claims to have known the Rubins quite well, says that he does not recall any opposition to the resolution from members of the family.

• • •

At a rally in East New York Sharpton delivers a fiery "Dump Giuliani" address, but mentions Ruth not once. Sharpton says it would have been inappropriate for him to "upstage this event, which was a rally for Charles Barron." Barron explains, "When we say 'Dump Giuliani,' obviously we mean 'Vote for Ruth Messinger.' It's just that he has so many more negatives than she has positives right now."

October 14

A consequence of the speed that young people rise through politics is the fascinating dynamic of twenty-somethings telling fifty-somethings what to do. Our finance director is twenty-six. Our advance director is twenty-seven. Our campaign manager is thirty. Each is convinced he knows his job better than the candidate. In some cases they're right, but even if they are, the candidate is still entitled to some deference. Taking orders from someone thirty years your junior is not something that comes easily to anyone. The smart staffers have a sense of self.

Ruth has lost confidence in our campaign manager over the last three months. For weeks, he was in an impossible position. Ruth demanded increased field operations. Jim ordered him to resist, but never took Ruth on directly. Exhausted by her continual demands that he could not meet, the campaign manager simply stopped talking to Ruth, incredibly marking the second candidate in a year with whom he was on nonspeaking terms. Ultimately, the situation became intractable, and he was pushed aside.

Our new campaign manager is Public Advocate Mark Green's political director, and he's a vast improvement. He holds both 8:00 morning meetings *and* 10:00 evening meetings. And instead of asking us all what we can "whack the mayor with," he asks us all "what we have for him." Sometimes, to change things, he asks "what we've got for him." All this for the bargain price of $2,000 a week, which is actually slightly less than his predecessor earned.

He is a manager without goals, process without substance. A political beast.

• • •

Our new manager is baptized by fire as Rudy and Ruth continue to spar about the Columbus Day Massacre. Ruth holds a press conference with Italian American supporters, including Alan Hevesi (who made it to the preparade Mass). "Rudy Giuliani will do anything in his political interest, no matter how it affects the city," Ruth declares. "There's no play, no matter how dirty, he won't use." We plan to keep this story going as long as we can.

Rudy delivers the apology of a man who believes his own infallibility: "I was not suggesting that anyone who has any reservations about going to Mass or a religious service should ever be required to go to it, or any pressure should be put on them to go to it. I think people have the right to make those choices themselves. It was probably a mistake to focus on the Mass. I should not have put the emphasis on the Mass because nobody should be pressured in any way to go to a religious service which they have any reservations about."

But he doesn't stop there. He continues: "The thing that I was puzzled about—and possibly somewhat offended about—was there were all of these Columbus Day celebrations all throughout the city. She didn't go to the Columbus Day celebration in Staten Island, she didn't go to the Columbus Day celebration in the Bronx. She dropped out of the Columbus Day celebration in Manhattan [after] the publicity was gone."

I hadn't realized there are five Columbus Day parades.

"I felt as a former grand marshal," Giuliani explains, "probably more offended by that than I should."

Name dropper.

He will not issue a blanket apology. He will not apologize to Ruth. Rudy's apology is limited, he says, to "whoever was offended."

Incredibly, after months of our crusading against abhorrent conditions in the public schools, double-digit unemployment, and a mayor who flaunts the campaign-finance law, this stupid, inconsequential issue generates Rudy's worst press of the campaign.

The *Times* and *News* write critical editorials. Ed Koch says the mayor will "put us all in handcuffs if he's re-elected." He calls Giuliani "venomous" and compares him to a tarantula.

Jimmy Breslin writes:

> Anyone who can mix up the secular and sacred and make claims that he is God by determining the meaning of such as a Mass is demonic. You can imagine what the guy has boiling inside him if he lets a thing like this out during an election campaign. In 100 years of this city, there hasn't been a man running around talking like this. He is a little man in search of a balcony.

On this one day, the city is united against the mayor.

Except for the *Post*'s Andrea Peyser, who faults Ruth for exploiting the issue.

• • •

Senator Moynihan, who endorsed us by press release on a Friday, is joining Rudy Giuliani in suing President Clinton to prevent him from using the line-item veto to strike an exception from the Medicaid bill that would cost New York City $2.6 billion. He doesn't even return calls from our office asking him to take time with Ruth during the day. Asked about the political significance of the event, Moynihan says, "I've taken an oath to uphold and defend the Constitution of the United States against all enemies foreign and domestic."

Hillary Clinton is coming to town for a fund-raiser, but will not consent to its being open to the press. She will only allow a photo opportunity at the Children's Defense Fund event, which stars Rosie O'Donnell and Glenn Close.

Ruth Messinger is alone.

October 15

October on the Messinger campaign has become a quiet purgatory. There will be no November surprise, no late media blitz, no last-minute turnaround. A *Daily News* poll shows Rudy with a 57–34 lead. He's ahead 55–35 among women, 48–41 among Democrats, 55–36 in Manhattan. A Zogby poll in the *Post* shows the race at 56–27. We don't even bother with tracking polls of our own anymore.

There won't even be the credibility and memory of a well-fought campaign.

"Get this over with, this worst ever of mayoral campaigns," Bob Herbert writes this morning in the *Times*. "There is no fun, no excitement, no charm, no charisma, and nothing in the way of new ideas. There should be a way to spare the voters this exercise in sustained dreariness." And Herbert doesn't have to live this race sixteen hours a day.

The *Post* drones on day after day. "Public education in New York City has a very long road to travel. Ruth Messinger most certainly isn't the one to show the way."

For most of us, the campaign has become a toothache; it causes the sort of pain that flares up from time to time but is mostly dull and annoying only for its persistence. People chat about what they will do after the campaign. The finance director and I mark time by the movie *Starship Troopers,* which is set to open two days after the election. Our deputies are planning a trip to Spain. Some people talk about what jobs they will seek after the election, but none can take any steps now to secure employment, since it would be unbecoming for staffers to do anything that might be interpreted by the press as an admission that the campaign is over. Jim doesn't yell so much anymore. Mostly he seems depressed. Sometimes he seems to be making efforts to repair some of his damaged relationships with people on the staff. Lee is as busy as ever, but clearly concerned about what is next for him. My staff has less and less to do. Today we roll posters for a women's rally. There is talk about whether the staff will be paid through November 15 as had been rumored, but it seems unlikely.

It seems that projections of city tax revenue increase by the day and Rudy is spending his Wall Street bonus like it's going out of style. Today he proposes $70 million in tax cuts for small corporations and families that pay for child care. It's a perfectly sound idea—we've proposed tax cuts for small businesses, too—but it couldn't be more frustrating. "It might be more honest and direct if he stood outside the voting booth on Election Day and gave everyone who was coming in a $20 bill," Ruth says.

Giuliani finally puts Columbus Day in the past. Elaborating on his apology, the mayor says, "Maybe I overreacted a bit. It was wrong to insert the notion of a religious service into anything that has to do with politics. I made a mistake and I'm sorry."

October 16

Today's doings offer a fine example of why politicians often sound as if they are saying nothing. Back in June, the president of the New York City Civil Service Retired Employees' Association, a huge union of retired civil-service workers, wrote Ruth that she had won the union's endorsement because of her support of variable supplements for retired city employees. Supplements are payments to pensioners designed to compensate for the devaluation of their retirement income as a result of inflation. Policemen and firefighters get them. Civil-service retirees don't.

There may be an ethical case to be made for supplements, but it's certainly not an issue about which many people care (except for those who get them or stand to get them), and we viewed this as an opening for us to be tagged with supporting yet another multimillion-dollar program. Ruth wanted the endorsement badly, but we persuaded her to write back to the union president indicating her trust that the endorsement was based on her whole mayoral platform and restating that her position on supplements was something she was willing to discuss. The union considered withdrawing the endorsement. It stood after a telephone conversation between Ruth and the president of the sort in which one side thinks it has gotten what it wanted and the other thinks it has given up nothing.

Today, before a mad throng of ten thousand senior citizens at Madison Square Garden, Ruth fires them up. "You deserve a fair hearing and a fair shake at City Hall. And in a Messinger administration you will."

Inspiring stuff.

October 17

Lee Jones and Fran Reiter are consecutive guests of Andrew Kirtzman on New York 1. (Reiter refuses to appear at the same time as Lee.) Every one of Kirtzman's questions in forty minutes of interviewing is a question about campaign strategy. According to the News Research Group Media Watch, during the first two weeks of October, 42 percent of stories about the campaign focused on strategic issues.

With the notable exception of Wayne Barrett of the *Village Voice*, there is no investigative reporting going on. Based on original research, Barrett's steady stream of stories covers topics ranging from manipulation of police complaint statistics to environmental commissioner Joel Miele's links to the mob. Barrett's book *City for Sale*, about corruption during the third Koch administration, helped enhance Giuliani's reputation as a prosecutor. Now Barrett is among his most persistent and vigilant critics. He is alone.

Newspapers report a great deal, but they investigate almost nothing. The press will report on any charge that is the product of a campaign's investigation. In rare cases, if the research is good and the campaign persuasive, the paper will pass the story off as the product of its own research. But no reporters are doing any investigative work on their own.

There are plenty of good stories to write. For example, what are the hidden costs of campaigns to taxpayers? Rudy is campaigning full-time now, Ruth has been for months. As far as I can tell, she hasn't set foot in the borough president's office in weeks. If they are doing their jobs, they must each be doing them from the car phone, since both are scheduled to the teeth. Do they have a right to a city paycheck during this time?

To what extent is it justifiable for their staffs to be involved in the campaigns? Rudy sent a photographer over to take pictures of the borough president's office in June accompanied by two city workers. Deputy Mayor Mastro sent the press a four-page single-spaced letter responding to our debate response on city stationery. Rudy's deputies regularly show up at his endorsement press conferences.

Ruth is equally culpable on this count. Someone from the borough president's office is with her at all times (in campaign jargon, the *body person*). Several of her staff members are at the campaign office during working hours helping out with field organizing.

Under the existing rules, this story will not be news unless one candidate raises it against the other.

Since both candidates are abusing the system, neither has any incentive to bring it up. But it is still a good story. It raises important issues. Perhaps candidates should be required to resign during their candidacies, as Bob Dole did when he resigned from his Senate seat in 1996. Perhaps city employees should be prohibited from working on political campaigns. And that's just the first story that comes to my mind. There are dozens of other important stories that aren't being written.

One obvious reason is that the press is lazy. It is easy to write stories about competing accusations by campaigns. Take each campaign's press release, get a quote or two, and you have a story. Speculating about motivations is even easier. It requires no work at all.

Investigative work is hard. It took hundreds of hours of work for us to find approximately $60,000 in additional illegal contributions that the Giuliani campaign accepted. News is a business like any other. Most editors do not have the luxury of allowing their reporters to spend weeks investigating a lead that may prove to be fruitless. They need quick results. So most of the hard stories never get written.

• • •

In the course of his discussion with Lee, Kirtzman responds to a statement by Lee about Ruth's prospects for winning the election by saying, "We're seeing professional spin tonight." It prompts me to think that the word "spin," like "love," has come to encompass so many different concepts that it is beginning to lack meaning. Perhaps we can refine the definition.

One type of spinning is arguing about what conclusions should be drawn from existing facts.

Two economists can look at a set of indicators and reach opposite conclusions about the strength of the U.S. economy. So too can different political analysts draw different conclusions from sets of poll data. When the mayor issued his management report, an annual statistical analysis of city performance, he gave himself straight A's. "This is really a remarkable performance," he said. We said it was "bad news for women, children, and the poor." Deputy Mayor Mastro accused us of lying, but as the *Times* acknowledged, we had simply taken statistics from the report. We spun a different conclusion from identical facts.

The second type of spinning is spinning facts themselves. When Rudy's people started spinning about the Cristyne Lategano situation, that was a different sort of argumentation than trying to convince people that rising unemployment is a sign of optimism. The ultimate issue in the Lategano situation was a question of fact: Did Rudy and Cristyne have an affair? The issue of what price Giuliani should pay if it were true is a question of opinion, but the truth of the underlying charge is a question of fact.

Spinning about conclusions and spinning about facts are quite different enterprises. The only thing that differentiates spinning about conclusions from ordinary arguing is that the spinner has an obvious bias; there is no intellectual honesty in the discussion. But everyone has biases in arguments all the time, so it doesn't seem like a big deal.

Spinning about facts is different. Unlike with a question of opinion, there is ultimate truth with a question of fact. There is no right or wrong answer to the question of what the repercussions should be for a public official who has shown infidelity, but there is an answer to the question of whether that person has in fact been unfaithful. The 1992 Clinton campaign raised spinning about facts to a new level of art. It applied all of the methods that had been used for argument-spin to fact-spin. It questioned Gennifer Flowers's credibility and showed her bias. Before that, the case would have been much simpler. People would have either believed or disbelieved Clinton's denial, and that would have been the end of it. Spinners then could have debated the argument of what the consequences of his answer should be.

My sense is that people have very different reactions to argument-spin and fact-spin. I certainly do. Spinning arguments is offensive only because it is boring. Spinning facts seems to obstruct the process of finding truth. Andrew Kirtzman and Adam Nagourney have conflated the concepts, I think. Everything is spin to them. It may all be, but in failing to differentiate between the different types of spin, they miss the important point that truth matters.

October 18

I must confess a mistake. There are, in fact, six Columbus Day parades. You can, I hope, understand my expectation that the celebration of Columbus Day was over, given that the holiday is now a week behind us. But I was wrong and I apologize. The Brooklyn Columbus Day Parade is today, and it is an important celebration of a historic moment and of a culture that is a vibrant part of the fabric of the city. I meant no offense.

Ruth and Rudy are both in the Brooklyn parade, and Rudy just cannot resist one more dig. "I think it's interesting," the mayor says, "that this is the only [Columbus Day] celebration she has participated in in the boroughs, and it comes after my discussion of her not doing it."

Columnist Sidney Zion says Giuliani's strategy is obvious. The mayor, he says, recognizes that Ruth already has the Italian Catholic vote locked up. "Ruth's long support for abortion probably tied up the Italian-Catholic vote before the campaign began. But if that didn't do it, her heartfelt support for gay marriages certainly did the trick."

October 19

With less than two weeks remaining, Jim thinks the time is right to bring out the big guns.

We're being consistently outspent on television. During the three weeks between October 4 and October 25, the Giuliani campaign is spending $380,000 on television, compared to our $256,000. The spread gets worse as Election Day approaches. That means, if we are going to hold our own, our ads will have to have greater impact than the mayor's. We think we have a powerful one and we're going to use virtually all of our remaining money on it.

The first twenty-five seconds of the ad are quotes from the mayor over sinister pictures of him, including a prolonged display of the "tell." Then:

> Rudy Giuliani cut $6 billion from our schools. Giuliani's education adviser explained, "Most of his constituents don't have kids in public schools." Giuliani cut the city hospital budget by 80 percent, laid off 1,600 doctors and nurses. He said, "They won't hurt health care." About massive cuts for the poor, Giuliani said, "The poor will eventually figure out that it's a lot easier to be homeless where it's warm."

Then a picture of Ruth walking up the steps to a house to shake hands with a tattooed man.

"Ruth Messinger. Because you don't have to be mean to be tough."

"Let that one filter out there for a few days," Jim says.

October 20

The *Times* is out in the field with a major poll. We all expect it to be another nail in the coffin, but early in the afternoon Adam Nagourney calls Jim with the preliminary results. The spread is 13 points, he says, but must be a mistake. The full results will no doubt show a margin more in line with the other polling. They don't. The spread is 13. The *Times* calls around to some other pollsters to try to account for the discrepancy, but finds no explanation, rejecting the obvious possibility, unthinkable to it, that the race could be tightening.

Could it be? The Zogby poll can be dismissed as Republican spinning. Quinnipiac employs Howard Rubinstein, a Giuliani supporter, as its publicist. But it's harder to explain away the Marist and New York 1 polls as not objective, especially when the basis of our pessimism is the longitudinal trends in the polls. Even if their questions are somehow biased against us, we're still doing worse than we were when those same questions were asked at earlier points in the campaign.

But voter attitudes change over time and many of those polls are already weeks old. We have an effective ad up, and Rudy no doubt hurt himself with the Columbus Week fiasco. The *Times* poll may also help to start changing the perception that the race is over. Once people start to think it is competitive, it may change the mix of likely voters and perhaps get the press to pay a little more attention. Maybe we can make a respectable showing. Maybe, just maybe, we can pull this thing off.

• • •

Former governor Hugh Carey, who pardoned John Hill during his tenure, endorses Rudy on the steps of City Hall. One of Carey's sons has a $144,000-a-year job as executive vice president and general counsel at the Economic Development Corporation.

Carey says it was fair for Rudy to question the party for John Hill. "I think the mayor made a comment about who was there at different places and times when it was felt fashionable to spend some time with those who were convicted. I think it's a fair comment as to what you do after hours, especially if you're talking about Elaine's."

Don't ask me what he means.

• • •

I take the opportunity on this otherwise sleepy day to attend our own press conference. Ruth is on the steps of the state courthouse hammering away at Giuliani's record of openness. Two weeks ago, Giuliani sued to prevent the release of a report stating the results of a judicially ordered review of the Administration for Children Services (ACS). Giuliani said the release of the report would diminish morale. The report, which the court ordered to be released, said that mismanagement in the agency endangers thousands of lives. Nearly 50 percent of kids are abused even after ACS takes over a case, because the agency closes files too quickly.

Last week, Public Advocate Mark Green won his lawsuit against Giuliani and forced the police department to turn over their disciplinary files. The overwhelming majority of abuse cases substantiated by the Civilian Complaint Review Board go unpunished by the police department. Yesterday state comptroller Carl McCall won a court order requiring Giuliani to release agency records, including those showing how the police department compiles crime statistics.

It's a good message, but seeing the presentation in person, I see a large reason why our campaign has developed the poor reputation it has. The courthouse is a gray, drab setting. Ruth's fake wood port-a-podium seems out of place. There are no people on the streets. There are two reporters, including only one from television, Andrew Kirtzman. Everyone else is from our campaign, and even that group is not very large. Ruth delivers her remarks to a grand total of eight people.

October 21

There will be no bump from the *New York Times* poll.

Adam Nagourney's story about the poll barely mentions that the race has tightened. The headline is "Poll Finds Most Voters Have No Opinion About Messinger," and the rest is more Giuliani spin. Nagourney's thesis is that the race "has not captured the attention of the city." Sixty percent of people had no opinion of Ruth, but "by almost every measure New Yorkers feel good about their city and its Mayor."

It is only at the end of the fourth paragraph that Nagourney mentions the head-to-head results, but even then he spins them from the mayor's perspective. "Mr. Giuliani's numbers could be even greater," he writes, "if the lack of excitement about Ms. Messinger's candidacy produced a low turnout among her potential supporters."

In one tautological sentence, entirely unsupported by evidence, Nagourney explains away the poll results. Any candidate's numbers could be greater if a lack of excitement about his or her opponent's candidacy produced a low turnout of that candidate's supporters. But the whole reason pollsters assess both individual favorable ratings and how respondents would vote in a head-to-head matchup is so that they don't have to speculate about how the different favorable ratings would translate into votes. Nagourney is dismissing the most important piece of data in the poll.

It looks to me like he's even mistaken about his basic premise that a majority of those surveyed have no opinion of Ruth. While Nagourney says 60 percent of people have no opinion of Ruth, he says 29 percent of people have no opinion of Rudy, which seems almost unthinkable. I've yet to meet a person in this city who doesn't have an opinion of the mayor. My guess is that Nagourney has conflated the concept of a neutral opinion with the very different concept of no opinion or knowledge. The conclusion is bolstered by the responses to some other questions in the survey. The *Times* asks which of the candidates will do better on various issues like education, poverty, and police brutality and what voters' impressions are of the individual candidates with respect to qualities like toughness and leadership. In every case more than 70 percent of the respondents offer an opinion on Ruth. In some cases it's bad. Voters think, 52–28, that Ruth cannot be trusted to deal with problems. In some cases it's good. By an overwhelming margin of 60–13, voters think Ruth cares about the needs of poor people (50–40 they think Rudy doesn't). But in every case the voters have an opinion. How could they possibly have an opinion of someone on individual issues as nuanced as particular character traits and not have an overall opinion?

This is where we pay the price for having lost the metabattle to convince the most influential political reporter in the city that this is a competitive campaign.

• • •

Jim is often angry, but usually his temper is directed at me or Lee or other members of the staff. He rarely shows his rage to Ruth and never to the press. Perhaps it's the *Times* story, perhaps something else, but he is past his limit. Jim lets loose with James Bradley of the *Village Voice*. Do you know why, he asks Bradley, 10 percent unemployment was on the front page of the *Times* in 1992, but barely made the newspapers this year?

"Because then journalists knew people were getting laid off. The elite in this town, the chattering classes, are very happy.

"New York," he says, "is becoming a cynical place run by a cynical man who doesn't give a shit. And he's proud of that. We've got a mean son of a bitch as mayor."

It is all part of Jim's worldview that race is the Rosetta Stone of politics—Giuliani is popular because, as Jim puts it, he keeps the sluice gates at 125th Street in Manhattan closed. It's a powerful theory, but he's not put it on the record before. Now he does. It's good, he tells Bradley, that Giuliani is a mean SOB. "He keeps all those people where they're supposed to be."

He mourns the lack of party support for Ruth to Adam Nagourney. "The true test of a party is when it's in a difficult situation—not when it's not. If that is true, this party has failed miserably."

"There's kind of a smarmy, rotten nature to this. It's not that it's just despicable, it's gratuitous. The constant bashing by Democrats of Ruth and her effort. While they are abandoning her in public, off the record they are trashing her to every reporter in town."

Jim even goes so far as to call Alan Hevesi "slimy," which seems like an understatement to all of us, but would be a remarkable public statement. It never makes it into the paper. Hevesi's consultant, Hank Morris, calls Jim later in the day and asks him to take back the comment. Out of professional courtesy, Jim agrees and asks Nagourney as another professional courtesy not to use the quote. Nagourney honors the request.

October 22

Politics aside, today is the best day of the campaign. At 8:00 in the morning, one of Ruth's staffers and I head out to LaGuardia Airport to pick up Robert Reich, the former Secretary of Labor, who is in town to endorse

Ruth for no immediately obvious reason. Reich tells me that he had Ruth's daughter Miriam as an economics student back at Harvard.

There's some time before the endorsement event, and Reich and I head off for a cup of coffee at an Au Bon Pain in midtown. He is the most impressive person I have ever met. I have only just begun reading Reich's memoir, *Locked in the Cabinet*, so many of my questions must seem tedious to him, but he answers them with patience. He loved being a cabinet officer, he says, but the time away from his family was too high a price to pay. I tell him about my increasing cynicism about politics. Reich nods in understanding, but tells me not to forget that politicians really can make a difference.

And as we begin talking about the issues in the campaign, I see that Reich believes what he says. His passion is obvious. He listens intently as I tell him the facts about the tax breaks the Giuliani administration has doled out to large corporations without any guarantees in return: $500 million in corporate welfare. He asks me what $500 million could buy for our schools. A thousand new teachers, I tell him, or new computers and Internet hookups for all of our schools. Reich nods again. As we head out to meet Ruth, he asks me, "Is it okay to say it's about time New York had a Jewish grandmother as mayor?"

"Just fine," I say. "You can say that many times if you like."

Reich delivers an impassioned speech. He calls the economic recovery lopsided and says that tax giveaways to large corporations could have been better invested in human capital, in improving education for the city's kids. "The question is what can New York do to make sure this success is shared by all. It isn't good enough, folks. And Ruth Messinger is concerned about the people who may not be getting all the benefits of this recovery."

When Reich heads off to his next speech, I am very sorry to see him go.

• • •

If there is a personality trait that is analogous to the retail view of the world, it is equivocation. Rudy Giuliani sees the world in black and white. Ruth Messinger sees it in grays. Ruth is too smart to believe that her saying something will make it true. Rudy Giuliani answers the question, once asked by the *Daily News,* "What will unemployment be in your administration?" without hesitation. Ruth Messinger cannot suffer its foolishness. She is too smart. She understands that results are achieved only through policies and accordingly thinks and speaks in terms of policies and nuances. But policy discussions do not play well in wholesale politics. Mandy and Jim have been fighting a continuous battle to get Ruth to speak in more active, results-oriented terms.

They recognized this as a problem as far back as the *Post* debate. Talking about homelessness, she said then, "What the mayor of this city needs to do, and what Rudy Giuliani should have done on the first day of his term, is to sit down with the advocates and with the judges and begin to negotiate agreements as to how we would provide for people who don't have homes."

In June she wrote this to Jim about a draft of the budget speech:

> I want the text and tone of this speech not to be dispositive, as in "I will do this," "I will merge that," but rather to suggest a real intention to consider and choose among several options that will make city government work better for everyone—taxpayers, residents, workers. "I will look to merge agencies whose functions are duplicative." I want that tone because I think it is important to convey that we will be prepared to act boldly, but also that we will do this with the input and ideas of the other players—from the private sector to Albany to labor leaders.

Jim and Mandy have tried to convince Ruth with some success that this is the language of a legislator, not an executive, but the old ways often show through. Asked by the *Times* editorial board what the first six months of a Messinger administration would be like, she says, "First of all, the appointments will be different. What I will do as Mayor, and I will certainly do in the first six months, is identify what are the biggest problems, what are the worst challenges facing the city." After years of thinking about being mayor, her instincts tell her to first change appointments and then hold a meeting.

Even Robert Reich, the most eloquent spokesperson our campaign has seen, cannot inspire Ruth to abandon the vestiges of her retail heritage. After Reich meticulously details the case against tax breaks for wealthy corporations, Ruth is asked what her policy on tax breaks would be. She says, "There are cases where it's appropriate, but the city has to figure what it's getting in return." It reduces Reich's argument to nothing.

• • •

Deputy Mayor Randy Levine says Ruth's opposition to a tax deal shows she "hasn't got the foggiest clue about running the economy," but candidate Giuliani equated the tax breaks to bribes in 1993. The outrage is not that the city offers tax incentives to some corporations to stay, but rather that the corporations that get them neither are needy (like Rupert Murdoch's News America, where we are today) nor, as in several cases including Bear Stearns, have any intention of leaving New York. What's more, as a report by Comptroller Hevesi shows, the city doesn't monitor the companies to ensure that they live up to their promises to keep a certain number of jobs in the city. Not to worry, though. Hevesi reports the program is "working well" as companies are living up to their obligations on their own.

• • •

The New York City Labor Council, which is headed by Democratic assemblyman Brian McLaughlin and encompasses 450 unions and 1.5 million workers citywide, endorsed Giuliani today, but it didn't hurt nearly as much as losing the endorsement of the Fire Alarm Dispatchers Benevolent Association. Ruth spent two years in court (successfully) fighting to save the city's fire alarm boxes from the mayor's budget cuts.

Rudy also earns the endorsement of Gus Bevona, the leader of the building unions, and is asked the quite reasonable question of how Bevona came to be the highest-paid union boss in the city. The mayor bristles. "This happens every time people endorse me, they become targets of this, and it is really unfortunate."

October 23

The *Post* does nicer work today than usual.

Columnist Eric Briendel calls Ruth a Communist. "The enduring legacy of the McCarthy era, he writes, is that it is taboo to call a Communist a Communist." Ruth, he says, is a Communist, plain and simple. As evidence he offers these facts: First, Ruth's mother was a member of the American Labor Party (ALP), created by FDR to ensure that New Deal supporters weren't driven out by Tammany Hall. After World War II, Briendel says, the ALP was taken over by Stalinists. Genuine Democrats defected. Briendel can find no evidence that Mrs. Wyler, Ruth's mom, defected. Second, in 1962, Ruth was a member of "Women's Strike for Peace," a group protesting JFK's nuclear-weapons policies. Briendel says it was a Communist front. Third, in the 1980s, Messinger was a cofounder of the U.S. Peace Council, the American affiliate of the KGB-created World Peace Council. Finally, in 1982, she abstained from a resolution condemning Poland's Communist regime for using anti-Semitism to discredit Lech Walesa.

It's a convincing case, I know, especially the parts about belonging to a peace council and opposing nuclear weapons, which must certainly be a Communist plot. All good capitalists love war and nukes. Ruth's mother was never in the ALP, but that should hardly weaken Briendel's case. She knows what it was, which must make her daughter a pinko.

The *Post* also quotes an off-the-record comment by our press deputy. Bill Clinton will be campaigning for us next week (we'll be sharing him with Jim McGreevey), but the location for the planned event is still in flux partially because of the New York City Marathon. "You don't want a record-setting pace by a runner destroyed—that would be the last nail in our coffin."

And the *Post* argues that Hevesi's report undermines Reich and Messinger's argument about tax breaks and jobs in the city. Even they, though, are usually above the headline they use for the story: "Big Shortcoming in Ruth's 'Jobless' Jab at Mayor."

October 24

I'm unqualified to offer any meaningful insight into what it is like for a woman to work on a campaign, but based on what I see and hear, it's not an experience that I would recommend. Day-to-day working conditions are tough for anyone to tolerate, but women have it a little bit worse. The staff of the campaign may be diverse, but the culture is not. Calling it the old boys' school dignifies it too much. It's more like a fraternity house. Looks impact hiring decisions. On the other side of the coin, although I've never seen an explicit example of discrimination, the facts speak for themselves about a glass ceiling. The campaign manager, finance director, comptroller, research director, press secretary, field director, and advance director are all men. Aside from Ruth's political director, who is a lifelong friend, the highest position in the campaign held by a woman is volunteer coordinator. The deputy finance director and scheduler (a difficult and important job) are women also. That's it.

As a result of the lack of women in positions of authority, many women regard the campaign as an old boys' crowd and feel excluded from basic information. Jim is not open by nature to begin with. In contrast to James Carville, who is known for his openness and for sharing strategy with everyone on the campaign, Jim is secretive. He keeps polls locked up in his office and does not openly discuss the most basic elements of our strategy, such as when our ads will be going on the air. It is especially disempowering for women.

As in any other organization, people's lives are most affected by their direct bosses, some of whom are quite reasonable. But some of the other higher-ups in the office like to be "taken care of." They routinely send people out to run errands for them—to get their lunch, drop off their laundry, get money for them from the bank, make dinner reservations, and anything else that comes to mind. By no coincidence, all of the people who are asked to do these sorts of things are women.

It seems to be a badge of honor among men in the office to see who can treat a woman the worst. Yesterday the campaign manager tapped on an empty cup, indicating to his assistant that he was thirsty for coffee. When another member of the campaign membership got wind of this, he shook his head. "That's so rude," he said, turning to bellow for his own assistant.

"I'm very good to her," he said.

They are all convinced they are good to their girls.

All the people who have quit the campaign so far have been women. In total, thirteen women have been hired to work on the campaign. Four have quit. Goodness knows how many could claim sexual harassment. One was pinned up against a wall late one night and forcibly kissed before repelling the attack. The man explained that it was the woman's fault, because he had twice bought her lunch and she should have understood the significance of that.

"I'm a thirty-five-year-old man," he explained.

The great irony is that Ruth Messinger is one of the most culturally sensitive people I have ever met. Her borough president's office is a model (some would say a caricature) of political correctness. They don't like us very much. We turn our noses up at them because of the long hours we work and how quickly we can turn things around, but I'm not sure I like us very much either.

October 25

Late in the afternoon, Jim calls me and Lee into his office. We expect him to be cheered by the Panamanian Day Parade, but he is not. A new poll by Marist has Rudy up 53–32, 58–27 among likely voters. Marist even asks a metaquestion of which Adam Nagourney would be proud. Seventy-two percent of Messinger's supporters think Ruth is likely to lose. The Marist poll confirms the result of a New York 1 poll showing Rudy up 56–32. The *Times* poll was an aberration.

"It's over," Jim says. He tells Lee to go in and tell Ruth the news.

"Evan," he says, "we won't make the kids work so hard anymore. I'm going to change my tone. I'm going to be nice."

• • •

Further proof of how little our message has penetrated. Bob Herbert's column today is about after-school crime and the need for after-school programs. He mentions Ruth not once.

October 27

The dementia of politics is deep. We've always regarded an economic downturn as a variable of sufficient magnitude to change the complexion of the race. When the stock market plunges today, we lament the news not because of what it signals for the economy, but rather for coming too late to make a difference in the campaign.

• • •

State Assembly Speaker Sheldon Silver, a Democrat, comes close today to calling Ruth a retail politician in so many words. He blames her unimpressive effort on her desire to "be all things to all people."

October 28

With yesterday's endorsement by the *New York Post*, all of the city's major dailies have lined up behind the mayor's reelection bid. The editorial boards fall over each other in praise of the mayor. "Mr. Giuliani's combative temperament is a bit like nuclear fission," writes the *Times*. "Harnessed the right way, it is a tool for progress, drilling through previously impervious bureaucratic and political barriers."

Newsday says "Giuliani proved the pessimists wrong." "No mayor in recent memory has been better for this city, and at a time when this city needed a great mayor most," adds the *Staten Island Advance*.

The *Daily News* says that Rudy "has proved to New Yorkers—indeed, to the world—that this rough-and-tumble city actually is governable. This achievement has earned him another enthusiastic *Daily News* endorsement—and a place of honor in the history books." The *Post* hopes for a wide margin of victory. "If any mayor has ever turned a town around, *this* mayor has turned *this* town around."

Even *El Diario*, the "champion of the Hispanic community," endorses Giuliani as *el candidato mas capaz para administrar una ciudad de matices inreiblemente diversos* (the candidate most capable of running an amazingly diverse city), though it notes that he has *practicamente olvidado* (virtually ignored) the minority community over the past four years.

The *News* argues that the mayor's "accomplishments would earn Giuliani four more years against virtually any challenger. Against Ruth Messinger, the lackluster Democrat, Giuliani deserves reelection by a landslide." The other papers agree. Ruth "cannot offer a credible rationale for her own candidacy," argues the *Post*. Giuliani, the *News* says, has created the sense that someone is in charge. "By contrast, the campaign slogan of Ruth Messinger could be 'Spare any change.' To vote for her would be to set the city back."

The *Times* says Ruth "failed to give voters a sharp sense of her own political philosophy" and that she "deserves to be remembered for her previous service to this city rather than for this uninspiring race."

El Diario expresses what seems to be implied by the *Times*. "Although Ruth Messinger has proven through hard work to be a capable and principled civic leader, she has been unfortunately repackaged by misguided consultants into a generic-brand politician for purposes of this campaign."

Only two papers have kind words for Ruth. The *Advance* calls her "an intelligent, dedicated and worthy public official, who has fought as hard as she can to make this a race. Some of her criticisms of the Mayor are well reasoned and well taken." And *Newsday* calls Messinger "a brilliant policy analyst, an admirable elected official and a very decent person," though it adds that the "painful lesson of the Messinger candidacy" is that this is "the end of the line for old-style Democratic politics." The *Amsterdam News* endorses Ruth as tepidly as Sharpton once did. It decries Giuliani, a "master" at the dangerous game of "fear, racism, and divisiveness," but has not a kind word to say about Ruth.

We suffer further indignities still. State assemblyman Brian McLaughlin, who gave the nominating address when Ruth was endorsed by the Queens Democratic organization, endorses Giuliani today. In a story about Giuliani's record on education, teachers' union president Sandra Feldman says she thinks Rudy "really is at the beginning of putting his mark on the school system in a positive way."

In the National Press, the *Washington Post* calls Ruth "hapless," which Jim likes to pronounce syllable by syllable for emphasis. David Brooks of the *Weekly Standard* says Ruth "is conducting the most lifeless, vacuous Democratic campaign in the city's history, maybe in the history of the world."

The latest polls by Quinnipiac and the *Daily News* show Giuliani leading 59–31 and 59–32, respectively. There is speculation in the press that Rudy may threaten Robert Wagner's all-time record of 68 percent of the vote, set in 1957.

But most disturbing of all is Dan Janison and Liz Willen's report in *Newsday* that our campaign may be short of a "critical resource," field staff. This follows yesterday's news that Council Speaker Peter Vallone ("In Slap At Messinger") is sending his army of two dozen volunteers to help Andrew Spano in the Westchester County Executive race. *Newsday* explains that "so-called pull operations get voters to the ballot booths, and attempt to distribute literature, hand out palm cards and serve as poll-watchers." The Giuliani forces, they report, will have an aggressive pull operation. They will also have "an Election Day 'rides program' through which voters can sign up for free transportation." *Palm cards* are baseball-card-size reminders of who is on which ticket. They usually pair a major candidate and a local candidate like "VOTE DEMOCRATS LINE B: CLINTON FOR PRESIDENT AND SCHLOMO FOR CITY COUNCIL," or, as ours read, "VOTE MESSINGER FOR MAYOR AND HEVESI FOR COMPTROLLER." They're useful for people who can't read down columns in the voting booths.

Janison and Willen are right. If we can't get the palm cards out next week, we're sunk.

October 29

The second and final Campaign Finance Board debate is hosted by ABC (in the same studio where they film *Live with Regis and Kathy Lee!*) and is for "contenders" only. The definition of "contenders" is sufficiently restrictive that Jules Polonetsky, who is polling at about 8 percent, will be excluded from the Public Advocate debate. Mercifully, that means the debate is canceled and not that Mark Green debates himself for an hour, though most agree he could do a job of it. Fortunately, though, it is not so restrictive that it excludes Ruth. She and Rudy face off against each other one-on-one for the first time in the campaign.

From the first question, it is clear the tone of the questions in this debate will be different from the first. "Citywide," the moderator says, "we found that voters are alarmed about our failing schools." They cut to a woman from the Bronx who says, "Schools are so overcrowded that kids are being taught in hallways, their books are outdated." Ruth, who has made education "a centerpiece" of her campaign, is asked why voters should believe that she can turn the schools around.

The debate is an epiphany of what could have been if only some people had paid attention to what we were saying. Political reporter Jay DeDapper asks Rudy about his $4-billion cut to the capital budget. Rudy says he merely continued a cut begun by David Dinkins, but DeDapper doesn't let him off the hook. He quotes the mayor saying in 1993 that "the decade of the '90s is a new era for our public schools." "What did that mean?" he asks Giuliani. And so it goes.

"Would you, Mr. Giuliani, want your son Andrew to be in a class of fifty-one students?" (Rudy prefers a class of fifty-one "in a great school" to "a classroom of three that wasn't doing the job.")

"New York City has the highest unemployment rate of major cities and the lowest job growth over the past four years. You take credit for the economy. Do you take blame for lagging job growth?" (Rudy willingly does.)

"What happens when the welfare laws require hundreds of thousands of people to enter the job market?"

"It's good news that crime is down dramatically, but some say at what cost?"

It is as if the past nine months have been a collective bad dream and that we have all awakened and left the *fucking hostile press environment* behind us. It is, if anything, unfair to the mayor. But he handles the adversity well.

Rudy is at his most affable. He does not become defensive, even when the adverse trend in the questioning becomes clear. For the first time in memory, he gives Ruth credit for an idea. "Although Ruth Messinger and I don't agree about much, we do agree about what should be done with principals." And he deems Ruth fit to be mayor, if not a desirable choice.

Giuliani says, "I don't agree with her ideas and I think she would take the city back to where it was four or five years ago, but I don't quarrel with her qualifications. She has had a distinguished public career." When Ruth immediately goes on the attack, Rudy interrupts and says, "That was a compliment, Ruth." Rudy gets big laughs (though Ruth points out that "it's only a compliment if you think backwards is a good direction"). Rudy brings the house down when he responds to Ruth's thoughts about what is wrong with being a bully by saying, "I think I'm a pretty nice guy."

Though everyone laughs, I think Rudy was serious.

The mayor grows testy on only a few occasions. When Ruth calls on him to sign the bill sitting on his desk to create an independent police monitor, Rudy snips that the "bill has absolutely nothing to do with police brutality" and that it remains an illegal bill. When confronted with a question about his inability to give others credit for shared successes, he is unable to give others credit for shared successes. "David Dinkins," he says, "supported Safe Streets, Safe Cities because he was forced to do so." Bill Bratton, he says, was not given the boot. "Bill Bratton moved on to another job." And he "takes offense" at the suggestion that he doesn't give police officers credit for the reduction in crime. But even those outbursts are controlled. His temper never shows.

Rudy even seems to hold the upper hand during the brief period where the candidates are allowed to ask questions of each other. Ruth again asks Rudy whether he will return the money from shady contributors, including Jay Fabrikant. Rudy says there could be no more convincing proof of his independence than the fact that Fabrikant gave him money and yet was turned down for a city contract. He, in turn, asks Ruth how she can responsibly pledge not to raise taxes when, as proven by the events of the past few days, it is impossible to predict how the economy will go.

I had wondered the same thing myself.

The average viewer might perceive that Ruth won the debate because of the tone of the questions, but Rudy minimized whatever damage there might have been by maintaining his cool and keeping the tone of the debate light. It is, in short, a masterful performance by Rudy Giuliani under difficult conditions.

• • •

One last go-around for old times' sake. In response to a yes or no question about whether the candidates supported single-officer patrol cars, Ruth said she did not and never had. In a press release titled "Messinger So Desperate for Support She Will Say Anything—No Matter How Untrue—to NYC Voters," the Giuliani campaign points out that a 1990 strategic policy statement from the borough president's office supported the idea. Minutes later, in a press release titled "Rudy So Out of Control He Will Say Anything—No Matter How Untrue—to NYC Voters," we point out that, in a fit of rage, Rudy threatened to force single-officer patrol cars upon the Police Benevolent Association during contract negotiations.

The campaign game is a lot like tic-tac-toe. It's easy to force a draw.

October 30

There's remarkably little coverage of the debate. David Seifman of the *Post* says the debate showed that Ruth "could have been a contender." Nagourney says Ruth "took the offensive whenever she could," but his front-page story is accompanied by a photo of Ruth and Dinkins bowing their heads that more than balances out whatever nice words he had. The panel of debate experts, including the debate coach at Regis High School and the author of "How to Read a Person Like a Book," again score the debate for the mayor. Messinger narrowly wins, 20.0–19.5 in sincerity, but Giuliani wins handily in body language, dramatic impact, and substance. Overall they score it 80.5–67.0 for the mayor.

• • •

There is persistent speculation in the press that Rudy is positioning himself for higher office. *New York* magazine is running a story this week about "Rudy's Oval Office Dream." The *Post* asks "How Does President Giuliani Grab You?" There is further speculation that Rudy may be picked as a vice-presidential candidate. ("I pity the guy who takes Rudy for vice-anything," Al Sharpton says. "He'll need a food taster.")

Ed Koch has reported that Giuliani has spoken to Republican leaders about a try for the Senate in 2000. On *Meet the Press,* host Tim Russert tells Koch that Rudy's people deny that the mayor has any thoughts of running against Moynihan.

"I'm telling you that I'm telling the truth and he is not," Koch says.

"The mayor is lying?" asks Russert.

"Well, in politics, you say 'dissembling.'"

• • •

With the outcome of the election a foregone conclusion, there is further speculation still about what will happen when term limits force Giuliani out of office in 2001. Fran Reiter is being mentioned as a possible Republican mayoral candidate. Freddie Ferrer, Alan Hevesi, Mark Green, Sal Albanese, Brian McLaughlin, and Floyd Flake are other likely candidates. Under one scenario, Mark Green could run for Senate in 2000 against Giuliani and by virtue of the rules of succession become mayor if Giuliani beat him and was unable to finish his term.

The only thing that is certain is that everyone will stay in the game. "Politics is like malaria," explains consultant Norman Adler. "Once you get it in your blood, it's very hard to get it out—even with medicine."

October 31

Even with a 27-point lead in the polls, Giuliani isn't letting up one bit. His campaign will be spending $900,000 on television ads during this last week of the campaign. We have $280,000. "It is more than saturation," Hank Sheinkopf says. "It is overkill, by any stretch of the imagination." But since the Giuliani campaign will have to return any unspent matching funds to the city, there is no incentive for him to hold back.

Giuliani invites neither Messinger nor Dinkins to the dedication of the Audubon Ballroom, where Malcolm X was assassinated thirty-two years ago, as a research center in Harlem. Both Ruth and Dinkins were instrumental in its creation.

And in an unabashed act of defiance, Rudy once again vetoes the revised bill for an independent police monitor. He says the City Council's revisions have not cured the bill's defects and that it still violates the city charter by impermissibly cutting into the mayor's powers.

• • •

Rudy may be going full steam ahead, but in our camp the tone has changed dramatically. Since his concession speech to me and Lee, Jim, true to his word, has changed his tone. He no longer yells and regularly spends time with the staff, now joking or asking them how he can help with the next step in their lives. Tonight, he is taking the research staff and a few others to dinner at one of the finest restaurants in the city.

Jim's tone with the press is less combative. His spin these days is that the race against Giuliani could not have been won by anyone on any strategy, an idea that the cynical among us believe is driven by a desire to protect his own professional reputation. He invites Joel Siegel of the *Daily News* into our headquarters to view twelve ads that we never got to air, which is striking given the near-paranoia with which he protected the secrecy of our ads and ad strategy—even within the campaign—during the earlier days of the race. "There were pieces to the argument we were going to make that we just never were able to get on the air," he tells Siegel. "We had plotted the race out. But without the money, you can't execute all of it."

Even our last ad seems to be more an attempt at having fun than making a serious argument. It shows a gradually inflating cartoon of Rudy Giuliani's face. "Is power going to Rudy Giuliani's head?" asks the announcer, with a whimsical lilt to his voice. "He inflated his own paycheck by $35,000, took hundreds of thousands in illegal contributions. Now Rudy's so high on himself, he's floating the idea of running for President." Giuliani's bloated head floats across the screen carrying a "Rudy for President" banner. Then it's punctured. "It's time to bring Rudy Giuliani back to Earth. On Election Day, send him a Messinger. Ruth Messinger."

Jim thinks the ad is funny and brilliant, but in my office we think it's a waste of money. Advertising the fact that Giuliani is thinking of running for president won't sway any voters. If we wanted to make an argument about the pay raise and illegal contributions, we should have just done so. This seems to trivialize the matter.

Nevertheless, Jim thinks it will "cut into Rudy's margins." Essentially the ad concedes that we are going to lose, but appeals to voters to keep it tight. The uncertain premise behind believing in the effectiveness of the ad is that some people will vote for Ruth not because they want to see her win, but because they don't want to see Rudy win by too much. I can't prove it, but my guess is that normal human beings don't engage in metathink.

• • •

There are parades in Brooklyn and Queens to celebrate Halloween. On New York 1, Andrew Kirtzman does a segment on political nightmares. He shows Ruth riding up to City Hall on her bicycle to the tune that accompanied the Wicked Witch of the West in *The Wizard of Oz*.

November 1

People ask me all the time how Ruth is holding up and I tell them, honestly, that she is doing quite well. She's maintaining a grueling schedule, even by her standards, and the press isn't getting any kinder, but she seems genuinely buoyant. I don't think she believes that it's likely she'll win, but clearly she still thinks she has a shot. All of these impossible circumstances will only be to her greater glory if she manages to pull the deal off.

The same people shake their heads in disbelief when I tell them all this, but what they don't realize is that Ruth is experiencing the campaign in a fundamentally different way than they are. I, like millions of other New Yorkers, get news about the race from newspapers and short segments on television. Our perception of where the race stands is shaped solely by polls and talking heads, all of whom have been foretelling doom for the Democrat for months.

Ruth experiences the campaign in the streets. She reads the polls and papers like anyone else, but she's also on the road ten hours a day and that shapes a subjective experience vastly different from the distilled reality of newspapers and television. The streets feel very different from any survey or poll. When I walked with Ruth to synagogue on Rosh Hashanah, at least a dozen people stopped her on the street to tell her they were with her. Her synagogue is on the Upper West Side, her stronghold, but, all the same, Ruth can't walk to the store without being accosted by someone telling her to kick the mayor's butt. In relative terms, these people represent a smaller percentage of the population than people with similar sentiments for the mayor, but in absolute terms they're a good-sized army. And few people, if any, have the nerve to come up to any candidate and say something negative. Ruth's experience, then, is unanimous and substantial personal support.

That support is sustaining Ruth through this last stretch of the campaign. It's this energy that allows Ruth or any candidate trailing in the polls to sincerely tell reporters that he or she is still confident about winning despite what the polls say. The truth is, better than 40 percent of the population would vote for anybody who carried the designation Democrat or Republican. But the adulation feels personal when you're on the receiving end. And because the comments are unanimously positive, candidates can convince themselves that the polls must be wrong.

During the primary, Sal Albanese cited his informal poll on a campaign stop on the Upper West Side as evidence that he was "getting votes by the process of elimination." Yesterday, Ruth told the press that she was "amazed at the number of people who came up to me and said you have my vote."

Neither she nor Sal was spinning. That is what the candidate experiences in a modern, television campaign. It is, I expect, what keeps politicians getting out of bed in the morning. And, in our case, it has nothing to do with reality.

• • •

Perhaps in response to our revelation of ads that never made it on the air, the Giuliani campaign shares their own stockpiled ads with Adam Nagourney. One particularly devastating ad opens with a quote from Ruth at the debate that the election "is not about the past." It then cuts to images of Ruth marching in Washington Heights for Kiko Garcia and hosting the party for John Hill. (Nagourney does not reveal how exactly they depict this.)

"In both quantity and quality of TV spots," Nagourney concludes, the race was "'no contest.'"

Mandy declines Nagourney's invitation to discuss the advertising. "I don't care to talk about it," she says.

November 2

There's lots of time to reflect these days, and I spend lots of it thinking again about political consultants.

At the very least, it seems to me, consultants should be getting much more attention as a group than they are. Consultants like Jim Andrews are a new species in its incipient stages. Political advisers are nothing new, of course. Franklin Roosevelt had the legendary James Farley. Harry Truman's

1948 campaign even had a research department to feed him negative factoids about Dewey. But Jim and his ilk are a different breed. The notion of a strategic political consultant whose sole responsibility is to *position* his or her client on major issues is a relatively recent phenomenon. And they are flourishing. My informal survey of the Campaigns and Elections directory indicates that although the number of political consulting businesses in the country has remained approximately the same over the past ten years, more than twice as many individuals and businesses provide strategic or general services (as opposed to a particular service like polling or speechwriting) than did a decade ago.

Someone should take notice of the fact that this thriving subspecies is changing the very nature of evolution. It used to be that politicians were, more or less, fixed commodities who prospered or suffered depending upon the attitudes of the day. Liberals were liberals. They won when people liked liberals and lost when they did not. Natural selection did its work. The fittest survived. Evolution was Darwinian.

Not so anymore. Thanks in large part to the efforts of strategic consultants, it is easier and, more important, more acceptable for political candidates to try to adapt themselves to the times. Depending on your view, a politician who tries to change his or her image to match the attitudes of the day may be paddling a rowboat through a gale, but the once unthinkable fact is that candidates now regularly succeed, for better or worse, in altering their images in fundamental ways. The nature of political survival is in flux. Evolution among politicians is becoming Lamarckian.

The magnitude of the impact of political consultants on this election seems laughable. Our opponent, a man who cut hundreds of millions of dollars from the public schools, has spent a plurality of his advertising dollars portraying himself as a friend of public education. My own candidate, a brilliant, lifelong advocate of social justice, has been massaged into a centrist who emphasized education and unemployment to the near exclusion of all other matters. When a man was savagely sodomized by city police officers, she said the mayor's handling of the situation was "right on target" and then went on to say how schools and jobs were the issues voters really cared about. We spent tens of thousands of dollars testing the idea of turning a small island in New York harbor into a casino, despite the fact that our candidate, just three years earlier, was described by one newspaper as casino gambling's "most vocal opponent in the city."

None of the examples proves anything by itself. Norman Siegel, president of the New York Civil Liberties Union and an outspoken critic of Giuliani, called the two days following the Louima assault "his best forty-eight hours as mayor of this city." In the aggregate, though, the examples show a great deal. A woman who had thought and done things for herself all her life grew, in the course of nine months, to instinctively look to others for answers to questions. In preparing for the final debate with Giuliani, we asked Ruth to name one thing she admired about the mayor. Unable to think of an answer, she turned to Jim, who mischievously exclaimed, "His hair!" When asked that exact question on an interview on CBS today, Ruth gave that exact answer.

My guess is that the old Ruth Messinger would have thought such an answer beneath her. This Ruth Messinger relies on her consultant's advice reflexively, depending on it even when it derived from a situation in which it was offered without a moment's thought or sincerity. Perhaps the modern political campaign demands a division of labor that frees the candidate from thinking through every single issue. When frustrated by Jim's pattern of criticizing what he perceives to be mistakes and his reluctance to affirm what course of action he believes we should follow, Ruth sometimes says, "I pay him to think about these things."

Our frustration with the press's complacency and unwillingness to inject itself into the arbitration of truth is misplaced in many respects. There are days when the political press seems to be operating in the world of metatruth, reporting not what is really true, but what campaigns say is true. In some sense, this is modern politics. Strategic consultants reside permanently in the world of metatruth. Our campaign never proposed the casino idea, but Ruth's prior inconsistent statements were never a serious concern for Jim. That's because strategic consultants are not concerned with what is true, but rather with what can be claimed to be true. They craft an image of a person that is distinct from the person's true self. It hardly seems fair to blame the press for buying into their worldview.

Time will tell what the lasting impact of the emergence of political strategists as a self-conscious profession will be, but there is every reason to think it will be quite profound. Who would ever have believed that the Bill Clinton many of us voted for in 1992 would be the same man to sign a welfare bill sending millions of Americans into poverty? There can be no question about the influence of consultants there. "Bill Clinton will sign a welfare bill," Robert Reich recalls Dick Morris saying in *Locked in the Cabinet*. When Reich and many of Clinton's advisers protested that the bill did not represent Clinton's true beliefs, Morris replied, "Bill Clinton can be anything he wants to be."

Morris is probably right. And whether it's cause or effect, an increasing share of the press seems to believe he is. But what is remarkable is that the press increasingly believes that these sorts of transformations are not only possible, but to be expected. It reports as if the strategizing is all there is to politics. When Ruth proposed during the campaign to open some city services to competition, the coverage focused almost exclusively on the strategic implications of the idea. Several papers asked consultants not associated with the campaign to comment on the tactical merit of the idea. Not one reporter investigated whether the idea itself was sound.

Surely strategic consultants are not to blame for the pervasive distrust of politicians in America, but the notion of politics they promulgate must at least be considered among possible contributing factors. At least when people voted for Adlai Stevenson or George McGovern, they knew (ideologically, at least) what they were getting. These days, there is every reason to believe that what politicians say today will be only slightly predictive of what they will say or do tomorrow. If strategic consultants have their way, politicians will become the ultimate anti-Burkians, instantly molding their views to match the mood of the day.

Perhaps someday the profession will subsume itself. A shrewd consultant might test this idea in a poll: "How would you feel if you learned that candidate Jones does not rely on polls in her decisionmaking?" I bet it would be pretty popular.

Trouble is, no one would believe it.

• • •

The decline in importance of the research department in these final days of the campaign is graphically illustrated at today's fund-raiser with Bill Clinton. My deputy and I are guarding a staircase. It is not even a very important staircase. People who ascend it will merely join another line at the top, where they will wait for an hour or so to be let into the main reception area. The people in real power on the campaign are guarding the staircase that leads people directly into the high-dollar room, where people will meet Clinton (and Ruth!) face to face.

My deputy and I are in a difficult situation because we don't really have a convincing rationale for keeping people at the foot of the stairs. We're told that the real reason is because it would be a fire hazard to let all of the people wait on the second floor. But everyone can see to the top of the stairs, and though it is quite crowded up there, it hardly seems as if another few dozen people will make any difference.

"Please stay calm," we say. "Everyone will get in eventually."

But the fact is they don't, and we both feel profoundly guilty later on. In order to make the reception appear crowded, the field staff has walled off half the room. As a result, many people, including our charges, don't get in at all. Those who do are crowded in like lemmings.

Clinton handles the group like a master. "There are lots of times," he says, "when it would have been comfortable for somebody who was the borough president of Manhattan to be somewhere else. But through the tough times when I was going through my own particular New York Marathon in 1992, she stuck by me and I'm standing with her tonight."

When a pinched AIDS activist tries to shout down Clinton, the president addresses him directly. "If you want to talk to me," he says, "go out there. But don't mess with the mayor's race; she doesn't deserve this." Besides, he says, "who do you think is more likely to care about the AIDS issue as mayor of New York?"

Riddled by guilt and unable to breathe, I leave after just a few minutes, but I'm pleased and amused by what I saw during a brief visit to the muckety-muck fund-raiser, the sort of thing that no one in the press will ever catch, but that makes politics seem real. Alan Hevesi, seeing Sharpton in person for perhaps the first time since the primary, walks over to the Reverend and offers him his hand.

Sharpton looks at Hevesi for a moment and turns away.

November 3

Bob Herbert asks whether "it is possible for New Yorkers to be less interested in a mayoral race." "Rain and Apathy Dog Mayoral Race As It Winds Down," says Adam Nagourney. But Ruth Messinger and Rudy Giuliani are campaigning to the end.

Rudy is spending the last days of the campaign on a forty-eight-hour bus tour of the city. "It's a mystical city between 2:00 and 6:00 A.M.," he explains.

What is the purpose of the campaign?

"I really do want to get into every neighborhood that I can, go to every part of the city and ask for people to vote for me," he tells the *Post*. "We're going to call it the 'Capital of the World Express,' and anyone who wants to ride with me can get on the bus."

To the *News*, he says, "We're going to reach out all over the city—to people of different races, different religions, different ethnic backgrounds, people who speak different languages." It will be good, he says, not only for the election, but for "healing for the community."

He tells Marcia Kramer of CBS:

> We still have people that are left out and we still have people that feel they aren't part of it. It's my job to reach them. That's why I'm really doing this forty-eight-hour tour. I want to go to the next term just reaching out to every neighborhood in the city and basically say that there's no neighborhood that we can't go to, no neighborhood that really shouldn't be part of this renaissance that New York City is going through.

"There are still people that feel left out," he explains to Adam Nagourney. "There are still people that feel that they are not included. And I want to say to them that I am going to dedicate the next four years . . . to try to make everyone feel that they are part of the success and possibilities of success in the city."

"I'm going to go everywhere," he exclaims today. "I want everyone in the city to feel a part of this wonderful feeling of success. It doesn't touch everyone, so we're going to try to reach out to everyone."

Personally, I think the tour is an excuse for him to eat.

"Very good, very lean," he says at Pastrami King in Queens, where he dines on corned beef and Dr. Brown's Cel-Ray. (Cel-Ray is a celery-flavored soda. Seriously.) "Delicious," he says of a free slice of VIPizza. He's eating constantly. The bus stops at Sylvia's Lindenwood Deli in East New York, visits Nathan's Famous in Coney Island for frankfurters, Lundy's restaurant in Sheepshead Bay for chowder and powdery rolls, Ferrara's near Times Square for cannoli, Kenny Rogers chicken, and the Blue Bay Diner in Staten Island. At 2:30 in the morning, they are at the Neptune Diner in Queens.

Even Rudy Giuliani cannot maintain this pace without showing signs of strain. "Are your feet okay?" he asks a woman soaking her nails at Plaza Nails. In the *Daily News* is a horrifying picture of a bleary-eyed Giuliani, in his Yankee hat and Yankee jacket, forcing a hug upon a bespectacled elderly woman who is shrinking back in revulsion. At an early morning assembly of sanitation workers, Giuliani sounds as if the spin has been ingrained into his very soul. "Even our sanitation trucks don't have graffiti!" he exclaims. "Four or five years ago, our sanitation trucks had graffiti!"

On the final evening the mayor and his staff are downright loopy. Depending on the ethnicity through which the bus is traveling, the loudspeakers play "The Macarena" or the theme from *Rocky.* In the wee hours of Election Eve, it is reported that the city's deputy mayors have their arms around each other's shoulders and are swaying to the music. Press secretary Sunny Mindel takes the microphone and exclaims, "For a city that never sleeps, we need a mayor that never sleeps."

"God bless you!" blares Randy Mastro.

Even the indefatigable Cristyne Lategano seems to have had too much. "Vote for Rudy on Tuesday," she says to no one in particular. "Maybe he can get some rest."

• • •

To the extent there is rational discourse going on in the Giuliani camp, it is to spin expectations about results. They are talking in terms of getting 60 percent of the vote. "Months back, I was saying Giuliani would win by 20 points. As it turned out, my prediction probably was way too conservative," says Guy Molinari. The only question remaining is whether this prediction is the product of irrational exuberance or reasoned evaluation.

• • •

Ruth is on her own round-the-clock tour of the city. Convincing myself that I should experience every aspect of campaigning at least once, I drag myself out of bed at 3:00 in the morning to meet Ruth at the United Parcel Service warehouse near my apartment, where she is to greet workers on the shift change.

As in the Rudy camp, Ruth and her entourage are giddy. Ruth proudly exclaims that she will get one hour of sleep, then return to the streets to vote and greet voters at a subway station.

As it turns out the UPS shift change doesn't happen until 4:00. I decide to pack it in. I can't imagine that anyone who goes to work at 4:00 in the morning is likely to waste precious sleep time voting in a stupid mayoral election. I certainly wouldn't.

November 4

Pea-size hail pelts the city, but I'll refrain from availing myself of the obvious metaphors, one way or the other. For me, Election Day is a reminder that all the stuff I've written about is dressing. Politics is still an intensely personal enterprise.

• • •

My minute in the voting booth is a revelation.

I've always bought into the idea of voting as an expression of civic virtue. During my nine years as a student and law clerk, I faithfully cast absentee ballots. When I returned home, I had my parents take a picture of me casting my first ballot in a real voting booth. But I never spent much time worrying about whom to vote for or thinking about why I made the decisions I did. I cast some votes more proudly than others—I liked voting for Clinton more the first time than the second, but I never even came close to voting for a Republican. Voting had always been a mechanical process. I was a Democrat. I voted for Democrats.

It felt different today. I voted for my first Republican, with no better reason than one might have for favoring one student-council candidate over another. Alan Hevesi had behaved dishonorably to Ruth and so his opponent, Anne Marie McEvoy, about whom I knew absolutely nothing, got my ballot. Mark Green had been nice to Ruth, so I voted for him.

It occurred to me as I voted for Ruth that, had I not worked on the campaign, I might have voted for Rudy Giuliani. Even after nine months on the campaign, my sense of Rudy Giuliani and Ruth Messinger was much the same as it had been back in January. Ruth Messinger was a smart, principled person. Rudy Giuliani was an intolerant man, but an effective administrator. Were they running for Senate against each other and I had not worked on the campaign, I'm sure that I would have voted for Ruth unhesitatingly. But in a mayoral race, I imagine that, though I would ultimately have voted for her, I would have given it a good amount of thought. Of course, at the same time, I would have voted for Alan Hevesi without a moment's deliberation.

But Rudy Giuliani and Ruth Messinger were no longer amalgams of policy positions; they were real human beings, whose strengths and flaws I knew too well. Rudy Giuliani got things done, but he cared not one whit for who he sacrificed along the way. At times, Rudy Giuliani acted on conviction when it was politically inexpedient for him to do so; at others he acted out of petty jealousy when it would have been politically expedient for him to act out of conviction. Ruth Messinger was an inclusive person without the slightest hint of prejudice, who was also willing to tolerate rampant sexism within her own campaign. Ruth Messinger was a smart, principled person who paid a man a quarter of a million dollars to think for her and at times seemed too willing to sacrifice principles for political gain.

Perhaps it is the case that no human being could withstand the degree of scrutiny to which I subjected Ruth Messinger and Rudy Giuliani and emerge intact. No man or woman is built to be in the public eye twenty-four hours a day, seven days a week. I had much more information than the average voter, but as I cast my ballot I realized that my experience was different only in degree from the ordinary citizen. The decision to vote, whether shaped by scientifically constructed television ads or personal knowledge, always comes down to the most basic emotion. I voted for Ruth Messinger simply because I liked her better.

• • •

Politics remains personal for Donna Hanover, who voted this afternoon, but wouldn't say for whom. She doesn't plan on being at Rudy's party tonight either.

"My wife makes her own decisions, as she has a right to do," the mayor says.

• • •

Our "victory party" is at the Hyatt. Our campaign manager is wearing a wireless headset and microphone that one might expect to belong to the producer of *Monday Night Football.* He is splitting his time tonight between our campaign and his mentor, Mark Green, who is having his own party next door. Green is likely to win by 70 points. We're likely to lose by 20. He is running around as if he has a great deal to do, but I can't imagine what it is.

Then, in an instant, it's all clear. With 1 percent of election districts reporting, Ruth is leading Giuliani 55–45. He must have known all along. The headset will be coming in very handy, indeed.

• • •

At 10:00 Ruth calls Rudy Giuliani to concede the race.

He asks her how she feels.

"Tired," she says, but not too tired to remind the mayor that she really believes that the city's schools need to be improved. The mayor agrees.

At 10:19, the race is over.

"Somewhere out there, a little girl is watching this," Ruth says. "And this message is for her: I didn't become mayor tonight, young lady, but you will. As sure as I'm standing here, you will. If just by reaching for it, just by giving it all I had I showed you that it could be done, I have succeeded."

After months of practice, she cannot help but stay on message (especially since Jim wrote the speech). "Tonight we lost a battle, but the war goes on. Our schools still don't work, still don't educate our kids—and they're still worth fighting for. Too many New Yorkers are still out of a job—and they're still worth fighting for."

• • •

Giuliani's victory speech is a giddy blur of self-congratulation and babble. He is so hoarse, he can barely be heard over the *Rocky* theme song, "Gonna Fly Now," playing in the background. He croaks:

> Thank you, I love you. Thank you New York, for reelecting me to a job I love so much. I give you my personal commitment we will be even more successful in the next four years as we have been in the last four. We did it. We turned

> this city around. Boy, did we turn this city around. Cynics made fun of us. But look where we are today. We molded together—together we molded a vision—we worked hard, very hard, to improve the quality of life for our great city.

"No more cocaine, no more heroin, no more marijuana!" he cries out to the crowd, which includes Hugh Carey, Floyd Flake, and sex therapist Ruth Westheimer.

And he vows to make the next four years more inclusive.

• • •

Though the campaign is over, the spinning continues. Giuliani, it appears, will fall short of his predictions of 60 percent, something Lee takes delight in pointing out. "I would expect the kind of margin they wanted isn't going to project Mayor Giuliani to the Senate or the White House, which is what they were hoping."

Randy Mastro will have none of it. "A landslide is a landslide is a landslide," he says.

The third "landslide" should clear up any ambiguity there.

• • •

As our victory party winds down, I am overwhelmed by weariness and relief. No one can yell at me anymore. No more seventeen-hour days. More time with my parents and girlfriend, who have patiently stuck it out for the past nine months.

Before we go, my father greets Sal Albanese. Though I had not realized it, my father, who is a high-school principal, worked with Albanese's sister when he was math chairman at Midwood High School in Brooklyn.

"Your father is a great principal," Albanese says, shaking my hand.

"He's a great father," I respond and think to myself that Sal could do it in 2001 and that maybe, just maybe, I'd be up for another ride. One little handshake and comment and Sal Albanese won a friend for life.

In the end, all politics is personal.

November 5

The tally of the 1997 New York City mayoral election shows that Rudy Giuliani beat Ruth Messinger 757,564 to 540,075 votes, or 57 to 41 percent. Absentee and affidavit ballots will not be counted for a week, but the Commissioner of Elections, Daniel DeFrancesco, does not think that they will alter the outcome of the election materially. Independence party candidate Sal Albanese collected 14,732 votes, approximately 1 percent of all votes cast. Turnout was 38 percent, the lowest in recent memory.

According to exit polling, Mayor Giuliani won among both genders. He carried a narrow 50–49 victory among women and was the overwhelming choice of men 58–39. He lost only among blacks, 79 percent of whom voted for Ruth Messinger versus 20 percent for the mayor. Whites backed Giuliani 76–21 percent.

The sluice gates, the sluice gates. Arrgh. Arrgh.

Among the 14 percent of voters who felt public schools mattered most, 80 percent voted for Messinger versus 18 percent for Giuliani. Among the 25 percent who thought crime and drugs were most important, 82 percent voted for Rudy versus 18 percent for Ruth. The small percentage of people who thought the economy mattered most backed Ruth timidly (53–42); the even smaller group that thought police brutality mattered most backed Ruth overwhelmingly (85–13).

Rudy Giuliani carried every borough except the Bronx.

One can already hear them talking about the need for an earlier and more aggressive field effort in 2001.

• • •

A *Times* editorial proclaims that "Mayor Rudolph Giuliani's reelection is a uniquely personal achievement. As a politician, he draws his legitimacy not from his party, but from his own history and a character that, in its frequently irritating intensity, mimics that of the city he governs. Ruth, they say, suffered from a 'mood-flattening stump style.'"

Gail Collins, also of the *Times*, says the 1997 elections delivered a resounding message: "Don't touch anything! You might break it!"

The *Daily Challenge* blames the *Times* for Messinger's defeat:

> Although the *Times* has traditionally been identified with liberalism and with candidates of the Democratic Party . . . this institution of neo-liberalism has revealed—or unveiled—its true role as a deceptive voice of neoconservatism. Our observations caused us to accurately predict that the *Times* was leaning towards an endorsement of Giuliani over Messinger when within the span of several months they published two front-page stories on Ruth Messinger which skillfully made mention of the fact that the outgoing Manhattan Borough President has a daughter Miriam, who happens not only to be a lesbian, but has a Black woman as her lover. And, to wit, they have a bi-racial child.

The *Amsterdam News* blames the press as a whole. Wilbert Tatum argues:

> Giuliani's victory is Pyrrhic and light years from a landslide. The anti-woman strategy worked with every group in this city with the exception of Blacks and Hispanics. Historians will ask one day: Why is that? Why was the press so down on her? There will first of all be some wiggleword answer like "We treated her just like we would a man." But when the record clearly bears out that this answer is a bald-faced lie, the crumbling Fourth Estate in this city will have no answer except pure and unadulterated hatred for and jealousy of strong females no matter where they dwell in our political horizon.

Lee essentially agrees with the black newspapers. "For an election to take place, and for an election to be competitive," he argues, "news organizations have to give candidates an opportunity to debate. You can argue that part of the problem for us is we didn't get traction. In order for us to get traction, we had to at least get on the racetrack."

Ellis Henican of *Newsday* says the campaign was over from "the day of the bicycle stunt."

Andrea Peyser says "Ruth Messinger in the end can't blame her trouncing on anyone except herself. When ideas failed, when her party turned its collective back, she transformed into the one thing she claimed to hate most: a bully."

Adam Nagourney says the election shows that "New York mayoral politics is moving away from ideology altogether. Today, it is performance and pragmatism, more than ideas and party affiliation, that matters most in mayoral elections."

State Democratic party chairman Judith Hope agrees. She says Rudy Giuliani and Bill Clinton are "both part of a new generation of politicians who are seen as problem-solvers first and partisan operatives second."

"It's the breakdown of the old party lines," summarizes Republican state senator Roy Goodman. "Performance counts. It's potentially a shift of tectonic consequences."

Washington Post columnist E. J. Dionne says that Giuliani's reelection was not a break with past, but rather represented continuity. "Voters, he says, "are in a back-to-basics mood."

Fred Siegel says "ideological liberalism is on the wane, but operational liberalism—the politics of big government—did well in this election."

Jim Andrews says Giuliani, "in effect, co-opted liberalism."

Lenora Fulani heralds the election as a sign of the strength of the rising Independence party. "Not since the creating of the Republican Party in the 19th century have we had a national third party." Though her candidate, Abe Hirschfeld, lost to Virginia Fields in the borough president's race, she is undeterredly buoyant. "What Abe has done here is consistent with the growing excitement of such a possibility." Perhaps the street issue will catch on in 2001.

As for campaign strategy, some blame our lack of field support. One member of our staff cited our first commercial as an example. "Look at the whole kids-learning-next-to-urinals thing. You know how many parent groups speak out about that in their day-to-day meetings? But you didn't have these people coming forward and saying that what Ruth Messinger was saying is right on."

Jim offered the view that Giuliani was unbeatable. "In hindsight," he told the *Observer,* "I don't know that Ruth could have done much differently. In this environment, it is very hard for any issue to gain traction, even though the issues are real."

"I'm not saying we couldn't have done better at this or better at that," he told Adam Nagourney. "I'm saying, fundamentally, it would not have made much difference. People just weren't listening. I don't think if you had substituted one candidate for another, it would have made all that much difference." Nagourney credited Jim's answer, though he noted that "there was, to be sure a measure of career preservation on the part of Messinger advisers who blamed their loss on forces beyond their control."

Others blamed Jim. "I didn't think that Andrews knew the key players in town and he felt that everyone was kind of in on the hustle," says Bill Lynch, David Dinkins's former deputy mayor who Jim had implied was on the hustle. "It's difficult enough to beat an incumbent mayor who's got the perception of things going well, crime is down, the economy is churning. The way you do it in this town is through coalition politics."

Wayne Barrett drew a different lesson. Back in September, he noted that of the $3.3 million we spent on the primary, only $631,000 went to media buys. We spent $1 million on headquarters and staff, $500,000 on consultants, $250,000 on polling and rent, and $2,200 a month for Jim's apartment and dry cleaning and got less than 20 percent of our total budget on the air. That figure is even more distressing when you consider, as the *Observer* notes, that Mandy Grunwald got a fixed fee based upon a projected amount of air time that we never met. Ultimately, her fee was 20 percent of air time actually purchased, an astonishing figure even by industry standards. That's not to blame Mandy. Had we exceeded our projections and put on more air time, she would have accepted a lower effective percentage. Still, it's a glaring indication of our inefficiency.

• • •

If there's a lesson to be learned from the insights of the Wednesday morning quarterbacks, it is that it is not easy to draw meaningful lessons from campaigns. Scientists derive theories from experiments they repeat hundreds of times, controlling as many variables as possible to focus on the matter with which they are concerned. Elections have a million variables and, as the diversity and contradictions among the opinions of the pundits show, reasonable people can draw different conclusions from the available evidence. A single election does not lend itself to scientific analysis.

A few things seem safe to say. One is that this would have been a difficult race for anyone to win. The decision to run is perhaps more important than any individual decision a candidate makes during a race. Ruth's decision to run was a mistake. There were others. We did a poor job at building coalitions. Our advance work was not what it should have been. Putting Ruth on a bicycle was an error. But all of those things would have mattered not one whit, I think, if we had put $2 million on television before August.

Fundamentally, I think, the strategy of the campaign was sound. As an ethical issue, there is good reason to take pause at Jim's decision—and Ruth's willingness—to move to the center and to emphasize television over field. But as a strategic matter, it is hard to question. Ruth could not have won as an old-style liberal. Perhaps she could also not win as a new-style moderate, but the polling showed that the former strategy would have led to certain defeat. We may not have done the best job of executing the strategy, but it was the right course under the circumstances. Out of self-interest or conviction, some people will use the example of our campaign to argue that field-driven campaigns are more effective or somehow necessary in New York. But who could possibly say how we would have done if we had spent a half million dollars on field instead of television. Perhaps better. Likely worse.

What is going on now is a human need to affix blame when things go wrong. Ruth lost, so she must have done things wrong. Perhaps she did, but the smart people will realize that, although there are lessons to be drawn from groups of campaigns, any one campaign can teach only so much. Ruth Messinger took on a secure incumbent and lost. What great lesson could possibly be learned from that?

November 18

I'm mad as I can be.

Since the election, like many people on the campaign, I've taken a vow of abstinence. No news whatsoever about mayoral politics. No Adam Nagourney articles. No New York 1, lest I discover that I actually have some interest in the programming. Not so much as a glimpse at the *Observer*. I have returned to reading newspapers the way I like to—back to front, spending a lot more time on the back than the front.

Today, I was tricked. Smack dab in the middle of a funny op-ed by Frank Rich in the *New York Times* about a celebrity tribute to the First Amendment is a little jab at the campaign. "The show," Rich writes, " felt like the Ruth Messinger campaign—a smug exercise in political nostalgia."

I'm only a bit mad about the fact that Rich has a negative view of the campaign—hardly a day goes by that a friend doesn't tell me what a bad campaign we ran. But I'm irate that Rich has dragged me back into the campaign. A nasty letter to the editor seems appropriate. Frank Rich has a lot of nerve drawing metaphors to real life events. A lot of nerve.

Still, what he writes is interesting. There are two separate claims in there really: that the campaign was smug and that the campaign relied exclusively on dated ideas, presumably, Rich would say, from the liberal agenda of the past. I won't dwell long on the strangeness of a year of campaigning being reduced to two words. I do wonder, though, how it can be that neither of the two words to which it was reduced has anything to do with reality.

The campaign certainly was not ever smug. There wasn't a day in nine months in the campaign when many, if any of us, thought we would win. Some days were less gloomy than others; some were almost optimistic, but internally we all always regarded our campaign as a long shot. And Ruth never said anything to the contrary.

And the campaign wasn't nostalgic or liberal. More than 80 percent of the campaign's energy went into promoting two main ideas: school reform and creating jobs. Ruth pledged not to raise taxes if elected. Ruth outlined a plan to privatize some city services and try to get more out of civil-service workers. When Ruth talked about crime, she praised Rudy's performance and called for more police on the streets.

One might reasonably ask whether the pledge not to raise taxes was responsible. One might reasonably ask whether it made sense for a woman who had fought for unions all her life to point to them as a way to save the city money. One might say that other issues should have been at the top of the agenda or that we should have said different things in different cases. But nothing the campaign ever said could justify the conclusion that Ruth's candidacy was an exercise in political nostalgia. As someone who watched Ruth Messinger's every move and heard at least secondhand virtually everything she said for nearly a year, the question I would ask is whether it was ethical, or even made sense, for a woman who had risen through city politics as a brilliant liberal to run as something other than what she had been. I don't know what the answer is to the question (I think it probably made fine sense) and I don't ascribe responsibility for the transformation, but I feel quite strongly that it is the right question to ask.

But, there it is: "a smug exercise in political nostalgia." That will be our footnote in history. Frank Rich probably gets too much of his news from newspapers and doesn't watch enough television to represent the average New Yorker, but it's proof that we lost the game. The game is something different from right and wrong. The game is deciding what you want to be and convincing people that is what you are. We wanted people to see Ruth as a compassionate, evenhanded, sensible moderate who cared about working people. Rudy wanted people to see her as a big-government, tax-and-spend liberal. People saw her as a tax-and-spend liberal. That's the game. We lost.

Politics doesn't score points for right and wrong.

Afterword

FOR THE NINE MONTHS I worked on the Messinger campaign, I answered one question more than any another: "Why?" Why was Ruth running against an unbeatable incumbent? Why was I working for Ruth? Given that I was working for Ruth, why wasn't I doing a better job? There were answers to all of these questions, which you know from having suffered through my account of the experience, but people rarely were interested in the details. Most would just shake their heads in disbelief that anyone would volunteer to be a deckhand on a ship everyone knew to be doomed to sink in icy waters.

When I set out to write this book, I answered a similar set of questions. Why was I writing a book about an unsuccessful campaign? Why would I think anyone would be interested in publishing such a book? It wasn't about the Messinger campaign, I would explain. It was a book about campaigns that was incidentally about the 1997 mayoral campaign. But people rarely were interested in details. For several months I placed my hope of publishing the book in a small academic press that had reviewed the draft manuscript favorably. The director of the house said they would publish the book, but changed her mind after her marketing director and a savvy friend from the Upper West Side—neither of whom had read the book—told her they did not think a book about the Messinger campaign would sell. It was only incidentally about the campaign, I explained again. But she wasn't interested in the details.

It took longer to write this book and find a publisher than it did to live the experience of working on the campaign. When both tasks were done, I allowed myself the indulgence of calling three people I had found to be especially compelling characters during the campaign and asking their reaction to some of the issues I raise here. The last of the three was Fran Reiter, who is currently head of the New York City Convention and Visitors Bureau. I wrote in November and explained the book and its spirit and that I was willing to observe any ground rules for our talk with which she felt comfortable.

A few weeks later, her assistant, who had worked on the Giuliani campaign, called me at the office. "Ms. Reiter cannot participate in any project that is critical of the mayor," he explained, "but she is very interested in one thing."

"What's that?" I asked.

"How were you able to publish a book about the Messinger campaign?"

"It isn't a book about the Messinger campaign," I said. "It's a book about campaigns that is incidentally about the 1997 mayoral campaign."

But he wasn't interested in the details.

• • •

Although Ms. Reiter was not accommodating, the other two people on my wish list were.

Adam Nagourney was generous with his time, exceedingly so, considering the fact that, as I explained to him, some of the book was critical of his work. A year had passed since Nagourney covered the mayoral campaign and, though he had covered the Schumer-D'Amato Senate race in the interval, Nagourney had some interesting insights.

He quite candidly said that he thought ours was "a really, really poor campaign" and that Ruth was up against tremendous odds running against Giuliani, who, he said, "managed to make the trains run on time." Nagourney clarified that he meant nothing by this other than to say that Giuliani was effective at delivering services to the middle class and that people gave him great credit for reducing crime in the city. In light of Giuliani's popularity, Nagourney wondered whether Ruth's decision to "move away from liberalism" made sense. Drawing attention to the homeless and other groups being left behind in the Giuliani reformation seemed to him to be strong issues that we had not tapped into nearly enough.

Our bathroom ad was "inept" in Nagourney's mind. Conditions in city schools were bad enough that there was "no reason to hype it up." The urinal "became a distraction." In Nagourney's opinion, it would have been better to "show kids in a really crowded room." That said, Nagourney would have covered the story from a straight news angle had it not been for Chancellor Crew's involvement in the debate. Nagourney was "stunned that a chancellor was so political and that he used such strong language." It was a compelling news story for which he made no apologies. Our mistake was to allow Crew an angle into the story by "staging a scene that could not be backed up with facts."

Nagourney, however, did regret his comment on television that we had "stumbled into the issue." Nagourney explained that, though he stands behind everything he writes, he is not infallible in impromptu television discussions. Nagourney seemed genuinely shocked when I told him how carefully we listened to everything he said and how much time we spent speculating about his motivations and state of mind. He recalled one conversation with Ruth that made him realize he had to be careful about what he said on a television show that hardly anyone was watching.

With respect to my central criticism that Nagourney sometimes passed off news analysis or opinion as fact, Nagourney conceded that he "pushes the envelope on that." "Good political reporting has a point of view," Nagourney said. And the *Times* "encourages you to offer a point of view if they trust you." At the same time, he conceded that in some cases, as when he called Sal Albanese an "unaccomplished campaigner," he was "pushing it as far as you can get away with." The difficult trick, he said, was to strike a balance between straight news reporting and offering greater insight, which he feels under pressure to do, since the "newspaper hires you to be an expert on the race."

I drew Nagourney's attention to some parallels between his coverage of Ruth Messinger and of Geraldine Ferraro in her 1998 bid for the Democratic nomination to challenge Al D'Amato. In a July article about the Senate campaign, Nagourney cited "many Democrats" as saying that Ferraro's "lagging finances" were a concern and that, unlike Charles Schumer and Mark Green, the other Democrats in the race, Ferraro had failed "to present any kind of unifying theme for her candidacy." In September he described her campaign as "listless." The fund-raising comment particularly irked the Ferraro camp, since Ferraro had as much money in the bank as Mark Green and was raising at nearly the same rate as Schumer, though she had started far behind him. As always, the spin was a question of perspective. Why was Ferraro's spin less valid than any other? Nagourney quite reasonably answered that the expectations had been set by Ferraro herself, who had declared that she would need $5 million for an effective Senate campaign.

Nagourney vehemently and convincingly denied that he has any bias against women candidates. He noted that the 1996 Dole campaign, which he covered, regularly complained about his coverage, and Dole, he said, was not a woman. We shared a laugh at the peculiarity of relying upon additional criticism as proof of his lack of prejudice, but this was only one piece of abundant evidence that the premise is flawed. Adam Nagourney was hardly the only person to find fault with the campaigns of Geraldine Ferraro and Ruth Messinger.

In short, Nagourney said that his overriding interest was in writing the best possible news story. He was conscious of not "turning people off voting" and, with ample justification, noted that he always reported campaign policy proposals with a minimum of editorializing. He made a conscious decision not to write about the Robert Kiley mishap during Ruth's budget speech, because he "did not want to distract" from a serious story.

The *Times* reporter had two regrets that he could recall. The "Mission Impossible" reference during the Caribbean Day Parade was unfair in his mind in retrospect, because it was not the result of any act of our campaign. Had we played the song, it would have been fair game, but we had not, and Nagourney regretted it the morning the story ran. When I reminded Nagourney of his story at the end of the campaign about disloyalty among Democrats, he also regretted allowing Jim to retract his comment about Alan Hevesi, which we both agreed would have made for a great story.

• • •

There were no surprises in my two hours with Sal Albanese. What you see is what you get, which is what makes Albanese so compelling. He is soft-spoken and honest, with appealing edges that have not yet been dulled by the homogenizing process of modern television politics. He seemed genuinely shocked by the size of our campaign and by the amount of time Ruth spent raising money. In comparison to Ruth's thirty-hour-a-week average of fund-raising time, Albanese estimated that he spent between one and two hours a week raising money. And although he knew of the Jim Andrewses of the world and thought there was good sense in much of what I told him of Jim's counsel to Ruth, he questioned the wisdom of relying heavily on political consultants.

Albanese "made a conscious decision not to poll early on." He defined his candidacy by his "core values." When we discussed whether it had made sense for him to have defined his candidacy by campaign-finance reform, a noble issue that does not poll well, Albanese said that if he ran again (which he plans to do), he would consider using polls to frame issues better, but still expressed a healthy skepticism of the "temptation of polling," which can be used to define a candidate's beliefs.

To Albanese, Ruth Messinger "compromised her core beliefs" during the campaign, a fact that was brought home to Sal by Messinger's speech on the budget and labor reforms. That speech, he said, was the result of "Ruth basically listening to people like Jim Andrews saying you have to be more moderate and was not something she instinctively believed in."

"It's not bad for people to evolve," Albanese said, "but it's wrong when the first question becomes what do I need to do to get elected. When the desire to get elected becomes the preeminent drive, it's tough to govern. You've got stand for something that you cannot abandon."

Albanese said that he never gave serious thought to going negative on Ruth. "People didn't even know who Sal Albanese was," he said, "and besides, Giuliani was the common enemy. I wasn't going to help Giuliani by spending money against Ruth." The one negative attack that Albanese launched against Messinger was based on a misunderstanding, as it turns out. When the Albanese campaign criticized Messinger for saying she had been a teacher, he thought that Ruth had been referring to her work as a lecturer at Hunter College. He had not realized that Ruth had taught in a community school. Albanese had not had the money to research his opponents and agreed that better research would have been a useful resource.

As it turns out, ours was not the only campaign with grievances against the press. For months, Sal said, he was "ignored." "We would hold press conferences, issue position papers and they would never be picked up in the press." Albanese felt that all of the papers, with the exception of *Newsday*, wanted Ruth to win the primary and then go on to be shellacked by Giuliani in the general election. They all knew that Albanese would be a stronger candidate. Two stories especially outraged Albanese. One was the *News* editorial, criticizing Albanese's position on workfare. Albanese wrote a rebuttal pointing out the factual inaccuracies in the piece, but the *News* would not print it.

The second was an article by Clifford Levy of the *Times* implying that there may have been something untoward in the bridge loan Albanese took out prior to receiving his matching funds. When Albanese in fact received the funds a few days later, he called Levy demanding a follow-up story. None was written. "There was an agenda at the *New York Times* to do everything in its power to minimize my candidacy." Moreover, Albanese felt that—especially in the budget speech—Ruth was "trying to convince the papers—which are anti-union—that she was not going to raise important labor issues." At the same time, Albanese—who refreshingly takes himself less than entirely seriously—recognized that he had "a case of candidatitis" and that there was probably no grand conspiracy against him. "I recognize," he said, "that raising money is a characteristic of political viability."

For the road, I asked Sal what he thought of our bathroom ad.

"I didn't think it was an effective ad," he said, "and was glad when Ruth put it up. I thought the press fairly panned it. It was not something that advanced her candidacy and visually it turned me off."

With that went my last, best hope of finding someone to say a nice word about my beloved urinal ad.

• • •

A few postmortems for the depraved among you. Ruth Messinger is president of the American Jewish World Service, a group based in New York that supports development programs in Third World countries and promotes Jewish education in the former Soviet Union. She also teaches classes at Hunter College and Queens College.

Lee Jones is a fellow in the Department of Housing and Urban Development in Virginia.

Jim Andrews had a successful year. His most prominent candidate, Don Siegelman, the lieutenant governor of Alabama, successfully challenged the incumbent, Fob James, who won some national notoriety for vowing to take a court decision striking down teacher-led prayer to the Supreme Court. A pledge to create a state lottery was the cornerstone of Siegelman's campaign. "I'm the only candidate who favors a lottery for education," Siegelman said. "If this state is going to change, we have to change our education system forever." Siegelman won. A few staffers from the Messinger campaign followed Jim to Alabama. Some playfully asked him what he would do after every state had a lottery.

In December 1977, the Giuliani administration floated the idea of turning Governors Island into a casino. After a flurry of unfavorable press, it dropped the idea.

Would-have-been Manhattan borough president Abe Hirschfeld is under indictment for allegedly hiring an intermediary to murder a former business partner for $75,000.

Abner Louima said that the police officers never said, "It's Giuliani time," and that the charge was a fabrication of his attorneys.

As best I can determine, New York City is still buying and fastening documents with Swingline staples.

There has been no news about gangs in months.

Board of Elections executive director Daniel DeFrancesco's ballot was disqualified this year. DeFrancesco, who votes by absentee ballot every year, improperly sealed his ballot with a strip of cellophane tape. DeFrancesco's was one of approximately 15,000 ballots that were challenged by Attorney General candidates Eliot Spitzer and Dennis Vacco. The State Board of Elections has made DeFrancesco's organization look efficient. Nearly two months after Election Day, the contest still has not been decided, and there is the prospect that the state will begin the New Year without an Attorney General.

Eric Ruano-Melendez ran for Senate and lost. Charles Schumer ran and won, which is one of several events that has thrown New York City politics into turmoil. When Daniel Patrick Moynihan announced that he would not seek reelection in 2000, he created the first open Senate seat in New York in a generation. Rudy Giuliani is said to be considering a Senate run, though he is given pause by the fact that under the city charter he would be succeeded by the Public Advocate, Mark Green, Giuliani's bitter rival (as if Rudy has any other sort of rival). The mayor is looking for ways to revise the charter to change the order of succession.

Green ran for Senate this year and could again in 2000, which could lead to the interesting possibility of a Green-Giuliani matchup. If Green were to win that race, he would ascend to the Senate. If he were to lose, he would ascend to the mayoralty. Green, though, is said to be focusing on a 2001 mayoral bid. Because of term limits, Green will be out as Public Advocate in 2001. So, too, will Alan Hevesi, Peter Vallone, Freddie Ferrer, and a gaggle of City Council members, almost all of whom, it seems, are considering runs for mayor. Hevesi, Ferrer, Green, Sharpton, and Albanese all seem certain to run. Vallone is a possibility. Subway gunman Bernhard Goetz has also thrown his hat into the ring. An animal-rights activist, Goetz supports vegetarian meals for schoolchildren and a ban on the feeding of animals to other live animals—though only south of 42nd Street. Goetz also opposes circumcision and supports the death penalty for first-time violent sex offenders. "I think given the choice between Messinger and Sharpton, I could be a viable candidate," Goetz says.

Eric Ruano-Melendez is biding his time, mulling his options.

On the Republican side, Fran Reiter is thought to be close to announcing a mayoral bid. Herman Badillo, the former congressman, Bronx borough president, and deputy mayor in the Koch administration, has switched parties and is said to be considering a mayoral run. Sixty-eight years old, Badillo ran for mayor five times as a Democrat.

As Norman Adler said, politics is like malaria.

• • •

I am working at a law firm in New York City. I read the sports pages first in the morning, but the campaign has left its mark. The central issue in the D'Amato-Schumer race was D'Amato's claim that Schumer had missed congressional votes because of his campaign for Senate. When D'Amato launched the attack, my first reaction was that it was the product of good research and would make a strong ad. Weeks later, when the Schumer campaign disclosed that D'Amato had missed votes in Nassau County during his own first run for Senate, I wondered why the Schumer research team had taken so long in responding and wondered even more how D'Amato could have launched such an attack without first determining whether he was susceptible to an effective response. It was only later that I noted to myself that at the core of these competing arguments was a matter of absolutely no significance. No one cares whether Chuck Schumer missed a vote on a resolution dedicating Holocaust Victims Day or Al D'Amato missed a vote on water rates in the Nassau County Board of Supervisors. But they conducted an entire campaign on the issue, spending tens of millions of dollars, until Al D'Amato called Chuck Schumer a "putzhead" when things really got substantive.

My most treasured memory from the campaign is my morning with Robert Reich. When I wrote him a note of thanks, he was kind enough to reply. "Thanks for your nice letter," he wrote. "I'm glad that the campaign was, in retrospect, a good experience for you. I've always felt that every intelligent person ought to spend part of his or her life in a political campaign. You will learn more about American politics than you ever wanted to know."

More indeed.

New York, New York
January 1999

Notes

Dates are 1997 unless otherwise indicated.

Part One:
Jams, Jellies, and Other Tools of the Trade

9 *February 2:* "a party that boasts": *Daily News,* "Dems Must Rise to Challenge," December 10, 1996; no truth to the rumor: *New York Times,* Herbert, December 13, 1996; "shapes up as hold your nose time": *New York Post,* Koch, February 14; "It's a miserable choice": *New York Times,* Firestone, March 22.

11 *February 6:* "When it comes to defense": Democratic National Committee Campaign Training Manual, Research Appendix (1995), 25.

17–18 *February 15:* Rollins said best campaign in thirty years, *Hotline,* November 8, 1993; "imposing order": *Louisville Courier-Journal,* Garrett, May 17, 1995; "cracking the whip": *Louisville Courier-Journal,* Cross, May 1, 1995; "most misleading TV ad of the year": *Louisville Courier-Journal,* Cross, May 10, 1995; pictures of Whitman: *Bergen Record,* Kiely, August 18, 1993; Millner "morally unfit": *Atlanta Journal and Constitution,* "A Miller-Millner Mudfest," August 15, 1994; sloganeering parrot: *Atlanta Journal and Constitution,* Foskett, August 10, 1994; "She hasn't a clue": *New York Times,* Sullivan, August 1, 1993; they got themselves an Uzi: *Village Voice,* Borges, January 2.

18–19 *February 16:* Stevenson buttons: *Newsday,* Voboril, September 21; "legendary lack of interest in fashion": *Sunday Times* (London), Allen-Mills, August 3.

22–23 *February 19:* "The facts had changed": *Newsday,* Janison and Willen, February 20; Sharpton "far and away the winner": *Daily News,* Liff and Zombardi, February 20.

23–24 *February 20:* "It is unfathomable to think": *New York Times,* Dowd, February 21; "Close your eyes": *Daily News,* Zion, February 20; "the leading contenders": *New York Times,* Nagourney, February 20; "I'm not suggesting": *Hotline,* "NYC Mayor: Dem Lovefest Focuses on Giuliani," *New York Post,* February 20; "It's spring training": *Bergen Record,* Blood, February 20; "Most politicians are half people": *New York Post,* Newfield, February 20.

24–26 *February 23:* Sharpton's sister lesbian: *Village Voice,* Schoofs, February 25; Sharpton called Koch a faggot: *Village Voice,* Schoofs, February 25; Jeffries on hand for announcement: *New York Times,* Hicks, March 14; "white interloper": *New York Post,* Siegel, September 14; Sharpton defrauded National Youth Movement: *New York Observer,* Conason, September 22; 1996 vote count: *New York Times,* Hicks, March 14; "You live long enough": *Washington Post,* Russakoff, March 28; Giuliani summons Jewish leaders: *Daily News,* Dwyer, March 4; "The Police Department is not going to be drawn": *Daily News,* Dwyer, March 4.

26–27 *February 25:* Joe Slade White's start: *Roll Call,* Keller, February 27; lived on Upper West Side: *Village Voice,* Bradley, February 25; "really bad rap": *New York Times,* Apple, December 16, 1986.

28 *February 26:* Morris on Goodman: *Daily News,* Allen and Lewis, March 4.

31–32 *March 2:* background on Albanese: *New York Times,* Hicks, May 25.

32–33 *March 3:* Rudia quote: *Daily News,* Liff and Siemaszko, March 3; "Data gathering is just not a priority": *Daily News,* Allen, March 23; "Had I gone ahead": *New York Times,* Kennedy, March 24; $27.3 million in lawsuits: *New York Times,* Sontag and Barry, September 17.

34–35 *March 4:* "his work with black candidates": *New York Times,* Nagourney, December 21, 1996; "boundless ego": *New York Post,* Peyser, March 5.

35–36 *March 5:* "You should be ashamed": *Newsday,* Janison, March 4; "In New York the competition for news": *Los Angeles Times,* Getlin, March 5, 1997.

38 *March 6:* "The introduction of the hollow-point bullet": *New York Times,* Kraus, March 6; "What we're really saying": *Daily News,* Liff, March 6.

38 *March 8:* Lypsinka on Rudia: *Village Voice,* Goldstein, March 24.

39 *March 9:* "has made a particular effort": *New York Times,* Nagourney, December 21, 1996.

41 *March 12:* "New Yorkers are more upbeat": *New York Times,* Nagourney, March 12.

44–45 *March 15:* 4,000 for 700 jobs: *New York Times,* Swarns, March 19; unemployment ranking: *Daily News,* "The Job Crunch," March 20; real wages: *Economist,* "Rudy Giuliani's Middle Way," March 22; "As for the rise in our unemployment rate": *New York Times,* Mastro, March 15.

45–46 *March 16:* growth in brutality settlements: *New York Times,* Herbert, March 24; $27.3 million in settlements: *New York Times,* Sontag and Barry, September 17; Livoti case: *Newsday,* Ramirez and Levitt, February 22; "a careful, well-thought-out, legally reasoned opinion": *Newsday,* Levitt, February 24; choke hold lasted more than a minute: *Newsday,* Levitt, February 24; "I think a lot of the information": *Newsday,* Rayman, June 26.

48 *March 17:* "If you want to be mayor": *New York Times,* Nagourney, March 18; "The St. Patrick's Day Parade provided": *New York Times,* Nagourney, March 18.

55 *March 20:* Giuliani promises review of incident: *Daily News,* Levitt, March 20; "set herself up": *New York Post,* March 20.

56 *March 22:* Giuliani allows historic agreement to expire: *New York Times,* Swarns, June 12; "least-known commissioner of all time": *New York Post,* Peyser, March 17; pregnant woman on EAU floor: *Staten Island Advance,* Patrick, March 15; "better job of outreach": *Newsday,* Janison, March 17.

57 *March 25:* Lowey study: *Daily News,* Goodman, September 10, 1996.

59 *March 27:* "It is inherently unfair": *Newsday,* Cheng, March 27; federal AIDS money forfeited: *Daily News,* Nicholson, March 27.

62 *April 2:* "personal jihad": *Daily News,* "Rudy Shudda Butted Out," July 25.

63 *April 4:* Sharpton on Farrakhan, *New York Times,* Nagourney, April 4.

66 *April 5:* "I think Ruth, Freddie and Sal": *New York Times,* Nagourney, April 6.

67–68 *April 6:* "This person came at them": *New York Post,* Stamey, Stirgus, and Massarella, April 7; O'Keefe said Garcia concealing a weapon: *New York Times,* July 5, 1992; accounts of Washington Heights crisis: *Newsday,* Vottman, July 8–9, 1992; Giuliani op-ed: *New York Times,* Giuliani, August 7, 1992.

69–70 *April 8:* celebrities occupy rent-controlled apartments: *New York Times,* Sontag, May 2; revisionist diversity defense of rent control: *New York Post,* Siegel, June 1; O'Connor on rent control: *New York Post,* Mosconi and Topousis, May 5; courageous and sensible: New York 1 *News,* April 8.

70–71 *April 9:* "The mayor's order": *New York Post,* "Rudy and the Scofflaw Diplomats," April 3; "If they'd like to leave": *Daily News,* Siegel and Feiden, April 11, 1997.

72–76 *April 10:* "if the priesthood had encompassed marriage": *New York Times,* Bearak and Fisher, October 19; "If you looked at our class": *Newsday,* Voboril, September 19, 1993; "fancy schvartze": *Newsday,* Voboril, September 19, 1993; "Do they really think I'm mean": *New York Times,* Manegold, September 7, 1993; "you would want him": *Village Voice,* Barrett, November 4, 1997; a hundred yards in the snow: *Times-Picayune,* February 15, 1995; "*very, very* few societies": *Spy,* Weiss, November 1988; "Nobody, no place celebrates Christmas": *Newsday,* Murphy, March 28; "I'm honest *and* intellectually honest": *New York,* May 25, 1987 (emphasis added).

78 *April 11:* Abrams threw a phone: *New York Times,* Firestone, January 13, 1998; "That was wrong then": memo from Scott Gale to Messinger, March 14.

80 *April 15:* "There's no possible way": *New York Times,* McFadden, April 8.

84 *April 17:* "Will I be running?": *Daily News,* Feiden, April 17; school visits: *Daily News,* Feiden, April 20.

85 *April 20:* "constrained by both the budget": Messinger memo to Andrews, January 20, 1997.

87–88 *April 21:* "There will be no patronage": *New York Observer,* Drucker, May 12; a dozen Giuliani campaign workers at EDC: *New York Observer,* Drucker, May 12; Carbonetti defaulted: *New York Observer,* Drucker, May 12; EDC bonuses: *Daily News,* Robbins and Calderone, June 15; "I've hired more people on merit": *New York Observer,* Drucker, May 12.

88 *April 22:* "When I look at the field of candidates": *Staten Island Advance,* Associated Press, "People in the News," April 23.

89 *April 23:* papers condemn secrecy: *New York Post,* "Carl McCall's Partisan Audits," April 1; *Newsday,* "Rudy Has Met the Enemy and His Name Is Giuliani," April 3; *Daily News,* April 2; *New York Observer,* "Let McCall's Auditors In," April 7; *New York Times,* Herbert, "The Big Bad Auditor," April 7; Pressman quote: *Los Angeles Times,* Getlin, March 5; "I've covered New York mayors": *Los Angeles Times,* Getlin, March 5; "The law provides for maximum access": *Daily News,* Ross and Sutton, April 24; "Although the press": *New York Times,* Sullivan, April 24.

90 *April 24:* "continuing paucity": Bell letter to Messinger, March 3; "I was surprised": Messinger letter to Bell, April 21.

90 *April 25:* Giuliani halts homeless referrals: *New York Times,* Firestone, 26, April 26.

91 *April 26:* Kuriansky quote: *Daily News,* Siegel, April 26.

92 *April 28:* "Mr. Giuliani won in 1993": *New York Times,* Weisman, April 28.

94 *May 1:* "work hard": *New York Post,* Seifman, May 1.

96–97 *May 3:* peace groups and draft counseling: *Westsider,* August 25, 1977; *New York Times,* Brozan, December 6, 1993; "nonstop carnival": *New York Times,* Bruni, October 12.

98 *May 5:* "It's a disgrace to the dead": *New York Post,* Hardt, Jr., May 7; "crushing schedule": *New York Post,* "Pedal-Pusher Ruth Conks Out Early," May 6; "I think Ruth is embarrassed": *New York Times,* Nagourney, "Charges Fly: She Snoozed! He's Unfit!" May 7.

99 *May 7:* colonial theme park proposal: *New York Observer,* Leonard, May 7; "A great deal of money": *Newsday,* Liff, March 16, 1994.

99–100 *May 8:* "Not even Jimmy Smits": *New York Times,* Kolbert, May 8; poll: *Daily News,* Siegel and Lombardi, May 8.

100–101 *May 10:* Andrews promotes Miller's lottery record: *Commercial Appeal,* Smothers, October 16, 1994; use of lottery money in other states: *Louisville Courier-Journal,* Cross, May 1, 1995.

102–104 *May 13:* "There is still a dream": *Staten Island Advance,* Patrick and Randall, May 14; "Freddie thinks": *New York Times,* Herbert, May 16; not a "terribly stable way of life": *Chief Leader,* Della Monica, April 8, 1994; "more conservative": *Chief Leader,* Della Monica, April 8, 1994; "They are faced with a situation": transcript of Reiter's remarks; Messinger "a force for good government": *Newsday,* Mangaliman, March 21, 1989.

Part Two: Polled in Every Direction

108–109 *May 14:* "Some politicians are": *New York Times,* Herbert, May 16.

111 *May 16:* "fast and loose": *Daily News,* "Ruth-less," May 17.

111 *May 17:* "The white press": *Amsterdam News,* Tatum, May 17.

111–112 *May 19:* Andrews profile: *New York Observer,* Durkin, May 19.

113 *May 20:* election action alert: *New York Times,* Nagourney, May 30.

114 *May 21:* poll: *New York Post,* Seifman, May 21.

114 *May 22:* "The city is in pretty decent shape": *Newsday,* Murphy, May 20; "We are focusing on education": *Newsday,* Kidsday, May 19.

114–115 *May 23:* "My first act": *Daily News,* Spitz, May 23.

115 *May 24:* Reiter smoked pot too: *Daily News,* Siegel and Lewis, May 24.

116 *May 26:* "They're alive": *Washington Post,* Harden and Dutt, May 25; "warped philosophy": *New York Times,* Firestone, May 31.

117 *May 27:* filing to divert attention: *Newsday,* Associated Press, May 23; Giuliani praises D'Amato: *Daily News,* Siegel, May 28; "ethics would be trashed": *Village Voice,* Barrett, November 4.

118 *May 29:* political memo: *New York Times,* Nagourney, May 29.

122 *June 3:* "that's a good question": *New York Post,* Rubinowitz, June 3; "I fully endorse": *Newsday,* Moses, June 4; "a pretty weak individual": *New York Post,* Rubinowitz, June 4; denouncement of endorsement: *New York Post,* "Pander Politics," June 4.

123 *June 4:* "Messinger wants to put": *Daily News,* Kriegel, June 16; text of ad: *New York Times,* Dao, June 10.

124–125 *June 5:* "I think Ruth has lost her mind": *New York Times,* Nagourney, June 6; Reiter refuses request for access: *New York Post*, Rubinowitz and Weiss, June 6.

127 *June 8:* Giuliani argues Messinger campaign in "disarray": *Newsday,* Moses and Janison, June 7.

127 *June 9:* reception of Ferrer: *New York Observer,* Durkin, June 16; "Whether it is primarily due": *New York Observer,* Durkin, June 16; "The rumor is": *New York Times,* Nagourney, June 9.

128 *June 10:* "woefully inadequate": *New York Post,* Topousis, Birnbaum, and Italiano, June 9; Giuliani tried to terminate Legal Aid contract: *New York Times,* Holloway, June 12.

128–129 *June 11:* Reading scores headlines: *Daily News,* Sugarman, June 11; *New York Post,* Buffa, June 11*; New York Times,* Steinberg, June 10; *Newsday,* "Coming Up Short?" June 13*; Newsday*, Polner, June 11; *Daily News,* "Crew's Control Showing Results," June 12; "an attempt to put a positive spin": *Newsday,* Polner, June 11; "it would be unfortunate": *New York Times,* Steinberg, June 10; "Let's call time out": *New York Times,* Steinberg, June 11.

130–131 *June 12:* "Brooklyn's answer to tough love": *Newsday,* Janison, May 30; "I don't think Messinger knows": *New York Observer,* Durkin, June 2; hiring of Joe Wiscovitch: *New York Observer,* Durkin, June 2; Messinger proposes teacher residency: *New York Post,* Topousis, June 13.

131–132 *June 13:* WABC waiting for Giuliani's call: *New York Post,* Seifman, March 8; "the question is": *Newsday,* Berkowitz, June 30, 1993; "If David Dinkins could do it": *Newsday,* Polner, July 26.

132 *June 14:* "decadent storm troopers of capitalism": Anti-Defamation League, "The Anti-Semitism of Black Demagogues and Extremists," 1992; Fulani welcomed Farrakhan: Berlet, Political Research Associates, "Clouds Blur the Rainbow: How Fred Newman and Lenora Fulani Use Totalitarian Deception to Manipulate Social and Political Activists," 1996; Jews "had to sell their souls": ADL, "Anti-Semitism," 1992; Golisano supported legalization: *Rochester Business Journal,* November 4, 1994; *New York Times*, Jones, October 29, 1994.

133 *June 15:* terms of rent deal: *Daily News,* Sorensen, Schaye, and Finnegan, June 16.

134 *June 16:* "Are you calling me anti-Semitic?": *New York Post,* Seifman, June 17.

137 *June 18:* Morris on poll results: *New York Post,* Rubinowitz, June 19; *Newsday,* Moses, June 19; *Daily News*, Lombardi, June 19; "Poll Shows Messinger Closing In on Giuliani": *Amsterdam News,* Browne, June 21; Fulani response: *Amsterdam News,* Fulani, June 21.

138 *June 19:* "local equivalent of Bosnia": *New York Observer,* Sargent, February 24; "On what? How to gain weight?": *New York*, Kirtzman, June 23–30; "I admire the good work": *New York,* Kirtzman, June 23–30.

140–141 *June 20:* "They seem to be buying": *Daily News,* Lewis and Siegel, June 19; "Rudy reading to kids": *Daily News,* Lewis and Siegel, June 19; text of EDC ads: *New York Times,* Firestone, June 20; "blatantly lay out campaign themes": *Newsday,* Murphy and Janison, June 20; pressure to pull ads: *New York Times,* Firestone, June 20; "The Straphangers are part": *Newsday,* Murphy and Janison, June 20.

143 *June 21:* Omansky to city: *New York Post,* Rubinowitz, June 21.

144–145 *June 22:* "Where's Ruth?": *Daily News,* Siegel, June 20; Messinger profile: *Daily News,* Lewis, June 22; "The campaign trail led": *Newsday,* Moses, June 21; "Nonlawyer Ruth Messinger": *New York Post,* Rubinowitz, June 21; "Messinger's malicious mouthpiece": *New York Post,* June 18.

147 *June 24:* theory of nonaggression pact: *Village Voice,* Barrett, June 3; Hevesi chief seen with Powers: *New York Post,* Seifman, May 31; Holtzman cleared: *Village Voice,* Shulman, July 22.

148 *June 25:* ad-box: *Newsday,* Cheng, "Giuliani Now the Education Mayor?" June 23; "Giuliani's TV commercial": *New York Post,* Hardt, Jr., June 22.

149–150 *June 26:* firefighters endorse Giuliani: *New York Times,* Greenhouse, June 24; principals endorse Giuliani: *Newsday,* Janison, June 21; pattern of endorsements: *New York Observer,* Drucker, June 23; *Village Voice,* Barrett, June 24.

151–152 *June 28:* police flyers: *New York Times,* Greenhouse, June 28; "It was beyond friendly": *New York Times,* Firestone, June 27; "Now that he's officially": *New York Post,* "Hevesi's Loss of Credibility," June 29.

152 *June 30:* "blatantly laying out campaign themes": *Newsday,* Murphy and Janison, June 20.

156–157 *July 1:* Giuliani working overtime: *New York Post,* Seifman and Buffa, July 1; "It's good news": *New York Times,* Cooper, July 1.

157 *July 2:* Sharpton in Washington, D.C.: *New York Times,* Van Gelder, July 5; "I think that's a mistake": *New York Times,* Van Gelder, July 3.

160–161 *July 6:* "no big deal": Channel 2 *News at Six,* July 7; "quite well": *New York Times,* Firestone, July 8; "ignorant" question: *New York Times,* Firestone, July 8; "She was a very big supporter": New York 1 *Road to City Hall;* "The Mayor's reelection plan": *Economist,* "A Tale of Two Cities: New York," September 27.

161–162 *July 7:* "good woman down" letter: *Daily News,* Finnegan, September 6; "one of the most substantive campaign exchanges": *Daily News,* Lewis and Siegel, July 8.

162 *July 8:* Maloney hiring: *Daily News,* Lewis, July 3.

164–165 *July 9:* feistiness of the campaigns: *Daily News,* Lewis, July 9; "adrift and divided": *New York Times,* Nagourney, July 9.

166 *July 11:* "The limousine liberal": *New York Times,* Nagourney, July 11; "I think Al Sharpton is right": *New York Post,* Topousis, July 11.

167–168 *July 12:* "The defecting Democrats": *New York Times,* Collins, July 10; "So if Messinger wants": *New York Post,* "Messinger Targets Wall Street," July 11; "In a 17 minute yadayadayada": *Daily News,* "Messinger for Mayor—of Mars," July 12.

169 *July 15:* town meeting about Governors Island: *New York Times,* Lueck, July 15; fund-raising totals: *Daily News,* Siegel, July 16; *New York Post,* Hardt, Jr., and Topousis, July 16.

170 *July 16:* unions in tank for Giuliani: *Village Voice,* Barrett, June 24.

172 *July 17:* "We have a limited budget": *Daily News,* Siegel, July 17.

173–174 *July 18:* "latest in a series": *New York Times,* Nagourney, July 17; "ruthless control freak": *New York Post,* Koch, July 18; "in choosing between": *New York Post,* Koch, July 18.

176–177 *July 19:* "Ideally, everyone would like to see": *New York Times,* "Ms. Messinger's Budget Blunder," July 18.

177–178 *July 20:* decision to distance from Crew a mistake: *New York Times,* Nagourney, July 20; "unless this political observer": Amsterdam *News,* Tatum, July 17–23; background on Hirschfeld: *New York Post,* Miller, May 7.

178–180 *July 21:* Owens says "rampant sexism": *Amsterdam News,* Browne, June 28; "They ran this explicitly sexist campaign": *Village Voice,* Schulman, July 22; building inspector check: *New York Post,* Topousis, July 22; Giuliani opposing immigrant law: *New York Times,* Firestone, July 19.

181–182 *July 23:* "a speech on budget issues": *New York Times,* "Ruth Messinger Gets Specific," July 23; lay off 8,000 police officers: *Newsday,* Polner, July 23; June unemployment rate: *New York Times,* Johnson, July 23; earlier unemployment increase: *New York Times,* Newman, December 7, 1991.

186 *July 25:* "I'm interested in seeing": *Newsday,* Ratish, July 25.

188 *July 26:* "He's an honest man": *Staten Island Advance,* "Kramer Endorses Giuliani," July 24.

189 *July 27:* "There will be at least as many": *Newsday,* Ratish, July 25; "Ruth refused to say": *New York Post,* Rubinowitz, July 25; "Messinger's Cop Chop": *New York Post,* July 25; "Messinger said her plan": *Newsday,* Ratish, July 25; "indications of haplessness": *New York Times,* Nagourney, July 27.

189–190 *July 28:* "a strategy to keep heat on Messinger": *New York Times,* Nagourney, July 28; "following the rules": *Newsday,* Polner, July 28.

192 *July 30:* "try to find out": *New York Observer,* Sargent, July 28.

193 *August 1:* "To make an exception": *New York Times,* "Discoverer of Cunanan Gains Reward," August 13; "You've done a lot of things": *New York Observer,* Sargent, July 28; "Let's really stop being stupid": *New York Observer,* Sargent, July 28.

194 *August 2:* one-fare poll: *Newsday,* Janison, July 30.

194–195 *August 3:* Lategano story: *Vanity Fair,* Conant, "The Ghost and Mr. Giuliani," September 1997.

200–202 *August 7:* Giuliani refuses questions about his marriage: *New York Times,* Firestone, August 5; "No, I'm not": *New York Post,* Seifman, August 4; "That's really a cheap question": *New York Post,* Hardt, Jr., and Denizer, August 7; "It's the worst kind": *Daily News,* Feiden, August 4; "Where are the sources?": *Newsday,* Janison and Rimbert, August 4; "The best thing for me to say": *New York Times,* Firestone,

August 5; "Allegations by unnamed sources": *Daily News,* Feiden, August 4; "Anytime anything comes out": *New York Post,* Seifman and Francescani, August 5; "Above all, my family": *New York Times,* Firestone, August 5; "Defiant Donna": *New York Post,* Seifman and Francescani, August 5; "We're talking beans": *Newsday,* Henican, August 6.

202 *August 8:* "Jesse, I've said everything": *Daily News,* Feiden, August 9.

203–204 *August 9:* ad text: *Newsday,* Janison, August 8; New York 1 poll: *Daily News,* Lombardi, August 10; street repair: *New York Post*, "Vanity Fair Shy on Street Smarts," August 21.

205 *August 10:* "New York's Loneliest Liberal": *Slate,* Traub, August 8; pulled ad: *New York Observer,* Durkin, August 18.

206–208 *August 11:* Jones press philosophy: *New York Observer,* Sargent, February 24; "[Klein's] entire body of prior work": *New York Post,* Seifman, August 9; Rodriguez platform: *Village Voice,* Ruscitti and Malamud, September 2; Rogers platform: *Daily News,* Rogers, August 27; background on Melendez: *Village Voice,* Ruscitti and Malamud, September 2; "The turnout's going to be low": *New York Times,* Perez-Peña, September 3.

208–209 *August 12:* Giuliani assumed responsibility: *New York Times,* Sexton, February 13; Barrios-Paoli on Giuliani's reason for acting: *New York Times,* Swarns, April 25; *New York Times,* Levy, April 26; Mastro denies seeing report: *New York Post,* Rubinowitz, April 24; "unfair political shots": *Staten Island Advance,* Associated Press, August 16.

209–210 *August 13:* Jonas said police attacked Abner: *New York Post,* Weiss and Massarella, August 13; CCRB statistics: *Daily News,* Marzulli, September 11; "I see this case": *Daily News,* Finnegan, August 14.

210–211 *August 14:* Jackson approached Stewart: *New York Post,* Koch, August 22; "The alleged conduct involved": *Daily News,* August 14; *Newsday,* Morrison, English and Janison, August 14; "it's Giuliani time": *Newsday,* Janison, August 14.

211–213 *August 15:* outreach to African Americans: *Daily News,* Feiden, August 16; "this is a new day": *New York Post,* Dunleavy, August 17; failed to act on Mollen Commission recommendations: *New York Times,* Kifner, August 25; "If I were Messinger": *Newsday,* McCarthy, August 16; "By the odd logic": *Newsday,* Janison, August 18; "very ugly police failure": *New York Times,* Firestone, August 15; "keep politics out of it": *Staten Island Advance,* Associated Press, August 16; "I think what the mayor has done": *Newsday,* Hurtado, August 16.

213 *August 16*: ad text: *Newsday,* Janison, August 13.

214 *August 17:* "To sum up": *Daily News,* Sharpton, August 13; Jackson endorses Sharpton: *New York Post,* Gregorian, August 13; "I am the only candidate": *Daily News,* Siegel, August 14.

215 *August 18:* Nagourney on Albanese: *New York Times,* Nagourney, August 18; Nagourney on Fields endorsement: *New York Times,* Nagourney, June 3.

217–218 *August 19:* Ruth "simply cannot win": *Daily News,* Finnegan and Siegel, August 20; Reiter response: *Newsday,* Janison and Murphy, August 21; "Giuliani Time": *Village Voice,* Dinkins, August 26; Giuliani on Schwarz: *New York Post,* Rubinowitz, August 21; "All these people are doing": *New York Times,* Nagourney, August 21; "We'll Take Manhattan": *Newsweek,* Adler, August 18; piece on activist mayors: *Time,* Cohen, August 18; Giuliani eyeing Senate seat: *New York Post,* Dicker, August 18; Giuliani promises job to Adams: *Staten Island Advance,* Nelson and Gavin, August 21.

218–220 *August 20:* "It would be naïve": *New York Post,* "Giuliani Time," August 21; poll: *New York Post,* Seifman, August 22; "It's beyond horrendous": *New York Post,* Seifman, August 24; "Messinger has imploded": *Daily News,* Zion, September 4;

Sheinkopf and Chapin: *Village Voice,* Bradley, September 9; "The mayor's race": *Daily News,* Siegel, August 24.

222–223 *August 22:* Omansky decision: *New York Times,* Firestone, August 23; McCall on cost of wasted police: *New York Times,* Roane, August 22; "A lot of people called": *Daily News,* Siegel, August 21.

224–225 *August 23:* job for Adams: *Staten Island Advance,* O'Shea, August 23; rat war: *Daily News,* Rein and Feiden, September 10; job for Wooten: *Newsday,* Polner, May 14; "I'm not going": *New York Times,* Krauss, August 23.

225–226 *August 24:* Messinger's "Giuliani time" speech: *New York Times,* Pierre-Pierre, August 25; *Daily News,* McPhee and Fan, August 25; "This is, like, misrepresentation": *Newsday,* Janison and Kershaw, August 25; Democrats "have not shown the aggressiveness: *New York Times,* Nagourney, August 25.

227 *August 25:* "Ruth Messinger's mayoral campaign has made": *Daily News,* "Ruth Less Than Meets the Eye," August 21; one of the top sinners: *New York Post,* Peyser, July 6; "Albanese charges she's distorting": *New York Times,* Nagourney, August 24.

228–229 *August 27:* "The longer you listen": *Daily News,* "Sal's Doleful Welfare Plan," August 27; 10 percent of workfare find jobs: *Newsday,* Moses, June 15.

230–232 *August 28:* "manufactured an illustration": *New York Times,* "How Not to Run a Campaign," August 28; "Schools Often Turn Bathrooms into Classrooms": *New York Times*, Sengupta, August 28; converted bathroom "has blackboards": *New York Times,* Sengupta, August 28; "nothing wrong" with the ad: *Daily News,* Fenner, Finnegan, and Siegel, August 29; Empire State survey: *Daily News,* Siegel, August 29; "You create an unfair depiction": *Daily News,* Siegel, August 28.

233 *August 29:* "Crime has gone down": *New York Times,* Kifner, August 30; "the dastardly deed": *New York Times,* Kifner, August 30.

234 *August 30:* "The anticipated low turnout": *New York Post,* Seifman, August 30.

236 *August 31:* "Do you feel that you're being discriminated against": *New York,* Kirtzman, "The Makeover: Ruth Gets Down (Sort of)," July 7.

236–237 *September 1:* "so buoyant": *New York Times,* Nagourney, September 2; "It's probably difficult": *New York Times,* Nagourney, September 1.

238–239 *September 2:* "Our problems in our education system": *Daily News,* Rein and Siegel, September 3; D'Amato recommendation of Giuliani for U.S. Attorney: *New York Times,* "Man in the News", April 13, 1983; "He will move to whatever drummer": *Daily News,* Claffey and Lombardi, December 11, 1996; Giuliani and D'Amato hug: *Daily News,* Claffey and Lombardi, December 11, 1996; "We have to stand up to the teachers' unions": *Newsday*, Janison, September 3.

239 *September 3:* "The Chancellor seemed particularly upset": *Riverdale Press,* "Fit Places for Learning?" September 4.

239–241 *September 4:* Albanese loan: *New York Times,* Levy, September 4; withdrawn Albanese endorsement: *Newsday,* Polner and Janison, September 4; "a vindication": *New York Times,* Kolbert, September 4; 10 percent "should more than accommodate": *New York Times,* Kolbert, September 4.

241–244 *September 5:* "For someone who has": *New York Times,* Nagourney, September 3; "It would make no sense": *Daily News,* Finnegan, September 5; "Several Democrats": *New York Times,* Nagourney, September 5; "at least contributed some comic relief": *New York Post,* "Now, Messinger as Victim," September 6; no *Post* endorsement: *New York Post,* "Disappointing Democrats," September 4; "none of the above": *Daily News,* "For Mayor, None of the Above," September 7; Sharpton "has fashioned the most sensible": *Caribbean News,* "Worthwhile Candidates in Democratic Primaries," September 9; Sharpton "as comfortable in a Brooks Brothers suit": *Amsterdam News,* Tatum, "Vote Sharpton, Ferrer and Fields Sept. 9," August 28-September 3; "Messinger shows a strong grasp": *Newsday,* "Best Democrat," September 4; "Who's more likely": *Newsday,* Janison, September 4; "It could be a Ruth poll": *Newsday*, Janison, September 4; "I don't think there's any doubt": *New York Times,* Firestone, September 5; "The CBC in league": *New York Times,* Firestone, September 5.

245–247 *September 6:* students turned away at Newtown High: *Newsday,* Cheng, September 4; school in dry-cleaning plant: *New York Post,* Alvarez, September 9; "It Was Nearly a Textbook Job": *Daily News,* Wasserman and Williams, September 4; "There hasn't been a chancellor": *Daily News,* Wasserman and Williams, September 4; Hevesi criticizes Sharpton: *Newsday,* Janison and Ratish, September 5; Drennan ad: *New York Times*, "World News Leaves 3 Candidates in the Shadows," September 6; LaGuardia ad: *New York Times,* "The Ad Campaign," September 6; D'Amato ad: *New York Post,* Francescani and Seifman, September 9.

249–251 *September 7:* Melendez on "corrupted lawyers": *New York Times,* Kolbert, September 8; "I don't want it for entertainment": *New York Times,* Nagourney, September 8; "asshole, but a successful asshole": *New York Post,* Hardt, Jr., September 28; "revenge of the nerd": *New Yorker,* "Giuliani Unbound," September 8.

251–253 *September 8:* unions "instrumental": *Daily News,* Siegel, September 7; "There isn't an overriding issue": *Daily News,* Siegel, September 7; Herbert analysis: *New York Times,* Herbert, September 7; "the candidates have raised": *Daily News,* Shipp, September 9; Koch holding his nose: *Daily News,* Feiden, September 9; Kerrison pity: *New York Post,* Kerrison, September 9; "Is that Liz Holtzman?": *New York Times,* Nagourney, September 9; "When it comes time for us to respond": *Daily News,* Siegel, September 8; "I'd like everyone to be clear": *New York Post,* Seifman and Topousis, September 8; "If they want to register": *New York Post,* Rubinowitz, September 9; turnout speculation: *Daily News,* Lombardi, September 9; if "they had a primary election": *Daily News,* Gonzalez, September 9; last-day poll: *Daily News,* Fan and Siegel, September 9.

255–256 *September 10:* "I want to thank the mainstream media": *New York Times,* Kolbert, September 11; "We are going to fly": *New York Times,* Holloway, September 10; "She skipped a debate": *New York Post,* Seifman, September 11.

256–261 *September 11:* "How to defeat Mr. Sharpton": *New York Times,* Nagourney, September 11; Giuliani says Messinger and Sharpton indistinguishable: *New York Times,* Firestone, September 10; "It does pose": *New York Post,* Seifman, September 11; "I am not going to get into an explanation": *Daily News,* Siegel, September 14; "if nothing else": *New York Post,* "Reluctant Ruth," September 12; "Why don't you listen": *New York Post*, Rubinowitz and Francescani, September 11; "eloquent spokesperson": *New York Post,* Rubinowitz and Francescani, September 11; Sharpton's overdue taxes: *Daily News,* Calderone and Robbins, September 11; Sharpton calls allegations racist: *New York Post,* Hardt, Jr., September 12; Sharpton says city owes hospital bill: *New York Post,* Seifman, September 13; Sharptons renew vows: *New York Times,* Firestone, September 12; *Staten Island Advance*, "Report: Al Sharpton Renewed Marriage Vows at Unification Church," September 12; Sharpton won primary: *Amsterdam News,* Tatum, "We Be Flying," September 11, citing *New York Times,* Herbert, September 11; Moore/Newport analysis: *Newsday,* Moore and Newport, November 8, 1993; Albanese calls Messinger campaign "fiasco": *Daily News,* Gonzalez, September 11; Grunwald and Andrews "biggest losers": *Crains*, "Election Winners . . . and the Losers," September 15; Messinger violated "enduring rule of politics": *New York Times,* Nagourney, September 15; Leventhal contributions: *New York Observer,* Drucker, June 30; Shulman ad: *Daily News*, Feiden, September 11; Giuliani campaign returning $290,000: *New York Times,* Levy, September 12.

263–265 *September 13:* Hevesi on Sharpton: *New York Post,* Hardt, Jr., and Orin, September 13; Hevesi cites his work in civil rights: *New York Times,* Nagourney, September 13; Giuliani says Sharpton lacks qualifications: *Daily News,* Finnegan, Feiden, and Siegel, September 15; "everybody darker than Liz Taylor": *New York Post,* Topousis and Stirgus, September 15; Albanese criticizes Hevesi: *New York Times,* Holloway, September 14; "white liberalism as a force": *Daily News,* Morris, September 15.

266–268 *September 14*: "Campaign Shifts into High Gear": *Daily News,* Siegel and Siemaszko, September 12; "I need your help": *New York Times,* Nagourney, September 15; Messinger street money: *New York Post,* Seifman, October 11; runoff poll: *Daily News,* Feiden, September 19; general-election poll: *Daily News,* Lombardi, September 12; Louima case makes no difference in vote: *New York Observer,* Durkin, September 15; "More and more": *Newsday,* Breslin, September 14.

268–270 *September 15:* Messinger kicked out of luncheon: *Newsday,* Janison and Ratish, September 16; "nothing is official until": *New York Post*, Topousis, September 16; spinner's no comment: *Newsday,* Moses, "Board of Elections Audited," May 8; "A nine looks like a zero": *Newsday,* Janison and Murphy, September 16; "a five can look like an eight": *New York Times,* Herszenhorn, September 16; "I'm taller": *Newsday,* Janison and Murphy, September 16; "I will not divide New York": *New York Post,* Seifman, Topousis, and Rubinowitz, September 16; minorities feel "robbed": *New York Post,* Seifman, Topousis, and Rubinowitz, September 16; "They don't understand": *New York Times,* Nagourney, September 16; "She'd win the runoff": *New York Times,* Nagourney, September 16.

270–272 *September 16:* "The water cooler's empty": *Daily News*, Breen and Sutton, September 18; "We're whipping people to death": *New York Times,* Nagourney, September 18; "Dixiecrat trick": *New York Times,* Haberman, September 19; Sharpton committed to supporting winner: *Daily News,* Fan, Allen, and Siemaszko, September 10; "I'm determined": *New York Times,* Nagourney, September 17; "Something doesn't smell right": *Newsday,* Murphy, September 17; "At best there's been some incompetence": *Daily News,* Rein, Finnegan, and Siegel, September 17; "Rudy is a hater": *Amsterdam News,* Tatum, "A Time Beyond Anger, A Time Beyond Giuliani," September 18; "To sort of be the nominee": *Daily News,* Rein, Finnegan, and Siegel, September 17; Giuliani on the debate: *Newsday,* Janison, September 7.

273 *September 17:* Board of Elections audit: *Newsday,* Moses, May 8.

Part Three: Into the Breach

277–280 *September 18:* "To a very, very large extent": *New York Post,* Seifman, September 19; "You think it lends character": *New York Times,* Firestone, September 19; "first fruit of months of research": *New York Times,* Nagourney, September 19; "one sex shop per block": *New York Post,* Seifman, September 19; "her proposal": *New York Post,* Seifman, September 19; "really issue oriented": *New York Times,* Firestone, September 19; Sharpton complaint: *New York Post,* Hardt, Jr., Rubinowitz, and Montero, September 19; Hardy to Chin: *New York Times,* Weiser, September, 19; "I don't know if I'd use the word ineptitude": *Daily News,* Siegel, September 19; "It's not over until the fat man sings": *New York Times,* Nagourney, September 19; "Ultimately we will unite": *New York Times,* Nagourney, September 19; "I have not been named": *New York Times,* Nagourney, September 19; Carbonetti background: *New York Observer,* Drucker, May 12; Messinger discussing subway crime: *Daily News,* Rutenberg, September 19.

282 *September 19:* "Faced with a critical political dilemma": *New York Times,* Rosenthal, September 19.

283–284 *September 21:* "I think it was outrageous": *New York Post,* Dicker, September 22; *New York Observer*/New York 1 poll: *New York Observer*, "Democrats Only Chance: Keep Sharpton Voters, *Observer* Poll Shows," September 22.

285–288 *September 22:* "not fit to hold any public office": *New York Times,* Nagourney, September 23; Giuliani press release: *Newsday*, Hurtado, Janison, and Murphy, September 23; Hill recalls party: *Daily News,* Rein, Finnegan, and Siegel, September 23; "apple-juice-and-cheese gathering": *New York Observer,* Durkin, September 29; "willful police riot": *New York Times,* Haberman, September 30; "a subterfuge": *New York Times,* Farrell, November 11, 1971; "Attica lurks as a dark shadow": *New York Times,* Haberman, September 30; *Village Voice,* Barrett, October 7; Badillo on Messinger party: *Village Voice,* Barrett, October 7; "If you throw a party": *New York Observer,* Durkin, September 29; "I don't think it makes sense": *New York Post,* Dicker and Rubinowitz, September 23; "I just happened to be in the area": *New York Times,* Herszenhorn, September 23.

289 *September 23:* "She said it": *New York Times,* Nagourney, September 24; Hill says Messinger out of town: *New York,* Tomasky, October 6; Barrett recalls get-togethers: *Village Voice,* Barrett, October 7.

290–291 *September 24: Times* criticism of Giuliani: *New York Times,* "The Mayor's Campaign Overkill," September 26; "by exaggerating her position on the subject": *New York Times,* Firestone, September 24; "an order of crow": *Daily News,* "Sex, Lies, and Video Tape," September 27; "literally mean opening up": *Daily News,* Rein and Finnegan, September 25; "They can attack me": *New York Post,* Rubinowitz, September 25; "a six can look like an eight": *New York Times,* Weiser, September 25; Marist poll: *New York Post,* Rubinowitz, September 25.

292 *September 25:* "We'd never do anything": *Newsday*, Janison, September 26.

293 *September 26:* "I give it to people": *New York Post,* Seifman, September 27.

293–294 *September 27:* Flake praises Giuliani: *Daily News,* Allen, September 28; Towns explains switch: *Daily News,* Allen, September 28; "excessive desire to criticize": *New York Observer,* Durkin, October 6; "top banana": *New York Post,* Topousis and Stirgus, September 29.

295 *September 28:* "My inclination is to pursue": *New York Times,* Hicks, September 29.

295–296 *September 29:* "mean Rudy": *New York Times,* Nagourney, September 29; "Rudy Giuliani Is a Colossal Asshole": *Esquire,* Sherrill, October 1997; "with an attitude and philosophy" like Messinger: *New York Times,* Nagourney, September 29; *Times* scorecard on second ad: *New York Times,* Herszenhorn, September 29; statute of limitations: *New York Times,* "Candidates in Search of a Story Line," September 28; "striking for its virulence": *New York Times,* Nagourney, September 29; "But there's a difference": *New York Times,* Nagourney, September 29.

298–300 *October 1:* Giuliani has Messinger disinvited: *Daily News,* Grant, August 26; "I think she's a perennial complainer": *Newsday,* Janison and Murphy, August 26; "We did not want to politicize": *New York Times,* Levy, September 28; "I think the fact is": *New York Post,* Topousis, September 30; photo of principal and Giuliani: *New York Times,* Nagourney, September 26; "Campaign activities are not typically permitted": *Daily News,* Rein and Finnegan, September 26; new bunker gear: *New York Times,* Kennedy, September 15; Giuliani has commissioners call hotline: *Newsday,* Levitt, September 15; "Even after I'd figured out": *Esquire,* Sherrill, October 1997; fired animal-services board members: *Newsday,* Moses, June 17; Queens building head transferred: *Newsday,* Murphy, September 16; sodomy charge a fabrication: *Daily News,* Dwyer, September 14; "Once again you betray your anticop bias": *Newsday,* Levitt, September 15; Dinowitz revenge: *Daily News,* Siegel, October 1.

301–302 *October 2:* "Public officials, both Democrats and Republicans": *Daily News,* Siegel, October 1; "most political, patronage-dedicated mayor": *Daily News,* Lombardi, October 4; "very simplistic": *Daily News,* Fan and Siegel, October 2; Quinnipiac poll: *New York Post,* Rubinowitz, October 2; *Newsday,* Janison, October 3; "I am going to launch": *New York Post,* Hardt, Jr., October 3.

302–304 *October 3:* Giuliani ad: *Daily News,* Lombardi and Finnegan, October 3; Polonetsky letter: *Newsday,* Willen, October 4; Albanese not campaigning as Independent: *New York Times,* Hicks, October 5; Giuliani would rather watch game: *Daily News,* Schwartzman and Allen, October 5; "That's just the reality of things": *Newsday,* Ramirez and Willen, October 5.

307–308 *October 5:* "We strive very, very hard": *New York Times,* Levy, October 5; "I can't swear to you": *New York Times,* Nagourney, October 6; "To talk about the election": *New York Times,* Nagourney, October 6; "This is an out-and-out lie": *Times,* Nagourney, October 6; "ugly, lying statements": *New York Times,* Nagourney, October 6; "Ruth Messinger has a very hard time": *Daily News,* Finnegan, Fan, and Siegel, October 7.

308 *October 6:* Albanese endorses Messinger: *New York Times,* Herszenhorn, October 7; *Newsday,* Janison, October 7; "I think the coverage sucks": *Daily News,* October 7.

309–310 *October 7:* Spence on gangs: *Daily News,* "Prober: Gangs Are Growing," October 8; Messinger letter to Reyes: *Newsday,* Polner, October 8; "If she believed Reyes acted improperly": *New York Post,* Rubinowitz and Seifman, October 8; "They are sleaze peddlers": *Daily News,* Finnegan and Siegel, October 8.

311–314 *October 8:*"As it happens": *New York Post,* Briendel, October 9; "paid political operatives": *Newsday,* Willen and Pollner, October 9; D'Arco identified Fugazy: *Village Voice,* Bastone, September 30; "Bill Fugazy's worked tirelessly": *Daily News,* Smith, June 6.

319 *October 9:* "personal, nasty and vicious": *New York Post,* Rubinowitz and Hardt, Jr., October 10; "replaced Leona Helmsley": *New York Post,* Hardt, Jr., and Merrigan, October 11.

319 *October 10:* "not the kind of debate": *New York Times,* "Two Views of New York," October 10; "put up a game fight": *New York Post,* Seifman, October 10; school programs as answer: *New York Post,* "Ruth's Time Warp," October 10; "blowing smoke": *Daily News,* "Ruth's Running as Fast as She Can," October 11; "a sycophant or an enemy": *Newsday*, Polner and Willen, October 11; Dinkins on Giuliani: *New York Post,* Rubinowitz and Hardt, Jr., October 10.

321–322 *October 11:* Fulani urges boycott: *Amsterdam News,* Fulani, October 9–15; Hirschfeld tree plan: *New York Times,* Hicks, October 23.

322–323 *October 12:* "rogues' gallery of donors": *Daily News,* Flynn and Robbins, October 12; "born to be rained on": *New York Times,* Herbert, October 12; little evidence of rise in gang violence: *New York Times,* Roane, October 12; 40 of 170 are gang members: *Daily News,* Coleman, Marzulli, and Smith, October 14; "the best alternative": *Daily News,* Finnegan, October 12; "no one equal to her deserving of support": *New York Times,* Nagourney, October 13.

324–325 *October 13:* "It is unthinkable to me": *New York Times,* Nagourney, October 14; "She attended four churches": *New York Post,* Topousis and Rubinowitz, October 14; "extraordinary viciousness": *New York Times,* Nagourney, October 14; "The campaign will decide what to do": *Newsday,* Polner and Janison, October 14; Hoenlein does not recall opposition: *Daily News,* Calderone, October 14; "we mean 'Vote for Ruth'": *New York Post,* Kuntzman, October 14.

326–327 *October 14:* "I was not suggesting": *Newsday,* Murphy and Janison, October 15; "The thing that I was puzzled about": *New York Post,* Hardt, Jr., and Topousis, October 15; "As a former grand marshal": *New York Times,* Nagourney, October

15; "put us all in handcuffs": *Newsday,* Murphy and Janison, October 15; Breslin on Giuliani: *Newsday,* Breslin, October 15; Peyser faults Messinger: *New York Post,* Peyser, October 15; "I've taken an oath": *New York Times*, Nagourney, October 17.

328 *October 15:* Poll: *Daily News,* Lombardi, October 16; "Get this over with": *New York Times,* Herbert, October 16; "Public education in New York City": *New York Post,* "Democrats and the Schools," October 16; "It might be more honest and direct": *Daily News,* Finnegan and Siegel, October 16; "Maybe I overreacted a bit": *Newsday,* Janison and Murphy, October 16.

329 *October 16:* "You deserve a fair hearing": *Village Voice,* Bradley, October 28.

329–331 *October 17:* 42 percent of stories on strategy: News Research Group, "Press Corps Changes Course: 'Strategy Replaces Scandal,'" October 15; manipulation of police statistics: *Village Voice,* Barrett, September 16; Miele mob ties: *Village Voice,* Barrett, October 14; "This is a really remarkable performance": *New York Times,* Firestone, September 18; Mastro says Messinger campaign lying: *New York Times,* Firestone, September 18.

332 *October 18:* "I think it's interesting": *Daily News,* Siegel, Allen, and Saltonstall, October 19; "Ruth's long support for abortion": *Daily News,* Zion, October 16.

334 *October 20:* Carey on Hill party: *New York Post,* Seifman, October 21.

335–336 *October 21:* poll: *New York Times,* Nagourney, October 21; "He keeps all those people": *Village Voice,* Bradley, October 28; "The true test of a party": *New York Times,* Nagourney, October 23.

338–339 *October 22:* "I want the text and tone": Messinger memo to Andrews, June 17; "First of all, the appointments will be different": *New York Times,* "Excerpts from Interview with Democratic Candiate," October 25; "There are cases where it's appropriate": *Newsday,* Janison, October 22; Hevesi says program "working well": *New York Post,* Wilner, September 29; *Newsday,* Janison, September 29; "This happens every time people endorse me": *Daily News,* Dwyer, October 30.

339–340 *October 23:* Messinger a Communist: *New York Post,* Briendel, October 23; "You don't want a record-setting pace": *New York Post,* Rubinowitz, October 23.

342 *October 27:* "be all things to all people": *New York Post,* Dicker, October 27.

342–344 *October 28:* "Mr. Giuliani's combative temperament": *New York Times,* "Re-elect Mayor Giuliani," October 26; "Giuliani proved the pessimists wrong": *Newsday,* "Encore," October 26; "No mayor in recent memory": *Staten Island Advance,* "For Mayor: Rudolph Giuliani," October 30; Rudy "has proved to New Yorkers": *Daily News,* "Don't Mess With Success," October 26; "If any mayor has ever": *New York Post,* "Why Rudy Giuliani," October 27; *"el candidato mas capaz": El Diario*, "Giuliani: *Cuatro Anos Mas,*" October 31; Messinger "cannot offer credible rationale": *New York Post,* "Why Rudy Giuliani," October 27; "By contrast, the campaign slogans": *Daily News,* "Don't Mess With Success," October 26; "failed to give voters": *New York Times,* "Re-elect Mayor Giuliani," October 26; "an intelligent, dedicated and worthy public official": *Staten Island Advance,* "For Mayor: Rudolph Giuliani," October 30; "a brilliant policy analyst": *Newsday,* "Encore," October 26; "master" of "fear, racism, and divisiveness": *Amsterdam News,* Tatum, "*Amsterdam News* Endorsements," October 30–November 5; "Rudy really is at the beginning": *New York Times,* Steinberg, October 28; "hapless": *Washington Post,* Brooks, October 29; Vallone staff to Westchester: *Daily News,* Finnegan, October 30; Giuliani Election Day plans: *Newsday,* Janison and Willen, October 29.

346–347 *October 30:* "took the offensive": *New York Times,* Nagourney, October 30; scores by debate experts: *Daily News,* "Comparing Giuliani and Messinger," October 30; "Politics is like malaria": *New York Times,* Kolbert, November 3.

347 *October 31:* "It is more than saturation": *New York Post,* Rubinowitz and Seifman, October 29.

350 *November 1:* "getting votes by the process of elimination": *New York Post,* Seifman, Rubinowitz, Gregorian, and Francescani, September 9; "amazed at the number of people": *Newsday,* Janison and Willen, October 29; unaired Giuliani campaign ads: *New York Times,* Nagourney, November 2; "I don't care to talk about it": *New York Times,* Nagourney, November 2.

351–354 *November 2:* "his best forty-eight hours": *New Yorker,* Klein, September 8; "There are lots of times": *Daily News,* Lombardi and Siegel, November 3.

354–356 *November 3:* New Yorkers less interested: *New York Times,* Herbert, November 2; "It's a mystical city": *Newsday,* Willen, November 1; "I really do want to get": *New York Post,* Rubinowitz and Seifman, October 31; "We're going to reach out": *Daily News,* Siegel, October 31; "There are still people that feel left out": *New York Times,* Nagourney, November 2; "I'm going to go everywhere": *New York Times,* Firestone, November 3; "Very good, very lean": *Newsday,* Duggan, October 28; "Even our sanitation trucks don't have graffiti": *New York Observer,* Durkin, November 10; Molinari prediction: *Staten Island Advance,* Patrick, November 2.

358–359 *November 4:* "My wife makes her own decisions": *Newsday,* Morrison and Kim, November 6; "I would expect the kind of margin": *New York Post,* Seifman and Rubinowitz, November 5.

360–363 *November 5:* "Mayor Rudolph Giuliani's reelection": *New York Times,* "Mayor Giuliani's Victory," November 5; "Don't touch anything!": *New York Times,* Collins, November 6; "Although the *Times*": *Daily Challenge,* "Brath, Mayoral Election Is About Race," November 6; "Giuliani's victory is pyrrhic": *Amsterdam News,* Tatum, "Rudy Beat Ruth . . . But How, and Why?" November 6–12; *Amsterdam News,* Boyd, November 6–12; "the day of the bicycle stunt": *Newsday,* Henican, November 5; "Ruth Messinger in the end": *New York Post,* Peyser, November 5; "New York mayoral politics": *New York Times,* Nagourney, November 6; voters "are in a back-to-basics mood": *Washington Post,* Dionne, December 2; "ideological liberalism": *Wall Street Journal,* "Urban Renaissance? Not Yet," November 6; Giuliani "co-opted liberalism": *New York Times,* Nagourney, November 5; sign of rise of Independence party: *Amsterdam News,* Boyd, November 6–12; "In hindsight": *New York Observer,* Drucker, November 17; "I'm not saying we couldn't have done better": *New York Times,* Nagourney, November 5; less than 20 percent of budget on air: *Village Voice,* Barrett, September 23.

364 *November 18:* "The show felt like the Ruth Messinger campaign": *New York Times,* Rich, November 25.

Afterword

369–373 "lagging finances were a concern": *New York Times,* Nagourney, July 18, 1998; listless campaign: *New York Times,* Nagourney, September 13, 1998; "I'm the only candidate": *Washington Post,* Edsall, June 4, 1998; Hirschfeld indicted: *Daily News,* Ross, Kriegel, and Goldiner, December 10, 1998.

Acknowledgments

I OWE DEBTS OF GRATITUDE to two sets of people: those who sustained me through the campaign and those who carried me through the process of writing this book.

The staff of the campaign was a unique, dedicated group of people who persevered with good humor in what was often an unpleasant environment. Working for the Messinger campaign was a great privilege. Friends like Giles Farley, Lee Jones, Roger Kosson, Libby Moroff, Pat Roach, and Kathy Viscardi made it a pleasure. My best friend from the campaign, Jordan Magill, had greater confidence in me than I had in myself at times. Special thanks to Ruth Messinger, who supported this project from its inception. As we lived through the campaign, neither she nor I imagined that she would be the subject of a book, and that, I am sure, must cause some ambivalence on her part. She has countenanced this endeavor, as she conducted herself throughout the campaign, with class and good cheer.

The path to the publication of this book was a bumpy one, but I was blessed with the patient support of many friends who carried me through some difficult disappointments along the way. Jennifer Apiscopa, Heather Beaudoin, Noam Bramson, Kari Butcher, Bruce Cooper, Peter Fante, Roslyn Goldstein, Lee Jones, Johannes Juette, Arthur Kaminsky, Ira Kaufman, Michelle Liblanc, Francis MacDonnell, Jordan Magill, Sherry Mandery, Mathew Mandery, Gary Saunders, Marla Simpson, and Ted Sturman read drafts of this book at various stages and offered comments, advice, and support that was always to the benefit of the project. Thanks to friends and former staffers Melanie Breen, Jen Kaiser, Melanie McEvoy, and Libby Moroff for thoughtful reflections on the campaign and filling in the gaps in the story. Thanks to Sal Albanese, Andrew Kirtzman, and Adam Nagourney for illuminating discussions about their own perceptions of the campaign.

Thanks to Leo Wiegman and Westview Press, who have treated me like family since I first contacted them in July.

Roslyn Goldstein, my guidance counselor from high school, has ungrudgingly continued in that role without pay for thirteen years beyond her obligation. Though after all this time I am still uncomfortable addressing her by her first name, she is a treasured friend and contributed to this book in many ways.

At difficult times throughout the campaign and the writing process, I depended, as I have since high school, on the utterly tasteless and childish sense of humor of my best friend, Ira Kaufman. Ira had ideas about the campaign that, if implemented, would, no doubt, have changed the course of history.

A disproportionate share of the burden of both the campaigning and writing experiences fell on Michelle Liblanc, whose reserve of love and patience seemed to be boundless.

This book is dedicated to my father, Mathew, my hero, role model, and friend, and my mother, Sherry, whose love, support, and unshakable confidence in me has sustained me in good times and bad. Ever since I was born, she has told me and anyone else unfortunate enough to be her captive audience that I would someday write a book. That she turned out to be right surprises no one more than me.

Evan J. Mandery

Author's Note

THE NAMES OF THE JUNIOR MEMBERS of the campaign staff have been changed.

E. J. M.

Index